346.0482 F

A User's Guide
Copyright

G000141679

Other titles in the '*A User's Guide*' series:

A User's Guide to Data Protection
Second Edition—July 2016
978 1 78451 249 1
£110

A User's Guide to Patents
Fourth Edition—November 2015
978 1 78043 489 6
£135

A User's Guide to Trademarks and Passing Off
Fourth Edition—May 2015
978 1 78043 685 2
£110

www.bloomsburyprofessional.com/usersguide

A User's Guide to Copyright

Seventh Edition

Consultant Editor: **Michael Flint**

General Editor: **Clive Thorne**,
Special Counsel, Baker Botts UK LLP

Assistant Editor: **Jonathan Cornthwaite**,
Partner, Wedlake Bell LLP

Contributors:

Rachel Alexander,
Partner, Wiggin LLP

Jonathan Cornthwaite,
Partner, Wedlake Bell LLP

Martin Delaney

Alexander Ross,
Partner, Wiggin LLP

Clive Thorne,
Special Counsel, Baker Botts UK LLP

Bloomsbury Professional

Bloomsbury Professional

An imprint of Bloomsbury Publishing Plc

Bloomsbury Professional Ltd	Bloomsbury Publishing Plc
41–43 Boltro Road	50 Bedford Square
Haywards Heath	London
RH16 1BJ	WC1B 3DP
UK	UK

www.bloomsbury.com

BLOOMSBURY and the Diana logo are trademarks of

Bloomsbury Publishing Plc

© Bloomsbury Professional Ltd 2017

British Library Cataloguing-in-Publication Data

A catalogue record for this book is available from the British Library.

ISBN:	PB:	978 1 84766 685 7
	Epdf:	978 1 52650 491 3
	Epub:	978 1 52650 490 6

Typeset by Phoenix Photosetting Ltd, Chatham, Kent
Printed and bound by CPI Group (UK) Ltd, Croydon, CR0 4YY

To find out more about our authors and books visit www.bloomsburyprofessional.com. Here you will find extracts, author information, details of forthcoming events and the option to sign up for our newsletters.

Preface

As was stated in the preface to the fourth edition, the purpose of this *User's Guide to Copyright* is to enable people whose jobs, businesses – or even hobbies – have any involvement with copyright law to acquire a general understanding of it. Part 1 of the *User's Guide* outlines copyright law generally, whilst Part 2 applies that law to particular industries, professions and areas of artistic endeavour. This *User's Guide* can be used to answer relatively straightforward questions of copyright law by reading the relevant chapter in Part 2 and referring as necessary to Part 1.

Over the years, this *User's Guide* has been found useful by those in business, lawyers and students of intellectual property (IP) law, not only in the United Kingdom but also in many other countries. For example, in 1998 a Japanese-translated version of the fourth edition was published in Tokyo.

The first edition of this work was published in 1979. The only UK copyright legislation then in force was the Copyright Act 1956 which had 51 sections, and a few statutory instruments introduced pursuant to that Act. Performers in those days had no copyright protection in their own performances, but were protected to some extent by the terms of the Performers' Protection Acts 1958–1972.

The Copyright, Designs and Patents Act 1988 ('CDPA') came into force on 1 August 1989. There have numerous amendments to the CDPA, especially those that implement Directives of the European Union. It now has over 300 sections. The case for a consolidation statute is now overwhelming.

This edition is considerably longer than the first edition. But it has not only been new legislation which has resulted in the extension of each new edition, for the arrival of the information age has added a considerable amount of new legislation and judicial decisions, both of the United Kingdom courts and the Court of Justice of the European Union.

This edition of the *User's Guide* takes account not only of changes in the law since the publication of the sixth edition in 2006, but also of the changes in relevant industries and, in particular, network communications.

Preface

I wrote the first three editions on my own but with guidance and help, not from lawyers, but from businesspeople in industries and professions where copyright is important. Clive Thorne (then a partner in Denton Hall Burgin & Warrens, now Dentons) joined me in writing the fourth edition of this work for which he revised and improved the chapters on design law. He continued to take responsibility for those chapters and that area of law in the fifth and sixth editions.

When the fifth edition was published in the year 2000 I had largely retired from the practice of law. Nicholas Fitzpatrick joined Clive Thorne and me in revising that edition of the book. In 2006 he edited the sixth edition. In particular, we have him to thank for the introduction of the cross-references and footnotes which have made the book more suitable for law students and lawyers who are not copyright law specialists.

This edition is focused even more strictly on copyright than previous editions – the chapters dealing with industrial design, breach of confidence and passing off, the protection of designs, character merchandising, the design of consumer goods and fashion goods, spare parts, and piracy and counterfeiting have been dropped. Industrial design law is significantly different from the rest of copyright law and is now the subject of a book entitled *A User's Guide to Design Law* (2010) by Clive Thorne. It was agreed that that those people dealing with design law issues would be better off referring to a book specifically on that subject rather than what can only be the somewhat limited exposition of that law in this book.

Clive Thorne is now the General Editor of the seventh edition of this work. He was responsible for Chapters 1 to 4, 6 to 8, 10, 16, 26 and 28. He is Special Counsel with Baker Botts LLP where he practises in all areas of intellectual property. He has a particular interest in the arbitration of IP disputes. Clive is on the WIPO and IMPRESS panels of arbitrators and has also been appointed to sit on ICC arbitration.

Jonathan Cornthwaite is the Assistant Editor of the seventh edition as a whole. In addition he was also responsible for Chapters 5, 9, 11, 13, 14, 15, 25 and 27. Jonathan is a solicitor and a partner at Wedlake Bell LLP. As well as IP law, he specialises in IT law, e-commerce law and competition law. He is the head of E-commerce Law in TELFA, the pan-European legal alliance of which Wedlake Bell is a founder member. Jonathan has published extensively on IP and IT subjects, and his books include *Marketing Law that Matters* published by Financial Times/Pitmans, and *The Internet and Intellectual Property* published by Monitor Press Limited.

Other solicitors specialising in copyright law have contributed very valuable revisions and updates to this edition. Their contributions not only take account of changes in copyright law and the way in which the industries and professions with which Part 2 of the book deals in detail are affected, but also have done much to simplify and clarify the book since the sixth edition.

A team of solicitors from media and technology firm Wiggin LLP were responsible for updating and rewriting Chapters 20 to 24. They were led by Alexander Ross and Rachel Alexander and included Deepti Burton, Sarah Drake, Tiffany Dale, David Naylor, Ross Sylvester, Ted Shapiro, Sunniva Hansson, Olivia Brown, Katharine Alexander, Rawa Kaftan, Matthew Dando.

Alexander Ross leads the music team at Wiggin LLP. He has been a music lawyer for over 20 years, and during that time has advised an eclectic mix of artists such as David Bowie, Bjork, Def Leppard, Elvis Costello and Joss Stone. As well as traditional talent work, he has extensive experience in licensing music for film, TV, computer games and other productions, and he is one of the few UK music lawyers with a true hands-on track record in digital music rights. Alexander sits on the Executive Committee of the International Association of Entertainment Lawyers.

Rachel Alexander is a partner in the IP litigation group at Wiggin LLP. She leads on many IP cases and advises on enforcement strategies, particularly in the online context. Rachel is a member of the Intellectual Property Lawyers Organisation. She was recognised as one of the IP Stars Top 250 Women in IP 2017 by Managing Intellectual Property.

Martin Delaney has edited Chapter 12 on collecting societies as well as Chapters 17 to 19. He is a recently-retired solicitor who spent 17 years as the Legal Director of the Copyright Licensing Agency. He was on the Legal Affairs Committee of the IFFRO (the international non-governmental organisation for collecting societies involved in printed media) and various UK Government committees looking at the reform of copyright.

Michael F Flint
15 October 2017

How to use the *User's Guide*

Copyright is encountered by people in a great many walks of life: from television executives to authors, architects, artists, film producers, school teachers and museum curators. The *User's Guide* is designed to assist people whose work or studies involve them in day-to-day dealings with copyright. It can be used to acquire a general understanding of copyright and also as a reference work for dealing with general copyright problems.

Both laymen and lawyers tend to regard copyright as a difficult subject which is best left to the specialist. Certainly copyright legislation in the UK is structured in a complex way, and the significant changes introduced since the last *User's Guide* do nothing to make matters simpler. It is hoped that the format of this book will overcome some of those difficulties. The *User's Guide* is, however, only a guide and is not intended to take the place of a legal adviser where problems of complexity arise. Some matters contained in the CDPA (and subsidiary legislation made under the CDPA), are not discussed at all, because they are of such a technical nature an expert legal adviser should always be consulted.

This seventh edition of the *User's Guide* has been extensively revised and updated. **Part 1** (Chapters 1 to 14) consists of a summary of the law of copyright. **Part 2** (Chapters 15 onwards) examines the way in which copyright law applies to certain organisations and occupations for which copyright plays an important role.

The Table of Incidence of Copyright in **Appendix 2** sets out the applicability of copyright for each type of work entitled to copyright protection. The table is for general reference only: copyright law has many exceptions, and no simple table can deal with all of them. When considering specific points, the text must be used in addition to the table. However, the table serves as a quick guide, or checklist, when reading one of the chapters in **Part 2** which deals with a specific type of organisation or activity.

We recommend that **Part 1** is read in full. If this is not possible in a particular situation, a reader with little or no copyright knowledge should at least first acquaint himself with **paragraph 1.02**: the basic principles of copyright.

Most chapters in **Part 2** contain a paragraph of definitions of the terms used in that chapter. Although these may not make easy reading, it is important to know the technical meaning of the terms used in copyright, because sometimes the technical meaning conveys something different from the usual and ordinary meaning of the same expression.

The *User's Guide* is also extensively cross-referenced. The footnotes refer back to case law, statutes, regulations and other parts of the *User's Guide* for further information on particular issues. Since, most frequently, the footnotes will refer to the CDPA, where we refer to 'section [x]' in a footnote, this will mean a section of the CDPA unless the footnote indicates otherwise.

Glossary of terms commonly used in the *User's Guide*

'the 1992 Regulations':	Copyright (Computer Programs) Regulations 1992, SI 1992/3233.
'the 1995 Regulations':	Duration of Copyright and Rights in Performances Regulations 1995, SI 1995/3297.
'the 1996 Regulations':	Copyright and Related Rights Regulations 1996, SI 1996/2967.
'the 1997 Regulations':	Copyright and Rights in Databases Regulations 1997, SI 1997/3032.
'the 2000 Regulations':	Conditional Access (Unauthorised Decoders) Regulations 2000, SI 2000/1175.
'the 2003 Regulations':	Copyright and Related Rights Regulations 2003, SI 2003/2498.
'the 2006 Regulations'	Performances (Moral Rights etc) Regulations 2006, SI 2006/18.
'the 2014 Regulations'	Copyright and Duration of Rights in Performances (Amendment) Regulations 2014, SI 2014/434.
'the Berne Convention':	Berne Convention for the Protection of Literary and Artistic Works 1886.
'the CDPA':	Copyright, Designs and Patents Act 1988.
'the CJEU':	Court of Justice of the European Union.
'the DPA':	Data Protection Act 1998.
'the DMCA':	US Digital Millennium Copyright Act 1998.
'the ECJ':	Court of Justice of the European Union.
'the EEA':	European Economic Area.
'the EU':	European Union.
'GATS':	General Agreement on Trade and Services.
'HRA':	Human Rights Act 1998.

Glossary of terms commonly used in the *User's Guide*

'the Phonograms Convention':	Convention for the Protection of Producers of Phonograms against the Unauthorised Duplication of their Phonograms 1971.
'the Rome Convention':	Rome Convention for the Protection of Performers, Producers and Broadcasting Organisations 1961.
'TRIPS':	Agreement on Trade Related Aspects of Intellectual Property Rights, Including Trade in Counterfeit Goods 1994.
'the UCC':	Universal Copyright Convention 1952.
'the UK':	United Kingdom.
'the USA':	United States of America.
'WIPO':	World Intellectual Property Organisation.
'the WIPO Treaties':	WIPO Copyright Treaty 1996 and the WIPO Performances and Phonograms Treaty 1996.
'the WTO':	World Trade Organisation.

Contents

[All chapter references are to paragraph number]

Contents

Contents

Contents

11   Rights in Performances

Contents

14   The protection of databases

Part 2 Copyright in use

15   Publishers and printers

Contents

Contents

Contents

Contents

Contents

25 Artists, photographers, art galleries, art dealers and museums

26 Architects and architecture

Contents

Table of statutes

Paragraph references printed in **bold** type indicate where the Act is set out in part or in full.

Table of statutes

Table of statutes

Table of statutes

Table of statutory instruments

Those paragraph numbers in **bold** type indicate where a Statutory Instrument is set out in part or in full.

Table of statutory instruments

Table of cases

Table of cases

C

Table of cases

Table of cases

Table of cases

Table of cases

Part 1
Copyright law

Chapter 1

What is copyright?

Introduction

1.01 This chapter sets out the basic principles of copyright law in the UK. These principles are elaborated in the following chapters of the *User's Guide*, which have been extensively updated and improved in this edition. In order to assist your use of the *User's Guide*, we recommend you refer to the section 'How to use the *User's Guide*', set out above.

The basic principles of copyright

1.02

- *Copyright is a property right, which is protected in the UK by virtue of the Copyright, Designs and Patents Act 1988 (CDPA).*
- Copyright subsists only in material which falls within one of those categories of work prescribed by the CDPA as being capable of copyright protection. These are as follows:
  - (a) literary works;
  - (b) dramatic works;
  - (c) musical works;
  - (d) artistic works;
  - (e) sound recordings;
  - (f) films;
  - (g) broadcasts;
  - (h) the typographical arrangement of published editions[1].

  Material which does not fall within any of these categories will have no copyright protection (ie it will not be a copyright work)[2].
- *There is no copyright in ideas*, only in the manner of their expression[3].

- *In the case of literary, dramatic, musical and artistic works the material must be original* in order to be entitled to copyright protection[4].
- *The material must have involved the use of skill and labour by the author*[5].
- *The work must usually be reduced to a material form*[6].
- *Copyright is owned independently of the physical material which records it.* For example, the owner of the manuscript of a play is not necessarily the owner of the copyright in the play[7].
- *There are no formalities to copyright protection in the UK.* Material does not have to be published, nor does it have to be registered, for it to have copyright protection[8].
- *If material is entitled to copyright, then the right which vests in the copyright owner is the right to prevent others from doing certain restricted acts.* The restricted acts are specified by the CDPA in relation to each category of work and differ for each category. If something is done in relation to copyright material, which is not one of the restricted acts specified for that type of work, then there will not be an infringement of copyright[9].
- *There are certain circumstances in which doing a restricted act without the authority of the copyright owner does not constitute an infringement of copyright*[10]. The most important of these general exceptions are:
  (a) 'fair dealing' defences[11];
  (b) use of less than a substantial part of a work[12].
  There are many other important exceptions, some of which differ according to the type of works[13].
- *Copyright subsists for defined periods which differ according to the category of work.* The standard copyright period is usually the life of the author plus 70 years[14].
- *In most cases the author, maker, producer or publisher of a work and the director of a film is its first owner,* but there are special rules which can override this general provision[15].
- *The author or maker of the material must be a 'qualifying person':* generally a citizen or resident of the UK or one of the countries which is a party to the Berne Convention or the Universal Copyright Convention[16].
- *Authors and directors (and performers) enjoy 'moral rights'* which include the right to be identified as author, the right to object to the derogatory treatment of a work and (for authors and directors) the right to prevent false attribution of a work[17].
- *Performers and persons having recording rights possess rights akin to copyright*[18].
- *Copyright should not be considered in isolation from other intellectual property rights*[19].

1   CDPA s 1(1).
2   Column I of the Table of Incidence of Copyright in **Appendix 2** sets out the different
     types of copyright works. **Chapter 2** will discuss in more detail what kinds of material
     are included within these categories.
3   See **paragraph 1.03** and **Chapter 3**.
4   See **paragraphs 3.01** ff.
5   Ibid.
6   See **paragraph 2.05**.
7   See **paragraph 9.01**.
8   See **paragraph 9.20**.
9   See Column III of the Table of Incidence of Copyright in **Appendix 2** for the restricted
     acts applicable to each type of work. **Chapter 6** discusses the restricted acts in more
     detail.
10   **Chapter 8**.
11   See **paragraphs 8.03** ff.
12   See **paragraph 7.06**.
13   See Column IV of the Table of Incidence of Copyright in **Appendix 2** for these
     exceptions. **Chapter 8** deals with them in more detail.
14   See Column II of the Table of Incidence of Copyright in **Appendix 2**, **Chapter 5**
     deals with the duration of copyright in more detail.
15   Column V of the Table of Incidence of Copyright in **Appendix 2** outlines the rules as
     to who is the first owner of copyright in relation to each type of work. **Chapter 9** deals
     with ownership and transmission of copyright in more detail.
16   **Chapter 4** deals with qualifying persons and international copyright.
17   **Chapter 10** deals in detail with moral rights.
18   See **Chapter 11**.
19   See **paragraph 1.04**.

The nature of copyright

1.03   The nature of copyright was summed up succinctly by the
Committees whose recommendations laid the basis for the Copyright
Act 1956 and the CDPA respectively:

'Copyright is a right given to or derived from works, and is not a right in
novelty of ideas. It is based on the right of an author, artist or composer to
prevent another person copying an original work. There is nothing in the
notion of copyright to prevent another person from producing an identical
result (and himself enjoying a copyright in that work) provided it is arrived at
by an independent process'[1].

'A writer writes an article about the making of bread. He puts words on paper.
He is not entitled to a monopoly in the writing of articles about the baking
of bread, but the law has long recognised that he has an interest not merely
in the manuscript, the words on paper which he produces, but in the skill
and labour involved in the choice of words and the exact way in which he
expresses his ideas by the words he chooses. If the author sells copies of his
article then again a purchaser of a copy can make such personal use of that
copy as he pleases. He can read it or sell it second-hand, if he can find anyone
who will buy it. If a reader of the original article is stimulated into writing
another article about bread the original author has no reason to complain. It
has long been recognised that only the original author ought to have the right

to reproduce the original article and sell the copies thus reproduced. If other people were free to do this they would be making a profit out of the skill and labour of the original author. It is for this reason that the law has long given to authors, for a specified term, certain exclusive rights in relation to so-called literary works. Such rights were recognised at common law at least as early as the fifteenth century'[2].

Phrased another way: 'Copyright protection shall extend to expressions and not to ideas, procedures, methods of operation or mathematical concepts as such'[3].

Copyright is a right to prevent other people copying an original work. It should be noted that it must be an original work, not just an original idea[4].

As for the word 'work', which appears frequently throughout this *User's Guide*, only those types of work which are expressly entitled to receive copyright protection under the CDPA are so entitled. Not everything which could be described in the everyday sense as being a 'work' is entitled to copyright. In this publication the word 'work' is used in the technical sense given to it by the CDPA[5].

Some writers have called for a simplification of UK copyright law, arguing that the complex structure of the legislation in the UK tends to undermine, rather than facilitate, the intentions of the copyright conventions and treaties which underpin copyright internationally.

1   Gregory Committee on Copyright Law 1952 (Cmd 8662).
2   Report of the Whitford Committee on Copyright and Design Law of 1977 (Cmnd 6732).
3   TRIPS Agreement, Sect 1 Act 9.2. For an interesting, if aged, discussion of the idea/expression dichotomy, see FW Grosheide, 'When ideas take shape' [1994] 6 EIPR 219. See also **paragraphs 4.17** ff.
4   This concept is considered further at **paragraphs 3.01** ff. The reader should also note that a similar formulation was adopted internationally by the TRIPS Agreement and the WIPO Copyright Treaty, see **paragraphs 4.20** ff.
5   A matter considered in more detail in **Chapter 2**, in particular **paragraph 2.12**.

Copyright and intellectual property generally

1.04   Copyright, designs, patents and trade marks are diverse rights which are, for convenience, usually grouped together under the headings of 'industrial property' or 'intellectual property'.

The CDPA

1.05   The principal UK copyright statute is the CDPA which came into force on 1 August 1989.

Part II of the CDPA, which deals with rights in performances, gives protection to performers and persons having recording rights. Its effect is to create rights analogous to copyright.

Statutory instruments

1.06 There are a number of rules and regulations contained in statutory instruments made under the CDPA. These have the effect in some cases of amending the CDPA and in particular of giving effect to EU law[1].

1   See **paragraph 1.08**.

Orders in Council

1.07 There are a number of Orders in Council extending the provisions of the CDPA to works originating outside the UK[1].

1   See **paragraph 4.09**.

EU law

1.08 The European Commission has adopted a number of Directives harmonising copyright laws (within the EU)[1]. The UK, like all EU Member States, has been required to amend its law to comply with these Directives by specified dates. Directives are binding on the Member States to which they are addressed although national authorities have the choice of the form and method of implementation into national law. The Commission may sue a Member State for non-implementation if the national authority has not incorporated the Directive into its law within the time limit specified in the Directive. Significantly, Directives are of *direct effect* in the sense that a citizen of a Member State may also sue his government before his or her national court for non-compliance with a Directive which has not been implemented within the requisite time period (provided the relevant provision is sufficiently clear, precise, unconditional and leaves no room for discretion in implementation)[2]. In the UK, EU Directives have been implemented by means of primary legislation eg Trade Marks Act 1995 or statutory instruments. EU legislation regarding copyright applies to all EEA States.

On 29 March 2017 the UK gave notice to the EU of its intention to leave the EU, under Art 50 of the Lisbon Treaty. Whatever the terms of departure it is probable that significant reforms to intellectual property law will be required.

1   See **paragraph 13.02**.
2   *Van Duyn v Home Office: 41/74 [1975] Ch 358, ECJ.*

International conventions

1.09 The UK is party to a number of conventions dealing with international copyright recognition and other matters of an international nature[1].

1   See **paragraph 4.12** ff.

Case law

1.10 There is a body of copyright-related common law consisting of the judgments delivered in relevant cases. Cases heard before implementation of the CDPA remain relevant. Additionally decisions of the Court of Justice of the European Union (CJEU) may be relevant and binding on UK courts.

Passing off, breach of confidence and privacy

1.11 The law relating to passing off, breach of confidence and privacy confers rights of action which can sometimes assist where copyright protection is not available. These are not matters which can, on the whole, be looked up in a statute[1], but have developed through a series of cases, and are contained in the judgments of those cases. They are based on common law and equity. As such these topics are in a constant state of evolution as judges modify the law in new cases which come before them.

1   Although the Human Rights Act 1998 and the Data Protection Act 1999 have had an impact on some of these issues.

The history of copyright in the UK

1.12 A short summary of the history of copyright may assist in understanding the present shape of the law.

Copyright effectively came into existence after the invention of printing. The first indications of copyright were the granting of licences by the Crown to printers giving them the right to print (ie copy), against the payment of fees to the Crown. In 1662 the Licensing Act was passed which prohibited the printing of any book which was not licensed and registered at the Stationers Company.

The first Copyright Act, the Statute of Anne, was passed in 1709. This gave protection for printed works for 21 years from the date of printing and unprinted works for 14 years. Again, books had to be registered at the Stationers Company.

The next important piece of copyright legislation was the Copyright Act 1842. This laid down the period of copyright as the life of the author and seven years after his death, or 42 years from the date of publication, whichever should be the longer.

The Copyright Act 1911 repealed the Copyright Act 1842 and itself remained in force until being repealed by the Copyright Act 1956. The 1956 Act re-enacted and continued in force some of the provisions of the 1911 Act.

In 1973, a departmental committee was set up, under the chairmanship of Mr Justice Whitford, to review the law of copyright and designs. Its report, *Copyright and Designs Law*, was published in 1977.

In 1981, the government published a Green Paper *Reform of the Law Relating to Copyright, Designs and Performers' Protection* followed by a White Paper *Intellectual Property and Innovation*. The White Paper dealt not only with copyright but also with patent and trade mark law. The Bill, which was to become the CDPA, was based upon the latter White Paper's proposals.

Since the CDPA came into force on 1 August 1989, very substantial changes have been made to it by statutory instrument. The effect of these regulations has been, amongst other things, to:

- modify the law relating to computer programs;
- extend the term of copyright;
- change the law regarding the authorship of films;
- introduce wide-ranging provisions dealing with the rental and lending, satellite broadcasting and cable transmission of copyright works;
- extend performer's rights;
- introduce the publication right;
- introduce specific provision relating to the copyright protection of databases and to create a new sui generis database right;
- enhance the protection afforded to conditional access technologies;
- amend copyright law in light of developments in *information society* services.

The structure of the CDPA

1.13 The following outline of the CDPA (and indeed all following references to the CDPA) deal with the CDPA as amended.

The CDPA is divided into seven parts: Part I Copyright; Part II Rights in Performances; Part III Design Right; Part IV Registered Designs; Part V Patent Agents and Trade Mark Agents; Part VI Patents; and Part VII Miscellaneous and General.

This *User's Guide* deals with Parts I and II in detail. It deals generally with Parts III and IV, not at all with Parts V and VI, and with Part VII only to the extent relevant to copyright users.

Part I of the CDPA is organised as follows:

- *Chapter I* deals with the subsistence, ownership and duration of copyright.
- *Chapter II* deals with the rights of copyright owners. The Chapter sets out and elaborates upon the acts which are restricted by copyright, and deals with issues of '*secondary infringement*' of copyright.

- *Chapter III* deals with acts permitted in relation to copyright works, ie those acts which can be performed without the consent of the copyright owner.
- *Chapter IIIA* deals with certain permitted uses of orphan works.
- *Chapter IV* sets out provisions dealing with moral rights.
- *Chapter V* considers 'dealings' with copyright works and describes how rights in copyright works and how moral rights may be assigned, licensed or passed on death.
- *Chapter VI* deals with remedies for infringement of copyright (both civil remedies and criminal sanctions).
- *Chapter VII* deals with licensing schemes and licensing bodies.
- *Chapter VIII* sets the provisions concerning the Copyright Tribunal.
- *Chapter IX* contains provisions dealing with the qualifications for, and extent of, copyright protection.
- *Chapter X* deals with Crown and Parliamentary copyright, other miscellaneous provisions dealing with, for example, folklore and, perhaps more importantly, the interpretation provisions in which terms not defined elsewhere in Part I are defined.

Part II of the CDPA deals with rights in performances[1].

Part VII is headed *Miscellaneous and General*. It deals with devices designed to circumvent copyright protection, the fraudulent reception of transmissions, the fraudulent application or use of trade marks, provisions for the benefit of the Hospital for Sick Children (the Peter Pan-saving provisions), and for certain international bodies. It also contains provisions dealing with the entry into force of the CDPA.

The *publication right*, which arises when a work is first published after its copyright period has expired, is not part of the amendments to the CDPA, but is to be found in reg 16 of the Copyright and Related Rights Regulations 1996 ('1996 Regulations')[2].

Similarly, *database right*, which subsists in a database if there has been a substantial investment in obtaining, verifying or presenting the contents of the database, is not included as an amendment to the CDPA, but instead is set out in Part III of the Copyright and Rights in Databases Regulations 1997 ('1997 Regulations')[3].

1   CDPA ss 180–212.
2   SI 1996/2967.
3   SI 1997/3032.

Copyright and Freedom of Expression: the Human Rights Act 1998

1.14   The nature of copyright is to reserve to the copyright owner the right to do certain 'restricted acts' in relation to his protected work. Within the legislative parameters, the copyright owner can use his property right in a work to restrain others from using it. In doing so, copyright limits the ability of others to express themselves (if doing so would involve using a copyright work without the authority of the owner in one of the ways restricted by copyright: eg copying without consent).

There is a clear tension between the exclusive rights enjoyed by a copyright owner and the rights to freedom of expression enshrined in the European Convention on Human Rights, as enacted in the UK by the HRA, which entered into force in October 2000.

By Article 10 of the ECHR:

'1. Everyone has the right to freedom of expression. This right shall include freedom to hold opinions and to receive and impart information and ideas without interference by public authority and regardless of frontiers
...

2. The exercise of these freedoms, since it carries with it duties and responsibilities, may be subject to such formalities, conditions, restrictions or penalties as are prescribed by law and are necessary in a democratic society ... for the protection of ... rights of others ...'.

In the Court of Appeal decision in *Ashdown v Telegraph Group Ltd*[1] the *Sunday Telegraph* published a minute drafted by an MP, Paddy Ashdown, which documented a confidential meeting between Mr Ashdown and the Prime Minister. The minute found its way to the *Sunday Telegraph* via a publisher to whom Mr Ashdown had entrusted a copy on a confidential basis. The *Sunday Telegraph* argued that their reproduction of the minute did not amount to an infringement since they should be entitled to enjoy one of the defences to infringement, either 'fair dealing' or 'public policy'[2]. Moreover, the *Sunday Telegraph* argued that the effect of the HRA was to require these defences to be applied in such a way as to preserve freedom of expression.

The court at first instance found against the newspaper, and the decision was upheld in the Court of Appeal. At first instance, Morritt VC found that the CDPA already balanced the rights of copyright owners and users. In other words, the legislation has (by initiating defences and exceptions to copyright infringement) balanced the competing demands of the right to enjoy property (ie copyright) and the right of freedom of expression. The Court of Appeal concluded that freedom of expression should not as a general rule have any effect on copyright enforcement. The Court did however recognise that rare circumstances arise where a freedom of expression will conflict with copyright protection, outside the ambit of the current exceptions set out in the CDPA. In those circumstances, the Court stated that it was necessary to apply the CDPA in a manner that accommodates the right of freedom of expression, looking closely at the facts of the case.

The decision exhibits the general reluctance of English courts to look outside and establish a balance between the competing interests of property and freedom of expression. Nevertheless, it illustrates that copyright law is subject to re-examination in light of the HRA, even if an active departure from existing copyright principles in favour of the freedom of expression would appear unlikely, except in rare circumstances.

1   [2001] EMLR 44, CA.
2   See **paragraph 2.16** and **Chapter 8**.

Chapter 2

Copyright works

Introduction

2.01   Copyright exists only in works which can be brought within one of the following categories:

- original literary, dramatic, musical and artistic works;
- sound recordings, films or broadcasts; or
- the typographical arrangement of published editions[1].

1   CDPA s 1(1).

Literary works

2.02   The CDPA defines a 'literary work' as:

'any work, other than a dramatic or musical work, which is written, spoken or sung, and accordingly includes:

(a)   a table or compilation other than a database;
(b)   a computer program;
(c)   preparatory design material for a computer program; and
(d)   database.'[1]

The expression 'literary work' covers works which are expressed in words or numerals irrespective of quality. Where a work, such as a novel, goes through a number of draft stages the components of each draft stage is capable of constituting a copyright work in its own right, quite distinct from each other draft and the final published edition[2]. It should be noted that for the purposes of the CDPA, maps, charts and plans are not literary works but are deemed to be artistic works[3]. The borderline between literary works and artistic works is sometimes unclear. In *ANACON Corpn Ltd v Environmental Research Technology Ltd*[4], for example, Mr Justice Jacob held that circuit diagrams are both literary works and artistic works. He said:

'My first thought was that it would be absurd to regard a circuit diagram as a literary work, but the more one thinks about the ambit of that expression, as used in the [CDPA] Act, the more one is driven to the conclusion that provided that it is all written down and contains information which can be read by somebody as opposed to appreciate it simply with the eye, the more one sees that that is just what it is'.

It is now established that tables, compilations, computer programs, preparatory design materials for computer programs and databases attract copyright protection, see Mr Justice Pumfrey in *Navitaire Inc v easyJet Airline Co Ltd*[5].

Not everything that is 'written, spoken or sung' is entitled to copyright. There must be a degree of originality[6].

Although copyright is *not a right in novelty of* ideas[7], in *Autospin (Oil Seals) Ltd v Beehive Spinning*[8], Mr Justice Laddie held:

'Copyright in a literary work gives protection not just to the words used but may also extend to the themes and ideas incorporated into it if they are efficiently substantial ... what the copyright protects is the relevant work and skill embodied in the work'.

The expression 'written, spoken or sung' was introduced by the CDPA. The inclusion of these words makes it clear that words spoken extempore (such as in an interview) will constitute a literary work at the time they are recorded. The author of such a literary work will be the speaker[9]. However, since such interviews are a common component of broadcasters' content, the CDPA contains an exception to copyright infringement for the benefit of broadcasters. Where a record of spoken words is made, in writing or otherwise, for the purpose of recording current events or broadcasting the whole or part of the work, the use of that recording (or copies of it) will not infringe the spoken literary work, provided that a number of conditions are met[10]. These are set out in detail elsewhere[11].

It has been long established that a wide variety of sometimes quite mundane material qualifies as literary work. Examples include street directories, mathematical tables, lists of stock exchange prices, grids and sequences of letters for competitions and betting coupons.

The CDPA (as amended by the Copyright and Rights in Databases Regulations 1997[12] ('1997 Regulations')) also specifically protects databases as a separate class of literary work (distinct from tables and compilations). The CDPA (as amended) defines a database as:

'a collection of independent works, data or other materials which –

(a) are arranged in a systematic or methodical way, and
(b) are individually accessible by electronic or other means'[13].

The amended CDPA imposes a requirement that a database can only be considered an original literary work if it (by reason of the selection or arrangement of its contents) constitutes the author's own intellectual creation[14]. The significance of this requirement is considered further in **Chapter 3**, but it is worth noting here that in implementing the Database Directive[15], the Parliamentary draftsmen have subtly increased the burden on a person seeking to establish that a database (as opposed to a table or compilation) qualifies for copyright protection.

Whether or not a database qualifies for copyright protection under the CDPA, the 1997 Regulations also introduced an additional sui generis property right, Database Right which subsists in a database if there has been a substantial investment in obtaining, verifying or presenting the contents of the database[16]. In brief, this right is infringed if a person extracts or re-utilises all or a substantial part of the contents of a database without the owner's consent[17]. The right expires at the end of 15 years from the end of the calendar year in which the making of the database was completed, except where the database is made public before the end of that period, in which event the right expires at the end of 15 years from the end of the year in which the database was made public[18].

Databases are now therefore subject to at least two possible tiers of protection. Compilations and tables receive yet another tier of protection. The result is a complex framework which brings with it a number of uncertainties[19].

1   CDPA s 3(1).
2   *Sweeney v MacMillan Publishers Ltd [2002] All ER(D)332.*
3   Dealt with in s 4 – the *'artistic works'* section, see **paragraph 2.06.**
4   [1994] FSR 659.
5   2004 EWHC 1725.
6   See **Chapter 3**.
7   See **paragraph 1.03**.
8   [1995] RPC 683.
9   See **paragraph 9.03**.
10 CDPA s 58.
11 See **paragraph 8.20**.
12 SI 1997/3032.
13 CDPA s 3A(1).
14 CDPA s 3A(2).
15 1996/9/EC.
16 1997 Regulations, reg 13(1).
17 1997 Regulations, reg 16.
18 1997 Regulations, reg 17.
19 For analysis, of the database right, see **Chapter 14**.

Dramatic works

2.03   Dramatic works are defined in the CDPA as follows: '"*dramatic work*" includes a work of dance or mime'[1].

This list is not exhaustive. Other works (eg radio plays, screenplays or even films) may also be dramatic works. A stage musical is a dramatic work. The 'book' of a musical comedy (ie the spoken words and lyrics) is both a dramatic and literary work. The music, considered separately from the book, is a musical work.

There must be some spoken words or action to perform or dance in order to differentiate a dramatic work from a literary work or a musical work. A description which is to be read, and is not written in a dramatic form, nor is intended for use in a dramatic way, would not be a dramatic work. On the other hand, the absence of dialogue (or indeed any spoken words) does not prevent a piece qualifying as a dramatic work. Dramatic incidents as well as spoken words are entitled to copyright.

The subject matter of the work must be sufficiently certain in order to qualify as a dramatic work. A screenplay will have dramatic elements (dialogue, directions etc), which are used to develop the plot. However the elements must be linked together in a way which is capable of performance. A television format was held to lack the necessary unity enabling it to be performed[2]. Similarly, in Canada, a sporting event was held not to be a dramatic work, notwithstanding that certain parts of the action were pre-planned[3]. In Australia the courts have upheld the existence of copyright in the format of a home renovation reality TV series, see: *Nine Films & Television Pty Ltd v Ninox Television Ltd*[4].

In 2000, the Court of Appeal held that the ordinary and natural meaning of a 'dramatic work' could be summarised as:

'a work of action, with or without words or music, which was capable of being performed before an audience'.

The Court held a film (as distinct from any dramatic work which may be recorded in the film)[5] may itself be capable of receiving protection as a dramatic work. Where a film contained a series of highly stylised 'jump shots', conveying the impression of a dance which was not actually capable of being performed and therefore not itself protectable as a dramatic work, the court held that the *film* itself (which was both a work of action and was quite capable of being performed) constituted a dramatic work in its own right and was capable of protection as such[6].

1   CDPA s 3(1).
2   *Green v Broadcasting Corporation of New Zealand [1989] RPC 700* and *Banner Universal Motion Pictures Ltd v Endemol Shine Group Ltd [2017] EWHC 2600.* See also **paragraph 2.14**.
3   *FWS Joint Sports Claimants v Copyright Board [1991] 22 IPR 429 (Fed Ct of Appeal), Canada.*
4   [2005] FCA 1404.
5   See **paragraph 2.08**.
6   *Norowzian v Arks Ltd (No2) [2000] FSR 363, CA.*

Musical works

2.04   For the purposes of the CDPA, a musical work is:

'a work consisting of music, exclusive of any words or action intended to be sung, spoken or performed with the music'[1].

Lyrics do not fall within the definition of a musical work, but instead are protected as literary works. However, musical annotations and directions on a score are part of the musical work.

In one case, the Court of Appeal considered whether 'performing editions of out-of-copyright musical works were themselves capable of constituting 'musical works' within s 3(1) of the CDPA. The court rejected an argument to the effect that to be a 'musical work' the editors would need to create new musical notation. Instead a wider test was to be preferred: what is required in order to assess whether a musical work based on an earlier work is itself capable of protection as a musical work is not a note by note textual comparison, but rather a comparison of the sounds which result[2].

The sounds are more important than the notes.

1   CDPA s 3(1).
2   *Sawkins v Hyperion Records Ltd [2005] EWCA 565, CA*. See also **paragraphs 3.01** and **20.04**.

Literary, dramatic and musical works – fixation

2.05   For copyright to subsist in a literary, dramatic or musical work it must be recorded in writing or otherwise. In other words, it must be reduced to some tangible form[1]. 'Writing' is defined in the CDPA as including:

> 'any form of notation or code, whether by hand or otherwise and regardless of the method by which, or the medium in or on which it is recorded ...'[2].

The intention is that any tangible form of recording of the work is sufficient to satisfy the requirement. Copyright exists in these works only from the time the work is recorded. A dance does not have dramatic copyright until it has been filmed or written down in some form, such as the shorthand notation of Benesch[3]. Equally, a melody will not have copyright protection until it is recorded or written down. So a dance or melody that is not recorded can be performed without copyright infringement. The question as to who owns the copyright if a work is first recorded by someone other than the author is considered below[4].

The requirement of fixation does not apply to artistic works[5].

1   CDPA s 3(2).
2   CDPA s 178.
3   See **paragraph 21.09**.
4   See **paragraph 9.03**.
5   See **paragraph 2.06**.

Artistic works

2.06   Under the CDPA, 'artistic works' means:

'(a) a graphic work, photograph, sculpture or collage, irrespective of artistic quality,
(b) a work of architecture being a building or a model for a building, or
(c) a work of artistic craftsmanship'[1].

It is worth noting that for an 'artistic work' to qualify for copyright protection, it need not, on the whole, have any artistic merit.

The CDPA sheds further light on the components of the definition of an artistic work[2]. So:

- a 'building' includes 'any fixed structure, and a part of a building or fixed structure';
- a 'graphic work' includes 'any painting, drawing, diagram, map, chart or plan' and 'any engraving, etching, lithograph, woodcut or similar work'[3]. In *Nova Productions Ltd v Mazooma Games Ltd*[4] Mr Justice Kitchin held that Bitmap (digital image) files and computer-generated composite frames constituted graphic works;
- a 'photograph' means 'a recording of light or other radiation on any medium on which an image is produced or from which an image may by any means be produced, and which is not part of a film'. This is a very wide definition, including such things as holograms, although significantly limited to still rather than moving images; and
- a 'sculpture' includes 'a cast or model made for the purposes of sculpture'.

The expression 'collage' is not defined in the CDPA, although the meaning has been considered in one case which held that the expression did not extend to a collection of articles arranged around a swimming pool to form the set for a photographic shoot[5]. Again, 'painting' and 'sculpture' are not defined, and therefore these terms bear their natural meaning. In one case it was held that 'painting' did not include the facial make-up of the 1980s pop star Adam Ant, although in principle there is no reason why make-up should not be capable of receiving protection, provided it is sufficiently original[6]. Again, in one case moulds for functional items were held not to be sculptures[7].

What amounts to a 'work of artistic craftsmanship' is not defined in the CDPA and accordingly this expression should also be given its ordinary and natural meaning. Both artistry *and* craftsmanship are required. So, although a graphic work, photograph, sculpture or collage will be protected 'irrespective of artistic quality', a work of craftsmanship (eg pottery) will be protected *only* if it has artistic quality[8].

Only architectural works and works of artistic craftsmanship require any artistic quality in order to fall within the definition of 'artistic work'. In the case of *Merlet v Mothercare Ltd*[9], the court held that a cape designed to be worn by a baby was a work of craftsmanship, but not of artistic craftsmanship, and consequently was not protected as a copyright work. Walton J held that the test as to whether something is a work of artistic craftsmanship, once it is established that it is a work of craftsmanship, is whether or not the artist-craftsman *intended* to create a work of art. It will be easier for a recognised artist to satisfy the court of his intentions than someone who has never attempted to sell his creations. It is also easier to bring hand-crafted works within the meaning of the expression, than machine-made works.

It is more important to ascertain the intention of the artist in creating the work, rather than the reaction of the viewer to the completed work, for it is usual in copyright law to ignore the question as to whether or not the work has any merit. However, in the *ANACON* case[10], Mr Justice Jacob said that, 'the essential nature of a graphic work, it is a thing to be looked at in some manner or another. It is to be looked at in itself.' A helpful analysis of what is meant by artistic craftsmanship is found in the Australian decision of *Swarbrick v Burge* [11].

Modern artists frequently use works in their art which do not fall within the technical definition of an artistic work described above (eg films, sound recordings, etc). Where one of these other types of works is used in an artistic context, we recommend reference to the particular parts of this *User's Guide* dealing with those other works. If it is to receive copyright protection, a work of art which does not fall within one of the above types of artistic work, must fall within one of the other categories of protected work considered in this chapter.

The requirement of fixation[12] does not apply to artistic works, so that an 'ephemeral work' (such as a sculpture created from rocks or debris below a tidal high water mark which is designed to be washed away by the next tide) is capable of being protected even if it is not recorded. 'Performance art' may receive protection as a dramatic work.

1   CDPA s 4(1).
2   CDPA s 4(2).
3   But query how this definition might cope with 'found' or 'ready made' pieces like those of Marcel Duchamp.
4   [2006] EWHC 24.
5   *Creation Records v News Group Newspapers Ltd [1997] EMLR 444*, see also **paragraph 6.04.**
6   *Merchandising Corpn of America Inc v Harpbond Ltd [1983] FSR 32.*
7   *Metix (UK) Ltd v GH Maughan (Plastics) Ltd [1997] FSR 718.*
8   *George Hensher Ltd v Restawile Upholstery (Lancs) Ltd [1976] AC 64, HL.* The *Hensher* decision has proved difficult authority, as demonstrated in the case of *Vermaat (t/a Cotton Productions) v Boncrest Ltd (No 1) [2001] FSR 5.* See further **Chapter 14.**
9   [1984] FSR 358.
10   See **paragraph 2.02.**
11   [2007] HCA 17.
12   See **paragraph 2.05.**

Sound recordings

2.07   A 'sound recording' is defined in the CDPA s 5A as:

'(a)   a recording of sounds, from which the sounds may be reproduced, or
(b)   the recording of the whole or any part of a literary, dramatic or musical
work, from which sounds reproducing the work or part may be produced,

regardless of the medium on which the recording is made or the method by
which the sounds are reproduced or produced'[1].

This is a technology-neutral definition intended to catch every type of
sound recording which is made now or in the future.

There are a number of points to be noted in relation to this definition
of sound recording:

(1)   it is not the physical disc or tape that receives copyright protection,
but rather the *recording* itself;
(2)   the definition is not limited to a recording of sounds. The first part of
the definition deals with traditional types of recording and includes
recordings of any sound (eg birdsong). The second part is limited to
recordings of literary, dramatic or musical works;
(3)   sound recordings are copyright works quite distinct from the
copyright in any compositions which they may record (which may
be protected as literary, dramatic or musical works);
(4)   sub-paragraph (*b*) of the definition has been included so as to
include, for example, a recording made directly from a synthesiser
of a musical work where the composer keys in his composition to
the synthesiser without actually producing a sound at that stage,
or of a literary or dramatic work where the synthesiser artificially
reproduces the human voice. Computer produced samples,
therefore, are entitled to protection as sound recordings. The same
paragraph is worded in such a way that a computer program which
can be played back so as to reproduce sounds in the form of a
meaningless noise to the human ear, would not be protected because
the noise will not constitute a sound reproducing a literary, dramatic
or musical work;
(5)   a sound recording does not qualify for copyright protection if, or to
the extent that, it is a copy of a previous sound recording[2].

The word 'record' does not appear in the CDPA (although it was
defined in the Copyright Act 1956, this definition is now irrelevant
except in relation to recordings made before the CDPA came into force).
Similarly, the word 'reproduction' is not defined in the CDPA. The
absence of a definition is likely to widen, rather than limit, the meaning
of the word.

1   CDPA s 5A(1).
2   CDPA s 5A(2).

Films

2.08 A film is 'a recording on any medium from which a moving image may by any means be produced'[1]. This too is a technology-neutral definition intended to cover all possible technical ways of recording moving images.

A film soundtrack is now treated as part of the film, following amendment of the CDPA by the Duration of Copyright and Rights in Performance Regulations 1995 ('1995 Regulations')[2]. Previously, the CDPA protected soundtracks separately simply as sound recordings, not as parts of films.

Copyright in a film is quite separate from the copyright in any literary, dramatic, musical or artistic work it may record. A film has copyright in its own right. So, the film of a live event or of abstract patterns (in which there is no copyright) will equally qualify as a 'film'.

Provided that a film constitutes a 'work of action' and is capable of being performed, it will also receive protection as a dramatic work in its own right, quite distinct from the acts it records[3]. This is interesting because at one time, it was generally thought that under the CDPA a film could only be copied by means of a technical reproduction of the film itself[4]. This position is suggested by the wording of the CDPA, which talks of copying in the context of a film as copying an 'image forming part of the film'[5] and provides that a film (or part of a film) which is simply a copy of a previous film has no copyright protection[6]. The traditional view was that whilst re-recording the same incidents featured in a previous film may infringe the copyright in underlying works (eg a screenplay), it would not infringe copyright in the earlier film itself. If a film is capable of receiving protection as a dramatic work in its own right, then replicating and re-shooting scenes from an earlier film is capable of infringing the earlier film (as distinct from the works appearing in it) if a substantial part is copied[7].

Copyright protection is not afforded to a film if, or to the extent that, it is a copy of another film[8].

Prior to the CDPA, the Copyright Act 1956 described 'films' as 'cinematograph films', an expression which carried a cumbersome definition. Films made before 1 June 1957 are not protected as cinematograph films at all, but as photographic works and dramatic works under the Copyright Act 1911. The law regarding old films can be complex and is beyond the scope of this *User's Guide*. Professional advice should be obtained when dealing with the copyright in such old films.

1   CDPA s 5B(1).
2   CDPA s 5A(2); SI 1995/3297.
3   *Norowzian v Arks Ltd (No2) [2000] FSR 363, CA*, see also **paragraph 2.03**.
4   For example, a still taken of the filmed image – see **paragraph 6.04**.
5   CDPA s 18(4).

6 CDPA s 5B(4).
7 See **paragraph 7.06**.
8 CDPA s 5B(4).

Broadcasts

2.09 The CDPA, as amended by the Copyright and Related Rights Regulations 2003 ('2003 Regulations')[1], defines a 'broadcast' as:

> 'an electronic transmission of visual images, sounds or other information which –
> (a) is transmitted for simultaneous reception by members of the public and is capable of being lawfully received by them, or
> (b) is transmitted at a time determined solely by the person making the transmission for presentation to members of the public,
> and which is not excepted by subsection (1A), and references to broadcasting shall be construed accordingly.
> (1A) Excepted from the definition of "broadcast" is any internet transmission unless it is –
> (a) a transmission taking place simultaneously on the internet and by other means,
> (b) a concurrent transmission of a live event, or
> (c) a transmission of recorded moving images or sounds forming part of a programme service offered by the person responsible for making the transmission, being a service in which programmes are transmitted at scheduled times determined by that person.'

Encrypted transmissions also constitute broadcasts, so long as the decoding equipment is available to members of the public by or with the authority of the person making the transmission or the person providing the contents of the transmission[2]. If the decoders are not made available to the public, then the transmission will not constitute a broadcast for the purposes of the CDPA.

A broadcast will not receive copyright protection if it infringes, or to the extent that it infringes, another broadcast[3].

The reception and immediate re-transmission of a broadcast is viewed as a separate broadcast to the one originally received[4].

The definition of 'broadcast' was substantially changed by the 2003 Regulations from that previously included in the CDPA. In order to give effect to the 2001 Directive (2001/29/EEC), the CDPA no longer distinguishes a 'broadcast' (formerly meaning, in basic terms, a wireless transmission), from a 'cable programme service' (broadly, a wireline transmission). The 2003 Regulations removed the significance of this distinction, categorising both forms of transmission as 'communications to the public'.

The new definitions of 'broadcast' and 'broadcasting' relate to transmissions by any electronic means (wireless or wireline), provided that those transmissions are transmitted for simultaneous public reception or at a time determined by the broadcaster. So:

- True video on demand (VOD) services will therefore not be classified as broadcasts, since the user determines the time at which the transmission is made[5].
- Near on demand services (whether provided by wireless or wireline means) appear most properly classified as broadcasts, since the service provider offers content over multiple channels at short intervals at a time determined by him[6].
- 'Enhanced' facilities included in broadcast streams such as multiple camera angles, drop down data streams or audio streams which are not truly 'interactive' features (given that they are usually broadcast simultaneously to all users as part of the primary transmission signal and individual streams then brought into view via user control of software in the set-top box) will constitute broadcasts for the purpose of the CDPA (as amended).

Content provided via websites will invariably be provided as a download or a stream.

Essentially, the CDPA now seeks to provide that only internet transmissions of conventional broadcast character will come within the definition of 'broadcast'. This means that the approach ensures that static web pages will not come within the scope of the concept but that copyright can subsist in images streamed via the internet at times determined by the person responsible for making the transmission.

Downloads occur when a user requests a transfer of, say, a music or video file sitting on a web server (ie an 'on demand' transfer) and will not therefore constitute a 'broadcast' for the purposes of the CDPA (as amended). However, 'streams' may or may not be classified as broadcasts. Streams (ie simultaneous display and downloads) occur when music or video is requested from a webpage and begins to play soon after the data transfer is initiated. The user's device is playing the content, essentially, as it receives it (although commonly part of the clip will be temporarily stored in the user's computer to 'buffer' against, for example, variations in transmission speed which might otherwise cause interruptions in the playout of the stream) rather than waiting for the entire clip to be transferred, and there is never a copy of the entire clip residing on the user's device as played parts are stored in transient memory rather than on any hard disk or other media.

An internet-delivered stream will constitute a broadcast for the purposes of the definition if the stream is delivered at scheduled times determined by the service provider. So:

- a real-time webcast where a user requesting the webcast joins the clip half-way through would be a broadcast for the purpose of a definition. So, if a user joining at 10.30pm a webcast of a music or sporting event which started at 10.00pm does not see the first

30 minutes of the event, that transmission will still constitute a broadcast;

- this should be contrasted with a stream that, when initiated, plays back music or a video clip and begins from the start 'on demand', which will not constitute a broadcast.

The words 'or other information' in the definition of 'broadcast' are designed to cover additional information included in the broadcast signal – for example, teletext transmissions or closed captioning. Other information might also include any 'pseudo-interactive' content, such as the 'enhanced' facilities described above.

Where users make available infringing copies of audio or video material via peer-to-peer services, their actions typically represent the provision of download facilities to others, and they would be treated in the same way as the operator of a traditional website hosting such content. This situation is complicated by more advanced peer-to-peer networks which permit a user to obtain a particular file more efficiently by copying different parts from different users simultaneously. However, despite technical differences in how different peer-to-peer systems facilitate the making available of a file to a very large number of other users, they involve individual transfers on demand, which would not constitute broadcasting. A possible exception to this relates to the emerging technology of peer-to-peer internet radio and television, where users on the network make their spare bandwidth available for 'live' transmissions. Newer peer-to-peer software applications[7] also raise difficult issues. Where peer-to-peer technologies permit 'simultaneous' transmission by the internet and other means (eg television), or the 'concurrent' transmission of a live event, this raises arguments that such services may themselves amount to a 'broadcast'. It is likely that very great consideration will need to be given to the correct meaning of 'concurrent' or 'simultaneous' in the context of such services.

1   SI 2003/2498.
2   CDPA s 6(2).
3   CDPA s 6(6).
4   CDPA s 6(5A).
5   See **paragraph 6.08** and, generally, **Chapter 24**.
6   See **paragraph 6.08** and, generally, **Chapter 24**.
7   For example, Coolstream, which allows users to upload files in streaming mode.

Cable programmes

2.10   The 2003 Regulations removed the previous definition of 'cable programme' included in the CDPA since, in the words of the former Copyright Directorate of the Patent Office:

'it is felt that there is no need to protect a "cable programme" as a species of copyright work other than where it is a "broadcast" as redefined, since any material included in an interactive cable service would seem already to be protected under other headings, ie as a literary, artistic, dramatic or musical work, sound recording or film.'[1]

1   Consultation Paper on implementation of the Directive in the UK, Patents Office, DTI, 7 August 2002.

Published editions of works[1]

2.11   Section 8 of the CDPA defines 'published edition' as meaning, in the context of copyright in the typographical arrangement of a published edition, 'a published edition of the whole or any part of one or more literary, dramatic or musical works'[2].

This definition expressly excludes editions which reproduce the typographical arrangements of previous editions of the same work[3] (ie duplicates of earlier editions). Without this exclusion, there could be perpetual copyright in a typographical arrangement because a new copyright period would commence with the publication of each new edition.

Because there is copyright in the typographical arrangements of published editions, publishers are able to sue for unauthorised copying of the published editions of literary, dramatic and musical works which do not themselves have copyright protection (because, for example, their copyright period has expired) where the typographical arrangements of the published editions of such works are themselves still in copyright. This is of particular importance to the publishers of novels, music, compositions etc where the works themselves are out of copyright.

In one case, Marks and Spencer copied and distributed a significant number of press cuttings to its staff. The owner of the typographical arrangement in the cuttings, the Newspaper Licensing Agency, claimed copyright infringement. It was held that when considering typographical arrangements of articles in a newspaper, the phrase 'typographical arrangement of a published edition' referred to the whole of or a page of a newspaper, not individual articles and that, in context, M&S had not copied a substantial part of the work[4].

1   For a history of typography, see Tariq Baloch, 'Typography in Law: From Mechanics to Aesthetics' [2001] 3 Ent LR.
2   CDPA s 8(1).
3   CDPA s 8(2).
4   *Newspaper Licensing Agency Ltd v Marks & Spencer plc* [2001] UKHL 38.

Only 'works' protected

2.12   It is essential, when considering any copyright problem, to decide first whether the material which is being copied is within one of the categories of work set out in the CDPA.

The case of *Tavener Rutledge Ltd v Trexapalm Ltd*[1] illustrates the essential principle that copyright can only exist in a work which can be brought within one of the categories defined in the CDPA. Tavener Rutledge sold lollipops under the name 'Kojak pops' for about two years without any permission from the owners of the Kojak television series. Trexapalm Ltd were intending to sell lollipops under the brand name 'Kojak Lollies', having been granted an exclusive licence from the owners of the television series to use that name. Tavener Rutledge sought an injunction restraining the passing off of Trexapalm's lollipops as those of Tavener Rutledge. Mr Justice Walton granted the injunction and in his judgment said that although in the USA there might be rights in invented names or fictional characters, English law did not recognise any such copyright. Therefore, one could not look to copyright to protect the use of such a name. It should be noted that the law of passing off and/or trade mark infringement may afford protection in cases where copyright law does not apply because the material does not come within the definition of a work.

1   [1977] RPC 275.

Real life events

2.13   There is no copyright in real life events, before they are reduced to writing or some other material form (such as the record of the telling of a story). However there *is* copyright in the *way* in which they are reduced into writing. So, in the case of *Harman Pictures NV v Osborne*[1], it was held that, although the events contained in a book by Cecil Woodham-Smith, entitled *The Reason Why* (an account of events surrounding the charge of the Light Brigade) were common to both that book and to John Osborne's screenplay for the film *The Charge of the Light Brigade*, there was, nevertheless, an infringement of the copyright in the book by the screenplay because the screenplay used the same characters and incidents in much the same order and arrangement as they appeared in the book. The case does not show that copyright exists in events, or that because someone has written down events he has a 'copyright' in those events. Copyright arose because of the *way* in which the events had been recorded into material form, which the court held had been copied by John Osborne. It follows that when real life events are resolved into material form, the result will be entitled to copyright but not the events themselves, as matters of fact[2].

Similar issues arise in the context of news reporting[3].

1   [1967] 2 All ER 324. See also *Ravenscroft v Herbert and New English Library Ltd [1980] RPC193* and *Poznanski v London Film Production Ltd [1937] MacG Cop Cas (1936–45) 107* and **paragraph 7.04.**
2   See also **paragraph 7.09.**
3   See **paragraph 16.05.**

Format rights

2.14   A programme format is essentially the formula by which a (usually episodic) television programme may be reproduced. The 'format' consists of the unifying elements of a series which are distinctive to the show and which are repeated from episode to episode. Common examples include game shows, chat shows and situation comedies. In the past, courts have been reluctant to extend protection to formats[1]. Notwithstanding that, in fact 'format rights' are commonly traded in the television industry. The popularity of 'reality TV' and the trade of such formats between UK and US-based companies has, in recent years, led to debates about the legal protectability of the formats of such shows as 'Survivor', 'I'm a Celebrity...', 'Pop Idol' and 'X Factor'[2].

The chances of a protectable copyright work existing in a format are enhanced where the format creator maintains a detailed record of the format. The key will be whether the format is sufficiently detailed and cohesive to be capable of being performed. If so, the format may receive protection as a dramatic work. Case law in other jurisdictions has shown that some courts have been prepared to extend copyright protection to formats. In Holland, for example, the Dutch Supreme Court held that the format for 'Survivor' was capable of copyright protection, albeit that the claimants failed to show that it was infringed by the format of 'Big Brother'[3].

In Brazil, Endemol were successful in establishing that TV SBT's show 'Cas Dos Artistas' ('The Artist's House') infringed its format of Big Brother. The judge pointed to the 'whopping similarity' of the formats, after Endemol had provided significant information on its own format to TV SBT during contractual negotiations.

Of course, these cases are not binding authority in the English courts, and although they do demonstrate that certain jurisdictions are more sympathetic to the protection of formats than the court in *Green v Broadcasting Corporation of New Zealand*[4] the same is not true for the English courts, where Laddie J recently cited with approval the dicta of Lord Bridge in *Green*:

> 'The protection which copyright gives creates a monopoly and there must be certainty in the subject matter of such copyright in order to avoid injustice to the rest of the world.'[5]

Even if copyright protection is not available, it may (depending on the circumstances) be possible for the format creator to take action for a breach of confidentiality or passing off. In practice, when format rights are traded, this is usually done through agreements which convey a variety of rights: including rights to confidential information, trade mark licences, 'know how', and contractual undertakings not to trade similar formats or co-operate with similar programmes within the same jurisdiction.

In March and April 1996 the Patent Office issued consultative documents proposing the introduction of copyright protection for the scheme or plan (ie a format) for a series of programmes recorded in a copyright work or works. The protection would only arise when the scheme or plan was 'sufficiently elaborated'. However, after assessing the outcome of a full consultative process, the Patent Office concluded that there was not sufficient industry support for the proposal and that the restricted acts of copying and adaptation together with the protection afforded by the laws of confidentiality and passing off provided sufficient protection for programme formats.

1   See **paragraph 2.03**.
2   For a recent discussion, see 'Format Rights, Not so Simple for Simon' [2005] Ent LR, 16(2) 32–34. See also *Celador Productions Ltd v Melville, Boone v ITV Network, Baccini v Celador Productions Ltd [2004] EWHC 2362* (re Who Wants to be a Millionaire), *Miles v ITV Networks Ltd [2003] All ER (D) 145* (re 'Dream Street').
3   Castaway Television Productions Ltd and Planet 24 Productions Ltd in dispute with Endemol.
4   See **paragraph 2.03**.
5   *IPC Media Ltd v Highbury-SPL Publishing Ltd [2004] EWHC 2984 (Ch)*. See also *Banner Universal Motion Pictures Ltd v Endemol Shine Group Ltd* [2017] EWHC 2600.

Image personality rights and copyright distinguished

2.15   As celebrities have sought increasing levels of control over the exploitation of their image for commercial purposes, more focus has been placed on the phenomenon of 'image' or 'personality' rights. Unlike copyright, there is not a high degree of harmonisation between different national laws on the issue of whether 'image rights' per se are capable of protection. In England, for example, they go largely unrecognised. If I own the photograph of a celebrity, I am free to exploit that photograph, provided that in doing so I do not infringe a right of privacy, engage in passing off, infringe a registered trademark or otherwise engage in misleading advertising.

My ability to exploit that photograph derives from my ownership of the copyright in the image. Copyright will subsist in a representation of the image of a celebrity as an artistic work[1]. If the image is taken from a photograph of the celebrity, then the first owner of copyright will be the photographer responsible for the picture, or their employer if they are an employee and the work is created in the course of their employment[2]. If the image is taken from a drawing of the celebrity, then the artist responsible for the drawing will be first owner of copyright in the image (again, unless they are an employee, in which case the employer is first owner of copyright).

1   See **paragraph 2.06**.
2   See **paragraph 9.11**.

Public policy and the denial of protection

2.16 Since copyright is a property right conferred by statute, if a work qualifies for protection in accordance with the statute, public policy will not intervene to deny the existence of copyright, notwithstanding that the work may not be particularly meritorious[1]. The courts have however, recently utilised the language of public policy in order to deny copyright protection to the 'business logic' of a computer program where that logic had been followed, albeit that no textual copying of the program itself had taken place. The court held that 'as a matter of policy, to permit the "business logic" of a program to attract protection through the literary copyright afforded to the program itself was an unjustifiable extension of copyright protection'[2].

Quite apart from the principles of copyright, the courts have an inherent jurisdiction to refuse to *enforce* copyright, where to do so would run contrary to public policy. The CDPA provides that 'nothing in this Part affects any rule of law preventing or restricting the enforcement of copyright, on grounds of public interest or otherwise'[3]. The courts have from time to time used this jurisdiction to deny copyright protection to works which are considered libellous, immoral, obscene, scandalous or irreligious, but have proved unwilling to allow public interest to be used as a general defence to copyright infringement[4]. So, where *The Sun* newspaper printed photographs taken from the security cameras of premises owed by Mr Al Fayed (showing the movements of Princess Diana and Dodi Fayed before their death) without authorisation, as part of a story which intended to convey that Mr Al Fayed had invented falsehoods about the events preceding their deaths, it was held that *The Sun* could not avoid copyright infringement by arguing there was a public interest in exposing those alleged falsehoods[5].

A work should also receive copyright protection, notwithstanding that the copyrights of others were infringed in making it[6]. Protecting an infringing work in this way may be advantageous to the owner of the work which has been infringed, since he may be entitled to an account of profits from the sales of the infringing work[7]. A typical example would be a sound recording which uses examples taken from other sound recordings without the authority of the copyright owners of those recordings.

1 See the *Hyde Park Residence* case below.
2 *Navitaire Inc v Easyjet Airline Co [2004] EWHC 1725 (Ch)*. See also **paragraph 6.04**.
3 CDPA s 171(3).
4 For example, *Stockdale v Onwhyn (1826) 5 B & C 173.*
5 *Hyde Park Residence Ltd v Yelland [2000] 3 WLR 215, CA.*
6 *Redwood Music Ltd v Chappell & Co Ltd [1982] RPC 109.*
7 See **paragraph 7.14**.

Chapter 3

Originality

Generally

3.01   Under English law if a literary, dramatic, musical or artistic work is to be entitled to copyright it must be original[1]. Originality in this context refers to the way in which the work is reduced to a material form and not to the originality of the *idea* upon which the work is based. In *University of London Press Ltd v Universal Tutorial Press Ltd*[2], Mr Justice Peterson held:

> 'The word "original" does not in this connection mean that the work must be the expression of original or inventive thought. Copyright Acts are not concerned with the originality of ideas, but with the expression of thought, and, in the case of "literary work", with the expression of thought in print or writing. The originality which is required relates to the expression of the thought. But the Act[3] does not require that the expression must be in an original or novel form, but that the work must not be copied from another work – that it should originate from the author.'

Again, in *Bookmakers Afternoon Greyhound Services Ltd v Wilf Gilbert (Staffs) Ltd*[4], Mr Justice Aldous said that:

> 'It is settled law that the word "original" does not require original or inventive thought but only that the work should not be copied and should originate from the author'.

The test frequently cited by courts for determining originality is that of the degree of 'skill and labour':

> 'It is the product of the labour, skill and capital of one man which must not be appropriated by another, not the elements, the raw material, if we may use the expression, upon which the labour and skill and capital of the first had been expended. To secure copyright for the product it is necessary that labour, skill and capital should be expended sufficiently to impart to the product some quality or character which the raw material did not possess, and which differentiates the product from the raw material.'

(Lord Atkinson in *MacMillan & Co v K & J Cooper*)[5].

There is no simple test to determine the extent of the skill and labour which must be devoted to a literary, dramatic, musical or artistic work in order to confer copyright protection upon it: 'It is a question of degree and will depend on the work produced and all the circumstances of the case'[6].

So, for example, in the case of 'compilation' literary works, originality has been considered 'a matter of degree depending on the amount of skill, judgment or labour that has been involved in making the compilation'[7].

In the context of databases, the CDPA[8] now provides that: 'a literary work consisting of a database is original if, and only if, by reason of the selection or arrangement of the contents of the database the database constitutes the author's own intellectual creation'[9]. This requirement for 'intellectual creation' signals a departure from traditional tests of originality[10], reflecting the European tradition of not offering copyright protection to databases which do not have literary or artistic merit[11]. Some writers have noted that similar language in the Software Directive[12] was not included in the regulations which implemented the Directive into UK law. However, it is safer to assume that some higher degree of originality is required in connection with databases than is necessary to establish protectability in the context of a non-database-related copying of work.

Copyright has been held to exist in football pools, timetables, lists of stock exchange prices[13], race cards[14] and mathematical tables[15] (the subject of cases where skill or labour has been applied to the compilation and organisation of information which is widely available). However, if such work is found to be a 'database', it will not qualify for copyright protection unless it meets the higher degree of originality test referred to above.

Artistic works have been considered differently. In *Interlego AG v Tyco Industries Inc*[16] Lord Oliver of Aylmerton, comparing the authorities concerning literary works (particularly compilations) and artistic works, stated:

'Originality in the context of literary copyright has been said in several well known cases to depend upon the degree of skill, labour and judgment involved in preparing a compilation ... skill, judgment or labour is likely to be decisive in the case of compilations. To apply that, however, as a universal test of originality in all copyright cases is not only unwarranted by the context in which the observations were made but palpably erroneous. Take the simplest case of artistic copyright, a painting or a photograph. It takes great skill, judgment and labour to produce a good copy by painting or to produce an enlarged photograph from a positive print, but no one would reasonably contend that the copy of the painting or enlargement was an "original" artistic work in which the copier is entitled to claim copyright. Skill, labour or judgment merely in the process of copying cannot confer originality'.

In the case of artistic works, the fact that a drawing is simple will not disqualify it for protection as an artistic work. In *British Northrop Ltd v Texteam Blackburn Ltd*[17] Megarry J had to consider whether drawings of such basic items as a rivet, screw, metal bar, washer etc were capable of being 'original' works. He said:

'A drawing which is simply traced from another drawing is not an original artistic work: a drawing which is made without any copying from anything originates with the artist ... It may indeed be that some thing may be drawn which cannot fairly be called a diagram or a drawing of any kind: a single straight line drawn with the aid of a ruler would not seem to me a very promising subject for copyright. But apart from cases of such barren and naked simplicity as that, I should be slow to exclude drawings from copyright on the mere score of simplicity. I do not think that the mere fact that a drawing is of an elementary and commonplace article makes it too simple to be the subject to copyright ... If simplicity were a disqualification, at some point there would come enough complexity to qualify. It is not that I am unable to see exactly where the [1956 Act] draws the line: it is that I cannot see that there is any intention to draw any line at all. Accordingly, I reject the defendants' contentions on this score.'

However, where a drawing contains only limited variations from an earlier drawing, the courts have proved cautious in affording protection. In *Interlego AG v Tyco Industries Inc*[18] Interlego sought to establish that small but technically important additions and emendations to design drawings created a new originality. This was rejected by the Privy Council, which held that the test for originality would only be satisfied if the new drawings were visually and significantly different or differed materially in their visual aspects from previous drawings. Lord Oliver of Aylmerton indicated:

'What is important about a drawing is what is visually significant and the re-drawing of an existing drawing with a few minimal visual alterations does not make it an original artistic work, however much labour and skill may have gone into the process of reproduction ...'

The fact that a drawing is substantially derived from earlier drawings does not deprive the new drawing of originality *per se*. In *SPE International Ltd v Professional Preparation Contractors (UK) Ltd*[19] it was held that although a substantial part of a drawing incorporated work from an earlier drawing, a substantial part was not so derived, and the differences in the new drawing did involve the expenditure of skill and effort necessary to confer on the new drawing (when considered as a whole) a quality which made it different from earlier drawings and was sufficiently original to deserve copyright protection.

More recently, it has been suggested that the dictum of Lord Oliver in *Interlego* should be confined to the subject matter of that case: technical drawings. In *Sawkins v Hyperion Records Ltd*[20], the court considered the issue of copyright in musical works. The plaintiff had created new 'performing editions' of several works which were themselves out of copyright. He registered his new editions with MCPS and PRS, and when Hyperon Records wanted to use his editions on a CD format, he sued for copyright and moral rights infringement. The Court of Appeal upheld Dr Sawkin's claims, emphasising that the test for originality is that the work 'originates' from the efforts of the author, as distinct from being 'slavishly copied' from another work. This is essentially a restatement of the 'sweat of the brow' test favoured by earlier case law[21].

Originality in the context of musical works is considered in further detail elsewhere in this *User's Guide*[22].

It is worth noting that there is no requirement for originality in the case of sound recordings, films, broadcasts, cable programmes and typographical arrangements of published editions. This is because they usually all involve some other act or work. For example, a sound recording will be a record of another work (a literary, dramatic or musical) or of a non-copyright sound (such as a bell ringing). Literary, dramatic, musical and artistic works (which are not adaptations), on the other hand, may exist independently.

EU Directives have incorporated a test for originality which differs from the long-established English test. The Court of Appeal in *SAS Institute Inc v World Programming Ltd*[23] has indicated that the EU test 'has raised rather than lowered the hurdle to obtaining copyright protection'. The EU test is 'whether the work comprises the expression of the author's own intellectual creation'. This arose from the Information Society Directive[24].

It is based on the principle that the protection of subject matter as authors' works presupposes that they are 'intellectual creations' which are original in the sense that they are the author's own intellectual creation. The leading CJEU case is *Infopaq International A/S v Danske Dagblades Forening*[25] which noted that the test applies to literary and artistic works as well as databases and photographs.

It has not been decided definitively whether the Directive and CJEU case law effects a substantial alteration to UK law. So in *The Newspaper Licensing Agency Ltd v Meltwater Holding BV*[26] both the Court of Appeal and Supreme Court held in applying *Infopaq* that the English law had not been qualified.

1   CDPA s 1.
2   [1916] 2 Ch 601.
3   Ie the Copyright Act 1911.
4   [1994] FRS 723.
5   (1923) LR 51 Ind App 109, PC.
6   *Greyhound Services* case, above. For an interesting discussion of originality in relation to the reconstruction of ancient texts, see Michael D Birnhack, 'The Dead Sea Scrolls Case: Who is the author' [2001] EIPR, Issue 3.
7   Per Lord Reid, *Ladbroke (Football) Ltd v William Hill (Football) Ltd [1964] 1 WLR 273 at 277, HL.*

8   As amended by the Copyright and Rights in Databases Regulations 1997, SI 1997/3032, '1997 Regulations'.

9   CDPA s 3A(2).

10 See *University of London Press Ltd* above which tended to see originality as meaning 'not a copy', rather than 'an intellectual creation'.

11 For further discussion of databases, see **paragraph 2.02** and **Chapter 14**.

12 Council Directive 91/250/EEC of 14 May 1991 on the legal protection of computer programs.

13 *Exchange Telegraph Co Ltd v Gregory & Co [1896] 1 QB 147.*

14 *Bookmakers' Afternoon Greyhound Services Ltd v Wilf Gilbert (Staffordshire) Ltd [1994] FSR 723.*

15 *Express Newspapers v Liverpool Daily Post and Echo [1985] FSR 306.*

16 [1988] RPC 343.

17 [1976] RPC 344.

18 [1989] AC 217.

19 [2002] EWHC 881.

20 [2005] EWCA Civ 565; see **paragraph 20.04**.

21 For a detailed analysis of this case see Richard Munden's commentary at IP & T Expert Commentary, 2005 [75].

22 See **paragraph 20.04**.

23 [2012] RPC 31.

24 Directive 2001/29/EC on the harmonisation of certain aspects of copyright and related rights in the information society.

25 [2012] EUECJ C-302/10 (17 January 2012).

26 [2013] EWCA Civ 890.

Titles and names

3.02   The title of a book, film or song will not have copyright protection in the UK unless it is so elaborate that sufficient skill and labour must have been involved in its invention so as to allow it to qualify as a literary work in its own right.

It was held, in a case which decided that the name 'Exxon' was not entitled to copyright protection, that for a name or title to have copyright protection: 'it must have qualities or characteristics in itself, if such a thing is possible, which would justify its recognition as an original literary work rather than merely as an invented word'[1].

In *Rose v Information Services Ltd*[2], Mr Rose, the publisher of 'The Lawyer's Diary', claimed he owned copyright in the title 'The Lawyer's Diary 1986' which was infringed by the words 'Law Diary 1986'. Dismissing the claim, Hoffmann J held that the words 'The Lawyer's Diary' 'were a simple and accurate description of the product. They were not a literary work of originality which qualified for literary protection'. He said that if the plaintiff was entitled to copyright protection it would be hard to see how the defendant could describe its product in a commercially acceptable form without being said to infringe the plaintiff's rights. In effect the plaintiff would have acquired a monopoly of part of the English language.

Newspaper headlines may also be protected as literary works pursuant to *Meltwater v Newspaper Licensing Agency*[3].

1   *Exxon Corpn v Exxon Insurance Consultants International Ltd [1982] Ch 119, CA.*
2   [1987] FSR 254.
3   [2013] UKSC 18.

Photographs

3.03   Photographs present particular problems in the context of originality. The CDPA treats photographs as artistic works irrespective of their artistic quality[1]. A photographic enlargement of an existing photograph is not entitled to copyright protection in its own right if it is merely a copy (since it will lack originality)[2], but if a person takes a photograph of an identical scene to that shown in another photograph, the second photograph is entitled to copyright in just the same way as the first photograph. The test for originality in a photograph will be low, and will turn on whether requisite skill and labour have been invested in factors such as the way in which the shot is composed, the angle at which the camera is pointing at the scene, the setting of the aperture and the calculation of the exposure.

The question of originality becomes more complex when considering photographs of other copyright works (eg paintings). The traditional view has been that, provided skill and labour is expended in taking a photograph, copyright will not be denied because the subject of the photograph is another work:

'All photographs are copies of some object, such as a painting or a statue, and it seems to me that a photograph taken from a picture is an original photograph'[3].

A US case casts doubt on this traditional view. In *Bridgeman Art Library Ltd v Corel* Corpn[4] the New York District Court (Southern District) held that the photograph of a painting which was 'in the public domain' and had been taken in such a way as to faithfully reproduce the painting lacked sufficient originality to be protected as a copyright work. However, at least one recent UK case suggests that the UK courts will not follow the lead set by *Bridgeman. Antiquesportfolio.com plc v Rodney Finch & Co*[5] concerned copyright in photographic images of three-dimensional objects (ie antiques as opposed to paintings). The judge held the photographs were original and attracted copyright protection[6].

The CJEU in *Painer v Standard VerlagsGmbH*[7] held that photographs are protected by copyright only if they are original in the sense that they are their author's own intellectual creation.

1   CDPA s 4.
2   See the dicta of Lord Oliver referred to in **paragraph 3.01**.

3 Graves' Case *(1869) 4 LR QB 715.*
4 36 F Supp 2d [9] and 25F Supp 2d 421 (SDN4) (1998).
5 [2001] FSR 345, [2000] All ER (D) 950.
6 For a discussion of this and the *Bridgeman* case, see Simon Stokes, 'Creativity Challenges Copyright', Managing IP Feb 2002.
7 Case C–145/10, [2012] ECDR 6.

Abridgements and arrangements

3.04 Copyright can exist in the abridgement of another copyright work, where the abridgement itself involves skill and labour, even though no original thought in terms of the content has been added[1]. Similarly, there can be copyright in the arrangement of a piece of music[2]. In order to obtain protection the contribution to the work made by the arranger is crucial. The CJEU recognised in *Infopaq*[3] that the author's own intellectual creation is evidenced from the form, the manner in which the work is prescribed and its linguistic expression.

1 *Macmillan & Co v Cooper (1923) 40 TLR 186, PC.*
2 *Redwood Music Ltd v Chappell & Co Ltd [1982] RPC 109.*
3 *Infopaq International A/S v Danske Dagblades Forening (C-5/08) [2010] FSR 20, ECJ.*

Independent creation

3.05 Copyright does not create a monopoly right over an idea, merely a right not to have a copyright work copied. So, if for example two people, acting independently of each other, produce identical directories, those directories will equally be entitled to copyright. Both works will be original in the sense that they owe their existence to the skill and labour of their compilers and will not infringe the other. However copyright may exist in an infringing work such as the unauthorised translation of an artistic work.

Identical subject matter

3.06 Similarly, if two different radio producers record a concert using their own equipment and quite independently of the other, there will be copyright in both recordings although the recordings will probably be identical in all material respects. On the other hand, a *copy* of one of those recordings would not in itself possess copyright[1]. Another example is that of an artist who paints a true copy of another painting. The copy infringes the copyright of the original painting and the copy does not itself acquire a new copyright, because it lacks the quality of originality[2].

1 See **paragraph 2.07**.
2 See **paragraph 3.01**; the position is different however in relation to adaptations, see **paragraph 6.09**.

Chapter 4

Qualification for protection and international copyright

Qualification

General

4.01 For copyright to subsist in any category of work it is necessary pursuant to the CDPA s 1(3) for the qualification requirements of the CDPA to be satisfied[1]. A work which is entitled to copyright protection in another country and which has passed all the other tests entitling it to copyright protection in the UK will nevertheless be unprotected under UK copyright law unless it meets the qualification requirements of the CDPA.

In summary, there are two bases for qualification for works coming into existence after 1 August 1989, being qualification by reference to:

- the author; or
- the country in which the work was first published; or

for works coming into existence before 1 August 1989 the 1956 Act applies and in particular the nationality of the author.

1 These are to be found in the CDPA, Ch IX, ss 153–162; see **paragraphs 4.02** ff.

Author: 'material time'

4.02 For the work to qualify for copyright protection the author must have been a qualifying person 'at the material time'[1]. What constitutes the 'material time' will depend upon the kind of work involved. The material time:

- *for unpublished literary, dramatic, musical or artistic works*, is when the work was made or, if the making of the work extends over a period, a substantial part of that period[2];

- *for published works*, is when the work was first published or, if the author died before that time, immediately before his death[3];
- *for sound recordings and films,* is when the sound recording or film is made[4];
- *for broadcasts,* is when the broadcast is made[5];
- *for published editions*, is when first published[6].

The question of when a literary, dramatic or musical work is made is considered elsewhere in this *User's Guide*[7]. The CDPA does not define when artistic works, sound recordings, films or broadcasts are made and therefore normal rules of construction will apply in respect of those categories of work.

1   CDPA s 154.
2   CDPA s 154(4)(a).
3   CDPA s 154(4)(b).
4   CDPA s 154(5)(a).
5   CDPA s 154(5)(b).
6   CDPA s 154(5)(d).
7   See **paragraph 2.05**.

Author: 'qualifying person'

4.03   The author of the work must be a 'qualifying person' at the material time. A 'qualifying person' is defined in some detail in the CDPA[1]. In summary, it includes a British citizen, a British Dependent Territories citizen, a British National (Overseas), a British Overseas citizen, a British subject or a British protected person within the meaning of the British Nationality Act 1981.

The expression also includes individuals domiciled or resident in the UK or another country to which the CDPA has been extended[2]. Bodies incorporated under the laws of the UK or another country to which the provisions of the CDPA have been extended, also come within the definition[3].

In the case of literary, dramatic, musical and artistic works, with certain exceptions[4] the author must be a natural person (as opposed to a legal person, such as a limited company). A 'legal person' may be the first copyright *owner* of such a work (because the copyright owner of a literary, dramatic, music or artistic work or a film made by an employee in the course of his or her employment, is the employer subject to any agreement to the contrary)[5], but for the purpose of deciding whether a work qualifies for copyright protection by reference to its author, it is necessary to consider the nationality, residence or domicile of the first *author* not the first owner. So, even if the employing body corporate does not qualify, the work will be entitled to protection in the UK if the actual author qualifies.

The question of authorship is more complex in the context of other categories of work (ie sound recordings, films, broadcasts and typographical arrangements). English law has traditionally protected the 'maker' of these works (ie the person who assumes the financial risk in making the work) although, as the flavour of UK law is effected by the implementation of EU Directives, this position is changing[6].

1   CDPA s 154(1)(a) ff.
2   CDPA s 154(1)(b); see **paragraph 4.08**.
3   CDPA s 154(1)(c).
4   Discussed further at **Chapter 8**.
5   CDPA s 11(2).
6   See **Chapter 9** for a fuller discussion of authorship issues.

Qualification in country of first publication

4.04   All types of work, except broadcasts, qualify for copyright protection if they have been *first published*[1]:

- in the UK; or
- in another country to which the relevant provisions of the CDPA have been *extended*[2]; or
- in another country to which the CDPA has been *applied* as regards that type of work[3].

A work will not be treated as 'first published' in a country which is not listed above simply because it is published elsewhere at the same time as it is published in one of the listed countries[4]. However, since it may be difficult to establish where publication first happened if a work is published in swift succession in several countries, the CDPA provides that publication will be deemed to be simultaneous if it takes place within 30 days following the first publication. So, if a work is published in the UK or another country to which the CDPA extends or has been applied within 30 days of its publication elsewhere, the publication will be regarded as simultaneous and the work will be entitled to copyright protection in the UK.

1   CDPA s 155.
2   See **paragraph 4.08**.
3   See **paragraph 4.09**.
4   CDPA s 155(3).

The meaning of 'publication'

4.05   Qualification for copyright protection in the UK by reference to the country of first publication applies to literary, dramatic, musical and artistic works, sound recordings, films and published editions.

'Publication' is defined in the CDPA as 'the issue of copies to the public'[1]. This definition applies to all categories of works except that a separate meaning is applicable in the context of 'the publication right'[2]. It is worth noting that in the case of literary, dramatic, musical and artistic works, publication specifically includes making available to the public by means of an electronic retrieval system[3]. A typical example of an electronic retrieval system is an online database.

A publication 'which is merely colourable and not intended to satisfy the reasonable requirements of the public' does not constitute publication. In *Francis, Day and Hunter v Feldman & Co*[4] sheet music of the song 'You Made Me Love You (I Didn't Want To Do It)' was printed in the USA. A few copies were sent to London and six were put on sale in a shop on Charing Cross Road within 30 days of the first copies being put on sale in New York (thus apparently satisfying the 30-day simultaneous publication rule referred to at **paragraph 4.04**). The court had to decide whether the copies offered for sale in London constituted publication. It held that the intention was to satisfy the reasonable demands of the public and therefore the song had been duly published in the UK. In each case the intention of the publisher, not necessarily the number of copies that are issued to the public, is important. The song had not been advertised and was not known in London, so six copies was sufficient to satisfy the reasonable demands of the public.

For this purpose publication means publication of the whole work, not just a substantial part of it. It will also be the latest published version[5].

There is a special provision for architecture: the construction of a building is to be treated as publication of a work of architecture or an artistic work incorporated in a building[6].

1   CDPA s 175(1)(a).
2   See **paragraphs 5.14** ff.
3   CDPA s 175(1)(b).
4   [1914] 2 Ch 728, CA.
5   *Sweeney v MacMillan Publishers [2002] RPC 35*.
6   CDPA s 175(3).

Acts not constituting publication

4.06 The CDPA specifically provides that some acts do not constitute publication[1]. These can be summarised as follows:

- *literary, dramatic and musical works*: performance or communication to the public of the work (otherwise than for the purposes of an electronic retrieval system)[2];
- *artistic works*: exhibition, the issue to the public of copies of a graphic work representing (or photographs of), a work of architecture in the form of a building or a model for a building, a sculpture or a work of artistic craftsmanship, the issue to the public of copies of a film including the work, communication to the public of the work (otherwise than for the purposes of an electronic retrieval system)[3];

- *sound recordings and films*: playing or showing the work in public, or the communication of the work to the public[4].

1   CDPA s 175(4).
2   CDPA s 175(4)(a).
3   CDPA s 175(4)(b).
4   CDPA s 175(4)(c).

Broadcasts – qualification for copyright protection by reference to the place of transmission

4.07   Broadcasts qualify for copyright protection if they are made from or sent from the UK or another country to which the CDPA is extended or applied[1].

1   CDPA s 156.

Extension of the CDPA overseas

4.08   The CDPA is extended to England and Wales, Scotland and Northern Ireland[1]. It has been further extended by Orders in Council to the Isle of Man. Guernsey and Jersey have now introduced their own Copyright Ordinances.

1   CDPA s 157.

Application of the CDPA overseas to foreign works

4.09   Provision is made in the CDPA to enable the government to *apply* the copyright protection afforded by Part I of the CDPA to works and people from countries to which the CDPA does not otherwise extend[1]. This is achieved by an Order in Council, implemented by statutory instrument. Orders need not apply protection uniformly to all classes of work. Indeed, the CDPA requires that an Order should *not* be extended to particular countries or classes of work unless the country in question is a member of the EU and/or one of the copyright conventions to which the UK is a party[2], except where satisfied that the country in question does or will give adequate protection to the class of works the Order relates to[3]. The intention is to give protection to works by authors from or first published in countries which give reciprocal protection to British works.

The latest such Order is the Copyright (Application to Other Countries) Order 2013[4], as amended by the Copyright and Performance (Application to Other Countries) (Amendment) Order 2015[5]. This Order applies protection to a variety of works from a number of different countries:

- The Order provides protection to literary, dramatic, musical and artistic works, films and published editions originating from Berne Convention countries, EU Member States, and other countries which are deemed to give adequate protection under their laws. The list of territories affected includes virtually all countries in the world.

- The Order protects sound recordings originating from the same list of countries referred to above, although protection is excluded for the playing of the work in public, or the broadcast of the work, unless the country of origin is a signatory of the Rome Convention[6], an EU Member State, or other country deemed to give adequate protection under its laws. Notably, the USA is excluded from protection, although this will change should the USA become a signatory to the Rome Convention.

- The Order protects broadcasts originating from a number of listed countries, which include the parties to the Rome Convention, the European Agreement on the Protection of Television Broadcasts and WTO/TRIPS[7], EU Member States, and other countries which are deemed to give adequate protection under their laws. Broadcasts are not uniformly protected in all such countries. In a small number of countries (ie Singapore, Indonesia and the EU Member States) protection is also extended to cable re-transmissions.

The CDPA also makes similar provision to extend rights in performances available under Part II of the CDPA to other countries[8].

This Order will be either replaced or amended by subsequent Orders adding or deleting countries to reflect membership of the international treaties, conventions and agreements which regulate international copyright protection.

1   CDPA s 159.
2   'Ie Convention countries', as to which see **paragraphs 4.12** ff.
3   CDPA s 159(3).
4   SI 2013/536.
5   SI 2015/216.
6   Cmnd 2425 – see **paragraph 4.18**.
7   See **paragraphs 4.17** ff.
8   CDPA s 208.

Denial of copyright protection

4.10   If a country fails to give adequate protection to British works, then an Order in Council may be passed which restricts the copyright protection in the UK afforded to works of authors connected with that country[1].

1   CDPA s 160.

Territorial waters, continental shelf, ships, aircraft and hovercraft

4.11 The CDPA treats the territorial waters of the UK as part of the UK. Acts done in the UK sector of the continental shelf on structures or vessels which are 'present there for purposes directly connected with the exploration of the seabed or subsoil or the exploitation of the natural resources' are deemed to have been done in the UK. So, if an oil rig which is in British territorial waters is used for the duplication of unauthorised video cassettes for commercial exploitation, or as a base for a radio station which broadcasts without the broadcaster obtaining licences for the broadcasts, there will be an infringement of UK copyright which could be the subject of civil and criminal proceedings in the UK[1].

Similarly, the CDPA applies to acts done on British-registered ships, aircraft or hovercraft as it applies to things done in the UK, wherever they are located[2].

1 CDPA s 161.
2 CDPA s 162.

International copyright: the Berne Convention and the Universal Copyright Convention

4.12 Copyright is created by national law. It follows that 'international copyright' as such does not exist. There are as many potential variations in the way a particular work may be protected in different parts of the world as there are territories. In most cases, the owner of copyright in a work who seeks to obtain relief against the unlawful exploitation of his work in another territory must enforce his rights under the law of the territory in which the infringement takes place. In an environment where works are generally exploited internationally, and commonly on a global basis (for example, via global networks such as the internet), it is vital that owners may effectively enforce their rights internationally. Territorial copyright has therefore become the subject of a number of international political agreements, regulating copyright issues and ensuring a degree of co-operation and legal uniformity between different territories regarding the works of their citizens. The three primary such international agreements are the Berne Convention, Universal Copyright Convention (UCC) and the TRIPS Agreement. The Berne Convention and the UCC have been subject to a number of amendments, principally necessary to update the law following technological developments. The last revisions of the Berne Convention were set out in the Paris Act of 1971, although more recently the Berne Convention was effectively revised by the WIPO Treaties as regards those countries which adhere to the WIPO Treaties[1].

The EU has also adopted a number of Directives intended to harmonise copyright law in the EEA[2].

1 Discussed at **paragraph 4.21**.
2 See **paragraphs 1.08** and **13.01**.

The 'national treatment' principle

4.13 The key principle which guides both the Berne Convention and the UCC is the principle of offering *national treatment* to the works of foreign nationals of other Convention countries. In short: a Convention country will offer the same or similar protection in its territory to the works of a foreign national originating from another Convention country as it will give to the works of its own nationals or which otherwise originate locally[1]. In practice the operation of this principle is restricted by two other principles: those of *minimum standards* and *reciprocity*[2].

1 Berne Convention Art 5(1) and UCC Art II(2).
2 See **paragraph 4.14**.

The principles of 'minimum standards' and 'reciprocity'

4.14 In certain respects the copyright protection offered by a Convention country to the work of a foreign national which originates outside that country may be more favourable than the protection afforded to the work of a local national or which otherwise originates locally. It is a requirement of both the Berne Convention and the UCC that members provide the nationals of other Convention countries with protection without any need to comply with local formalities such as deposit or registration notwithstanding that domestic nationals and/or works first published locally must comply with such provisions[1]. The most significant territory in which formalities are required is the USA. In this respect, for example, the literary work of a UK author first published in the UK may receive superior protection in the USA to the work of a US author first published in the USA if the latter has failed to comply with local formalities. However, under the UCC, a foreign national will only be deemed to have satisfied local formalities if the work in question bears an appropriate 'copyright symbol'[2].

1 Berne Convention Art 5, UCC Art III(I).
2 As to which see **paragraph 4.16**.

Differences between the Berne Convention and the UCC

4.15 The principal difference between the two Conventions is the minimum term of copyright protection they provide. Under the Berne Convention, the minimum period of copyright accorded to literary, dramatic, musical and artistic works is the life of the author plus 50 years. Under the UCC, the minimum term is the life of the author plus 25 years[1]. Both Conventions provide that signatories may provide for a greater degree of protection than that provided for in the Conventions, and Convention countries often do.

1   Article 4(2).

Copyright symbol

4.16 It is important to note that under the UCC, if a work is to avoid the necessity of complying with domestic formalities which may operate as a precondition of copyright protection in other UCC countries[1], it is vital that from the time of first publication of the work in question, all copies published with the authority of the author or other copyright proprietor must bear the © symbol accompanied by the name of the copyright proprietor and the year of first publication. This notice must be placed in such a manner and location as to give reasonable notice of the copyright claim[2]. Failure to put this symbol on a work published in a Berne Convention country will not prejudice copyright in the other Berne Convention countries. However, it may result in the work losing copyright and going into the public domain in those UCC countries which are not Berne Convention countries and which require formalities as a condition to copyright protection.

1   See **paragraph 4.14**.
2   Article III(i).

Other international copyright Conventions and agreements

4.17 The UK is a party to a number of other significant international agreements, including the following.

(a) The Rome Convention

4.18 In summary, the Rome Convention conveys rights protecting performers (with regard to the affixation and exploitation of recordings of their performances), phonogram producers (regarding the unauthorised reproduction of their phonograms – essentially audio records and cassettes) and broadcasters[1]. 'Broadcast' for these purposes means 'wireless' transmission, excluding cable transmission and re-transmissions (which were not contemplated). The minimum period of protection is 20 years from the end of the year of fixation, performance or broadcast (as relevant). Like the Berne Convention and the UCC, this Convention is based on the principle of 'national treatment'[2]. Again, like the UCC, the Rome Convention excuses phonogram producers from compliance with local formalities, provided that either the phonograms or their containers show a ℗ notice and the year of first publication.

There is also a requirement to identify the producer, his successor in title or exclusive licensee[3].

1   To authorise re-broadcasting, affixation and reproduction of their broadcasts, and the communication of their broadcasts to premises against payment of an admission fee.
2   See **paragraph 4.13**.
3   Article 11.

(b)   The Phonograms Convention

4.19   This Convention focuses on measures to combat phonogram piracy. In essence, the Convention requires members to protect producers against the making and importation of unauthorised copies of phonograms for public distribution, and the public distribution of such phonograms. Like the Rome Convention, the Phonograms Convention requires a minimum 20-year period of protection[1], and similar notice requirements in order to fulfil local formality requirements. Unlike Rome, however, the level of protection is not based on 'national treatment'. Signatories are required to afford the minimum level of protection prescribed by the Convention to phonograms from other Member States, even if local law is less protective.

1   Article 4.

(c)   The WTO, TRIPS and GATS

4.20   The agreement establishing the WTO was signed in Marrakesh, Morocco on 15 April 1994[1]. The principal *objectives* of the WTO are to raise standards of living, ensure full employment, expand production and trade and allow optimal use of the world's resources. The WTO *functions* include the development of an integrated multilateral trading system, the settlement of trade disputes, the provision of a forum for negotiations on trade relations, the review of trade policies and a greater coherence in global policy making.

The TRIPS Agreement was entered into as part of and is annexed to, the WTO agreement. Both became effective on 1 January 1995. The aim of the TRIPS Agreement is to reduce distortions and impediments to international trade and to ensure adequate and effective intellectual property protection without creating barriers to trade. The ambit of the TRIPS Agreement includes copyright and related rights, trade marks, geographical indications (eg an indication of the region from which a product originates, such as Champagne), industrial designs, patents, topographies of integrated circuits, protection of 'know how' and the control of anti-competitive practices. Enforcement issues are also dealt with.

The Treaty is expressed not to derogate from existing Conventions. Its terms are based on the principles of 'national treatment'[2] and 'most favoured nations treatment' (ie that, subject to certain exceptions, any protection given by a member to the nationals of another country will be given to the other members of TRIPS). It is worth summarising the provisions of the TRIPS Agreement relating to copyright:

- *Principle* copyright protection is expressed to 'extend to expressions and not to ideas, procedures, methods of operation or mathematical concepts as such'[3].
- *Computer programs* whether in source or object code are protected as literary works[4].
- *Compilations* of data or other materials, whether in machine readable or other form, which by reason of the selection or arrangement of its content constitute intellectual creations, are protected as such[5].
- *Rental rights* in computer programs, cinematographic works and phonograms are required to be protected for authors, phonogram producers and 'and any other right holders in phonograms' respectively, and their successors in title, subject to certain limitations[6].
- *Performers* should have the possibility of preventing the fixation of their performances, or the reproduction of a fixation, on a phonogram. With regard to live performances, a performer should have the possibility of preventing unauthorised (wireless) broadcast and 'communication to the public'[7].
- *Phonogram producers* should enjoy the right to authorise the reproduction of their phonograms[8].
- *Broadcasting organisations* should have the right to prohibit the fixation of their broadcasts, the reproduction of fixations, the wireless rebroadcast of their broadcasts and the communication to the public of television broadcasts.
- *Term:* wherever the term for protection of a copyright work is not based on the life of a person, the term must be not less than 50 years from the end of the year of authorised publication, or, if not published within 50 years of its making, not less than 50 years from the end of the year of its making. Photographs and works of applied art are excluded from this provision[9]. For performers and phonogram producers the protection is set at 50 years from the end of the year of fixation or performance. For broadcasting organisations the term of protection required is at least 20 years from the end of the year of broadcast[10].

The General Agreement on Trade in Services (GATS) came into force in 1995 as a result of the Uruguay Round negotiations to extend the multilateral trading system of the WTO to services. All members of the WTO are signatories to the GATS and have committed to further rounds of GATS negotiations, the first of which started in 2000.

The members of the WTO are automatically members of the TRIPS Agreement.

1   'The Marrakesh Act'.
2   See **paragraph 4.13**.
3   Article 9.
4   Article 10.
5   Article 10.
6   Articles 11 and 14(4).
7   Articles 14(1).
8   Articles 14(2).
9   Article 12.
10 Article 14(5).

(d) The WIPO Treaties

4.21   The WIPO Treaties arose as a consequence of the need to update the provisions of the Berne Convention, Rome Convention and the Phonograms Convention in light of advances in technology and in line with the TRIPS Agreement.

The WIPO Copyright Treaty 1996 (in line with TRIPS) confirms the principle that copyright protection extends to expressions and not ideas, procedures of operation or mathematical concepts as such[1]. Computer programs and compilations (of data or other materials in any form, which constitute intellectual creations by reason of their selection or arrangement) receive protection. Authors of literary and artistic works also receive newly recognised rights: the exclusive right to authorise 'the making available to the public' of the original and copies of their work and the 'communication to the public' of their works (by wired or wireless means, eg by means of 'on demand' online transmission)[2] for authors of computer programs and films and works included in phonograms a limited right to authorise commercial lending rental[3]. The Treaty also contains provisions designed to ensure adequate remedies are available against infringers who would circumvent technical methods of preventing unauthorised use or, for example, remove rights management information (designed to track the use of a work for the purpose of calculating remuneration).

The WIPO Performances and Phonograms Treaty 1996 protects performers and phonogram producers[4]. Parties are required to provide protection on the basis of 'national treatment'[5]. The Treaty recognises a number of rights in performances: namely performers' moral rights in affixations of their live aural performances on phonograms, and a performer's exclusive rights to authorise reproduction, making available to the public (again by wired or wireless means) and commercial rental of originals and copies of their performances embodied on phonograms[6]. Performers also receive the exclusive right to authorise the fixation of their performance and to authorise the broadcast and 'communication to the public' of affixed performances (except where the performance is already a broadcast performance)[7]. For phonogram producers, the Treaty provides similar exclusive rights to authorise reproduction, making available to the public (again by wired or wireless means) and commercial rental of originals and copies of their phonograms[8]. The Treaty provides for a single equitable remuneration right for performers and/or producers, leaving it to the discretion of signatories as to whether this is shared between producer and performer, or allocated to one or other of them[9]. In accordance with TRIPS, the minimum period of protection to be afforded to performers and phonogram producers is 50 years from the end of the year of affixation or (in the case of the rights of producers in published phonograms) publications[10]. As with the WIPO Copyright Treaty, this Treaty includes provisions targeted against the circumvention of technical methods of preventing unauthorised use or, for example, the removal of rights management information.

The WIPO Treaties did not address the issue of 'exhaustion of rights' (which remains to be determined by national governments[11]), and whether reproduction includes the kind of temporary storage required for the operation of electronic systems. Nor was any protection of audio-visual performers provided for.

1   Article 2.
2   Articles 6 and 8.
3   Article 7.
4   Article 3.
5   Article 4.
6   Articles 5 and 7–10.
7   Article 6.
8   Chapter 3.
9   Article 15.
10 Article 17.
11 See **paragraphs 6.05** and **13.04**.

Summary

4.22   For copyright users in the UK, the practical consequence of the UK's membership of the various international agreements is to achieve international protection for the works of UK authors, producers and performers. However, it is of vital importance, in order to ensure that such protection is available in as many territories as possible, for users to ensure from the outset that all copies of their work distributed with their authority bear the correct © or ℗ notices identified at **paragraphs 4.16** and **4.18**[1].

1   The UK is party to a number of other Conventions and agreements which are not discussed in detail here but which include the Convention Relating to the Distribution of Programme-Carrying Signals Transmitted by Satellite 1974 (dealing with the transmission of broadcasts by satellite). The UK is also a member of a number of Conventions from the Council of Europe, including the European Agreement Concerning Programme Exchanges By Means of Television Films 1958, the

Agreement on the Protection of Television Broadcasts 1960, the European Agreement for the Prevention of Broadcasts Transmitted from Stations Outside National Territories 1965 and the European Convention Relating to Questions of Copyright Law and Neighbouring Rights in the Framework of Transfrontier Broadcasting by Satellite 1994.

Chapter 5

Term of copyright and publication right

Introduction

5.01 Copyright in a work, like its author, will not live forever. Public policy has set a balance between the private interests of authors and their estates on the one hand, and the public interest in having access to works on the other. For the copyright user, to know whether a work is still 'in copyright' (ie whether it still attracts copyright protection) is vital. Once copyright expires, it 'enters the public domain' as a general rule and becomes freely exploitable.

Under the Conventions considered in **Chapter 4**, we saw that international standards have been agreed regarding the duration of copyright. Of these, the longest period is set by the Berne Convention, which sets the minimum period of protection for literary, dramatic, musical and artistic works at 50 years 'post mortem auctoris', or 'after the death of the author' (an expression often shortened to *pma*).

However, the Conventions only set minimum standards, and consequently the period of protection still varies from country to country. Within the European Union, the effects of that variation were seen as an impediment to the common market. Consequently the standards have been harmonised by a series of EU Directives.

The following table sets out a simple summary showing the copyright duration of works produced on or after 1 August 1989. Different rules will apply to works produced before this date.

Type of original work	Copyright duration
Literary, dramatic, musical and artistic works (including photographs)	70 years from the end of the calendar year in which the author died.

Type of original work	Copyright duration
Sound recordings	50 years from the end of the calendar year in which it was made; or if during that period it is published, 70 years from the end of the calendar year of publication; or if during that period it is not published but is played or communicated in public, 70 years from the end of the calendar year in which it was first so made available.
Films	70 years from the end of the calendar year in which occurred the death of the last to survive of the principal director, the author of the screenplay, the author of the dialogue, and the composer of the music specifically created for and used in the film.
Broadcasts	50 years from the end of the calendar year in which the broadcast was made. In the case of repeats, copyright expires at the same time as the original.
Typographical arrangements	25 years from the end of the calendar year in which the edition was first published.
Works of unknown authorship	70 years from the end of the calendar year in which it was made, or 70 years from the end of the calendar year in which it was made available to the public if it was made so available.
Computer-generated literary, dramatic, musical and artistic works	50 years from the end of the calendar year in which it was made.

The position becomes more complex for the user who needs to establish whether an older work which s/he wants to exploit is still in copyright, and depending on the age of the work, it may be necessary to apply one of a number of historic Copyright Act provisions in order to determine the copyright period remaining in the work.

In this chapter, we touch on the circumstances in which copyrights are revived or extended as a consequence of the amendments to the CDPA, and if so, who owns the revived or extended rights. We also consider what period of protection will apply to various categories of work of different ages.

Literary, dramatic, musical and artistic works

5.02 The general rule[1] is that copyright subsists in these works (if original) until the expiry of the period of 70 years from the end of the calendar year in which the author died[2].

1   CDPA s 12(2).
2   There are exceptions for works of unknown authorship, computer-generated works
    and works of joint authorship, which are dealt with below.

Unpublished literary, dramatic, musical and artistic works

5.03   Certain works (including literary, dramatic and musical works, engravings whose author has died, and photographs taken on or after 1 June 1957) that were still unpublished when the CPDA came into force will remain in copyright until the end of 2039[1].

In 2014 HM Government consulted on reducing the duration of copyright in respect of these and other works, but announced in 2015 that it would not be taking any action at the moment to reduce that duration.

1   CPDA Sch 1, para 12(4).

Computer-generated works

5.04   The copyright in a computer-generated work subsists until the end of the period of 50 years from the end of the calendar year in which it was made[1].

1   CDPA s 12(7).

Sound recordings

5.05   The general rule is that the copyright in a sound recording subsists until the end of the period of 50 years from the end of the calendar year in which the recording was made, and it then expires[1]. However, if during that 50-year period the recording is published or made available to the public by being played in public or communicated to the public, copyright will endure for 70 years from the end of the calendar year in which the first publication or making available (as the case may be) occurred (although for these purposes no account is to be taken of any unauthorised act)[2].

Where the author of the sound recording is not a national of an EEA state, the duration of copyright is that to which the sound recording is entitled in the country of which the author is a national, provided that it is not longer than the period set out above in this paragraph[3].

1   CDPA s 13A(2)(a).
2   CDPA s 13A(2)(b) and (c).
3   See s 13A(4).

Copyright in sound recordings made before 1 August 1989

5.06   The copyright in a sound recording made before 1 June 1957 subsisted until the expiration of 50 years from the end of the calendar year in which it was made.

The copyright in a sound recording made between 1 June 1957 and 1 August 1989 expires at the end of the fiftieth year from the end of the calendar year when it was first published.

The copyright in sound recordings made during this period, which remained unpublished on 1 August 1989, expires on 31 December 2039, unless it has been published in the meantime; in this latter case it will remain in copyright for a period of 50 years from the end of the calendar year in which publication takes place[1].

1   CDPA Sch 1, para 12(5)(a).

Films made before 1 June 1957

5.07   Because, before 1 June 1957, films were treated as dramatic works and photographs for copyright purposes[1], the period of protection was the life of the writer or writers of the screenplay plus 50 years and, for the photographic element, the period was 50 years from the end of the calendar year in which the photograph was taken.

1   There was no separate film copyright.

Films made between 1 June 1957 and 1 August 1989

5.08   The period of copyright for a cinematograph film made between these dates differed according to whether the film was registered under Part III of the Cinematograph Films Act 1938 or Part II of the Films Act 1960 as a 'British' film, or whether it was not so registrable.

Copyright subsisted in a film which was so registrable, continued to subsist until the film was registered, and continued thereafter until the end of the period of 50 years from the end of the calendar year in which it was registered. The copyright period for registered films remains unchanged.

In the case of films which were not registrable under the Films Act 1960, copyright continued until the film was published and thereafter until the end of the period of 50 years from the end of the calendar year which included the date of its first publication.

The position under the CDPA for a film made before 1 August 1989 and which was neither registered nor published before that date, is that the copyright period will expire on 31 December 2039 unless it has been released in the meantime; in this latter case it will remain in copyright for a period of 50 years from the end of the calendar year in which it is released.

Films made after 31 December 1995

5.09   The copyright period for these films is 70 years from the end of the calendar year in which the death occurs of the last to die of the following persons:

- the principal director;
- the author of the screenplay;
- the author of the dialogue;
- the composer of music specially created for and used in the film[1].

If the identity of some but not all of these persons is not known, then the reference to the last to die is construed as a reference to the last known person to die[2].

Where the country of origin of a film is not an EEA state, and the producer and director of the film are not EEA state nationals, the duration of copyright is that to which the film is entitled in the country of origin provided that it is not longer than that set out above[3].

If there are no known persons falling within these categories, then the period is 70 years from the end of the calendar year in which the film was made, or (if it was 'made available to the public' within that period) 70 years from the end of the calendar year in which it was first made[4]. This provision may for example, apply to films made (ie videos recorded) by security cameras if such films are entitled to copyright protection.

1   CDPA s 13B(2).
2   CDPA s 13B(3).
3   CDPA s 13B(7).
4   CDPA s 13B(4).

Broadcasts

5.10   The copyright in a broadcast subsists until the expiry of the period of 50 years from the end of the calendar year in which it was made[1]. The copyright period is not extended by repeats or reinstated by broadcasts made after the end of the copyright period[2].

1   CDPA s 14(2).
2   CDPA s 14(5).

Published editions

5.11   Published editions are, in effect, typographical arrangements of literary, dramatic, or musical works[1]. The copyright in a published edition subsists for 25 years from the end of the calendar year in which it was first published[2].

1   See **paragraph 2.11**.
2   CDPA s 15(2).

Anonymous and pseudonymous, literary, dramatic and artistic works (except photographs)

5.12   A work is anonymous or pseudonymous[1] if the identity of the author is unknown, or, in the case of a work of joint authorship, if the identity of none of the authors is known[2].

The identity of an author is regarded as unknown if it is not possible to ascertain his or her identity by reasonable enquiry. If his or her identity is once known, it shall not subsequently be regarded as unknown[3].

The position with regard to anonymous and pseudonymous works made after 1 January 1996 is that the copyright period is 70 years from the end of the calendar year in which the work was made, or (if the work was made available to the public in that period), 70 years from the end of the calendar year in which it was so made available.

Once the identity of the author is known, the normal 70 years pma rule will apply.

The expression 'made available to the public' includes (amongst other things), in the case of:

- *literary, dramatic or musical works* – performance in public or broadcasts of the works;
- *artistic works* – exhibition in public;
- *films* – showing the work in public or including it in a communication to the public.

The use of the word 'include' in this definition means that other methods of making the work available to the public, such as publication in a written form, must also be taken into account.

If at any time before the end of this period it is possible for a person who had no previous knowledge of the fact to ascertain the identity by reasonable enquiry, then the full period of copyright will apply to the work.

1 CDPA s 9(4) uses the expression 'of unknown authorship'.
2 CDPA s 9(4).
3 CDPA s 9(5).

Unpublished works – publication right

5.13 Publication right applies only to literary, dramatic, musical and artistic works and films[1]. Consequently, the word 'work' is used in connection with it to refer only to *those* classes of works.

Publication right was introduced into the CDPA by the Copyright and Related Rights Regulations 1996 ('the 1996 Regulations')[2], as subsequently amended, and applies only from 1 December 1996.

A person who, *after the expiry of copyright protection*, publishes for the first time a previously unpublished work becomes the first owner of the publication right in that work, which is an intellectual property right comparable to copyright[3].

'Publication' as used in this context means:

'... any making available to the public, in particular –

(a) the issue of copies to the public;
(b) making the work available by means of an electronic retrieval system;

(c) the rental or lending of copies of the work to the public;

(d) the performance, exhibition or showing of the work in public; or

(e) communicating the work to the public.'[4]

An unauthorised act will not amount to publication[5].

Given that publication right only arises in the case of works in which the copyright has expired before they are published, it is necessary for the Regulations to specify who can give the consent for an authorised act after the copyright has expired. For the purposes of the 1996 Regulations, an unauthorised act means 'an act done without the consent of the owner of the physical medium in which the work is embodied or on which it is recorded'[6].

It is important to bear in mind that the definition of an unauthorised act in relation to the publication right has no relevance whatsoever to the definition of an unauthorised act in relation to a work which is in copyright. Except in the context of publication right, ownership of the physical medium in which the work is embodied or on which it is recorded (such as a canvas which bears a painting or a compact disc on which music has been recorded) carries with it no right whatsoever in copyright law[7].

Publication right will be of little value to owners of unpublished manuscripts and musical scores until the year 2040, because unpublished literary and musical works enjoyed perpetual copyright until the CDPA came into force and introduced a copyright period that was not dependent on publication[8]. There is, however, immediate copyright value in artistic works (including photographs) in respect of which the copyright period was not dependent on publication but was 50 years pma.

1 Publication right is also considered at **paragraphs 9.10** and **25.23**.
2 SI 1996/2967.
3 1996 Regulations, reg 16(1).
4 1996 Regulations, reg 16(2).
5 1996 Regulations, reg 16(3).
6 1996 Regulations, reg 16(3).
7 See **paragraph 9.03**.
8 See **paragraph 5.03**.

The qualification for publication right

5.14 A work qualifies for publication right protection only if:

* its first publication was in the EEA; and
* the publisher of the work was, at the time of first publication, a national of an EEA state[1].

It will be noted that these requirements are not in the alternative: both must be satisfied.

1 See 1996 Regulations, reg 16(4).

Period of publication right

5.15 Publication right expires at the end of the period of 25 years from the end of the calendar year in which the work was first published[1].

There is no publication right in works in which Crown copyright or Parliamentary copyright subsisted but in which copyright expired before the works were published[2].

1   1996 Regulations, reg 16(6).
2   1996 Regulations, reg 16(5).

Application of copyright provisions to publication right

5.16 Certain copyright provisions are applied to the publication right by reg 17 of the 1996 Regulations.

These provisions are:

- the rights of the copyright owner[1];
- the exceptions and defences to copyright actions[2];
- dealings with rights in copyright works[3];
- remedies for infringement[4];
- copyright licensing[5].

There are some minor variations in the way that these provisions are applied to publication right which do not merit detailed discussion here[6]. Most deal with presumptions which can be made in the case of an action for infringement.

1   See **Chapter 6**.
2   See **Chapter 8**.
3   See **Chapter 9**.
4   See **Chapter 7**.
5   See **Chapters 9** and **12**.
6   See 1996 Regulations, reg 17.

Works of joint authorship and co-authorship

5.17 A work of joint authorship means a work that is produced by the collaboration of two or more authors, in which the contribution of each author is not separate from the contribution of the others[1]; and a work of co-authorship means a work produced by the collaboration of the author of a musical work and the author of a literary work where the two works are created in order to be used together[2]. The term of copyright in such works is to be determined by reference to the date of death of the last surviving author. For example, in the case of literary, dramatic, musical or artistic works which are 'joint works', the term of copyright continues until the end of the period of 70 years from the end of the calendar year in which the last surviving author dies[3].

1 CDPA s 10(1).
2 CDPA s 10A(1).
3 CDPA s 12(8).

Crown copyright

5.18 The basic position is that any copyright to which a work 'made by Her Majesty or by an officer or servant of the Crown in the course of his duties' is entitled will be owned by the Crown[1]. In the case of a literary, dramatic, musical or artistic work, copyright will subsist for 125 years from the end of the calendar year in which it was made unless it is 'published commercially' before the end of the period of 75 years from the end of the calendar year in which it was made. In that case copyright will subsist for 50 years from the end of the calendar year in which it was first so published. 'Commercial publication' is defined in the CDPA as:

'(a) issuing copies of the work to the public at a time when copies made in advance of the receipt of orders are generally available to the public, or

(b) making the work available to the public by means of an electronic retrieval system'[2].

The copyright period for works of Crown copyright which are not literary, dramatic, musical or artistic works is the same as that for non-Crown copyright works.

The copyright existing in every Act of Parliament, Act of the Scottish Parliament, Measure of the National Assembly for Wales, Act of the National Assembly for Wales, Act of the Northern Ireland Assembly and Measure of the General Synod of the Church of England will be Crown copyright, and will subsist until the end of the period of 50 years from the end of the calendar year in which Royal Assent was given or (in the case of a Measure of the National Assembly for Wales) in which the Measure was approved by Her Majesty in Council.

1 CDPA ss 163–167 which concern Crown and Parliamentary copyright are dealt with only generally in this *User's Guide*.
2 CDPA s 175(2).

Parliamentary copyright

5.19 The 70 years pma period does not apply to Parliamentary copyright works. The duration of Parliamentary copyright[1] can be summarised as follows:

- *Works made by or under the direction or control of the House of Commons or the House of Lords:*
  (a) literary, dramatic, musical and artistic works: 50 years from the end of the year in which the work is made;

(b) other works: the normal copyright period applicable to the relevant category of work under the CDPA.

- Bills of either House cease to be in copyright when they receive Royal Assent (ie they become Acts of Parliament) or, if they do not receive Royal Assent, on the withdrawal or rejection of the Bill or the end of the session. A Bill will regain its copyright protection if it is reintroduced in a subsequent session;
- *The devolved Assemblies*: the CDPA[2] provides for copyright in bills of the Scottish Parliament, the Northern Ireland Assembly and the National Assembly for Wales, and in proposed Measures of the National Assembly for Wales.

1   Parliamentary copyright is dealt with in ss 165–167 of the CDPA.
2   CDPA ss 166A–166D.

Copyright vesting in certain international organisations

5.20   The 'international organisations' in question are those to be specified in statutory instruments, of which the only one at present is the Copyright (International Organisation) Order 1989[1], which confers copyright protection on works originating with the United Nations, its Specialised Agencies or the Organisation of American States, which would not otherwise enjoy copyright in the UK. These works are protected for 50 years from the end of the calendar year in which they were made[2].

1   SI 1989/989.
2   CDPA s 168(3).

Peter Pan and the Hospital for Sick Children

5.21   Sir James Barrie, who wrote the play *Peter Pan*, died in 1937. The copyright in the play expired on 31 December 1987, at which time the copyright was vested in the Trustees for the Hospital for Sick Children. The CDPA provides that, notwithstanding the expiration of the copyright in the play, the Trustees are to continue to receive royalties payable in respect of any public performance, commercial publication, or communication to the public of the whole or any substantial part of the work or an adaptation of it[1]. The royalty is to be determined by agreement, or failing agreement by the Copyright Tribunal. The Trustees are not given power to grant exclusive licences in *Peter Pan*; their right is to receive royalties only.

1   CDPA s 301 and Sch 6.

Universities' and colleges' perpetual copyright

5.22 The perpetual copyright conferred on universities and colleges by the Copyright Act 1775 will now expire on 31 December 2039[1].

1 CDPA Sch 1, para 13(1).

Performances

5.23 For the duration of rights in performances see **paragraphs 11.17–11.18**.

Chapter 6

Restricted acts and acts of secondary infringement

Introduction

6.01 Copyright is a personal property right which allows the owner the exclusive right to undertake, and authorise others to undertake, a number of activities in relation to his work. By s 2 of the CDPA:

> 'the owner of copyright in a work of any description has the exclusive right to do the acts ... restricted by the copyright in a work of that description'[1].

Since the owner is exclusively entitled to permit these activities, anyone who undertakes a 'restricted act' without his authorisation will be liable for infringement of copyright regardless of the intention or knowledge of the infringer[2]. The ability to sell or license the right to perform these restricted acts is the basis of all economic activity utilising copyright[3].

In addition to the restricted acts, a number of activities *may* constitute copyright infringement if the person undertaking the act of infringement does so with knowledge or has reason to believe that the infringing article is an infringement[4]. Doing these acts will constitute a *secondary* infringement of copyright.

1 See **Chapter 7** for a discussion of infringement issues.
2 See **paragraph 7.03**.
3 See **Chapter 9** for a discussion of issues regarding the transfer of rights.
4 See **paragraph 7.23**.

The restricted acts summarised

6.02 Under the CDPA, the restricted acts in relation to a work are:

- copying the work;
- issuing copies of the work to the public;

- renting or lending copies of the work to the public;
- performing, showing or playing the work in public;
- communicating the work to the public;
- making an adaptation of the work or doing any of the above acts in relation to an adaptation[1].

1 CDPA s 16(1).

Authorisation

6.03 Copyright in a work is infringed by a person who without the licence of the copyright owner does, *or authorises another* to do, any of the acts restricted by copyright'[1]. For these purposes, facilitating the doing of an act differs from procuring the doing of an act[2]. So in a case relating to a 'dual' cassette tape recorder the House of Lords held that:

> 'sales and advertisements to the public generally of a machine which may be used for lawful or unlawful purposes, including infringement of copyright, cannot be said to "procure" infringements of copyright by members of the public who use the machine to copy pre-recorded tapes'[3].

Some acts may involve multiple infringements. For example, the functioning of the internet involves a variety of processes, several of which will involve restricted acts. Posting an audio-visual work on to an internet website will involve the 'uploading' of a work to a computer file server that is connected to the internet. Accessing this work will involve 'downloading' the work from the server. The transmission of images to the public via the internet or the immediate re-transmission of a broadcast signal containing work, made by means of the internet, will also amount to a 'communication to the public' of the work.

Briefly, there are at least four technical processes involved in 'webcasting':

- acquisition (capturing the data);
- digitisation and encoding (to make it compatible with one of the playback forms);
- hosting (storage on the hard drive ready for access by users); and
- delivery to the user.

These processes may involve the restricted acts of:

- copying (capturing the data, digitisation, uploading to the ISP server, downloading)[4];
- public performance (if the webcast is shown in public)[5];
- communication to the public.

Until recently, it was widely thought that the principles laid down in *CBS Songs Ltd v Amstrad Consumer Electronics plc* made it unlikely that a website which offers peer-to-peer software for download by others, but which does not itself directly engage in unauthorised copying, could be construed as 'authorising' the infringing activities of the software users. However, recent cases in the US and Australia (both common law jurisdictions) indicate a willingness of the courts in those jurisdictions to find that distributing such software may itself amount to infringing activity, raising the possibility that an English court may re-evaluate the Amstrad decision in light of peer-to-peer file sharing[6].

In *Universal Music Australia v Sharman License Holdings,* the Australian Federal Court found that Sharman Networks had infringed copyright by authorising its users to engage in unauthorised copying of music files. Sharman had encouraged users of its Kazaa software to 'Join the Revolution', and encouraged users to 'defy the record companies by ignoring copyright constraints'. Sharman was ordered to utilise filtering technologies which either stops users from sharing files that match a list provided by record companies, or which allows users only to see licensed works) and to put 'maximum pressure' on current users to upgrade to the filtered version.

1 See s 16(2).
2 *Belegging-en Exploitatiemaatschappij BV v Witten Industrial Diamonds Ltd [1979] FSR 59 at 65,* CA.
3 *CBS Songs Ltd v Amstrad Consumer Electronics plc [1988] 2 All ER 484,* per Lord Templeman.
4 See **paragraph 6.04**.
5 See **paragraph 6.08**.
6 *MGM Studios v Grokster* 545 US 913 (2005) and *Universal Music Australia v Sharman License Holdings [2005] FCA 1242 (5 September 2005).*

Copying

6.04 The CDPA provides that what amounts to copying will depend on the work in question[1]:

- *Literary, dramatic, musical and artistic works*: Copying a literary, dramatic, musical or artistic work means *reproducing it in any material form*. This includes storing it in any medium by electronic means, such as on the memory of a computer[2]. For artistic works, copying includes making a three-dimensional work from a two-dimensional work and vice versa (eg making a drawing from a sculpture)[3]. A special exemption exists in relation to the taking of photographs in buildings[4].
- *Films and broadcasts*: Copying a film or broadcast includes making a photograph of the whole or any substantial part of any image forming part of it[5]. Although this is not an exhaustive definition, it confirms that a 'video grab' (ie the reproduction of a still taken from a moving video image) will amount to copying, notwithstanding that the single image which is 'grabbed' may be a very insignificant part of the whole work[6]. Interestingly the CDPA contains no express

provision confirming that these works will be copied if they are stored by electronic means (in contrast to the works referred to in the previous paragraph), although this seems to be implicit.

- *Published editions*: Copying the typographical arrangement of a published edition of a work means 'making a facsimile copy', which includes copies that have been enlarged or reduced in size[7]. The House of Lords held in *Newspaper Licensing Agency Ltd v Marks & Spencer plc* that works comprising a number of literary works such as newspapers were entitled to copyright in the 'edition' ie what the publisher offers to the public rather than an individual article or column[8].

- *Photographs*: Copyright in a photograph can be infringed where a facsimile copy is taken of it by some photographic means. However, a photograph can also be infringed if reproduced by another method (eg a painting). The test is whether a substantial part of the photograph has been replicated. If A sets up a scene to be photographed and B also photographs the same scene. B has not infringed A's photograph, since he has not copied the photograph, but the scene. There is no causal link between the works created by A and B[9].

No special guidance is offered in the CDPA with regard to the copying of sound recordings, although these, like the works discussed above, are subject to the general principles regarding infringement discussed in **Chapter 7**.

Although the CDPA does not specifically address the technological processes comprising the functionality of the internet, copying includes storing the work in any medium by 'electronic means'[10]. The word 'electronic' is very widely defined by the CDPA as meaning 'actuated by electric, magnetic, electro-magnetic, electro-chemical, or electro-mechanical energy'[11] and would include computer hard drives, CD-ROMs and DVDs. So, when a digital copy is made of a work without the permission of the owner, the copier will infringe copyright.

In its original form, the CDPA makes it clear that copying will include copying which is transient or incidental to some other use[12]. In the digital environment this form of copying is integral to the operation of digital networks. Unlike most other means of communication (the fax machine excluded), downloading a digital transmission from a digital network like the internet, or uploading material from a digital storage device like a CD-ROM *inevitably* involves copying. In both cases a copy will be made on the memory of the user's computer and in the former case on any of a number of computers used in the process of conveying the information to the end user. This created complex legal problems for online service providers, who transfer (and in the process of so doing make 'cache' copies of) countless amounts of data that almost certainly contain unauthorised copies.

For that reason the CDPA has now been amended so as to specifically exclude the making of transient copies as part of networked communications from infringing copyright under certain circumstances[13].

Computer programs are protected as literary works[14], but a series of cases has limited the extent to which computer programs may be infringed by anything other than straightforward textual copying. In one case, the court was invited to consider whether an online booking system created for easyJet infringed the copyright of another booking system by appropriating the 'business logic' of the earlier system[15]. It was not disputed that the underlying software did not resemble that of the earlier system, except that it acted on similar inputs with similar results. The court was invited to draw an analogy with 'non-textual copying' in the context of the plot of a book[16]. The claim of non-textual copying failed. A computer program has no theme, events or narrative flow like a plot, simply a series of pre-defined operations intended to achieve a desired result, and no actual code had been copied. To extend the literary copyright in a computer program to restrain use of 'business logic' would be an extension of protection which ran counter to public policy[17].

1   CDPA s 17(2). See **paragraph 21.06** for a consideration of copying lighting designs in the context of plays, and **Chapter 25** regarding the copying of artistic works generally.
2   CDPA s 17(2).
3   CDPA s 17(3); see **paragraph 25.05**.
4   See **paragraph 8.24**.
5   CDPA s 17(4).
6   See however the exceptions to copyright infringement considered at **Chapter 8** and in particular **paragraph 8.34**.
7   CDPA ss 17(5) and 178.
8   [2001] UKHL 38.
9   *Creation Records v News Group Newspapers Ltd [1997] EMLR 444*; see also **paragraph 2.06**.
10   CDPA s 17(2).
11   CDPA s 178.
12   CDPA s 17(6).
13   See **paragraph 8.02**.
14   See **paragraph 2.02**.
15   *Navitaire Inc v (1) EasyJet Airline Co (2) Bulletproof Technologies Inc [2006] RPC 3*, Pumfrey J.
16   The court considered *Jarrold v Houlston [1857] 3 Kay & J 708*.
17   Se **paragraph 2.16**.

The issue of copies to the public

6.05   *Issuing copies to the public* is an act restricted by the copyright in every category of copyright work. For the purposes of the CDPA, the phrase: 'issue to the public of copies of a work' means:

'(a) the act of putting into circulation in the EEA copies not previously put into circulation in the EEA by or with the consent of the copyright owner, or

(b) the act of putting into circulation outside the EEA copies not previously put into circulation in the EEA or elsewhere'[1].

For these purposes 'copies' will include electronic copies[2]. However the act of 'putting into circulation' suggests a *tangible* copy (such as a CD or DVD) which is itself circulated rather than, say, a computer file which is communicated from A to B via the internet, since any further circulation of that file would be of a further copy of that file, not the file itself.

The following activities do not qualify as issuing copies to the public for the purposes of this restricted act:

'(a) any subsequent distribution, sale, hiring or loan of copies previously put into circulation (but see section 18A: infringement by rental or lending), or

(b) any subsequent importation of such copies into the United Kingdom or another EEA state,

except as far as paragraph (a) of [section 18] subsection (2) applies to putting into circulation in the EEA copies previously put into circulation outside the EEA'[3].

This wording is confusing even for experienced practitioners, and has done nothing to ease the frequent misunderstandings amongst users in relation to this area of law. The current language arose from amendments made to the CDPA implementing the Rental and Lending Directive[4]. Its intention was to introduce into the CDPA the concept of 'exhaustion of rights' between the Member States of the EU.

In accordance with Community principles, when goods have been circulated in any part of the Community there should, broadly, be no impediment to the movement of those same goods within any other part of the Community. This conflicts with the territorial nature of copyright law and the ECJ has developed a doctrine of European exhaustion of rights to address this issue[5]. Consequently, the first circulation of copies of a copyright work within the EEA with the authorisation of the owner is said to 'exhaust' the owner's right to control any further distribution, sale, hiring or loan *of those same copies* to the public within the EEA. The copyright owner cannot, for example, claim copyright infringement because copies he has authorised for sale in France are subsequently issued for sale into the UK, since this kind of 'parallel importing' is necessary to ensure the free movement of goods and services within the Community envisaged by the Treaty of Rome[6].

At the same time, the wording attempts to exclude any suggestion of adopting a policy of full 'international exhaustion of rights' (which would exhaust the right of a copyright owner to restrict the further distribution, sale, hiring or loan of copies of his work after the first authorised issuing of such copies to the public with his authorisation anywhere in the world, regardless of where that subsequent distribution takes place geographically). The Rental and Lending Directive, for example, specifically provides that the 'distribution right' in certain categories of work is not exhausted within the Community unless the first sale in the Community was made with the owner's consent[7]. A copyright owner can, for example, claim copyright infringement because copies he authorised for sale in the US were subsequently imported for sale into the UK. A doctrine of 'international exhaustion' has been discussed in the context of multilateral trade agreements, but its introduction currently remains unlikely since it would fundamentally attack the practice of exclusive territorial licensing practised in almost all industries involving the distribution of copyright works.

Two trade mark cases are of interest since they track a similar debate in relation to exhaustion of rights. Consistent with the principles outlined above, in *Silhouette International Schmied GmbH & Co KG v Hartlauer Handelsgesellschaft GmbH*[8] the ECJ ruled out the possibility of a Member State introducing a concept of international exhaustion of rights in the context of trade marks. However, in the UK, in a subsequent decision[8], Laddie J (whilst acknowledging that there is no international exhaustion of rights) observed that an owner may be said to have given implied consent to the importation of goods into the EEA where he has sold the goods outside the EEA without restricting the right of the purchaser to distribute and onward sell the goods in question. In practice then, it is important, in deciding whether rights have been exhausted in relation to particular goods within the EEA, to consider all the circumstances in which they were sold, including the nature of the goods, the terms of any contract of sale and the provisions of applicable law. For the user who wishes to ensure that no implied consent may be deemed to be given, it will be important to ensure that (for products circulated for distribution outside the EEA) any distribution agreement expressly limits the territory for sale and excludes importation of the products into different jurisdictions.

It should be noted that nothing in the CDPA limits the right of a copyright owner to prevent the issuing of *further* copies of the same work to the public. So, if the author of a book authorises his publisher to issue 1000 copies to the public in the UK and these are sold, the author's copyright is infringed if the publisher issues further copies of the book without the further authorisation of the author.

The effect of s 18 of the CDPA can be summarised as follows:

- copies already circulating in the EEA with the consent of the copyright owner can be distributed, sold, hired or lent or imported into the UK or another EEA state without the copyright owner's authorisation;

- copies already circulating outside the EEA but not circulated in the EEA, can only be sold, distributed etc in the EEA with the copyright owner's authorisation;

- copies already circulating in the EEA without the copyright owner's consent (for example, where they were placed on the market in a Member State where the copyright period had expired) may not be imported etc into the UK without the copyright owner's authorisation;

- the act of issuing copies to the public does not in itself exhaust any other right of the copyright owner to authorise 'restricted acts' (such as, for example, rental and lending or communication to the public).

1   CDPA s 18(2).
2   CDPA s 18(3).
3   CDPA s 18(3).
4   Directive 2006/115/EC.
5   See **paragraph 13.04**.
6   See **paragraph 6.11** and **Chapter 13**.
7   Article 9(2).
8   *C-355/96: [1999] Ch 77*.
9   *Zino Davidoff SA v A & G Imports Ltd [2000] Ch 127*.

Rental and lending

6.06 The rental and lending rights are conferred by the CDPA s 18A. The position is that both rental and lending of copies of a work to the public are now restricted acts. The rights exist only in respect of literary, dramatic and musical works, and artistic works (subject to certain exclusions regarding works of architecture in the form of buildings, or models of buildings, and works of applied, as opposed to fine art), films and sound recordings[1]. 'Rental' for these purposes means:

'making a copy of the work available for use, on terms that it will or may be returned, for direct or indirect economic or commercial advantage'[2].

And 'lending' means:

'making a copy of the work available for use, on terms that it will or may be returned, otherwise than for direct or indirect economic or commercial advantage, through an establishment which is accessible to the public'[3].

For the avoidance of doubt, the CDPA specifically provides that the expressions 'rental' and 'lending' do not include[4]:

'(a) making available for the purpose of public performance, playing or showing in public, or communication to the public;
(b) making available for the purpose of exhibition in public; or
(c) making available for on-the-spot reference use.'

Moreover, 'lending' is expressly stated to exclude 'making available between establishments which are accessible to the public'[5]. So, one public library may lend a book to another public library without infringing the restricted act of lending. Where lending by an establishment accessible to the public (for example, a public library) gives rise to a payment, the amount of which does not go beyond what is necessary to cover the operating costs of the establishment, there is no direct or indirect economic or commercial advantage for the purposes of the definitions of 'rental' and 'lending'. In other words, if the library is careful to establish that its charges are only sufficient to recover its costs, then the fact that a public library is being paid does not convert its 'lending' into 'rental'[6].

Since implementation of the Rental and Lending Directive[7], the authors of literary, dramatic, musical and artistic works, and film directors, also have a right to receive 'equitable remuneration' from the rental of their works, notwithstanding that the rental right itself is transferred by the author to, say, the producer of a film[8]. This right cannot be waived and cannot be assigned except to a collecting society (for the purposes of collecting it for the author). Any attempt in an agreement to exclude or restrict the right to equitable remuneration will be void[9].

The level of equitable remuneration is to be set by the parties; in the absence of agreement, the Copyright Tribunal may settle the amount[10]. In the film industry (where the rental of works remains commonplace) this provision has had a significant effect, with producers commonly attempting to reduce the uncertainty inherent in the vague notion of 'equitable remuneration' by adopting contractual devices intended, more or less, to absolve themselves and those taking title under them from any obligation to pay further amounts in respect of such rights.

Since a communication to the public (either as part of a broadcast or an on-demand service) is excluded from the definition of rental and lending, it follows that the author of the work included in such an electronic transmission will not by virtue of the transmission obtain a right to receive equitable remuneration. Rental and lending are intended to relate to the making available of hard copies, not files transmitted by means of networked computer systems.

1   CDPA s 18A(1).
2   CDPA s 18A(2)(a).
3   CDPA s 18A(2)(b).
4   CDPA s 18A(3).
5   CDPA s 18A(4).
6   See **Chapter 18**.
7   Directive 2006/115/EC implemented by the Copyright and Related Rights Regulations 1996 (SI 1996/2967).
8   CDPA s 93B(1).
9   CDPA s 93B(5).
10 **Chapter 12**.

Performance, playing or showing of a work in public

6.07 The restricted act of 'performance' applies only to the copyright in literary, dramatic or musical works[1]. 'Performance' includes delivery (in the case of lectures, addresses, speeches and sermons), but also includes any method of visual or acoustic presentation, including presentation by means of a sound recording, film or broadcast of the work[2].

The 'playing or showing of a work in public' is also restricted in relation to sound recordings, films and broadcasts[3]. So, for example, to show the transmission of a film on a television set or other monitor 'live' before an audience, or to play a sound recording on a radio in public, will amount to a public performance, playing or showing of the work, (although the reader should note that there are significant qualifications to these principles considered fully below).

However, the CDPA specifically provides that:

'Where copyright in a work is infringed by its being performed, played or shown in public by means of apparatus for receiving visual images or sounds conveyed by electronic means, the person by whom the visual images or sounds are sent, and in the case of a performance the performers, shall not be regarded as responsible for the infringement'[4].

This wording is 'technology neutral' and protects broadcasters, cable operators and internet service providers against any liability for making a 'public performance' if the service is displayed on a monitor in public.

The act of broadcasting itself is not a 'performance', notwithstanding that the broadcast will be received by the 'public at large'[5]. Communication to the public (including broadcasting) is a separate restricted act[6].

In determining whether a performance is 'in public' for the purposes of s 19 of the CDPA, the courts have repeatedly stated that the issue is a question of fact to be determined in each case. However, the meaning and scope of the words 'in public' is a question of law which in less obvious cases may need to be investigated.

The phrase has been the subject of numerous judicial decisions which stress that the determining factor in deciding whether a performance is in public should be a matter of 'common sense'[7]. Accordingly, while certain factors may be important in borderline cases[8], the courts will give very little weight to arguments based on such factors if a performance is clearly 'in public' in accordance with the ordinary meaning of the words[9].

The starting point for determining the meaning of 'in public' is that it is the character of the audience which is all-important: performance in public means a performance to an audience which is not domestic or quasi-domestic in character[10]. In the leading case of *Jennings v Stephens*[11] it is said that the question depends 'solely upon the character of the audience' and that factors such as whether visitors are present, whether an entrance fee is charged and the number of the audience are not decisive. However, it is clear from subsequent cases that these and other factors may help shed some light on whether the audience is domestic or quasi-domestic in a difficult case.

The question to be asked is whether the performance is 'part of the domestic or home life of the members of the audience' or whether the audience form a 'domestic circle' or whether the members of the audience are 'bound to one another by any domestic or quasi-domestic tie'. On the other side of the line lie performances which are part of the audience's 'non-domestic or outside life'[12]. An Australian case similarly puts the question as whether the 'persons coming together to form the audience are bound together by a domestic or private tie, or by an aspect of their public life.'[13]

The cases treat the issue of whether membership of the audience is open to the public as a strongly relevant factor and it is clear that this does not have to mean the public at large but can refer to a portion or section of the public. For example, where there was a performance at a private club which was sufficiently exclusive that most of the public could not afford the membership fees (or, indeed, satisfy the membership requirements) this was held to be a public performance – one of the reasons given was that a section of the public were 'able to become members'[14]. In a hotel, a live performance was 'in public', since any paying member of the public (whether paying for accommodation or dinner) was able to become a member of the audience[15].

Some of the more detailed analysis in the cases[16] look at economic arguments – essentially asking what the copyright owner's monopoly created by the exclusive right to authorise public performance is intended to cover. In *PRS v Harlequin Record Shops*, the judge recognised[17] the defendant's argument that 'a most important consideration is whether the performance injures the [copyright owner] or interferes with his proprietary rights' and 'whether the performance is given to audiences for performances to which the [copyright owner] would expect to receive a fee'. The fact that historically a fee has not been charged will not be decisive since 'one of the rights which [the copyright owner] possesses is the right to decide whether or not to charge a fee for performances'. In that case, the evidence was that a prudent record shop owner would be likely to pay for a licence rather than have performance stopped, and this was seen as relevant to whether the copyright owner would be injured; in another case the question of whether some of the audience members would be willing to pay for the performance was relevant to whether the copyright owner was suffering a loss[18].

The following audiences have been treated as non-domestic, so as to render a performance 'in public':

- the members of a proprietary club – where membership was exclusive but open to a section of the public who met the membership criteria[19];
- the members of a Women's Institute watching a play put on by another branch – membership was in theory open to all women in the catchment area of the branch[20];
- the staff in a factory – the general public not being able to attend[21];
- in an Australian case, a single person in an hotel room – on the basis that the viewer is there as a guest of the hotel and not as an individual in a private or domestic situation[22].

Furthermore, the viewing of films in prisons and oil rigs is generally regarded as 'in public', despite the fact that the residents of those places will live (for the time being at least) on the premises and despite the fact that no entrance fee is charged. It is suggested that the viewers are not there in their 'private and domestic' capacity but on another basis, ie the fact they have been incarcerated/employed there. By contrast it has been told that the putting on of a play by children or adults at home would be domestic and private. Therefore not public[23].

The CDPA contains an important qualification to the general principle regarding the performance of broadcasts. Where a broadcast is shown or played in public to an audience who does not pay for admission (such as for example, on a 'big screen' like those commonly displayed in sports and other bars) the copyright in the broadcast or in any sound recording or film which is included in the broadcast will not be infringed, provided the performance is before a non paying audience[24]. For these purposes, an audience is considered to be paying:

'(a) if they have paid for admission to a place of which that place forms part; or

(b) if the goods or services are supplied at that place (or a place of which it forms part) –
   (i) at prices which are substantially attributable to the facilities afforded for seeing or hearing the broadcast […], or
   (ii) at prices exceeding those usually charged there and which are partly attributable to those facilities'[25].

So, if a pub landlord charges increased beer prices instead of charging for admission to a room with a 'big screen', he will be deemed to be showing the broadcast to a paying audience and will be infringing copyright unless he obtains appropriate authorisations[26].

The CDPA specifies that a number of categories of people will not be regarded as having paid for admission, namely:

- residents and inmates;
- members of clubs and societies, where the payment is made only for membership and the provision of facilities for seeing or hearing

the broadcast of cable programme, which is only incidental to the main purpose of the club or society[27].

What amounts to a 'broadcast' for these purposes is considered elsewhere[28].

It is important to note that, since implementation of the 2003 Regulations, this exception does *not* (except in certain limited cases, referred to below) permit the use of sound recordings without an appropriate licence if the recording is an 'excepted sound recording'. 'An excepted sound recording' is one:

'(a) whose author is not the author of the broadcast in which it is included; and

(b) which is a recording of music with or without words spoken or sung.'[29]

This essentially includes all commercial music. The only cases in which such music may be played in public as part of a broadcast without a licence is where the playing or showing of the broadcast in public:

'(b) is necessary for the purpose of —
   (i) repairing equipment for the reception of broadcasts;
   (ii) demonstrating that a repair to such equipment has been carried out; or
   (iii) demonstrating such equipment which is being sold or let for hire or offered or exposed for sale or hire.'[30]

The effect of the amendments to s 72 of the CDPA made by the Copyright and Related Rights Regulations 2003, SI 2003/2498 ('2003 Regulations') has therefore been to require that bars and other profit-making organisations that relay broadcasts (eg via radio or television) on the premises to customers who have not paid for admission will now require a licence in respect of the public performance of sound recordings contained in broadcasts in addition to their existing PRS (Performing Rights Society) licence for the public performance of the musical compositions in the broadcast. Previously, a PRS licence in respect of the public performance of the musical works was all that was needed[31].

Performance is not a restricted act in the context of 'artistic works'[32].

1   CDPA s 19(1).
2   CDPA s 19(2).
3   CDPA s 19(3).
4   CDPA s 19(4).
5   This issue is considered in further detail in **paragraph 24.17**.
6   See **paragraph 6.08**.
7   *Ernest Tucker v PRS [1943] Ch 167.*
8   For example, whether the general public is invited, whether an entrance fee is charged, whether guests are present, the number of persons present.
9   See eg *Ernest Turner*, above and *PRS v Harlequin Record Shops [1979] 2 All ER 828.*
10 *Jennings v Stephens [1936] 1 All ER 409.*
11 *Jennings v Stephens*, above.

12 *Jennings v Stephens*, above.
13 *Australian Performing Rights Association v Commonwealth Bank of Australia (1992) 25 IPR 157.*
14 *Harms Incorporated v Martan's Club [1927] 1 Ch 526.*
15 *PRS v Hawthorn's Hotel (Bournemouth) [1933] Ch 855.*
16 For example, *Jennings v Stephens, Ernest Turner v PRS, PRS v Harlequin Record Shops*, above.
17 The judge appears to accept that these are valid arguments but was of the opinion that they would only be important in a difficult or borderline case – where the performance is clearly 'in public' then it was not proper to rely on them in order to turn a performance into something it is not.
18 *Harms v Martan's Club*, above.
19 *Harms v Martan's Club*, above.
20 *Jennings v Stephens*, above.
21 *Ernest Turner v PRS*, above.
22 *Rank Film Production v Dodds [1983] 2 NSWLR 553.*
23 *Duck v Bates [1884] 13 QBD 843.*
24 CDPA s 72(1).
25 CDPA s 72(2).
26 See **paragraph 24.17**.
27 CDPA s 72(3).
28 See **paragraphs 2.09** and **2.10**.
29 CDPA s 72(1A).
30 CDPA s 72(1B).
31 See **Chapters 20** and **23** for a discussion of music and performance issues.
32 See **paragraph 21.04**.

Communication to the public

6.08   The 2003 Regulations substantially amended CDPA s 20 to deal with the provision of 'Information Society' services[1].

A new restricted act of 'communication to the public' was introduced. Communication to the public is an act restricted in a literary, dramatic, musical or artistic work, a sound recording or film, or a broadcast[2].

A 'communication to the public' means a communication to the public by electronic transmission, and in relation to a work includes the broadcasting of the work and making the work available to the public in such a way that members of the public may access it from a place and at a time individually chosen by them[3] (ie an on-demand, or other interactive service).

Previously, there was considerable debate about the legal status of an internet or mobile transmission, and how that transmission might be considered for the purposes of copyright law in the UK. The earlier definition of 'broadcast' was clearly not intended to capture 'point to point' transmissions, and the only relevant case in the UK which suggested that elements of the process of 'hypertext linking' could be construed as a cable programme service[4], was of somewhat limited authority.

The concept of communication to the public covers the placement of material on a web-server for access by members of the public – whether by downloading or streaming – at a time individually chosen by them. Webcasts however may fall under the category of a broadcast, as tuning into an ongoing stream is analogous to tuning into a television or radio programme; and if they do not, they are certainly within the concept of a 'communication to the public'.

There has already been some controversy over the future interpretation of the communication right; in particular the 'making available' issue.

The EU Commission has taken the view that the critical copyright restricted act is the 'making available' of the work to the public, ie 'the offering of work on a publicly accessible site, which precedes the stage of its on-demand transmission. It is not relevant whether any person actually has retrieved it or not.' The Commission's view is that the term 'communication to the public' does not cover so-called near video on demand, where the offer of a non-interactive programme is broadcast several times in parallel at short intervals. On this view, BSkyB, for example, does not 'make available' films on the Sky Box Office channel. Interestingly, the Patent Office seems to disagree with the Commission, and takes the view that a delay of no more than 15 minutes is de minimis, and that a service such as Sky Box Office is effectively 'making available' films. In the view of the authors, the Commission's view is to be preferred on this issue.

To make a work available on an interactive basis some form of initial fixation (ie upload) must take place. To do this it follows that a certain amount of copying must take place. Many copies may be made in making a work available: on the initial server, at transmission points and at the reception point. What is not clear and what will need to be addressed are questions such as:

- Where and when does the making available take place, and which parties are making available?
- Are the parties responsible for the initial uploader and/or all the ISPs in the chain?

The Patent Office in its comments on the implementation of the 2003 Regulations stated that 'some right owner organisations suggested that the implementing legislation should seek to identify the points or points at which an act of 'making available' is to be regarded as having taken place. However, 'the Government does not feel that this is necessary or that it would be appropriate particularly given that the [2001 Directive] does not seek to expand upon this aspect'.

1 In order to give effect to these changes the definition of 'broadcasting' which previously existed in the CDPA was modified, and the references in the CDPA to 'cable programme services' and 'cable programmes' were deleted entirely. The Copyright and Related Rights Regulations 2003 (SI 2003/2498).

2   CDPA s 20(1).
3   CDPA s 20(2).
4   *Shetland Times Ltd v Wills [1997] FSR 604.*

Adaptations or acts done in relation to adaptations

6.09   This restricted act applies only to literary, dramatic or musical works. The meaning varies dependent upon the category of work in question.

In relation to literary (other than computer programs and databases) and dramatic works 'adaptation' is specially defined as follows:

'(i)   a translation of the work;
(ii)   a version of a dramatic work in which it is converted into a non-dramatic work or, as the case may be, of a non-dramatic work in which it is converted into a dramatic work;
(iii) a version of the work in which the story or action is conveyed wholly or mainly by means of pictures in a form suitable for reproduction in a book, or in a newspaper, magazine or similar periodical'[1].

In the case of musical works, 'adaptation' means: 'an arrangement or transcription of the work'[2].

In relation to computer programs and those databases which receive copyright protection as such[3], an adaptation will mean any arrangement, altered version, or translation of the database or program in question[4].

In the case of computer programs, a 'translation' will include a version of the program which 'is converted into or out of a computer language or code or into a different computer language or code'[5].

An adaptation will itself have copyright if it has sufficient originality, even if the person making the adaptation has no licence from the copyright owner in the original work and is therefore infringing one of the restricted acts, such as copying, in making the adaptation. So, the CDPA provides that doing any of the other restricted acts to the adaptation, including making a further adaptation of the adaptation, will breach the copyright in that adaptation[6].

The restricted act of making an adaptation does not apply to artistic works, so that an artist can effectively imitate the style of another artist without infringing that artist's copyright. But he must not, in the process of so doing, make a copy of the original work.

1   CDPA s 21(3)(a), see also **paragraph 21.11**.
2   CDPA s 21(3)(b).
3   See **paragraph 2.02** and **Chapter 14**.
4   CDPA s 21(3).
5   CDPA s 21(4).
6   CDPA s 21(2).

Secondary infringement: importing, possessing, dealing with or providing means for making infringing copies

6.10 In addition to the 'restricted acts', the following acts will constitute 'secondary infringements' of copyright:

- *Importation*: the importation of an article (other than for private or domestic use) into the UK or any other country to which the CDPA extends or applies, if the importer knew or had reason to believe that the article was an 'infringing copy' of a work[1].
- *Dealing with infringing copies*: a person may not:
  - (a) possess in the course of a business;
  - (b) sell or let for hire, or offer or expose for sale or hire;
  - (c) in the course of a business exhibit in public or distribute; or
  - (d) distribute otherwise in the course of a business to such an extent as to effect prejudicially the owner of the copyright;

  an article which is or which he has reason to believe is an 'infringing copy' of a work[2].

  Possession in the course of business means possession in the ordinary course of a business, otherwise solicitors acting for copyright owners who are in possession of infringing video tapes which they had seized on behalf of their client would be liable for an infringement under this sub-section. In the case of *LA Gear Inc v Hi-Tech Sports plc*[3] it was held that where the articles were not on view and were only shown to those who requested a sight of them, they were not offered for sale nor exposed for sale. Moreover, a brochure and a price list had been prepared, but this, it was held, was inviting offers for sale rather than actually offering for sale.
- *Articles used to make infringing copies*: a person may not:
  - (a) make;
  - (b) import into the UK;
  - (c) possess in the course of a business; or
  - (d) sell or let for hire, or expose for sale or hire;

  an article specifically designed or adapted for making copies of that work knowing or having reason to believe that it is to be used for making 'infringing copies'[4].
- *Transmission of infringing copies:* the transmission of a work by means of a telecommunication system (otherwise than by communication to the public) knowing or having reason to believe that 'infringing copies' were made by means of the reception of the transmission in the UK or elsewhere[5]. E-mailing an infringing copy to a third party could also amount to a secondary infringement on the same basis.

The last of these acts of secondary infringement was introduced by the CDPA. For these purposes 'Telecommunication system' means 'a system for conveying visual images, sounds or other information by electronic means[6], and therefore has a very wide meaning. The most common case of secondary infringement likely to be encountered under this section is the sending of documents by fax machines. Although the sender does not make a copy on his machine he knows that a copy will be made on the recipient's fax machine.

'Dealing' with an article which is an infringing copy suggests the existence of physical 'articles' which infringe copyright. The question of what constitutes an 'article' for this purpose is difficult in the context of electronic copies. Arguably, a copy held on a hard disk of a computer, or even a temporary copy held on a computer's RAM could be an 'article'. However, it is difficult to envisage how the recipient of such a copy could 'deal' with it except by making further copies – in which case he would in any event commit a primary act of copyright infringement[7].

1   CDPA s 22.
2   CDPA s 23.
3   [1992] FSR 121, CA.
4   CDPA s 24(1).
5   CDPA s 24(2).
6   CDPA s 178.
7   See **paragraph 6.04**.

Infringing copies

6.11   The expression 'infringing copy' has a lengthy definition in the CDPA[1].

In the first place, an article is an infringing copy 'if its making constituted an infringement of the copyright in the work'[2].

An article made outside the UK, the making of which would have constituted an infringement of the copyright in the work had it been made in the UK, or a breach of an exclusive licence agreement relating to that work, will be an infringing copy if it has been, or is proposed to be, imported into the UK. For example, where a licence has been granted by a copyright owner resident outside the UK, to a person in the UK, giving that person the exclusive right to make copies in the UK, then copies which have been perfectly legally made outside the UK (either by the copyright owner himself, or other non-UK resident licensees), will become infringing copies if they are brought into the UK without the permission of the UK licensee[3].

There is an important exception to this rule, which is necessary by reason of the UK's membership of the EU. An article which may lawfully be imported into the UK by virtue of any enforceable Community right under the European Communities Act 1972 is not an infringing copy. Under Art 30 of the Treaty of Rome, goods must be able to circulate freely throughout the common market. Therefore, even if exclusive licences for the manufacture of goods have been granted to

UK licensees, goods made elsewhere within the EEA can be imported into the UK without becoming infringing copies[4].

Various parts of the CDPA specify that copies made other than in accordance with various 'permitted' acts should be construed as 'infringing copies'[5]. For example, following the 2003 Regulations, any copy produced by a person in reliance on the 'time shifting' exception to copyright infringement will be treated as an 'infringing copy' if it is subsequently 'dealt with' (ie sold, let for hire, offered or exposed for sale or hire or communicated to the public)[6].

One recent case considered the issue of whether a transient copy of game software held on the RAM of a Sony Playstation games console without the authorisation of the copyright holder was capable of being considered an 'infringing copy' (in circumstances where it was necessary to establish that such a copy had been made in order to trigger those provisions of the CDPA which restrict the use of articles designed to circumvent technical anti-copying measures)[7]. The court found that the silicon RAM chip contained in the games console and on which the transitory copy was made was an article, and that whilst it contained an unauthorised copy it was also an infringing article: nothing in the CDPA suggests that an object containing an ephemeral copy should not be considered an article[8].

1   CDPA s 27.
2   CDPA s 27(2).
3   CDPA s 27(3)(b).
4   See also **paragraph 6.05** and generally, **Chapter 13**.
5   These include copies which are to be treated as 'infringing copies' by virtue of ss 31A(6) and (9), 31B(9) and (10), 32(5), 35(3), 36(5), 56(2), 63(2), 68(4), 70(2) and orders under s 141. See **Chapter 8**.
6   CDPA s 70(2), see **paragraph 8.33**.
7   *Sony Computer Entertainment Inc v Ball [2005] 3 FSR 160*.
8   *Sony Computer Entertainment Inc v Ball [2005] 3 FSR 160* at 161.

Secondary infringement: use of premises for infringing performances

6.12 A person who gives permission for a place of public entertainment to be used for the performance of a literary, dramatic or musical work which constitutes an infringing performance will be liable for the infringement unless, when he gives permission, he believes on reasonable grounds that the performance will not infringe copyright[1].

For these purposes, a 'place of public entertainment' includes premises which are occupied mainly for other purposes, but are, from time to time, made available on hire for the purposes of public entertainment[2]. This, for example, would include a pub which was occasionally used for live musical performances. If the performers did not have a licence from the owners of the music copyright, not only would the performers themselves be infringing the restricted act of performing a work in public, but the owner of the pub, if he knew or had reason to believe that the performers had not obtained a licence from the copyright owners, would also be liable for infringement of the copyright in the music.

It should, however, be noted that this act of secondary infringement applies only to performances of literary, dramatic or musical works and not, for example, to films or sound recordings.

1 CDPA s 25(1).
2 CDPA s 25(2).

Secondary infringement: provision of apparatus for infringing performances

6.13   Where any work is infringed by a public performance of the work (the restricted act applicable to literary, dramatic and musical works) or by the playing or showing of the work in public (the restricted act applicable to sound recordings, films, broadcasts or cable programmes) or by means of apparatus for playing sound recordings, showing films or receiving visual images or sounds conveyed by electronic means, the following persons are also liable for the infringement:

*   the supplier of the apparatus or any substantial part of it;
*   an occupier of premises who gave permission for the apparatus to be brought onto the premises;
*   the person who supplied a copy of a sound recording or film used to infringe copyright.

In each case the person must be shown to have known or had reason to believe, that the apparatus was likely to be used so as to infringe copyright[1].

1 CDPA s 26.

Secondary infringement: knowledge and belief

6.14   In order to establish liability for secondary infringement the copyright owner must prove that the infringer had knowledge or reason to believe that he is dealing in an infringing copy. This is a question of fact. In *LA Gear v Hi-Tech Sports*[1] the Court of Appeal indicated that the existence of knowledge was an objective test. The claimant must demonstrate that the infringer must possess sufficient facts from which a reasonable man would arrive at the necessary belief or knowledge. For the avoidance of doubt written notice should always be given to the infringer who should have a reasonable time to evaluate the information.

1 [1992] FSR 121.

Chapter 7

Infringement of copyright and remedies

Primary and secondary infringement: a summary

7.01 When deciding whether a copyright infringement has occurred, it is necessary to establish that:

- an act of infringement has been carried out by the defendant;
- the infringed work falls within one of the categories of work in which copyright exists[1];
- the infringed work is still within the term of copyright[2];
- a restricted act has been undertaken without the authorisation of the owner[3] (ie a primary infringement has been committed) and/or an act which amounts to a secondary infringement has been committed with 'knowledge'[4]; and
- no exception or defence to copyright infringement is available to the defendant[5].

If any of the above elements are not established, an action for infringement will not succeed.

1 See **paragraphs 2.01** ff.
2 See **Chapter 5**.
3 See **paragraphs 6.02–6.09**.
4 See **paragraphs 6.10–6.14**.
5 See **Chapter 8**.

Proving infringement

7.02 Copyright does not provide an exclusive or monopoly right in an idea[1]. For example, if an author writes a literary work identical to one created earlier by somebody else, this will not amount to an infringement if the defendant has never heard the earlier melody and has created the alleged infringing work independently.

When a person claims that a copyright infringement has occurred, he has the burden of showing that, on the balance of probabilities, this is the case. Except in cases of flagrancy (when a whole work has been intentionally reproduced without authorisation), it will usually be necessary to look at the surrounding facts to see if an infringement can be shown. The claimant will need to show both that the degree of similarity between the works is substantial enough to constitute infringement[2] and that the alleged infringer had *access* to the infringed work. If substantial similarity can be shown, the practical burden of proof will transfer to the alleged infringer to rebut the claim that he had access, or to show that notwithstanding access he did not copy (eg because the two works were based upon a common public domain news story reported in the press[3]). Expert witnesses are often called, in difficult cases, to provide evidence regarding the level of similarity to assist the court in establishing whether copying has taken place.

In some cases, it is the copying of an unusual style or even mistakes which can provide evidence of copying. For that reason, it is common for the owners of copyright works (such as compilations) which require little originality in order to receive protection to deliberately insert false information for the purpose of detecting infringements. In *Waterlow Directories v Reed Information Services Ltd*[4], for example, the claimants were alerted to an unauthorised copying of its legal directory when mailings were received at a false 'seed' address, incorporated by the claimant in its own directory, from a competitor seeking to copy entries in order to compile its own database.

In *IBCOS Computers Ltd v Barclays Mercantile Highland Finance Ltd*[5] the presence of copied mistakes in the coding of a computer program enabled the court to establish that copying had taken place.

1   See **paragraph 7.04**.
2   See **paragraph 7.06**.
3   See **paragraph 7.10**.
4   [1992] FSR 409.
5   [1994] FSR 275.

Intention: strict liability

7.03   In cases of primary infringement it is not necessary to show that the infringer *intended* to infringe. In one case, *Sony Music Entertainment (UK) Ltd v EasyInternetcafe Ltd*[1], the defendant operated an internet café which provided a 'CD burning' service allowing customers to download material from the internet onto CD-R. The café proprietor instructed its employees not to look at the files downloaded by customers. The café proprietor was sued for copyright infringement by the owners of musical tracks downloaded by customers. In his defence, the proprietor claimed (amongst other things) that he was an 'involuntary copier'. He did not know infringing acts were taking place. Although his copying devices were controlled by human employees, these were, in effect automatons. This argument was rejected by Mr Justice Peter Smith:

> 'If a high street printer copies material, which contains infringing copyright material (for example a pirated PhD thesis) the printer will be liable. He will not know that the material is infringing for obvious reasons. Nevertheless, he is liable. I do not see how it can be said to be different because he chooses not to know'.[2]

In the popular music industry, it is often said 'everybody copies everybody', since the structure of many popular compositions are based on a limited pool of cultural and musical references which are frequently reinvigorated by new treatments. Nevertheless, if a songwriter or composer draws on an influence so closely that his work is substantially similar, he will infringe copyright even if he does so unconsciously[3].

However, if someone who infringes a work can show that he did not know (or have reason to know) that the work was in copyright, this will have an impact on the remedies available to the claimant[4].

In the leading case of *Francis Day & Hunter Ltd v Bron*[5], it was claimed that the opening bars of a song, 'In a Little Spanish Town', composed in 1929, had been copied in a song entitled 'Why', composed in 1959. The evidence of the composer of 'Why' was that he had not seen or studied or, in his recollection, played the music of 'In a Little Spanish Town', nor had he ever to his knowledge heard it (although he admitted he might have heard it at a younger age). This evidence was accepted. The trial judge found that he had insufficient factual material concerning the similarity of the works. It was not right to draw an inference in the absence of direct evidence, and in the face of the composer's denial that he had sufficient knowledge or memory of 'In a Little Spanish Town', that he copied it without knowing that he was doing so, rather than to conclude that the similarity arose from coincidence. Accordingly, the judge held that the infringement of copyright was not established. The case went to appeal.

On appeal Willmer LJ said:

> 'if subconscious copying is to be found, there must be proof (or at least a strong inference) of de facto familiarity with the work alleged to be copied'.

Diplock LJ (as he then was) said:

> 'If the existence of the copyright work has no causal connection with the production of the alleged infringing work, even though the latter be identical with the former, there is no infringement of copyright. In my view, however, it is equally clear law that neither intention to infringe, nor knowledge that he is infringing on the part of the defendant is a necessary ingredient in the cause of action for infringement of copyright. Once the two elements of sufficient objective similarity and casual connection are established, it is no defence

that the defendant was unaware (and could not have been aware) that what he was doing infringed the copyright in the plaintiff's work'.

In the *Da Vinci Code* case, *Baignet v The Random House Group Ltd*[6] the Court of Appeal stressed that copyright was infringed whether or not the defendant appreciated that what he was doing infringed copyright or whether he intended to infringe.

1 [2003] EWHC 62.
2 Per Mr Justice Peter Smith, *Sony Music Entertainment (UK) Ltd v EasyInternetcafe Ltd*, above.
3 See **paragraph 7.06**.
4 See **paragraphs 7.12** ff.
5 [1963] 2 All ER 16, CA.
6 [2007] EWCA Civ 247.

Use of ideas and characters

7.04 Copyright, is generally concerned with the protection of form, not of ideas[1]. There is no infringement of copyright if the ideas in one work are used in another. It is sometimes said that there will be no infringement of a literary or dramatic work, even if the plot is followed in another work, provided different words are used. This is incorrect. The test is whether the copier, in following the original, made substantial use of the skill and labour of the original. Copyright exists not only in the series and order of certain selected works, but also in the organisation of the ideas and the manner of their presentation. In the case of a novel or play, the plot is presented by means of a series of dramatic incidents. If these incidents are reproduced, even with different language, an infringement will take place. The organisation and selection of these incidents to create the plot requires skill and labour. To determine whether the use of the plot in another work is an infringement will require an examination of the way (ie the form) in which the alleged infringer has presented his plot to determine whether he merely borrowed the concept of the plot and used his own skill and labour in expressing its form. In this context, the words from Mr Justice Laddie's judgment in *Autospin (Oil Seals) Ltd v Beehive Spinning*[2], are relevant[3].

A related question is: to what extent can the writer of, say, a novel, play or screenplay control the re-use of the characters, recast into different scenarios by other writers?

Although there is little by way of dicta considering this issue, in *Pozanski v London Film Production Ltd*[4], a case concerning alleged plagiarism of a play based on Catherine the Great in a subsequent filmed work, the claimants argued that there was copyright (inter alia) in certain characterisations in the work, and that that copyright was infringed by the defendants when they followed the selection and treatment of the subject, scenarios and characters of the claimant. Crossman LJ held:

'I do not find myself driven to the conclusion that the selection or treatment was a copying of [the plaintiff's] selection and treatment. I find that if and so far as there are any similarities they are mainly in ideas which are not the subject matter of copyright, and the treatment and development of these ideas are quite different from the treatment and development in the [plaintiff's work].'

The conclusion that can be drawn from this is that an English court will not find that there is a breach of copyright where the idea or character is used from an original work and developed in a different direction for the new work. For example if a literary character is taken by another author and used for a different book which tells a different story entirely then this will not be copyright infringement, although such an action may result in an accusation of moral rights infringement (false attribution or derogatory treatment[5]), or a claim for 'passing off'.

Of course where there is copying of a character and the same story is retold that may be an infringement of copyright in the original literary work as a whole, provided a substantial part of the original work is taken[6].

In *Ravenscroft v Herbert*[7] Brightman J found infringement by way of non-textual copying and that this constituted infringement as much as literal copying. More recently in *IPC Media Ltd v Highbury Leisure Publishing Ltd*[8] Laddie J held that:

'The law of copyright has never gone as far as to protect general themes, styles or ideas. Such general concepts are not put out of bounds to others by the law of copyright.'

1   See **paragraph 1.03**.
2   [1995] RPC 683.
3   See **paragraph 2.02**.
4   (1937) MacG Cop Cas (1936–45) 107.
5   See **Chapter 10**.
6   See also **paragraphs 2.02** and **2.13**.
7   [1980] RPC 193. In an unreported interlocutory judgment in that case Templeman J took a different approach to that taken by Brightman J at trial and doubted whether infringement existed.
8   [2005] EWHC 317.

Parodies

7.05   A parody, which uses an idea from an existing work, but which also uses substantial new skill and labour, does not infringe the copyright in the original work. A parody, however, which uses the same work, will be an infringement[1].

There must be no reproduction of a substantial part of the original work. So, a parody of a song entitled 'Rock-a-Billy' using the words 'Rock-a-Philip, Rock' in the chorus of the parody in the same way as the words of the song were used, was held not to infringe the copyright in 'Rock-a-Billy'[2]. On the other hand, a label for a bottle substantially the same as the Schweppes Indian tonic water bottle, except that the name used was 'Schlurppes', was held to infringe the copyright in the Schweppes label, even though it was accepted that the 'Schlurppes' label was a parody[3]. This is subject to the permitted act of 'caricature, parody or pastiche' introduced as of 1 October 2014 by the CDPA s 30A.

1 See also **paragraph 1.14**.
2 *Joy Music Ltd v Sunday Pictorial Newspapers (1920) Ltd [1960] 2 QB 60*.
3 *Schweppes Ltd v Wellingtons Ltd [1984] FSR 210*.

'Substantial part'

7.06 For copying to constitute an infringement, it must be substantial[1];

'What amounts to a "substantial" part for these purposes must be assessed upon the basis of quality rather than quantity'[2].

If the most vital part of a work is copied (even though it may not be a very large part), it will nevertheless be considered to be a substantial part for the purpose of deciding whether or not there is an infringement.

The question is always whether the alleged infringer has used a substantial part of the skill and labour of the original maker for the making of the copy. To take a few examples:

- in the context of a literary work, four lines from Kipling's 'If' used in a Sanatogen advertisement, were held to be a substantial part[3];
- in the context of a dramatic work, an episode in a full-length feature film consisting of dramatic events and accompanying dialogue, taken from four pages of a book of 126 pages, was held to be a substantial part[4];
- in the context of a musical work, an extract of 60 seconds' duration from 'Colonel Bogey' constituted a substantial part[5];
- in the context of a film, the copying of a style or technique (such as an editing technique) will not amount to an infringement of copyright unless a substantial part of the 'essence and originality' of the film has been appropriated[6];
- in the context of a published edition, cuttings from articles in various newspapers were held, in context, not to constitute a substantial part of the newspapers concerned[7].

In the context of a film, television broadcast or cable programme, taking a photograph of the whole or any substantial part of any image is an infringement[8]. 'Video grab' (the photographing of a still taken from a moving video image) will amount to copying, notwithstanding that the single image which is 'grabbed' may be a very insignificant part of the whole work[9].

The question of what constitutes a 'substantial part' was considered at length by the House of Lords' in *Designers Guild v Russell Williams*[10].

That case concerned a fabric design launched by the defendant under the name 'Marquante', in 1996, which was similar (but not identical) to the claimant's design 'Ixia' released in 1995. Four of five law lords gave reasoned judgments in favour of the claimant and their judgments offer limited guidance, although Lord Scott, finding for the claimant, restated with approval Laddie's test for determining whether an altered copy constitutes an infringement, as follows:

> 'Has the infringer incorporated a substantial part of the independent skill, labour etc. constituted by the original author in creating the copyright work?'[11]

Elsewhere, the judgments suggest that in an altered copying case, the finding of copying will usually depend on the extent and nature of the similarities between the work, and that if the similarities are enough to justify a conclusion that copying has occurred, then that infringing design must incorporate a substantial part of the original design.

Lord Hoffmann suggests that the question is whether the alleged copy contains 'sufficient of the author's skill and labour as to attract copyright protection'. Although not expressly stated in his judgment, some writers have used this dictum as support for a new test for determining whether a substantial part has been copied: namely, 'Is the amount of material copied sufficient to constitute a copyright work in its own right as an original work?'[12]

The EU Information Society Directive[13] now governs the restricted act of reproduction of a copyright work. Article 2 defines this reproduction right by reference to reproduction 'in whole or in part' but does not define this. In *Infopaq*[14] the CJEU held that the expression has to be defined in accordance with the overall objectives of the Directive and international law. It went on to state that parts of a work are protected since they share the originality of the whole. The Directive should be interpreted broadly so that a small part of a work if it contains the expression of the intellectual creation of the author would be protectable from infringement.

It is unclear whether in practice this test is significantly different from the long-standing UK test. In *Baigent v The Random House Group Ltd*[15] Mummery LJ warned against a precise definition of 'substantial part'.

1 CDPA s 16(3).
2 House of Lords in *Ladbroke (Football) Ltd v William Hill (Football) Ltd [1964] 1 WLR 273*.
3 *Kipling v Genatosan Ltd (1917-1923) Macg Cop Cas 203*.
4 *Fernald v Jay Lewis Production Ltd [1975] FSR 499*.
5 *Hawkes & Son Ltd v Paramount Film Service Ltd [1934] Ch 593*.
6 *Norowzian v Arks Ltd (No 2) [2000] FSR 363, CA* (see the further discussion of this case set out in **paragraphs 2.03** and **2.08**).
7 *Newspaper Licensing Agency v Marks & Spencer plc [2000] NLJR 900, CA*, see **paragraph 2.11**.
8 CDPA s 17(4); *Spelling Goldberg Productions Inc v BPC Publishing Ltd [1981] RPC 283, CA*.

9 See **paragraph 6.04** and the exceptions to copyright infringement considered at **Chapter 8** and in particular **paragraph 8.34**.

10 [2001] FSR 113.

11 Laddie, Prescott and Vitoria, *Modern Law of Copyright and Designs* (3rd ed, 2000), 3.137.

12 For an interesting discussion on this issue, see Mark Chacksfield, 'The Hedgehog and the Fox, a Substantial Part of the Law of Copyright' [2001] EIPR 259.

13 2001/29/EC.

14 Case C-5/08 [2009] ECR 1-6569.

15 [2007] EWCA Civ 247.

Quotations

7.07 Where a work contains quotations from another work, but the quotations do not constitute a substantial part of the work from which they are taken, the use of the quotations will not constitute an infringement of copyright. Whether or not they constitute a substantial part of the other work is a question of fact in each case[1].

1 See **paragraphs 7.06** and **16.06**.

Proof of damage unnecessary

7.08 In order to succeed in an action for infringement of copyright, it is not necessary to prove damage, although the fact that there has been damage caused by the infringement will inevitably affect the amount of damages awarded by a court. The claimant may in any event be able to sustain an account of profits from the infringer[1].

1 See **paragraph 7.12**.

Factual sources

7.09 A common problem arises where a work is based upon a factual event (eg a film or documentary based on real life events). Factual information is not, of itself, a 'work' capable of copyright protection[1]. Indeed, in a news context, there is a significant public interest in making information available as widely as possible. However, if the *expression* given to the story in one account is copied, then an infringement may be said to have occurred. The problem becomes acute for users who wish to create biographical films or other works based on events which are well documented in previous news reports or biographies. Such activities will often require the devotion of significant budgets, which may be at risk from claims of copyright infringement from earlier biographers whose works may be used as research tools. The question in these cases is no different from that stated above, namely: has the alleged infringer used a substantial part of the skill and labour of another? In practice it is common for film producers creating such a film to acquire the rights in an earlier biography, or to hire the consultancy services of a key figure in the factual events, in part to rebut any allegation of infringement, notwithstanding that the film may not be substantially based on these contributions.

Exceptions to copyright infringement also exist in the context of news reporting and these are considered further in **Chapter 8**.

1   See **paragraphs 1.02** and **2.13**.

Liability for infringement

7.10   Who is liable for infringement of copyright? The CDPA[1] provides that copyright in a work is infringed by any person who, without the licence of the owner, does, or authorises another person to do, any of the restricted acts. In short liability falls upon any person who, without the consent of the owner of the copyright in question:

- does any of the restricted acts in relation to the work in the UK or any other country to which CDPA extends;
- authorises any other person to do any such act[2];
- commits any act of secondary infringement with knowledge[3].

1   CDPA s 16(2).
2   See **paragraph 6.03**.
3   See **paragraphs 6.10–6.14**.

Remedies for infringement

7.11   There are two types of remedies for breach of copyright: civil remedies (including damages, an injunction, an account of the profits gained by the defendant as a result of the infringement, delivery up of infringing articles, etc)[1] or criminal proceedings[2].

1   CDPA s 96 ff.
2   CDPA s 107.

Damages

7.12   There are a number of defences to claims for damages. There is a limited defence under the CDPA s 97(1) so that someone who infringes a work can show in the circumstances that he did not know (or have reason to know) that the work was in copyright, a claimant should not be entitled to damages for the infringement[1]. This is an objective test: would a reasonable man with the knowledge of the infringer have believed the work is in copyright?[2] The onus is upon the infringer to prove this defence.

In *Infabrics Ltd v Jaytex Ltd*[3] Buckley LJ said:

'It is, in my opinion, incumbent upon anyone who proposes to make use of any artistic work in a way which might infringe copyright, if it subsists in the work, to make such enquiries and investigation as he reasonably can satisfy himself that the work is free of copyright ... If no adequate enquiries or investigations are made it must, it seems to me, be difficult to suppose that the person proposing to use the work has no grounds for suspecting that it may be subject to copyright'.

The defence of not knowing, or having reason to believe, therefore, is unlikely to be available, except in those cases:

- where the work is very old and might be out of copyright; or
- where it is the sort of work which it would be reasonable to assume did not have copyright protection; or
- where it is of foreign origin and is unlikely to be entitled to protection under UK law.

In each case, the court will take into account all the relevant circumstances. The defence has not been made available in circumstances:

- where the defendant knew, believed or suspected that copyright subsisted, but belonged to someone other than the claimant[4];
- where the defendant makes a mistake as to the owner of the copyright from whom authorisation must be obtained, and obtains consent to publish from the wrong person[5];
- where the defendant proves that the publication occurred in circumstances where it is common practice to publish without the owner's consent[6];
- where the defendant assumes that, because the work was published anonymously, it is not entitled to copyright protection.

1   CDPA s 97(1).
2   *LA Gear Inc v Hi-Tec Sports plc [1992] FSR 121.*
3   [1980] FSR 161, CA.
4   *John Lane Bodley Head Ltd v Associated Newspapers Ltd [1936] 1 KB 715.*
5   *Byrne v Statist Co [1914] 1 KB 622.*
6   *Banier v News Group Newspapers Ltd [1997] FSR 812.*

Damages for flagrancy

7.13   Under certain circumstances the court, in assessing damages for infringement, has power under the CDPA s 97(2) to award additional damages (ie damages which go beyond the actual damage suffered as a result of the infringement). The court must have regard to all the circumstances and, in particular, to the flagrancy of the infringement and to the benefit which accrued to the defendant by reason of the infringement[1]. What is not clear is whether these damages should be compensatory or punitive[2].

In the case of *Cala Homes (South) Ltd v Alfred McAlpine Homes East Ltd*[3], it was held that:

- the power to award additional damages is not limited to cases where the infringer knows or has reason to believe that copyright has been infringed (which is not the same thing as not knowing that the work in question was in copyright);
- it is not necessary that there should be both flagrancy and benefit accruing to the defendant;
- additional damages are designed to allow the court to register in terms of a financial penalty its disapproval of the behaviour of the infringer.

In *Redrow Homes Ltd v Bett Bros*[4] it was held that additional damages can be awarded if there is an award of damages, but not if there is only an award of account of profits (see below). The additional damages are not available if the claimant does not seek compensatory damages.

If an infringement is careless rather than deliberate, additional damages will not be appropriate[5]. Nor are additional damages available where a clip was broadcast by the defendant in the belief that its broadcast was permissible, in the public interest, and did not compete with the rights-holder's use of the work[6].

1 CDPA s 97(2). 'Flagrancy' implies scandalous conduct, deceit etc, including deliberate and calculated copyright infringements, and 'benefit' implies a financial benefit in excess of the damages he would otherwise have to pay: *Ravenscroft v Herbert [1980] RPC 193*. See also *Technomed Ltd v Bluecrest Health Screening [2017] EWHC 2142*.
2 Although not a decided point, obiter dicta of Lord Clyde *in Redrow Homes Ltd v Bett Bros* (see n 4 below) suggests his view that these damages were aggravated, at 209F per Lord Clyde. Amounts awarded by courts under s 97(2) have typically been modest.
3 [1995] FSR 818.
4 [1999] 1 AC 197, HL overruling *Cala Homes*, above.
5 *Noah v Shuba [1991] FSR 14*, per Mummery J.
6 *ProSieben Media AG v Carlton UK Television Ltd [1998] FSR 43*.

Account of profits

7.14 Instead of damages, a claimant can apply for an account of profits. This is an 'equitable' remedy and as such, the remedy may not be awarded if the claimant has not himself acted equitably. So, by way of example, an account of profits may not be ordered by the court when there has been a delay on the part of the claimant in claiming the account. However, the fact that damages would be an adequate remedy is not of itself enough to deter the request. The aim is to prevent an infringer from being unjustly enriched by his activities. The remedy is most useful, and likely to be available, in the cases of simple, deliberate infringement. The account of profits which will be applied for is of net profit[1].

A claimant is not entitled to claim for both damages and an account of profits. In the case of *Minnesota Mining and Manufacturing Co Ltd v C Jeffries Pty*[2], the claimant was allowed discovery of the defendant's accounts before having to make an election as to whether to claim damages or an account of profits. In *Island Records v Tring International*[3] the court held that after judgment on liability a successful claimant would normally be entitled to disclosure from the defendant to enable an informed election as to damages or an account of profits.

1   *Pike v Nicholas (1869) 5 Ch App 251.*
2   [1993] FSR189 (Aus).
3   *Island Records v Tring International plc* [1995] FSR 560.

Delivery up and forfeiture

7.15   In addition to damages or an account of profits, the owner (or exclusive licensee) of copyright may apply to the court to require a person who has been dealing with articles which infringe the copyright to deliver up to him the infringing copies (for example, books, records etc), as if he had been the owner of them since the time when they had been made[1]. Generally this right must be exercised by applying for a court order within six years from the date on which the infringing copy or article in question was made[2]. This limitation is subject to two caveats. First, if the copyright owner is under a 'disability' then an application may be made at any time within six years after the date on which he ceased to be under the disability (for these purposes 'disability' means insanity or minority). Second, if the copyright owner was prevented by fraud or concealment from discovering the facts entitling him to apply for an order, an application may be made at any time within six years after the copyright owner could, with reasonable diligence, have discovered the facts.

The owner has a similar right to delivery up of any article specifically designed or adapted for making copies of a particular copyright work, provided that the person against whom the order is sought, knew or had reason to believe, that the article would be so used[3].

Alternatively, the court can order the disposal of infringing copies[4]. Again, this remedy is at the discretion of the court and will not be awarded if the harm it does to the infringer would be out of proportion to the interests of justice served by making the order[5].

1   CDPA s 99(1)(a).
2   Ie prior to expiry of the limitation period by such action, Limitation Act 1980.
3   CDPA s 99(1)(b).
4   CDPA ss 114, 204 and 231.
5   *Ocular Sciences Ltd v Aspect Vision Care Ltd [1997] RPC 289.*

Injunctions and interim injunctions

7.16   An injunction can be obtained to restrain a copyright infringement, although an injunction will not be available if the court consider that damages would provide adequate relief in the circumstances.

An interim (or 'interlocutory') injunction may be available to restrain an infringement pending trial, provided that the claimant is able to establish that he has a sufficiently serious claim which is not frivolous or vexatious, and that on the balance of convenience the likely damage from the claimed infringement will exceed the harm caused to the claimed infringer by the injunction[1].

1   *NWL Ltd v Woods [1979] 1 WLR 1294.*

Who may sue?

7.17   An action for copyright infringement may be brought by the owner of the copyright, or by a person to whom an 'exclusive licence' has been granted[1].

For the purposes of CDPA, an 'exclusive licence' means a licence in writing, signed by or on behalf of an owner or prospective owner of copyright, authorising the licensee to the exclusion of all other persons (including the licensor), to exercise a right which would be exercisable exclusively by the owner of the copyright[2]. So, for example, if two publishing houses are given licences to publish a work in the UK (neither, therefore, having an exclusive licence), any action against a third party publisher who publishes an infringing work in the UK must be brought by the original owner – not by one of the two licensed publishers.

1   CDPA ss 96 and 101; see **paragraph 9.29**.
2   CDPA s 92(1).

Technical provisions concerning claimants and defendants in civil actions

7.18   Part I, Chapter VI of CDPA contains provisions regarding the rights of claimants and defendants in relation to civil actions, some of which have been mentioned above, which are generally of a technical nature. For example, ss 101 and 102 deal with the rights and remedies of exclusive licensees in infringement proceedings; ss 104–106 deal with presumptions which apply in proceedings for infringement of copyright and which apply in the absence of evidence to the contrary being forthcoming. These sections and similar issues of a technical nature are not, therefore, dealt with in detail here.

Criminal proceedings

7.19 The provisions of CDPA regarding penalties and summary proceedings in respect of dealings which infringe copyright are set out in ss 107–110 of CDPA.

In brief, any person who:

'(a) makes for sale or hire; or
(b) imports into the United Kingdom, otherwise than for his private and domestic use, or
(c) possesses in the course of business with a view to committing any act infringing the copyright, or
(d) in the course of a business—
    (i) sells or lets for hire, or
    (ii) offers or exposes for sale or hire, or
    (iii) exhibits in public, or
    (iv) distributes, or
(e) distributes otherwise than in the course of a business to such an extent as to affect prejudicially the owner of the copyright;

an article which is, and which he knows or has reason to believe is, an infringing copy of a copyright work'

shall be guilty of an offence[1].

In addition, any person who makes, or has in his possession, an article specifically designed or adapted for making infringing copies of a particular copyright work, is guilty of an offence, if he knew or had reason to believe it was to be so used[2].

Furthermore, a person who infringes copyright in a work by communicating the work to the public in the course of business, or otherwise than in the course of a business to such an extent as to affect prejudicially the owner of the copyright, commits an offence if he knows or has reason to believe that, by doing so, he is infringing copyright in that work[3]. This provision, which was implemented by the Copyright and Related Rights Regulations 2003[4] ('2003 Regulations'), facilitates, for example, criminal proceedings against large-scale 'uploaders' of infringing material to peer-to-peer internet services.

Where copyright is infringed (otherwise than by reception of a communication to the public):

- by the public performance of a literary, dramatic or musical work; or
- by the playing or showing in public of a sound recording or film,

any person who caused the work to be so performed, played or shown is guilty of an offence if he knew or had reason to believe that copyright would be infringed.

A Law Commission consultation paper in 1999 provisionally recommended that the consent of the Director of Public Prosecutions should be required prior to any private prosecution for copyright infringement. Following responses opposing this suggestion, however, the Law Commission decided not to pursue this point, and private prosecutions may still be taken. In circumstances of genuine piracy, this remedy can be an effective weapon in the hands of copyright holders.

1   CDPA s 107(1).
2   CDPA s 107(2).
3   CDPA s 107(2A).
4   SI 2003/2498.

Penalties in criminal proceedings

7.20   The penalty on summary conviction for the offences set out in (a), (b), (d)(iv) and (e) of **paragraph 7.19**, or of communicating the work to the public (again as detailed in **paragraph 7.19**) is a fine not exceeding level 5 on the 'standard scale', or imprisonment for a term of six months (or three months in relation to an infringing communication to the public), or both[1]. If convicted on indictment the penalty is an unrestricted fine and/or imprisonment for up to ten years (or two years in relation to an infringing communication to the public). The other offences set out in **paragraph 7.19** must be dealt with summarily and the penalty on conviction is imprisonment for a term not exceeding six months or a fine not exceeding 'level 5 on the standard scale', or both.

The court may order that any article in the possession of a person who is charged with an offence under s 107, whether he is convicted of it or not, but which appears to the court to be an infringing copy, or to be an article used or intended to be used for making infringing copies, is to be delivered up to the owner of the copyright in question or such other person as the court may direct[2]. In *R v Carter*[3], the Court of Appeal, Criminal Division expressed the view that piratcal infringement was equivalent to the offence of theft and the conviction should generally attract at least a short prison sentence.

1   CDPA s 107(4) and s 107(4A).
2   CDPA s 108.
3   [1993] FSR 303.

Notice to HM Revenue & Customs

7.21   The copyright owner of a published literary, dramatic or musical work can give notice to HM Revenue & Customs ('HMRC'):

*   that he is the owner of the copyright in the work; and
*   that during a period specified in the notice he requests HMRC to treat as prohibited goods printed copies of the work which are infringing copies[1].

The owner of the copyright in a sound recording or film may give notice in writing to HMRC that he is the copyright owner of the work and that infringing copies of the work are expected to arrive in the UK at a time and place specified in the notice. He may request by the notice that HMRC treats the copies as prohibited copies. During the period that a notice is in force (and there is no limit) the only copies that may be imported are those for private and domestic use.

1   CDPA s 111.

Company directors and officers liable for infringement

7.22   Where an offence is committed under s 107 of the CDPA by a company, and it is proved that the offence was committed with the consent or connivance of a director, manager, secretary or other similar officer of the body, or a person purporting to act in any such capacity, that person as well as the company, is guilty of the offence and liable to be proceeded against and punished accordingly[1].

1   CDPA s 110(1).

'Knowing or having reason to believe'

7.23   In cases of secondary infringement and criminal prosecutions, it is necessary to show that the defendant knew or had reason to believe that there was an infringement or offence committed. What constitutes 'reason to believe' will depend on the circumstances in each case and the owner can assist his case by positive action. When a copyright owner becomes aware that pirated copies of his work are on the market he would be well advised to give notice to traders of that fact with such details as are available to enable traders to identify the pirated versions. Proof of receipt of such a notice or information should constitute 'reason to believe' that the trader was dealing with a pirated copy and therefore guilty of secondary infringement and liable for a criminal offence. Consequently such a notice can be a powerful disincentive to further trading in the article in question.

The Enforcement of Intellectual Property Rights Directive

7.24   The European Commission, the European Parliament and Council agreed, on 26 April 2004, the terms of the Enforcement of Intellectual Property Rights Directive[1] which was introduced into UK law by the Intellectual Property (Enforcement etc) Regulations 2006[2].

In response to rising levels of piracy and counterfeiting, the Directive aims to harmonise national laws in relation to the enforcement of intellectual property rights and build upon Member States' international obligations.

The Directive is based on 'existing best practice' in Member States (ie it adopts the best practices already used by Member States and seeks to harmonise them). It covers infringements of all intellectual property rights, both copyright and industrial property, such as trade marks, designs or patents[3].

Article 4 stipulates that rights holders, other persons authorised to sue on those rights, for example licensees, collective rights-management bodies and trade associations, can seek redress under the Directive if their rights have been infringed.

The Directive is limited to civil sanctions for commercial or large-scale infringement, rather than one-off infringements by individuals. It contains no criminal sanctions, although Member States are free to implement them if they wish. The measures, procedures and remedies it will extend throughout the EU include, among others, injunctions to halt the sale of counterfeit or pirate goods, provisional measures such as precautionary seizure of suspected offenders' bank accounts, evidence-gathering powers for judicial authorities and powers to force offenders to pay damages for lost income to rights holders. In certain circumstances, if the infringer has acted unintentionally and without negligence, then compensation may be awarded to the rights holder if other measures will cause the infringer disproportionate harm. A right of information allows judges to order certain persons to reveal the names and addresses of those involved in distributing the illegal goods or services, along with details of the quantities and prices involved. Member States are encouraged to introduce preventative measures such as the publication of judicial decisions and the development of professional codes of conduct.

As many of the sanctions already exist in the UK, the Directive is unlikely to have a great impact on UK copyright law.

More generally, the Directive forms part of a broad-based approach by the European Commission to tackle counterfeiting and piracy. The Directive complements Council Regulation 1383/2003 under which customs officials have been given increased powers to stop the flow of and seize counterfeit and pirated goods[4].

The Court of Appeal in *Hollister Inc v Medik Ostoney Supplies Ltd*[5] summarised the principles to be applied and in particular 'proportionality'.

Article 15 of the Directive is the authority for 'Publicity Orders' whereby the successful claimant would be entitled at the expense of the infringer publication of a notice of the infringement. This was considered in *Samsung v Apple Inc*[6].

1   2004/48/EC.
2   SI 2006/1028.
3   Article 1.

4   Council Regulation 1383/2003 replaced Regulation 3295/94 on the export and re-export of goods infringing intellectual property rights with effect from 1 July 2004, and the UK has dealt with the changes in the Goods Infringing Intellectual Property Rights (Customs) Regulations 2004 (SI 2004/1473).
5   [2012] EWCA Civ 1419.
6   [2012] EWCA Civ 1339.

Chapter 8

Exceptions and defences to copyright actions

Acts permitted in relation to a copyright work

8.01 Public policy demands that several categories of use are specifically permitted by CDPA in relation to copyright works. A user who undertakes one of these 'permitted uses' will not infringe copyright in the work, notwithstanding that his activity would otherwise appear to be a restricted act. At the heart of these permitted uses is the concept of 'fair dealing'. The most important permitted uses are:

* making of temporary copies;
* fair dealing for purposes of research or private study;
* fair dealing for purposes of criticism, review and news reporting;
* incidental inclusion of works;
* making a single copy available for personal use (by the visually impaired);
* certain educational uses;
* certain uses by libraries and archives;
* certain uses for the purposes of public administration (such as use for Parliamentary and judicial proceedings);
* reproduction of own or personal copies (the private use exception).

In addition, there are a number of specific exceptions relating to computer programs, database designs and typefaces, as well as a number of miscellaneous exceptions which are considered below and elaborated on in the relevant chapters in **Part 2** of this *User's Guide*.

Apart from the activities referred to above, case law suggests that the courts will not recognise any other general 'public interest' defence to copyright infringement[1]. This reflects the fact that what is being protected is a statutory property right in a work, as opposed to, say, the confidentiality in information passed in the course of a confidential relationship.

The 'fair dealing' exceptions to copyright infringement were substantially amended by the Copyright and Related Rights Regulations 2003[2] ('2003 Regulations'), which implemented the 2001 Copyright Directive[3].

The 2001 Directive radically overhauled the exceptions to copyright infringement which EU Member States could include in local law. However, of the 20 exceptions which the EU permit to be included, only one is *mandatory* on Member States: the exemption for transient copies (referred to below). Of the remaining non-mandatory exceptions, the UK Patent Office has elected not to expand the pre-existing exceptions available in the UK under CDPA (although several of those exceptions have altered in scope[4]). The fact that a widely differing scope of exceptions is now available across different Member States has had the effect of perpetuating a lack of harmonisation on important issues (most obviously in relation to private copying[5]) across Europe[6].

The 2001 Directive implemented the so-called 'three-step test' to determine the circumstances in which exceptions to copyright infringement are permissible[7]. Specifically, under the 2001 Directive, exceptions and limitations may only be applied:

- in special cases;
- which do not conflict with the normal exploitation of the work or other subject-matter; and
- which do not unreasonably prejudice the legitimate interests of the rightsholder[8].

In the UK, the Patent Office was lobbied by rights holders to directly incorporate this test in UK law, as a means of limiting the scope of the exceptions available in the UK. However, the Government elected not to do so, on the basis that the 'three-step test' was relevant in framing the exceptions, rather than in the application of the exceptions once incorporated into UK law.

Broadly, the changes made to the UK law on fair dealing implemented by the 2003 Regulations are as follows:

- *Fair dealing for the purposes of research and private study:* the 'research' element must now be non-commercial and subject to acknowledgement. The 'private study' element must also include study for a non-commercial purpose[9].
- *Fair dealing for the purpose of criticism, review and news reporting* must now be in relation to work 'lawfully made available to the public'. The provisions on source acknowledgement have also been altered[10].
- *The other fair dealing exceptions* (for things done for the purposes of instruction and examinations, recording of broadcasts by educational establishments, reprographic copying by educational establishments,

copying by librarians or archivists, recordings of folk songs) have been modified to operate only for 'non-commercial purposes'[11].

- A *new exception* has been introduced to permit observing, studying and testing functions of computer programs[12].

On 1 October 2014 the Copyright and Rights in Performance (Personal Copies for Private Use) Regulations 2014[13] came into force to introduce an exception permitting individuals to make copies of a work if it was the individual's own copy of the work and for non-commercial or private use.

1   See **paragraph 2.16**.
2   SI 2003/2498.
3   Directive 2001/29/EC on the harmonisation of certain aspects of copyright and related rights in the information society.
4   See below.
5   2001 Directive, Art 5(2)(b). The private copying exemption, which provides for a system of 'fair compensation' for rights holders, forms the basis for the levy systems in operation in certain other European jurisdictions.
6   For a further examination of the 'non-mandatory' exemptions, see Carstan Schaal, 'The Copyright Exceptions of Art 5(2)(a) and (b) of the EU Directive 2001/29' [2003] 5 Ent LR. Harmonisation of these exceptions is on the agenda for the Commission's review of the 2001 Directive, scheduled for completion in 2007.
7   The 'three-step test' is found in international treaties (eg Art 13 of the TRIPS Agreement and Art 10, WIPO Copyright Treaty). For a further discussion of the 'three-step test' see Ute Decker, 'The Three Step Test', Copyright World, February 2001.
8   2001 Directive Art 5.5.
9   See **paragraph 8.03**.
10   See **paragraph 8.04**.
11   See **paragraphs 8.10** ff.
12   See **paragraphs 8.03, 8.13** and **28.19** ff.
13   SI 2014/2361.

Mandatory exception: making of temporary copies

8.02   Copyright in a literary work (other than a computer program or a database), or in a dramatic, musical or artistic work, or the typographical arrangement of a published edition, or in a sound recording or a film, is *not* infringed by making a temporary copy which is:

'transient or incidental, which is an integral and essential part of a technological process and the sole purpose of which is to enable–

(a)   a transmission of the work in a network between third parties by an intermediary; or

(b)   a lawful use of the work;

and which has no independent economic significance.'[1]

The purpose of this exception, is to enable the temporary acts of reproduction (browsing, caching, etc) which are integral to the operation of the digital networks such as the internet. The exception was considered mandatory by the Commission because it is necessary to enable transmission systems to function effectively[2].

It is worth noting that the exception does not apply to computer programs or databases, a position which the Patent Office has agreed to monitor.

1 CDPA s 28A.
2 For a detailed discussion of caching and the mandatory exception, albeit predating the 2003 Regulations, see P Bernt Hugenholtz, 'Caching and Copyright: the Right of Temporary Copying' [2000] EIPR, Issue 10.

Fair dealing

Research and private study

8.03 Fair dealing for 'research for a non-commercial purpose' is a defence available only in respect of the infringement of literary, dramatic, musical and artistic works. No fair dealing with these works will constitute an infringement of copyright in the work, provided that it is accompanied by a sufficient acknowledgement[1]. No acknowledgement is required if impossible 'for reasons of practicality or otherwise'[2]. The acknowledgement may take the form of identification of the work or its title and the author.

Similarly, fair dealing with a literary, dramatic, musical or artistic work for the purposes of *private study* does not infringe copyright in the work. Fair dealing for private study does not require an acknowledgement. For these purposes, 'private study' excludes any study which is directly or indirectly for a commercial purpose[3]. 'Study' has been held to have its ordinary meaning. Where fair dealing involves copying (and fair dealing can involve actions other than copying, such as, for example, broadcasting) and if the copying is done by somebody other than the researcher, or the student himself, then the exception does *not* apply:

- if a librarian, or a person acting on behalf of a librarian, does anything which is not permitted under any regulations made by the Secretary of State relating to copying by libraries and archives[4];
- in any other case, if the person doing the copying knows, or has reason to believe, that the copying will result in copies of substantially the same material being provided to more than one person, at substantially the same time and for substantially the same purpose. So, for example, a person researching a legal matter may not make copies of a textbook dealing with that issue to provide to a number of his colleagues who are also researching the same issue[5].

Nor is it fair dealing:

- to convert a computer program expressed in low-level language into a version expressed in high-level language; or

- incidentally, in the course of so converting the program, to copy it[6];
- to observe, study or test the functioning of a computer program in order to determine the ideas and principles which undertake any elements of the program[7].

However, if certain conditions[8] are complied with, it is not an infringement of copyright to do these acts[9].

Guidelines issued by the Patent Office indicate that all research done by businesses operating for profit are likely to be considered as being conducted for a commercial purpose. Even research undertaken by non-profit organisations will fall outside the exception if it is for a commercial purpose. This is a particular issue for universities, whose facilities have increasingly been used on a 'contracted-out' basis by commercial companies in support of their commercial activities. However, the impact extends beyond these activities, and would include, for example:

- work done for spin off companies owned by a university;
- work undertaken by an author contributing to a scholarly journal for which the author is paid or receives royalties;
- work undertaken to prepare for a paid conference speech.

In short, the impact of this change in law is, therefore, to require many people conducting commercial activities to obtain licences in order to continue activities they had previously undertaken without the necessity for a licence.

The Society of Authors publishes influential guidance as to what it would consider to be fair dealing for the purposes of criticism and review in relation to a literary work, which may provide a useful rule of thumb for publishers. In brief this amounts (in the case of poems) to no more than one quarter of the whole poem or 40 lines (whichever is shorter) and, (in the case of prose) to 400 words for a single extract, or 800 words over a series of extracts each of no more than 300 words[10].

1   CDPA s 29(1C).
2   CDPA s 29(1B).
3   CDPA s 29(1).
4   This question is dealt with in more detail in **Chapter 18**.
5   CDPA s 29(3).
6   CDPA s 29(4).
7   CDPA s 29(4A).
8   CDPA s 50B (decompilation) and s 50BA (observing, studying and testing).
9   This is discussed more fully in **Chapter 28**.
10 See **Appendix 1**.

Criticism, review and news reporting

8.04   Fair dealing is permitted with any work for the purpose of criticism or review of that or another work or of a performance of a work, provided that it is accompanied by a sufficient acknowledgement *and provided that the work has been made available to the public*[1].

The words in italics were added by the 2003 Regulations, and effectively limit the ambit of this exception. It will no longer be permissible, for example, for a biographer to include previously unpublished letters in his work without licence in reliance on this exception[2].

The amended CDPA includes a non-exhaustive list of circumstances which will be deemed included within the scope of the phrase 'made available to the public'. This includes the issue of copies to the public, making the work available by an electronic retrieval system, rental and lending, performance, exhibition, playing or showing the work in public, or the communication of the work to the public. In each case, however, when determining whether the work has been made available to the public, no account is to be given to an unauthorised act[3].

Further amendment was made by the Copyright and Rights in Performances (Annotation and Parody) Regulations 2014 with the object of not unduly restricting the use of quotations for reasonable purposes that cause minimal harm to copyright owners[4].

Case law has given the words 'criticism' and 'review' their dictionary definitions. Criticism may extend to matters other than literary criticism, such as ideas contained in the work, or events surrounding it[5]. So, in one case, Channel 4 successfully argued that the inclusion of a clip from the film *A Clockwork Orange* in a programme considering the merits of the decision to withhold the work from distribution in the UK, was fair dealing. The question in each case will be whether the use is genuinely one of criticism or review.

In the context of news reporting, the CDPA provides that:

'(2) Fair dealing with a work (other than a photograph) for the purpose of reporting current events does not infringe any copyright in the work provided that (subject to subsection (3)) it is accompanied by a sufficient acknowledgement.

(3) No acknowledgement is required in connection with the reporting of current events by means of a sound recording, film or broadcast where this would be impossible for reasons of practicality or otherwise.'[6]

So, in the case of *BBC v BSB Ltd*[7] it was held that the showing of excerpts from BBC broadcasts of World Cup football matches, to which the BBC had the exclusive broadcasting rights in the UK, constituted fair dealing for the purpose of reporting current events. The excerpts varied in length from 14 to 37 seconds and were used in successive news bulletins over a period of 24 hours following the match in question. They were accompanied by a verbal report of the incidents and an acknowledgement of the source of the film. Scott J accepted that for the purposes of the CDPA, fair dealing is largely 'a matter of impression'.

It is worth noting that a photograph can be reproduced for the purposes of criticism or review, but not for the purpose of reporting current events.

The intention of the legislation is to prevent, for example, newspapers or magazines reproducing photographs for reporting current events which have appeared in competitors' publications. On the other hand a painting can be reproduced for this purpose, if, for example, it had been stolen and the reproduction was for the purpose of illustrating the report of the theft.

Also, the reproduction of stills taken from a film and printed as if they are photographs in order to report a current event may be fair dealing, provided a sufficient acknowledgement is made[8].

The terms 'criticism' and 'review', or 'reporting current events' were recently described as of wide and indefinite scope so that 'any attempt to plot their precise boundaries was doomed to failure'[9]. Consequently, these broad concepts are often relied upon as a first line of defence against many claims of copyright infringement. A good example of this phenomenon was the recent case of *IPC Media Ltd v News Group Newspapers Ltd*[10]. The case concerned the an advert published by the Sun newspaper which included a reproduction of the cover of a TV listings magazine belonging to the claimant, alongside a picture of a publication owned by the defendant. The aim was comparative advertising, although the defendant argued that its use of the claimant's material was for the purpose of 'criticism and review' of the claimant's product. The court held that the use was not 'fair'. It was using the copyright material to advance its own commercial interests at the expense of the other. All that was required to criticise the claimant's product was to identify it, which did not require the reproduction of its cover.

1   CDPA s 30(1).
2   It may still be possible to do so in reliance on the 'news reporting' exemption in appropriate circumstances.
3   CDPA s 30(1).
4   SI 2014/2356.
5   For example, *Time Warner Entertainments Ltd v Channel 4 Television Corpn plc [1994] EMLR 1*.
6   CDPA s 30.
7   [1992] Ch 141.
8   *Hyde Park Residence Ltd v Yelland [2000] 3 WLR 215, CA.*
9   *Pro Sieben Media AG (formerly Pro Sieben Television AG) v Carlton UK Television Ltd and Twenty Twenty Television Ltd [1999] EMLR 109, CA.*
10 [2005] EWHC 317, ChD.

Substantial use in relation to fair dealing

8.05   It is not necessary to decide whether use of a work constitutes fair dealing, until it has been determined that a substantial part of a work has been used[1]. Once that is established, it is necessary to examine whether the use is in fact fair.

1   See **paragraph 7.06**.

Use must be fair: motive and substantial part

8.06 The expression 'fair dealing' is not defined in the CDPA, although it is clear that for a defence of fair dealing to succeed, the use must be fair in the circumstances. The courts have considered this to be an objective 'jury test'. A number of factors have been considered relevant to determine fairness, but three are particularly important:

- the number and extent of quotations and extracts used;
- the use made of them; and
- the proportion the extracts bear to the new work[1].

The test for fairness is objective. The question is not whether the alleged infringer honestly believes his activities fall within one of the 'fair dealing' provisions, but whether the court does. The fairness of his motivations and intentions are important, but the focus of the court's concern should be the likely affect on the claimant[2].

The amount and significance of the material taken is key. The court must consider whether, on balance, the nature and the extent of the copying was within the bounds of what was reasonable and appropriate. This will clearly vary widely depending on the circumstances, but as a rule of thumb, the more substantial the copying is, the less likely a defence of fair dealing is likely to succeed. In *PCR Ltd v Dow Jones Telerate Ltd*[3], for example, a news reporter's use of quotes from another's report in the course of reporting a current event was not fair dealing, because she used more material than was reasonable or appropriate to report the event in question.

Another difficult area is that of art criticism. A large market has developed in glossy 'coffee-table' books, reproducing works of art. Many of these books have been published on the assumption that the subject artworks can be reproduced without authorisation from the copyright owner, because the use is for the purpose of criticism and review. Frequently such books include a modest amount of art criticism to support the images in the book. In each case it will be necessary to consider whether, in context, the use is fair. In cases where artists, or their descendants, and the Design and Artists Copyright Society (DACS) have challenged this form of use, they have achieved some success[4].

In other jurisdictions the operation of internet search engines has raised issues as to what sort of use may be 'fair'. In *Leslie A Kelly v Arribasoft Corpn*[5], the court was asked to consider whether the inclusion of images in a visual search engine infringed copyright in the images. The search engine in question (unusual, in that it used visual images rather than text) produced a lot of 'thumbnail' versions of images relating to a search inquiry, produced by maintaining an indexed database of millions of images, obtained via the use of 'crawler' software (trawling the internet for relevant images). Some 35 of the claimant's images appeared on the defendant's database. The judge found a prima facie case of copyright infringement, but considered that the defendant's use of the images would be 'fair use'. It is unlikely the same decision would result in the UK however, since 'fair dealing' defences are more narrowly defined in the UK than the general US doctrine of 'fair use'; nevertheless, in light of the implementation of the Human Rights Act 1998, such an outcome is not impossible[6].

Under the CDPA, a criticism or review which uses part of an unpublished work is able to rely on the defence of fair dealing.

In the context of news reporting, one recent case identified three principles which should be considered central in establishing whether the dealing is 'fair':

* the motive of the infringer;
* the extent and purpose of the use;
* whether the extent of use was necessary in order to report the current event in question[7].

In the same case, the fact that certain stills which had been used by a newspaper had not previously been published or physically distributed, and had been misappropriated, was considered important in finding that use was not fair dealing: 'Misappropriation and use of other people's property is not likely to be regarded as fair dealing'[8].

1   Lord Denning, *Hubbard v Vosper [1972] 2 QB 84, CA.*
2   *Pro Sieben Media AG (formerly Pro Sieben Television AG) v Carlton UK Television Ltd and Twenty Twenty Television Ltd* [1999] EMLR 109, CA.
3   [1998] EMLR 407.
4   A case involving the descendants of Matisse (supported by DACS) against the publisher Phaidon resulted in a settlement on terms preventing Phaidon printing such books without a licence, and required a payment of retrospective licence fees.
5   US District Court, Central District of California, 18 March 2004.
6   See **paragraph 1.14**.
7   *Hyde Park Residence Ltd v Yelland [2000] 3 WLR 215, CA*, per Aldous LJ.
8   Ibid, per Mance LJ.

Sufficient acknowledgement

8.07   A 'sufficient acknowledgement' is required when there is a fair dealing for the purposes of criticism, review or reporting current events or the reading in public of extracts from literary or dramatic works. For these purposes 'sufficient acknowledgement' means an acknowledgement which identifies the work by title or other description, unless:

* in the case of a published work, it is published anonymously;
* in the case of an unpublished work, it is not possible for a person to ascertain the identity of the author by reasonable inquiry[1].

1   CDPA s 178.

Incidental inclusion

8.08   Copyright works are often included incidentally in other works. In fact, for example, filmed images often include a huge variety of diverse material. The incidental inclusion of any work in an artistic work, sound recording, film or broadcast does not infringe the copyright in the earlier work and nor will issuing the resulting work to the public, or playing, showing the work or its communication to the public[1].

This 'incidental inclusion' exception is very important to those users who make works potentially featuring a large number of visual images or sounds (such as photographers and film producers). However, where musical works are included, the position is qualified. A musical work, or words spoken or sung with music, or so much of a sound recording or broadcast as includes a musical work or such words, will not be treated as incidentally included in another work if it is deliberately included[2]. The producer of a television transmission from a concert hall, for example, could not claim to incidentally include the music performed at the concert in his programme. However, if music is played on loud speakers for the benefit of the audience at a sporting event, the inclusion of the music in the transmission of the event will be 'incidental inclusion' because it cannot be excluded. On the same basis, if music can be incidentally heard whilst a commentator sums up a match, there will be no infringement.

What 'incidental' means will depend on all the circumstances of the case. In *FA Premier League Ltd v Panini*[3] the defendant, without authorisation from the claimant, published a sticker album featuring images of footballers in their playing strip bearing the logos of the club and the FA Premier League. The claimant had exclusively authorised another person to include such logos in another sticker album. The defendant claimed its use of the club strip was 'incidental'. The court held that the following factors were relevant:

- 'incidental inclusion' does not only mean unintentional or non-deliberate inclusion;
- in considering whether the inclusion was an infringement, it is necessary to consider how the artwork which includes the relevant material was created;
- an inclusion can be incidental, notwithstanding that the material was an integral part of the final work.

The test of whether the use of the work was incidental should include a consideration of why the material was included. Was there a commercial reason?

On these tests, the court held for the claimant. In order for the stickers to be collectable, the players had to appear in their strip. The inclusion of the relevant material was therefore essential, not incidental[4].

1   CDPA s 31(1) and (2).
2   CDPA s 31(3).
3   [2003] EWCA Civ 995.
4   It was considered that in any event, the sticker albums were probably literary works, to which the defence under s 31 does not apply.

Disabled persons

8.09 A number of provisions were added to the CDPA by the Copyright and Rights in Performance Regulations 2014[1] providing exemptions from copyright infringements for the benefit of the disabled. The Regulations extended the provisions previously applicable to 'visually impaired persons' to 'disabled persons':

* If a disabled person (defined as a person with a 'physical or mental impairment') lawfully possesses a copy of a literary, dramatic, musical or artistic work, or a published edition which is not 'accessible' to him because of his impairment, it will not be an infringement of copyright for an accessible copy to be made inter alia for his personal use[2].

* Such 'accessible copies' must be accompanied by a statement that they are made pursuant to s 31A of the CDPA, a sufficient acknowledgement, and may not be charged at a price which exceeds the cost of making or supplying the copies[3].

* The CDPA also provides that if a person holds an 'accessible copy' and is not a disabled person or a person who lawfully possesses a legitimate copy and intends to transfer the accessible copy to a disabled person, then the accessible copy will be deemed an infringing copy[4]. Any transfer of an accessible copy to another person will infringe copyright unless the transferor has reasonable grounds to believe the transferee is a disabled person or a person who lawfully possesses a legitimate copy and intends to transfer the accessible copy to a disabled person[5]. If an accessible copy is subsequently 'dealt with' (ie sold, let for hire, offered or exposed for sale or hire, or communicated to the public) it will be treated as an infringing copy[6] for the purpose of that and subsequent dealings.

* If an 'authorised body' (ie an educational establishment or a body that is not conducted for profit[7]) lawfully possesses a copy of a commercially published literary, dramatic, musical or artistic work, or a commercially published edition, it will not be an infringement of copyright for the body to make, or supply, accessible copies for the personal use of disabled persons[8].

* Such 'accessible copies' must be accompanied by a statement that they are made available pursuant to s 31B of the CDPA, and a sufficient acknowledgement[9]. The authorised body must not make a charge for supplying the copy in excess of the cost of making and supplying the copy[10].

- An authorised body, if an educational establishment, must ensure that the copies are only used for educational purposes[11]. The copy must be copy protected (unless the owner agrees otherwise)[12]. The copy will be treated as an infringing copy if the authorised body ceases to be entitled to make or supply it[13]. If the copy is subsequently dealt with it will be treated as an infringing copy for that and subsequent dealings[14].

1   SI 2014/1384.
2   CDPA s 31A(2). NB this exception does not apply to musical works or databases if making the accessible copy would involve recording a performance of the music or infringing copyright in the database – s 31A(2). Nor does it apply if 'accessible copies' have already been made commercially available with the authority of the copyright owner – s 31A(3).
3   CDPA s 31A(3).
4   CDPA s 31A(4).
5   CDPA s 31A(5).
6   CDPA s 31A(6).
7   CDPA s 31B(6).
8   CDPA s 31B(1). NB This exception does not apply to broadcasts.
9   CDPA s 31B(7).
10 CDPA s 31B(10).
11 CDPA s 31B(6).
12 CDPA s 31B(8).
13 CDPA s 31B(9).
14 CDPA s 31B(11).

Education, libraries and archives

8.10   A number of exceptions set out in the CDPA specifically relate to educational activities[1] and these may be summarised as follows:

- things done for purposes of instruction or examination[2];
- anthologies for educational use[3];
- performing, playing or showing works in course of activities in educational establishment[4];
- recording by educational establishments of broadcasts[5];
- reprographic copying for educational establishments of passages from published works[6];
- lending by educational establishments[7].

As discussed above[8], it is now a feature of the CDPA that these uses must be non commercial in nature.

1   CDPA ss 32–36A; these exceptions are considered in detail in **Chapter 17**.
2   CDPA s 32 (as amended by the Copyright and Rights in Performances (Research, Education, Libraries and Archives) Regulations 2014, SI 2014/1372).
3   CDPA s 33.
4   CDPA s 34.
5   CDPA s 35.
6   CDPA s 36.
7   CDPA s 36A.
8   See **paragraph 8.01**.

Libraries and archives

8.11 The CDPA also provides a number of exceptions to copyright infringement applicable in the context of libraries and archives[1]:

- copying by librarians: articles in periodicals;
- restriction on production of multiple copies of the same material;
- lending of copies by libraries or archives[2];
- copying by librarians: supply of copies to other libraries[3];
- copying by librarians or archivists: replacement copies of works[4];
- copying by librarians or archivists: certain unpublished works[5];
- copies of work required to be made as a condition of export[6];
- legal deposit libraries[7];
- making work available through dedicated terminals[8].

These exceptions are considered in detail elsewhere[9].

1 See **paragraphs 18.03–18.07.**
2 CDPA s 40A(1), (1A).
3 CDPA s 41.
4 CDPA s 42.
5 CDPA s 43.
6 CDPA s 44.
7 CDPA s 44A.
8 CDPA s 40B.
9 See **Chapter 18.**

Public administration

8.12 The CDPA sets out a number of uses which may be applied to copyright works for the purposes of public administration without the licence of the copyright owner[1]. The provisions are detailed but can be summarised as follows:

- *Parliamentary and judicial procedure:* copyright is not infringed by anything done for the purposes of Parliamentary or judicial proceedings or for the proceedings of a Royal Commission or statutory enquiry[2].
- *Public inspection:* material open to public inspection pursuant to a statutory requirement or on a statutory register may, under certain circumstances, be copied[3].
- *Public issues:* material which is communicated to the Crown in the course of public business may be copied by the Crown[4].
- *Public records:* material comprised in public records within the meaning of the Public Records Act 1958, the Public Records (Scotland) Act 1937, the Public Records (Northern Ireland) Act 1923 or in Welsh public records (as defined in the Government of Wales Act 1998) may be copied[5].

- *Statutory authority:* when the doing of a particular act is specifically authorised by an Act of Parliament, then the doing of that act does not infringe copyright[6].

This is a short summary of complex provisions and a user who proposes to make or issue copies to the public in reliance on these public administrative exceptions is recommended to undertake a detailed review of the CDPA.

One point of general interest is that where material which is open to public inspection contains information about matters of general scientific, technical, commercial or economic interest, copyright is not infringed by the copying or the issuing to the public of copies of that material, although the authority of the person who is required to make the material open to public inspection must be obtained[7].

1   CDPA ss 45–49.
2   CDPA ss 45 and 46.
3   CDPA s 47.
4   CDPA s 48.
5   CDPA s 49.
6   CDPA s 50.
7   CDPA s 47(3).

Computer programs: lawful users

8.13   A person who may lawfully use a copy of a computer program will not infringe copyright by making back-up copies 'which it is necessary for him to have for the purposes of his lawful use'[1]. The CDPA, defines a 'lawful user' as a person who has a right to use the program 'whether under a licence to do any acts restricted by the copyright in the programme or otherwise'[2]. If the user is entitled by this provision to make a back-up copy, then any term or condition in an agreement which purports to prohibit or restrict him from doing so will be irrelevant, and void[3].

Similarly, a lawful user of a computer program will not infringe copyright by 'decompiling' the program, provided that a number of conditions are met[4], nor is it an infringement of copyright for a lawful user of a copy of a computer program to observe, study or test the functioning of the program in order to determine the ideas and principles which undertake any element of the program if he does so while performing any of the acts of trading, displaying, running, transmitting or storing a program which he is entitled to do[5].

Lastly, copyright is not infringed by a lawful user who copies or adapts a computer program, 'provided that the copying or adapting – (a) is necessary for his lawful use; and (b) is not prohibited under any term or condition of an agreement regulating the circumstances in which his use is lawful'.

1   CDPA s 50A.
2   CDPA s 50A(2).
3   CDPA ss 50A(3) and 296A; see **paragraph 28.17**.
4   These conditions are considered in detail at **paragraph 28.18**.
5   CDPA s 50BA; see **paragraph 28.19**.

Databases

8.14   The CDPA provides that:

'It is not infringement of copyright in a database for a person who has a right to use the database or any part of the database, (whether under a licence to do any of the acts restricted by the copyright in the database or otherwise) to do, in the exercise of that right, anything which is necessary for the purposes of access to and use of the contents of the database or of that part of the database.'[1]

The term in any contract which purports to prohibit or restrict the user of a database from undertaking this permitted act, will be irrelevant and void[2].

1   CDPA s 50D(1).
2   CDPA ss 50D(2) and 296B.

Designs

8.15   The CDPA contains a number of permitted acts in relation to design documents and models, designs derived from artistic works and things done in reliance on registration of designs, which are not considered in detail in this *User's Guide*[1].

1   CDPA ss 51–53 (s 52 repealed by the Enterprise and Regulatory Reform Act 2013, subject to savings as specified in SI 2016/593).

Typefaces

8.16   The CDPA makes a special exemption for the use of a typeface (which is protectable as an artistic work) in the ordinary course of printing. Since this is particularly relevant to printers and publishers, this exception is discussed in more detail elsewhere in this *User's Guide*[1].

1   See **paragraph 15.14**.

Works in electronic form

8.17   The purchaser of a copy of a work in 'electronic form' may copy or adapt the work, or make copies of the adaptation, in connection with his use of the work, provided that it has been purchased on terms which (expressly or impliedly) allow him so to do, or else he is permitted to by virtue of any rule of law[1].

For the purposes of the CDPA, 'electronic' means actuated by electric, magnetic, electro-magnetic, electro-chemical or electro-mechanical energy and 'in electronic form' means in a form usable only by 'electronic means'[2].

If the seller has not imposed any express terms which prohibit the transfer of the purchaser's copy, or imposed obligations which continue after a transfer, or prohibit the assignment of any licence, or terminate any licence on a transfer, then anything the purchaser is allowed to do may also be done by a subsequent transferee without infringement of copyright. However, any copies or adaptations made by the purchaser which are not transferred must be destroyed, because they will be treated as infringing copies for all purposes after the transfer. If there are express terms (which themselves lay down the terms on which the transferee may do things which the purchaser was permitted to do) then the transferee is bound by those latter terms. Normally, a transferee is not bound by the terms of sale between the transferor and his vendor. This is a special provision introduced by the CDPA, and applies only in these particular circumstances[3].

The same rules apply when the originally purchased copy is no longer usable and what is transferred is a further copy used in its place[4]. The provisions also apply on subsequent transfers.

Section 56 was introduced into the CDPA primarily to deal with computer programs, but the definition of 'electronic form' is wide enough that it will cover any types of work (such as musical works, films or sound recordings) which are carried on CD-ROMs, DVDs, magnetic tapes or compact discs or any other electronic carriers.

Usually, there are very clear express terms, both on the covers and on the actual carrier in the case of films on video tape or DVD and sound recordings on compact discs, to the effect that they may not be copied. However, in the case of computer programs, the express terms of sale normally clearly state what may be done with them and these should be referred to if the purchaser wishes to rely on the exceptions contained in s 56 dealing with works in electronic form.

The CDPA contains additional provisions relating to the making of back-up copies, decompilation and observing, studying and testing the functioning of computer programs[5].

1   CDPA s 56.
2   CDPA s 178.
3   CDPA s 56(2).
4   CDPA s 56(3).
5   See **paragraph 8.13** and **Chapter 28**.

Miscellaneous permitted acts

General

8.18 A number of 'miscellaneous' acts are specifically permitted by the CDPA in respect of copyright works[1]. Some of these are of particular relevance to specific industry sectors and will be discussed further in **Part 2** of this *User's Guide*, however, because they are of broad application, it is worth noting these exceptions here.

1 CDPA ss 57–75 with the exception of ss 67, 73, 73A and 74 which have been repealed.

Anonymous or pseudonymous literary, dramatic, musical and artistic works

8.19 When it is not possible by reasonable enquiry to ascertain the identity of an author and it is reasonable to assume that copyright has expired or that the author died 70 or more years ago, then there is no infringement by any act done in relation to that work. This does not apply to Crown copyright works and works vested in international organisations[1].

If the work in question is a joint work, then the exception only applies if it is not possible to ascertain the identity of any of the authors[2].

This exception is particularly relevant in the context of the quotations[3].

1 See **paragraphs 5.18** and **5.20**.
2 CDPA s 57.
3 See **paragraph 16.06**.

Use of notes or recordings of spoken words

8.20 The definition of a literary work in the CDPA includes a work which is spoken or sung[1]. If, for example, a journalist tapes an interview, the words spoken by the interviewee have copyright as they are recorded and the copyright belongs to the interviewee[2].

However:

'where a record of spoken words is made, whether in writing or otherwise for the purpose –

(a) of reporting current events, or
(b) of communicating to the public the whole or part of the work,

it is not an infringement of any copyright in the words as a literary work to use the record or material taken from it (or to copy the record, or any such material, and use the copy) for that purpose…'[3].

This exception is subject to the following proviso, namely that:

'(a) the record is a direct record of the spoken words and is not taken from a previous record or from a broadcast;
(b) the making of the record was not prohibited by the speaker and, where copyright already subsisted in the work, did not infringe copyright;

(c) the use made of the record or material taken from it is not of a kind prohibited by or on behalf of the speaker or copyright owner before the record was made; and

(d) the use is by or with the authority of a person who is lawfully in possession of the record'[4].

In short, provided that the interviewee does not object to the making of the recording and it is used only for the purpose of recording current events or broadcasting, then the journalist will be able to use the record without infringing the copyright in the spoken words. But the copyright in the spoken words as recorded by the journalist will belong to the speaker.

1 See **paragraph 2.02**.
2 See **paragraph 2.05**.
3 CDPA s 58(1).
4 CDPA s 58(2).

Public reading or recitation

8.21 The reading or recitation in public by one person of a reasonable extract from a published literary or dramatic work does not constitute an infringement of the copyright in the work, provided that it is accompanied by a sufficient acknowledgement[1]. Similarly, copyright in a published literary or dramatic work is not infringed by the making of a sound recording of such a reasonable extract from it, or by its communication to the public, or a reading or recitation of such extract, provided that the recording or communication to the public consists mainly of material in relation to which it is not necessary to rely on this exception[2].

It is interesting to note that the CDPA provides that the communication to the public must not consist 'mainly of material in relation to which' it is necessary to rely on the exception. This can be read as meaning that the programme must not consist of the readings of a series of reasonable extracts from a number of different literary and dramatic works (not necessarily readings of extracts from a particular work). No definition of what amounts to a 'reasonable extract' is offered by the CDPA.

1 CDPA s 59(1). See also **paragraph 21.14** for a consideration of the use of extracts in dramatic performances.
2 CDPA s 59(2).

Abstracts of scientific or technical articles

8.22 If a scientific or technical article appears in a periodical accompanied by an 'abstract' indicating the content of the article, the copyright in the article or the abstract will not be infringed by copying the extract or issuing copies of it to the public. This exception does not apply to the extent that a licensing scheme is established under the CDPA[1] to grant licences to undertake this activity[2].

1   CDPA s 143.
2   CDPA s 60.

Recordings of folksongs

8.23   The words and music of a song may be recorded for the archive of a body designated by Order of the Secretary of State, provided that the song is unpublished and of unknown authorship at the time the recording is made, and provided that the recording does not infringe any other copyright (eg another sound recording) or the rights of performers[1]. Copies of such recordings may be made and supplied by archivists on conditions prescribed by the Secretary of State, including a requirement that the archivist is satisfied the recording is needed for research and private study, and no person is given more than one copy of any particular recording[2].

1   CDPA s 61(1) and (2).
2   CDPA s 61(3) and (4). A number of bodies have been designated for this purpose and these are considered in further detail at **paragraph 18.10**.

Representations of artworks on public display

8.24   The CDPA contains specific provisions relating to buildings, sculptures, models for buildings and works of artistic craftsmanship (ie an artistic work which is not a painting, sculpture, drawing, engraving, photograph or work of architecture) where permanently situated 'in a public place or in premises open to the public'[1]. The copyright in any such work is not infringed by:

'(a)   making a graphic work representing it,
(b)   making a photograph or film of it, or
(c)   making a broadcast of a visual image of it.'[2]

Copyright will not be infringed by issuing to the public, or the communication to the public of anything made pursuant to this exception[3].

So, a film or television broadcast (live or pre-recorded), for example, may make use of buildings and other such works which are in public parks, houses which are open to the public (whether or not an admission fee is charged), galleries, museums, etc without any express licence from the owner of the copyright in those works. If the works are situated on private premises, permission will be required from the owner of the premises in order to enter them for the purpose of making the television broadcast or film, but this is unrelated to any question of copyright.

Models of buildings (or parts of buildings) are frequently used as sets in the film and television industry. A licence from the copyright owner of a building still 'in copyright' must be obtained before making such a model, because the exception does not extend to making models, which would infringe the restricted act of copying.

The Design and Artists Copyright Society Ltd (DACS) was formed with the intention of protecting artists whose works are used in films and broadcasts (among other uses). Further information may be obtained from DACS[4].

1   The CDPA does not define what does or does not qualify as being 'in a public place'. For example, there is no clarification as to whether a work of art situated on private property, but clearly visible from public land, could be construed as 'being in a public place'.
2   CDPA s 62(2). See also **paragraph 26.11**.
3   CDPA s 62(3).
4   See **Appendix 1**.

Advertisements for sale of artistic works

8.25   Copyright in an artistic work is not infringed by making copies to advertise its sale. However, a copy made for this purpose will be an infringing copy if it is subsequently dealt with (ie sold, let for hire, offered or exposed for sale or hire, exhibited in public, distributed or communicated to the public) for any other purpose[1].

1   CDPA s 63.

Subsequent works by the same artist

8.26   There are clear public policy reasons why copyright should not be used to inhibit an artist's creative development. The author of an artistic work who no longer owns the copyright in his earlier work, will not be deemed to infringe his earlier work by copying it, unless he repeats or imitates the main design in his earlier work[1].

1   CDPA s 64.

Reconstruction of buildings

8.27   Anything done for the purpose of reconstructing a building will not infringe copyright in the building itself, or in any drawings or plans by which the building was constructed[1].

1   CDPA s 65. See **paragraph 26.12**.

Lending to the public

8.28   The rental or lending of a literary, dramatic, musical, artist work (other than a work of architecture or applied art) or a film or sound recording will infringe copyright in the work unless it is authorised[1]. However, the Secretary of State may order compulsory licensing subject to reasonable payment[2]. This power has not been exercised as at the time of writing.

1   CDPA s 18A. See **paragraph 6.06**.
2   CDPA s 66.

Miscellaneous permitted acts: films

8.29   Copyright in a film will not be infringed by any act which is done at a time when, or in pursuance of arrangements made at a time, when:

'(a)   it is not possible by reasonable inquiry to ascertain the identity of any of the persons [by reference to whose life the copyright period is ascertained],[1] and

(b)   it is reasonable to assume–

(i)   that the copyright has expired, or

(ii)   that the last to die of those persons died 70 years or more before the beginning of the calendar year in which the act is done or the arrangements are made.'[2]

This exception will not apply where the film is Crown copyright or is the copyright of an international organisation, pursuant to s 168 of the CDPA[3].

1   See **paragraph 5.09**.
2   CDPA s 66A(1).
3   See **paragraph 9.09**.

Sound recordings

8.30   The amended CDPA also provides that: 'It is not an infringement of the copyright in a sound recording to play it as part of the activities of, or for the benefit of, a club, society or other organisation if the following conditions are met'[1]:

'The conditions are:

(a)   that the organisation is not established or conducted for profit and its main objects are charitable or are otherwise concerned with the advancement of religion, education or social welfare,

(b)   that the sound recording is played by a person who is acting primarily and directly for the benefit of the organisation and who is not acting with a view to gain,

(c)   that the proceeds of any charge for admission to the place where the recording is to be heard are applied solely for the purposes of the organisation; and

(d)   that the proceeds from any goods or services sold by, or on behalf of, the organisation –

(i)   in the place where the sound recording is heard, and
(ii) on the occasion when the sound recording is played,

are applied solely for the purposes of the organisation'[2].

This modifies the position prior to the 2003 Regulations, which allowed the free playing of sound recordings in 'not for profit' clubs even if, say, the premises had been licensed to a third party. Now if such venues are hired out for a fee and commercial music is played, a licence will be required in the relevant sound recordings from Phonographic Performance Limited (PPL).

1   CDPA s 67(1).
2   CDPA s 67(2).

'Ephemeral recordings' for broadcasts[1]

8.31   The technical process of preparing a broadcast may involve various technical acts of copying. The CDPA provides for this[2] by making it clear that where a person is authorised (by licence or assignment) to include a literary, dramatic, or musical work (or an adaptation of one of those works), an artistic work, sound recording or film in a broadcast, he will be deemed to be authorised to undertake a number of acts for the purpose of his broadcast, namely:

*   for literary, dramatic, musical works and adaptations to make a sound recording or film[3];
*   for artistic works to make a photograph or film[4];
*   for sound recordings and films to make a copy[5].

These are the so-called 'ephemeral rights'. It should be noted that the ephemeral right does not extend to making further reproductions from the original recording. Moreover, the recording, photograph, copy or film made by the licensee must be destroyed within the 28-day period beginning on the day on which the recording is first used for broadcasting the work, and may not be used for any other purpose[6]. If the owner of the copyright agrees, the 28-day period can be extended.

The ephemeral right does not vest any rights beyond the right to make a recording, photograph, film or copy (as relevant), which must be destroyed within 28 days. If, therefore, a television station is given a licence to broadcast a play expressly limited to its area, then the ephemeral right exception would additionally entitle it to pre-record the play, but it would not be entitled to use the recording for any other purpose (for example, such as transmitting to another area or selling the tape to a station in another country).

Retaining the recording beyond the 28-day period infringes the copyright in the material which has been recorded, entitling the owner of the copyright to damages for breach of copyright and to destruction, or delivery up, of the offending recording[7].

1   See **Chapter 24**.
2   CDPA s 68.
3   CDPA s 68(2)(a).
4   CDPA s 68(2)(b).
5   CDPA s 68(2)(c).
6   CDPA s 68(3).
7   CDPA s 68(4).

Supervision of broadcasts and other services

8.32   The Broadcasting Acts 1990 and 1996 and the Communications Act 2003 contain provisions for the making of copies of transmission services by regulatory bodies (now OFCOM and the Governors of the BBC) for the purposes of maintaining supervision and control. The making of such copies does not require a licence from the authors.

Time shifting

8.33   A record of a broadcast may be made *in domestic premises* for private and domestic use, solely for the purpose of enabling it to be viewed or listened to at a more convenient time, without infringing the copyright in the broadcast, or works included in it[1].

The requirement that the copy must be for 'private and domestic use' was found in one recent case to prevent the operator of a commercial copying service from relying on this defence in making copies for customers of material taken from the internet:

> '... the interposition of the defendant in the copying exercise for commercial gain is fatal to this defence. The copying is done by the defendant and the defendant is not copying it for the purpose of private and domestic use. It is copying for the purpose of selling [a CD-R]'[2].

For the same reason, the words 'in domestic premises' were added to the provisions of the CDPA by the 2003 Regulations. It is now clear that 'time shifting' is not a defence which can be used to excuse activities which take place on commercial premises.

The availability of a 'time shifting' defence to persons downloading from the internet was thrown into sharp focus by the *EasyInternetcafe* decision[3]. In particular there was a concern that the defence could aggravate the impact of unauthorised peer-to-peer copying. However, the 2003 Regulations added a new sub-section, to prevent individuals who copy broadcasts in domestic premises, purportedly for 'private and domestic use', being able to rely on the section where such a copy is subsequently 'dealt' with. Under s 70(2) of the CDPA (as amended) such copies will be treated as infringing copies for the purposes of that dealing and if that dealing infringes copyright, copies shall be treated as infringing copies for all subsequent purposes. 'Dealt with' is defined to mean sold or let for hire, offered or exposed for sale or hire or communicated to the public.

The 2003 Regulations also limited the ambit of this exception to the copying of *broadcasts* only. This can be distinguished from the position prior to the 2003 Regulations, whereby the 'time shifting' exemption extended to both broadcast and cable programme services[4]. The *EasyInternetcafe* decision had found (based on the authority of the *Shetland Times* case[5]) that the unauthorised downloading of copyright material from the internet may be excused by the 'time shifting' exception set out in s 70 because the processes of the internet could be construed as a cable programme service. It is now clear that some, but by no means all, applications of the internet are caught by the definition of 'broadcast' (which is intended to capture only services 'transmitted for simultaneous reception by members of the public' or 'at a time determined solely by the person making the transmission'[6]). The functioning, for example, of an internet-based peer-to-peer service would not typically appear to amount to a broadcast for the purposes of the CDPA (as amended), since material is made available 'on demand'. It follows that since the implementation of the 2003 Regulations copying material from internet-based services without authorisation is no longer permitted by 'time shifting' except in those circumstances (such as the 'live' streaming of an event or a scheduled internet communication)[7] which may now be construed as broadcasts under the CDPA. Some writers have commented that the process of 'capping' television programmes (by recording them onto digital files for communication and download via peer-to-peer networks) could be construed as 'time shifting' for the purposes of the CDPA. The authors would respectfully disagree that that reflects the current position under English law. The fact that the material included in a download started life as an authorised broadcast may excuse the making of a copy by the 'uploader', but would not excuse the further distribution of that copy by the uploader via a peer-to-peer network, nor the download of a file made available 'on demand' over such a network[8].

It is worth noting that 'at a convenient time' does not mean 'at only one other convenient time' since, on the general rule of statutory construction, the singular will imply the plural and vice versa unless the context so requires.

1   CDPA s 70.
2   *Sony Music Entertainment (UK) Ltd v EasyInternetcafe Ltd (unreported, 28 January 2003)*, per Peter Smith J.
3   Ibid.
4   See **paragraph 2.10** for a discussion of cable programmes.
5   See **paragraph 6.08** for a brief discussion of the *Shetland Times* case.

6   See **paragraph 2.09**.
7   See **paragraph 2.09**.
8   The same may not be the case in relation to peer-to-peer streaming services.

Photographs of broadcasts

8.34 Taking photographs, for private and domestic use, of images from a broadcast is permitted and does not infringe the copyright in the broadcast or in any film included in it[1].

1   CDPA s 71.

Transmissions to public and non-paying audiences

8.35 Where a broadcast service is shown or played in public to an audience who does not pay for admission (such as, for example, on a 'big screen' like those commonly displayed in sports and other bars) the copyright in the broadcast, or in any sound recording (other than an 'excepted sound recording' – essentially commercial music) or film which is included in the broadcast will not be infringed, provided the performance is before a non-paying audience[1]. This provision is considered in detail elsewhere in this *User's Guide*[2].

1   CDPA s 72(1).
2   See **paragraphs 6.07** and **24.17**.

Recording of broadcasts for archival purposes

8.36 Broadcasts may be copied for archival purposes. Again, these copies may only be made by designated bodies nominated by Statutory Instrument[1]. The Copyright (Recording for Archives of Designated Class of Broadcasts and Cable Programmes) (Designated Bodies) Order 1993 nominates the following as such bodies:

- the British Film Institute;
- the British Library;
- the British Medical Association;
- the British Music Information Centre;
- the Imperial War Museum;
- the Music Performance Research Centre;
- the National Library of Wales;
- the Scottish Film Council.

1   CDPA s 75.

Adaptations

8.37 Where one of the permitted acts is performed in relation to an adaptation of a literary, dramatic or musical work, then the copyright in the work from which the adaptation was made is not infringed any more than the copyright in the adaptation itself[1].

1   CDPA s 76.

Revived copyright: action taken before copyright revived

8.38   No act done before 1 January 1996 will be regarded as infringing revived copyright in a work[1]. Moreover, if arrangements were made before 1 January 1995 but after copyright had expired in a work to undertake an activity which would have infringed copyright in a work had it been in copyright, then those actions will not be an infringement[2]. There is no explanation in the Duration of Copyright and Rights in Performance Regulations 1995[3] ('1995 Regulations') as to what is meant by 'arrangement' (eg there is no indication that the arrangement must be in writing).

Similarly, it is not an infringement of revived copyright in a work to:

- issue to the public after 1 January 1996 copies of the work made before 1 July 1995, if at the time when they were made copyright did not subsist in the work[4];
- do anything after 1 January 1996 in relation to a literary, dramatic, musical or artistic work or a film made after that date or made in pursuance of arrangements made before 1 January 1996 which contains a copy of that work or is an adaptation of that work if:
  (a)   the copy or adaptation was made before 1 July 1995 and at a time when copyright did not subsist in the work; or
  (b)   the copy or adaptation was made pursuant to arrangements made before 1 July 1995 at a time when copyright did not subsist in the work[5].
  It should be noted that these latter provisions deal only with copies and adaptations. A film of a book is not a copy or adaptation for this purpose, but results from the exercise of the restricted act of making a film;
- do, after 1 January 1996, anything which is a restricted act in relation to the work (such as making a film of a book) if the act is done at a time when, or done in pursuance of arrangements made at a time when, the name and address of a person entitled to authorise the act cannot by reasonable enquiry be ascertained[6].
- do any of the acts restricted by copyright in respect of a revived copyright work provided that payments of a reasonable royalty are made to the copyright owner or such other remuneration as may be agreed or determined in default of agreement by the Copyright Tribunal[7].

1   Duration of Copyright and Rights in Performance Regulations 1995, SI 1995/3297,
    reg 23(1). As to revived copyright, see **paragraph 9.19**.
2   Duration of Copyright and Rights in Performance Regulations 1995, SI 1995/3297,
    reg 23(2)(a).
3   SI 1995/3297.
4   1995 Regulations, reg 23(2)(b).
5   1995 Regulations, reg 23(3).
6   1995 Regulations, reg 23(4).
7   1995 Regulations, reg 24.

Chapter 9

Ownership, transmission and licensing of copyright

Distinction between copyright and objects

9.01 It is important to distinguish between ownership of copyright on the one hand, and on the other hand ownership of the object on which the copyright work has been reduced to material form. It is a common misapprehension that the owner of the object is also the owner of the copyright. For example, if an artist draws a picture in a fan's autograph book, the copyright in the drawing would not belong to the owner of the autograph book: although the latter would be entitled to retain physical possession of the object (ie the book), the copyright in the drawing would remain with the artist.

Basic rules of authorship and ownership

9.02 The basic rules as to authorship and ownership of a copyright work are that the author is the person who creates the work, and the first owner of copyright in the work is the author[1].

Even if the creation of a literary, dramatic, musical or artistic work has been specifically commissioned, the ownership of the legal title to the copyright will normally remain with the author unless there is a specific contractual provision vesting the copyright in the person commissioning the work[2].

However, there are special rules regarding the authorship of sound recordings, films, broadcasts and typographical arrangements and also in relation to works of joint authorship and co-authorship[3]. There are also exceptions to the basic ownership rules in the case of Crown copyright, Parliamentary copyright and the copyright of certain international organisations and works made by employees[4].

1   CDPA s 11(1).
2   In contrast with the position prior to the CDPA, as to which see **paragraph 9.15**.
3   See **paragraphs 9.04–9.08**.
4   See **paragraphs 9.09** and **9.11**.

Literary, dramatic, musical and artistic works and computer-generated works

9.03   The basic rules of authorship and ownership of copyright works apply to literary, dramatic, musical and artistic works. However, the person who *creates* the work may not be the same person who *records* it for the first time. In each case the question will be: who is responsible for the expression that is recorded? In the case of a literary or a dramatic work, it is commonly said that the person who creates the language will be the author, but that will not always be the case. In each situation it will be a question of determining on the facts who is responsible for the protectable elements. So:

> 'a mere copyist of written matter is not an "author" … a person to whom the words are dictated for the purpose of being written down is not an "author". He is the mere agent or clerk of the person dictating, and requires to possess no art beyond that of knowing how to write'[1].

To take a number of examples:

- *The secretary*: If a secretary records the words dictated by someone else, the person dictating the text will be the owner of copyright[2].
- *The reporter*: If a reporter takes down the words of another, but uses his or her own skill and labour to turn those words into an original article, s/he will be the author[3].
- *The story collaborator*: If a person collaborates on a literary or dramatic work, it is possible that s/he will acquire copyright in his or her contribution. If the work consists of detailed elements of plot construction and characterisation, for example, which are sufficiently distinct and original to amount to protectable works[4], then this will receive protection[5]. The circumstances in which a contribution will receive copyright protection in these circumstances are uncommon.

The CDPA makes special provision for literary, dramatic, musical and artistic works that are 'computer-generated works', the author of which will be the person by whom the arrangements necessary for the creation of the work are undertaken[6].

For these purposes a computer-generated work means a literary, dramatic, musical or artistic work which is 'generated by computer in circumstances such that there is no human author of the work'[7]. A typical computer-generated work would be a list of names and addresses, such as to be found in a classified directory, where a computer rather than a person sorts the names and addresses into a certain order and manner.

Such a list will itself have copyright. The person (probably a company) that employed the people who obtain the names and addresses and input the data will be the copyright owner.

Particular issues relating to the ownership of artistic works, especially photographs, are considered elsewhere in this *User's Guide*[8].

1   *Walter v Lane [1900] AC 539*, per Lord James.
2   *Donoghue v Allied Newspapers Ltd [1938] Ch 106*.
3   *Express Newspapers plc v News (UK) plc [1990] FSR 359.*
4   See **paragraph 2.03**.
5   See **paragraph 7.04**.
6   CDPA s 9(3).
7   CDPA s 178.
8   See **paragraph 25.14**.

Sound recordings

9.04   The author of a sound recording is the person who creates the sound recording (ie the producer). 'Producer' is defined in the CDPA as meaning 'the person by whom the arrangements necessary for the making of the sound recording ... are undertaken'[1].

1   CDPA s 178.

Films made after 30 June 1994

9.05   The authors of a film made after 30 June 1994 are the producer and the principal director[1]. A film is treated as a work of joint authorship unless the producer and principal director are the same person. 'Producer' is defined as for a sound recording[2] (ie the person by whom the arrangements necessary for the making of the film are undertaken). There is no definition of 'director' or 'principal director' in the CDPA. It should be noted that, since 30 June 1994, the rule that the employer is the first owner of the copyright in a work made by an employee in the course of his employment also applies to films[3].

Copyright works embodied in films	First owner in the absence of any agreement to the contrary
Film	In a film made since 30 June 1994 the producer and director are the first owner. In a film made before 1 July 1994 the first owner is the producer
Sound recording – the soundtrack when not accompanying the film	As above
Musical work – musical score, songs in the film	Composer/songwriter

Copyright works embodied in films	First owner in the absence of any agreement to the contrary
Literary work – ie script, song lyrics	Author of the work
Dramatic work – provided the film constitutes a work of action and is capable of being performed	Author of the work
Design right in the set design	Set designer
Rights in performances	Actors

1   CDPA s 9(2)(ab).
2   See **paragraph 9.04**.
3   See **paragraph 9.11**.

Broadcasts

9.06   The author of a broadcast is the person 'making the broadcast'[1]. If the broadcast consists of the relay of another broadcast by reception and immediate re-transmission, then the author of the original broadcast will also be the author of the relay broadcast[2].

Under the CDPA, the person making a broadcast, broadcasting a work or including a work in a broadcast is:

- the person transmitting the programme, if s/he has responsibility to any extent for its contents; and
- any person providing the programme who makes, with the person transmitting it, the arrangements necessary for its transmission,

and in this context references to a programme include references to any item included in a broadcast[3].

1   CDPA s 9(2)(b).
2   CDPA s 9(2)(b).
3   CDPA s 6(3); see **paragraph 24.03**.

Typographical arrangements of published editions

9.07   The publisher is the author of the typographical arrangement of a published edition[1].

1   CDPA s 9(2)(d).

Works of joint authorship and co-authorship

9.08   A work of joint authorship means a work produced by the collaboration of two or more authors in which the contribution of each is not distinct from that of the others[1]. So, if, for example the lyricist and composer of a song actually work together in writing the words, then the words will be a joint work, so long as the contribution of each was not distinct from that of the other. But if one of the writers composes the chorus and the other the verses (eg as in the case of a number of Lennon and McCartney compositions), there would not be a work of joint authorship because their respective contributions would be distinct: it would, instead, be a work of co-authorship[2].

In one case, the members of the band Spandau Ballet claimed a right to participate in publishing royalties from the band's songs which had been written by Gary Kemp. One of the arguments advanced by the other band members was that they were joint authors because of their contributions in rehearsal. Park J held that the other band members' contribution (which was to the performance and interpretation of the compositions) was not 'the right kind of skill and labour' required. Although there had been improvisation of some elements of the songs in rehearsal, the melody, choral structure and rhythm had been created by Mr Kemp[3].

A more recent, and even higher-profile, court case involving conflicting entitlements to musical copyright was *Fisher v Brooker et al*[4], which involved litigation instituted by Gary Fisher claiming entitlement to the musical copyright in his organ solo that featured in *A Whiter Shade of Pale*, the best-known work by the band Procol Harum. At the conclusion of protracted litigation that reached the House of Lords it was held that Mr Fisher was indeed the co-author of the musical copyright in that work, and was a joint owner – as to 40% – of the musical copyright in it.

The question of who will be a joint author is sometimes a difficult one. In the case of *Cala Homes (South) Ltd v Alfred McAlpine Homes East Ltd*[5] the employee of a building company gave a very detailed brief to a firm of technical draughtsmen as to the design of certain houses and even as to the choice of material. He did not, however, actually put pen to paper. Laddie J held that:

> 'to have regard merely to who pushed the pen is too narrow a view of authorship. What is protected by copyright in a drawing or a literary work is more than just the skill of making marks on paper or some other medium. It is both the words or lines and the skill and effort involved in creating, selecting or gathering together the detailed concepts, data or emotions which those words or lines have fixed in some tangible form which is protected. It is wrong to think that any person who carries out the mechanical act of fixation is an author. There may well be skill and expertise in drawing clearly and well but that does not mean that it is only that skill and expertise which is relevant. Where two or more people collaborate in the creation of a work and each contributes a significant part of the skill and labour protected by the copyright, then they are joint authors'.

Accordingly, Laddie J held that in spite of the fact that the builders' executive did not actually draw the designs, he was a joint author.

Nevertheless, it is essential that there is 'direct responsibility for what actually appears on the paper', and to that extent, at least one subsequent case has noted that the facts of *Cala* are exceptional. In *Ray v Classic FM*[6], the court set out three criteria for joint ownership: collaboration, significant creative input, and a constitution which is not distinct from that of other authors' work. The question is: *can the putative author be said to have contributed the right kind of skill and labour, and if so, was his contribution enough to amount to joint authorship?* In one case, for example, a member of a team had worked on the development of a software program. It was held that his case for joint authorship would hold prospects of success only if he had made a substantial contribution to the detailed idea or program structure. In circumstances where he had little input into the actual coding, his claim failed[7].

The difficulties of joint authorship were considered in detail in the case of *Brighton v Jones*[8], a case which concerned the play *Stones in His Pockets*, written by the defendant. The court held that the contribution made by the claimant, a theatrical director, was not of a nature to make her a joint author of the script, for it had always been the defendant who created the words.

Cases such as this and the more recent case of *Minder Music Ltd v Sharples*[9] illustrate how important it is to reduce to an express written agreement the contributors' respective entitlements to co-created works.

Some writers have suggested that the proliferation of interactive works presents a special problem for the law regarding joint authorship. In recent years, for example, the development of broadband internet-based gaming services has resulted in a new generation of online multi-player games, based on complex interactive environments formed by the game provider, but populated by thousands of characters whose attributes are, at least in part, determined by the game-player himself. Such games usually utilise a 'client/server' architecture. In short, one computer program operates on the player's personal computer, and another operates on a centralised server to which gamers obtain 'live' simultaneous access. The server-based software determines the parameters (or 'logic') of the game (the virtual environment), whilst the software based on the player's personal computer stores the player's game-based information and communicates that to the server. Players can, within the parameters pre-set by the server software, 'create' original items (names, characteristics, even assets such as originally designed buildings etc). However, on the principles set out above, it does not appear to the authors possible for game players to acquire, by virtue of their input, any position of joint authorship of the game which they join. Nevertheless, it is possible for the player to generate valuable assets (and indeed such assets have been traded on online auction sites such as eBay). For that reason, the terms and conditions which game players are required to accept before joining such digital environments are likely to include a full assignment of any intellectual property rights which might be generated by the player in participating in the game.

A film is to be treated as a work of joint authorship unless the producer and principal director are the same person[10].

1   CDPA s 10(1).
2   CDPA s 10A(1).
3   *Hadley v Kemp [1999] EMLR 589.*
4   [2009] UKHL 41.
5   [1995] FSR 818.
6   *Ray v Classic FM plc [1998] FSR 622.*
7   *Pierce v Promco SA [1999] ITCLR 233.*
8   [2004] EWHC 1157(Ch).
9   [2015] EWHC 1454.
10   CDPA s 10(1A). In *Slater v Wimmer [2012] EWPCC 7*, whose subject was film footage of a skydive over Mount Everest, the claimant (principal director) and the defendant (producer) were held to be joint authors.

First ownership of Crown and Parliamentary copyright

9.09   The above rules do not apply to Crown copyright or Parliamentary copyright, or to copyright of certain international organisations.

In the case of Crown copyright, the Crown is the first owner of the copyright in a work made by an officer or servant of the Crown, in the course of his or her duties[1].

In the case of Parliamentary copyright, where a work is made by or under the direction or control of the House of Commons or the House of Lords, the House by whom, or under whose direction or control, the work is made is the first owner of any copyright in the work, and, if the work is made by or under the direction or control of both Houses, then the two Houses are joint first owners of copyright[2]. There are some variants to this rule relating to the ownership of copyright in Parliamentary Bills which are beyond the scope of this *User's Guide.*

Modifications to s 165 of the CDPA were introduced by the Parliamentary Copyright (Scottish Parliament) Order 1999[3], so that its provisions apply (as modified) to works made by or under the direction or control of the Scottish Parliament.

Certain international organisations are the first owners of copyright in original literary, dramatic, musical or artistic work made by their respective officers or employees[4].

1   CDPA s 163.
2   CDPA s 165(1)(b).
3   SI 1999/676.
4   CDPA s 168.

Ownership of publication right

9.10   Publication right is discussed at **paragraphs 5.13** ff above. The owner of the publication right is the person who publishes for the first time a previously unpublished work in which the copyright has expired, with the consent of the owner of the physical medium in which the work is embodied or on which it is recorded[1]. Thus, if a book publisher publishes a collection of photographs taken in the nineteenth century with the consent of the owners of the actual photographs, the owner of the publication right would be the publisher, not the owners of the photographs.

1　1996 Regulations, reg 16(1).

Works created in the course of employment

9.11　The most common exception to the rule that the person who creates a work is its first owner arises in respect of works created in the course of employment.

When a literary, dramatic, musical, artistic work or film[1] is created by an employee in the course of his or her employment, under a contract of service, the employer is the first owner of the copyright in the work subject to any agreement to the contrary[2]. So for example, if an advertising executive writes the text of an advertisement in the course of his or her employment, the copyright in that text will (subject as aforesaid) vest in his or her employer[3].

Under the CDPA an employee who produces a copyright work in his or her personal time will own the work. However, some contracts of employment vest in the employer the copyright in all works written during the period of employment, whether or not they are written during the course of employment. For the employee who wishes to retain rights in works created in his or her personal time, it will be vital to ensure that his or her employment contract adequately deals with the question of the ownership of the copyright therein.

It should however be noted that special circumstances that import a relationship of agency or trust can produce different results. For example, if the work in question is created by an employee as an agent for its principal, the latter may own the relevant copyrights[4]; in a situation where a work is created by the founder of a company in anticipation of its incorporation, it can be deemed to be held on trust for the company by the founder[5]; and, depending on the circumstances, a subsidiary company may be held to have acted as agent for its parent in granting a copyright licence[6].

1　But not a sound recording.
2　CDPA s 11(2).
3　See **paragraph 27.03**.
4　*Cyprotex Discovery Ltd v University of Sheffield [2004] EWCA Civ 380.*
5　*Vitof Ltd v Altoft [2006] EWHC 1678.*
6　*VLM Holdings Ltd v Ravensworth Digital Services Ltd [2013] EWHC 228 (Ch).*

Assignment by terms of employment and engagement

9.12 The provisions regarding first ownership by employers referred to at **paragraph 9.11** apply only to literary, dramatic, musical and artistic works and films. So, an individual record producer who undertakes the arrangements necessary for a record to be made will be the first owner of the copyright in the sound recordings that s/he produces, whether or not s/he does so in the course of employment. Consequently, for any record company employing his or her services and wishing to own the product of those services, it is all the more vital that an agreement setting out a full assignment of the producer's rights in his or her work is entered into. The terms upon which a person is employed can vary the provisions of the CDPA.

In any event, where an author is hired on a 'contract for services', such as a freelance consultancy agreement, it is vital (and common practice) that where the prospective owner wishes to make further use of a copyright work produced by the author, it must indicate the ownership position of the work and take appropriate rights. For example, in *Ray v Classic FM plc*[1] a radio station wished to make use overseas of a database which it had engaged the defendant to prepare. The consultancy agreement was silent as to ownership of the database. Although the court held that some rights to use the work were implicit in the arrangement, it refused to infer that these rights extended to the additional use sought. The case provides a salutary reminder of the need for good professional advice in drawing up such agreements, even when they appear to be basic.

By contrast, in *Griggs Group v Ross Evans*[2], the court *was* prepared to imply a beneficial assignment of copyright to the commissioner of artwork. The court granted a declaration to a person commissioning artwork from the defendant, because it was necessary to imply a term requiring such a beneficial assignment in order to give business efficacy to the commissioning arrangement. An exclusive licence would be insufficient for the purpose:

> 'Where a freelance designer is commissioned to create a logo for a client... the designer will have an implicit task if he were to contend that he is free to assign the copyright to a competitor...in order to give business efficiency to the contract, it will rarely be enough to imply a term that the client shall enjoy a...licence...'.

Also, in *Fresh Trading Ltd v Deepend Fresh Recovery Ltd*[3], a case that involved a dispute over the ownership of copyright in the logo relating to the INNOCENT smoothie business, the court also held that there had been an equitable assignment of the copyright to the claimant that had commissioned the creation of the logo for its business. In another case[4] involving the commissioning of logo artwork the court ruled that the party commissioning the work was entitled to the legal interest in the copyright. Comparable rulings have been made in respect of software copyright[5].

Very different approaches, however, can be adopted by the courts depending on the facts: for example, in *Clearsprings Management Ltd v Business Linx Ltd*[6] (which involved a dispute as to the ownership of copyright in computer programs) and *Orvec International Ltd v Linfoots Ltd*[7] (which involved a dispute as to the ownership of the artistic copyright in a photograph), the court in each case was prepared to imply in favour of the commissioner no more than a non-exclusive licence. *Celebrity Pictures Ltd v B Hannah Ltd*[8] also involved a dispute over the copyright in commissioned photographs, in which the court ruled in favour of the photographer, not the commissioner.

1   See **paragraph 9.08**.
2   *R Griggs Group Ltd, R Griggs and Co Ltd and Airwair Ltd v Ross Evans, Raben Footwear Pty Ltd, Ronny Leopold Lewy and Gary Lewy [2003] EWHC 2914 (Ch), [2005] EWCA Civ 11, CA.*
3   [2015] EWHC 52.
4   *Atelier Eighty Two Ltd v Kilnworx Climbing Centre CIC [2015] EWHC 2291 (IPEC).*
5   See for example *Destra Software Ltd v Comada (UK) LLP [2013] EWHC 1575 (Pat).*
6   [2005] EWHC 1487.
7   [2014] EWHC 1970.
8   [2012] EWPCC 32.

Ownership in works created before 1 August 1989

9.13   The general rule is that the ownership of copyright at the time of its creation is determined by reference to the law in force at that time. This means that for works created during the life of the Copyright Act 1956[1], ownership is determined by the terms of that Act, and that for works created during the life of the Copyright Act 1911[2], the latter remains relevant. Earlier works are governed by still earlier Acts. Under the 1956 Act there were significant differences in the first ownership rules from those contained in the CDPA. The Copyright and Related Rights Regulations 1996[3] ('1996 Regulations') also changed the rules as to the ownership of films with effect from 1 July 1994. What follows is a discussion of particular issues arising in respect of older works[4].

1   Ie from 1 June 1957 to 31 July 1989.
2   Ie from I July 1912 to 31 May 1957.
3   SI 1996/2967.
4   **Paragraphs 9.14–9.17**.

Films made before 1 July 1994

9.14   The first owner of a film made after 1 June 1957 and before 1 July 1994 was the person by whom the arrangements necessary for the making of the film were undertaken.

Before 1 July 1957 films were not protected as a separate category of protected work as such, and ownership vested in the owners or their component parts (ie the writers of the screenplay, composers of the musical score, and the cinematographer). Specialist expert advice should be sought if it is important to ascertain the first owner of such a film, as the law involved is beyond the scope of this *User's Guide*.

Commissioned works: pre-CDPA

9.15 Before the CDPA, the copyright in photographs, portraits and engravings which were made under commission from a third party vested in the person who commissioned the work. It was necessary that the commission was made for valuable consideration (ie money or money's worth). This provision could be varied by agreement. For example, artists who painted portraits under commission might require the person commissioning the portrait to enter into an agreement providing that certain aspects of the copyright should remain vested in the painter.

It should be noted that this exception applied only to photographs, portraits and engravings. This produced some strange anomalies. If a painter was commissioned to paint a picture of a house by the person who owned it, the copyright in the painting remained in the artist, unless there was an express agreement to the contrary. The person commissioning the painting was entitled to own the painting and keep it in his or her house; but s/he would not have been entitled to license reproductions of it for magazines etc. That right remained with the artist. Similarly, if a theatrical impresario commissioned a musical play from a freelance composer and writer, the rights in the play would not have vested in the impresario, unless s/he took an express assignment. Alternatively, s/he could have employed the composer and writer as full-time employees under contracts of service, in which case copyright would have vested in the impresario as employer[1].

1   See **paragraph 9.11**.

Photographs: pre-CDPA

9.16 Before the CDPA there was a special exception regarding the ownership of copyright in photographs. The owner in this case was the person who owned the material on which the photograph was processed. In the case of an ordinary photograph this was the negative. If an instant camera was used, then the owner of the roll of film would be the owner of the copyright in the photograph. The owner of the copyright was not the person who took the photograph. It will be recalled, though, that the copyright in a photograph commissioned by a third party vested in the person who ordered the taking of the photograph[1]. This rule overrode the provision that the owner of the material upon which the photograph was taken was the owner of the copyright in it.

1   See **paragraph 9.15**.

Sound recordings: pre-CDPA

9.17   Prior to the CDPA, the rules as to the ownership of copyright in sound recordings were similar to those which applied to photographs. That is to say, the owner of the material upon which the recording was made was the owner of the copyright in the sound recording. There was an exception in the case of soundtracks of films (which the Copyright Act 1956 excluded from the definition of sound recordings), the copyright in which vested in the owner of the copyright in the film.

On the other hand, the rule regarding ownership of the copyright in the commissioned recordings differed from that applicable to photographs. If a sound recording was commissioned, the ownership remained with the person who owned the record at the time when the recording was made and not with the person who commissioned the record – unless the contract between them provided otherwise.

Ownership of extended copyright

9.18   The period of 'extended copyright' is the 20-year period following the date on which copyright would have expired under the CDPA, before the period of protection was extended from 50 years to 70 year pma[1] by the Duration of Copyright and Rights in Performances Regulations 1995 ('1995 Regulations')[2].

The owner of extended copyright is the person who was the owner of the copyright in the work immediately before 1 January 1996. However, if his or her ownership was for a period of less than the whole of the 50 years pma under the original 1988 provisions, then the extended copyright will be owned by the person who owned the balance of the original 50 years' pma period[3].

By way of illustration:

- A assigns the film copyright in her novel in 1960 to XYZ Films Ltd. A dies in 1965. Therefore, the original copyright period would have expired in 2015 but it is now extended to 2035. XYZ Films Ltd owns the extended copyright.
- B assigns the copyright in his original screenplay to XYZ Films Ltd in 1960 on condition that, if a second film is not made by the year 2000, the rights will revert to him. The other facts are as above. In this case, B's heirs have the benefit of the extended copyright because it is part of the reversionary interest expectant on the termination of the original period granted to XYZ Films Ltd.

1   *Post-mortem auctoris*, 'after the death of the author'.
2   SI 1995/3297.
3   1995 Regulations, reg 18.

Ownership of revived copyright

9.19   The person who was the owner of the copyright in a work immediately before it expired ('the former copyright owner') is from 1 January 1996 the owner of any revived copyright in the work[1]. And 'revived copyright' means any copyright which subsists by virtue of the 1995 Regulations after having expired under the 1988 provisions or any earlier copyright enactment[2]. However, if the former copyright owner had died before that date, or in the case of a company had ceased to exist, then the revived copyright vests (in the case of a film) in the principal director of the film or his personal representatives and (in any other case) in the author of the work or his personal representatives.

By way of illustration:

*   C assigns the copyright in a novel to X in 1935. C dies in 1940. Copyright expires in 1990 (50 years pma). X is therefore the former copyright owner and will own the revived copyright from 1 January 1996.

*   D assigns the copyright in a novel or any other copyright work, except a film, to Y in 1935. D dies in 1940. Copyright expires in 1990. Y dies in 1993 or, Y being a company, is struck off the register in 1993 (mere winding-up proceedings are not enough for the company to cease to exist). Y having been the former copyright owner, the revived copyright will vest in the heirs of D and not in the heirs of Y.

*   E directs a film and F photographs it in 1940[3]. XYZ Films Ltd as assignee and employer owned the rights in the services of E and F. It therefore owned the dramatic and photographic rights in the film and effectively was copyright owner of the film. E dies in 1943 and F dies in 1944, therefore, the term of dramatic copyright in the film expires in 1993 and the photographic copyright in 1994. XYZ Films Ltd is the owner of the revived copyright. If XYZ Ltd has been struck off the Companies House register in 1995, the heirs of E, (the director of the film) will become the owners of the revived copyright in the entire film.

1   1995 Regulations, reg 19.
2   1995 Regulations, reg 17.
3   See **paragraph 2.08** – as the film was made before the Copyright Act 1956 came into force, it would have been protected as a dramatic and artistic work, not as a film.

Registration

9.20   There is no copyright registry in the UK, but many years ago it was necessary to register copyright material at the Stationers Company[1]. The Stationers Company maintained a register of copyrights (being originally the right to print) from the sixteenth century. The Registry finally ceased to be of any importance when the Copyright Act 1911 came into force. It is sometimes thought that it is necessary to register one's work with a lawyer or bank in order to establish copyright. This misconception probably arises because it is useful to have some evidence of the date when the work came into existence, in case a very similar work comes into existence elsewhere at a later date. The ability to prove the date upon which a work came into existence can be of considerable value in an infringement action. The Stationers Hall Registry still exists, although since February 2000 works may no longer be registered there. The Registry continues to maintain its database in relation to works previously registered, which can be valuable in establishing the date upon which a registered work came into existence. This may equally be accomplished by sending a copy of the work to oneself (or to a bank, solicitor etc) by registered mail or recorded delivery and leaving it sealed.

1   See **paragraph 1.12**.

Assignments and exclusive copyright licences: what do 'sole' and 'exclusive' mean?

9.21   The transmission of copyright may be effected by assignment, by will, or by operation of law, as personal or movable property[1].

The owner can also grant contractual rights (ie licences) to undertake restricted acts in respect of his or her copyright work. If that licence is exclusive (in the sense that it authorises the licensee to do a particular act to the exclusion of all others, including the grantor himself or herself) then the CDPA provides that the exclusive licensee will have enhanced rights not available to other licensees[2].

The expressions 'sole' and 'exclusive' are often used together in intellectual property licences. However, whilst the word 'exclusive' has the clear statutory meaning referred to above, 'sole' is not defined in intellectual property legislation at all. Instead, it is generally accepted that a 'sole licence' is one that grants rights to the licensee to the exclusion of everyone except the licensor. This accords with the meaning of 'sole' in other areas, for example in agency contracts. This is contrary to the meaning of an 'exclusive licence' (above), in the sense that a 'sole licence' allows the licensor to exploit rights under a licence, whereas an 'exclusive licence' expressly prevents it from doing so. The definitions also overlap in the sense that they both prevent the rest of the world (outside the licensor and licensee relationship) from exploiting the rights.

'Sole' and 'exclusive' were historically used in legislation such as the Copyright Act 1842, but seem to have been superseded by a more precise definition of 'exclusive' in legislation and a more precise definition of 'sole' in practice.

In consequence, the words 'sole' and 'exclusive' should not be used together in copyright licences.

1   CDPA s 90(1). For a relatively recent Court of Appeal analysis of an assignment of musical copyright see *BSI Enterprises Ltd v Blue Mountain Music Ltd [2015] EWCA Civ 1151.*
2   See **paragraph 9.29**.

Assignments limited to part of copyright

9.22   A copyright owner may want to transfer particular rights in his or her work to different people (eg because they possess particular skills necessary to exploit those rights fully). A novelist, for example, may want to allow publisher A to reproduce his or her novel and sell those copies to the public, and film producer B to adapt it into a screenplay (ie a dramatic work) to be recorded on film. Alternatively, a promoter of a sports event may require the television broadcaster who records the event to assign to him or her the right to exploit the television feed (signal) or recording in all media other than television, recognising that other licensees may be better placed to exploit it in other media (eg the internet). Indeed the promoter may go one step further and allow the television broadcaster to exploit the TV rights in a certain part of the world only, say the United Kingdom, and require the rights in respect of exploitation in the rest of the world to be assigned to the promoter for onward licensing to overseas broadcasters.

The law recognises that copyright may be sold off in these separate packages, and the CDPA provides that the owner can effect partial assignments which apply:

- to one or more, but not all, of the things that the owner is exclusively entitled to do with regard to the work; or
- to part, but not the whole, of the period during which the copyright subsists[1].

So, for example, a novelist may assign to a publisher the right to distribute copies of his or her book for a period shorter than the life of copyright, after which the rights revert to the novelist. However, s/he could not assign to the publisher the right to distribute copies of the book in only part of the UK (since a geographical limitation is not contemplated by the CDPA as one by which copyright for the UK can be divided). So, a document purporting to assign copyright in Surrey, for example, will not be an effective assignment, although it could take effect as a licence.

1   CDPA s 90(2).

Assignments and exclusive licences must be in writing

9.23 Assignments and exclusive licences of copyright must be in writing and signed by or on behalf of the assignor[1]; a non-exclusive licence, however, need not be in writing.

1 CDPA ss 90(3) and 92(1).

Assignment of future copyright

9.24 It is possible to assign copyright which has not yet come into existence[1]. Indeed this is entirely usual when, for example, a film producer commissions a writer to create a screenplay.

1 CDPA s 91(1); see **paragraph 22.03**, and *B4U Network (Europe) Ltd v Performing Right Society Ltd [2013] EWCA Civ 1236*.

Assignments of extended or revived copyright made before 1 January 1996

9.25 Where an agreement made before 1 January 1996 purports to assign the extended or revived copyright to another person, that will be an effective assignment, provided that it is signed by or on behalf of the prospective owner of the copyright. The assignment does not have to be of the whole of the extended or revived copyright, but may be a partial assignment[1].

In any event it is common to find wording in agreements for the sale, for example, of film rights or musical compositions, which have very wide language capable of encompassing extended or revived copyright. In *Redwood Music Ltd v Francis Day and Hunter Ltd*[2] the judge had to consider a large number of assignments of songs in order to determine whether the wording was wide enough to include the reversionary copyright. If the wording of an assignment shows a clear intention to assign not only the copyright for the period under current legislation, but also any extensions etc, then a court may hold that reg 20 of the 1995 Regulations will be effective even though the words 'extended' or 'revived copyright' do not appear in the granting clause in the assignment. It is probable that the words 'extended' or 'revived' will have been used, however, because lawyers working for entertainment industry companies have long been aware of the way in which copyright legislation can be changed and will usually take steps to ensure that if there is any additional copyright period their clients will gain the benefit from it.

1 1995 Regulations, reg 20.
2 [1978] RPC 429.

Presumption of transfer of rental right to film producers by authors

9.26   Where an agreement concerning film production is concluded between an author of a literary, dramatic, musical or artistic work (excluding the author of a screenplay or any dialogue or music specially created for the film) and a film producer, the author is presumed to have transferred to the film producer his or her rental right[1].

This provision came into effect on 1 December 1996, and the presumption applies in relation to agreements concluded before 1 December 1996. However, the exclusion of the presumption in relation to the screenplay, dialogue or music specially created for the film does not apply to films made before 1 December 1996.

1   CDPA s 93A(1).

Right to equitable remuneration where rental right is transferred

9.27   The 1996 Regulations introduced a right for authors to receive 'equitable remuneration' from the exploitation of their rental rights under certain circumstances[1]. The amount of equitable remuneration is to be agreed, or failing agreement, is to be determined by the Copyright Tribunal.

The right applies only to authors who have transferred their rental right concerning a sound recording or a film to the producer of the sound recording of the film. In such an event, the author retains the right to equitable remuneration, which cannot be assigned by him or her except to a collecting society, or by testamentary disposition or 'by operation of law'[2]. This last phrase means that the right could pass (for example) to third parties as a result of a bankruptcy of the author, or to his trustees, if s/he ceases to be of sound mind.

The equitable remuneration is payable by the person for the time being entitled to the rental right (usually the distributors of the film or sound recording)[3].

1   CDPA s 93B.
2   CDPA s 93B(2).
3   CDPA s 93B(3).

Distinction between assignments and licences

9.28   One of the main differences between an assignment and a licence is that an assignee becomes the owner of the copyright (ie s/he becomes owner of the *property* in the copyright conferred by the CDPA), whereas a licence does not convey any property rights, only the *personal* contractual authority of the copyright owner to exercise certain rights to which the owner is otherwise exclusively entitled. Even so, a licence granted by a copyright owner will bind anyone to whom the owner may subsequently assign his or her copyright, except for a purchaser in good faith for valuable consideration without actual or constructive notice of the licence or someone who acquires rights from such a purchaser[1]. So:

- If an owner (O) assigns his or her copyright to an assignee (A) and later purports to assign the same copyright to a third party (B), the later purported assignment is ineffective to transfer any rights, since O has already divested himself or herself of the rights and has nothing to left to assign. B's only remedy will be against O (ie a contractual claim), whether or not B had notice of the earlier assignment to A.
- If O has granted an exclusive licence to a licensee (L) and later assigns his or her copyright (including the rights exclusively licensed to L) to B, the licence will not be binding on B unless B had actual or constructive notice of L's licence. If not, L's only remedy will be against O (ie a contractual claim).
- If a licensee assigns his or her rights to a third party, and his or her own head licence is terminated by O, the assignment of rights that s/he has entered into will fail, as will, for example, any sub-licence agreement entered into by the assignee. If the head licence is terminated by reason of a breach by the assignee or one of his or her sub-licensees it will make no difference that the terms of the assignment and/or sub-licence neglected to mention the restriction which brought about termination. The assignee and sub-licensee's rights fail since a licensee cannot itself grant more than s/he has been granted[2].

The other main difference between assignments and licences is that, as a general rule, only the property owner can enforce copyright against third parties. Since a licensee's rights are contractual, the basic rule of 'privity of contract' under English law is that s/he can only enforce them against the licensor. In essence, 'privity of contract' means that only the parties to an agreement can sue or be sued under its terms. So, if a contract between A and B purports to grant rights over A in favour of C, C cannot usually enforce the obligation against A unless it is possible to construe some direct agreement between A and C, such as a collateral agreement. Moreover, if B brings proceedings for breach of contract against A, he or she can only claim damages for his own loss, not the loss of any third party on that third party's behalf. This position is modified in two key respects:

(a) *Exclusive licensees*: under the CDPA an exclusive licensee has enhanced statutory rights[3].

(b) *Third party beneficiaries*: third parties may benefit from any contract in accordance with the terms of the Contracts (Rights of Third Parties) Act 1999 ('the 1999 Act'). In essence, the 1999 Act gives a third party the right to enforce the term of a contract which confers a benefit on it. For the third party to be able to enforce its rights, it must be expressly identified in the contract (by name or as a member of a class answering a particular description); however, the third party need not be in existence when the contract is made. For example if a contract refers to the conferral of rights on suppliers, such suppliers may not yet have been chosen and appointed by the parties.

The third party can only enforce a term of a contract subject to and in accordance with the other relevant terms of the contract. In other words, the term being enforced should not be construed in isolation from the rest of the contract. The third party will be entitled to all the remedies to which the other parties are entitled; therefore, conversely the third party will also be under a duty to mitigate any loss that it may suffer under any breach of contract.

Crucially, the parties to a contract cannot vary or remove the third party's rights under the contract once the latter have crystallised. Those rights are deemed to have crystallised when the third party has communicated its agreement to the term of the contract, or when the party against whom the term is enforceable by the third party (ie the promissor) becomes aware that the third party has relied on the term, or when the promissor can reasonably be expected to have foreseen that the third party would rely on the term and has in fact relied on the term. For that reason, since the 1999 Act, most licence agreements will normally contain a clause such as:

'The parties confirm that it is not their intention that the terms of this Agreement should create any right enforceable by third parties pursuant to the Contracts (Rights of Third Parties) Act 1999.'

1   CDPA s 90(4).
2   *Monty Python Pictures Ltd v Paragon Entertainment Corpn [1998] EMLR 640.*
3   As to which see **paragraph 9.29**.

Exclusive, non-exclusive and implied licences

9.29   Although no licence conveys property rights, under the CDPA an exclusive licensee does have certain rights akin to those of an owner. In short, an exclusive licensee 'has, except against the copyright owner, the same rights and remedies in respect of matters occurring after the grant of the licence as if the licence had been an assignment'[1].

So, if an owner of the copyright in a work within the UK (O) exclusively licenses to a licensee (L) the right to exploit it, and a third party (T) later, without authority, purports to exercise some of those rights during the life of L's licence, then O and/or L could take action against T to prevent its infringing activity and/or to recover compensation. A non-exclusive licensee on the other hand would usually have no standing against a third party[2], with the effect that if it wishes to enforce its rights against T, the co-operation of O will be required. Commonly, licences of copyright contractually require an agreed level of co-operation in such matters from the licensor.

Although formalities are required in respect of the creation of an exclusive licence[3], none are required to create a non-exclusive licence.

If the terms of a licence are not reduced to writing, or otherwise specifically agreed, a licence to use material may still be implied in the circumstances[4]. In a contractual setting, a licence, like any other term, will only be implied in order to give 'business efficacy' to the arrangement, not because it would be reasonable to do so. The question will be whether the party would, had it been reminded by an 'officious bystander' during their negotiations of the need for the licence, have agreed that it was necessary[5]. The extent of the licence recognised will be the minimum necessary to give effect to the initially-intended arrangement. In other words, the courts will not intervene to improve on the commercial deal, but they will impose a term necessary to give effect to it. So, where A and B agree terms by which B may supply work for a particular use to A under terms which allow B to retain copyright, a licence for the particular use will be implied, but, if so, that licence will not extended to other uses not contemplated by the parties at the time of the contract[6]. It may also be possible to imply the existence or terms of a licence from a course of conduct or negotiations[7] or industry custom, on the same principles which apply to other contractual terms.

1   CDPA s 101(1).
2   Subject to the points made at **paragraph 9.28**.
3   See **paragraph 9.23**.
4   See for example *JHP Ltd v BBC Worldwide Ltd [2008] EWHC 757 (Ch)*; *Wilkinson v London SHA [2012] EWPCC 48*; and *Noemalife SPA v Infinitt UK Ltd [2013] EWHC 2376 (TCC)*.
5   *Liverpool City Council v Irwin [1977] AC 239.*
6   *Ray v Classic FM plc [1988] FSR 622.*
7   *Helme v Maher [2015] EWHC 3151 (IPEC).*

Licences of uncontemplated technologies

9.30   When licensing copyright works, it is necessary to ensure that the drafting is sufficiently wide to cover the specific uses envisaged for the work. Any copyright licence should clearly state the rights to be granted. However, questions sometimes arise as to whether a particular technology or distribution mechanism, which was not specifically contemplated by the parties to a copyright licence at the time of signature, will be included in the licence. This has been the subject of numerous disputes (eg in the context of video, CD, and more recently the internet). In each case, the answer will depend upon the manifest intention of the parties as that may be understood by construing the contract. The key to establishing this intention is to determine the meaning that the agreement would convey:

'... to a reasonable person having all the background knowledge which would reasonably have been available to the parties in the situation they were in at time of the contract'[1].

Is the plain wording of the grant wide enough to catch the technology concerned? If it is, then the technology may be deemed included within the licence even though it was not specifically in the contemplation of the parties at the time of entering into the agreement, nor could have been (since it had not been invented). So, by way of example, a grant of 'the exclusive right of production' in 1880 was held to include producing a film of the work, even though film had not been invented[2].

If the contractual wording is ambiguous, then it will be necessary to consider all the terms of the agreement to establish whether these terms suggest that the parties did not intend to include the disputed right. If particular terms do not make sense in the context of the new medium, or if payment provisions are unworkable, then these are likely to be taken as indications that the parties did not intend to grant the rights.

One common device employed to overcome this kind of problem is to use 'technology-neutral' wording such as 'all methods of transmission known or hereafter devised' in licences. Some caution is urged in relation to the use of such words, since certain jurisdictions do not consider this kind of wording to bind the parties regarding technologies not in their contemplation at the time of contract. Clearly, in any event, for a licensor, this type of wording is to be avoided if possible.

1   *Investors Compensation Scheme Ltd v West Bromwich Building Society [1998] 1 WLR 896, HL*, per Lord Hoffmann.
2   *Serra v Famous Lasky Film Service Ltd (1921) WN 347*. There are a number of other examples, including *Barstow v Terry [1924] 2 Ch 316, Hospital for Sick Children v Walt Disney Productions Inc [1968] Ch 52; JC Williamson Ltd v Metro Goldwyn Mayer Theatres Ltd (1937) 56 CLR 567*, and *MGN Ltd v Grisbrook [2010] EWCA Civ 1399*.

Licences of extended or revived copyright

9.31   The copyright owner can grant a licence of extended or revived copyright before the date upon which it has arisen (ie before the expiry of the original copyright period). However such a licence is vulnerable to the purchase of the copyright by a purchaser in good faith without actual or constructive notice who is not aware of the licence and therefore is not bound by it[1]. Licences which were in existence immediately before 1 January 1996 and which were not due to expire before the end of the old copyright period, continue to have effect during the period of any extended copyright[2]. This is, however, subject to any agreement which might exist to the contrary.

These same provisions apply to waivers or assertions of moral rights and to 'any term or condition of an agreement relating to the exploitation of a copyright work'[3]. Therefore, if five years before the end of the copyright period, the heirs of an author granted a licence of the television rights in a novel to a television company, unless there was some wording indicating a different intention, that licence would be effective not only for the five-year term but for the full 20-year extended copyright period.

Any copyright licence which is imposed by the Copyright Tribunal is equally effective in similar circumstances.

1 See **paragraph 9.28**.
2 1995 Regulations, reg 20(2).
3 1995 Regulations, reg 21(2).

Other forms of transmission – insolvency and death

9.32 When the owner of copyright becomes bankrupt, his or her copyright passes by operation of law to the trustee in bankruptcy, without any assignment in writing by execution of law. Copyright can be bequeathed by will like any other property[1].

1 CDPA s 90(1).

Reversion of works assigned before 1 June 1957

9.33 If a copyright work was assigned or licensed before 1 June 1957[1] it may be affected by a provision originally contained in the Copyright Act 1911 which remains in force in respect of works assigned or licensed before the Copyright Act 1956 came into force. Under the provisions of the 1911 Act, assignments or licences made by the author of a work in his lifetime are only effective (whatever the terms of the assignment or licence) for the period of his or her life and 25 years after death. Grants made by his or her executors or heirs of his or her copyright are not affected by these provisions.

There is an exception in the case of 'collective works'. This expression applies to encyclopedias, newspapers, anthologies etc.

Although it is not settled law, it is probably the case that authors who had made assignments before 1 June 1957 could assign the reversion after that date. This is certainly the case under the CDPA in respect of assignments of the reversion made after 31 July 1989.

1 Ie when the Copyright Act 1956 came into force.

Dealings with copyright within the European Union

9.34 There is an inherent tension between the exclusive (and territorial) rights which vest in a copyright owner, and the tendency of EU law to seek the elimination of market barriers within the European Union. The result has been a considerable body of legislation and case law. It is vital for users who enter into agreements for the exploitation of copyright works within the EU to appreciate the impact of these developments, which are considered in detail in **Chapter 13**.

Moral rights

9.35 Moral rights are not assignable[1].

1 CDPA s 94. For further discussion of these rights see **paragraph 10.28**.

Performers' property rights

9.36 The transmission of performers' rights is dealt with elsewhere in this *User's Guide*[1].

1 See **paragraphs 11.11–11.14**.

Partners

9.37 Unless a partnership deed states anything to the contrary, the copyright in all work produced during the currency of a partnership is a partnership asset[1], and, like other assets, is owned and passes in accordance with the general provisions of the partnership deed concerning assets. To avoid dissemination of shares in copyright, it is usually desirable to provide that, upon the death or retirement of a partner, his or her share in the copyright should vest in the surviving partners. Alternatively, partners could, in their respective wills, leave their shares in the copyright to their surviving partners.

1 See for example *Coward v Phaestos Ltd [2013] EWHC 1292 (Ch)*.

Chapter 10

Moral rights

Introduction

10.01 European jurisdictions, in contrast to common law jurisdictions, have long distinguished between an author's *economic* rights (broadly equating to his right to control the exploitation of his work and thereby receive compensation by selling rights to others) and his *moral* rights (essentially rights to remain linked to his creation, such as to be recognised as author and to object to treatments of his work which would tend to undermine his integrity). Prior to the CDPA, these rights received no statutory protection in the UK[1].

The CDPA introduced moral rights into UK law for the first time, providing four categories of rights[2]:

- the right to be identified as author (or director) – the *paternity* right[3];
- the right to object to a derogatory treatment of work – the *integrity right*[4];
- the right not to have work falsely attributed – the *false attribution right*[5];
- the right of privacy to certain photographs and films – the *privacy right*[6].

1 Although certain common law rights, such as passing off, served similar functions.
2 CDPA, Ch IV, ss 77–89.
3 CDPA s 77 and **paragraphs 10.02–10.11**.
4 CDPA s 80 and **paragraphs 10.12–10.20**.
5 CDPA s 84 and **paragraphs 10.21–10.23**.
6 CDPA s 85 and **paragraphs 10.24–10.26**.

Paternity right

10.02 The paternity right essentially provides its owner with the right to be identified as the author (or in the case of films, the director) of his work to the viewer, listener or purchaser of a copy of his work, whenever the work is exploited. The details of the right differ depending on the category of work in question. The author (or director) is required to specifically assert this right in order to gain protection[1].

1 See **paragraph 10.08**.

Paternity right: who is protected?

10.03 The authors of literary, dramatic, musical or artistic works and the directors of films have the right to be identified as the author (or director) of their work. Producers of sound recordings and authors of broadcasts and typographical arrangements have no paternity rights. All the works must be entitled to copyright protection[1].

1 CDPA s 77(1).

Paternity right: literary and dramatic works

10.04 In the case of literary works or dramatic works[1], the author has the right to be identified when his work is:

- published commercially;
- performed in public;
- communicated to the public;
- included in copies of a film or sound recording which are issued to the public[2].

1 Excluding words intended to be sung with music.
2 CDPA s 77(2).

Paternity rights: musical works and lyrics

10.05 The author of musical works and lyrics has the right to be identified when:

- his work is published commercially[1];
- copies of a sound recording of his work are issued to the public; or
- a film of which the soundtrack including his work, is shown in public, or copies of such film are issued to the public[2].

1 See **paragraph 10.07** for a discussion of 'commercial publication'.
2 CDPA s 77(3).

Paternity right: artistic works

10.06 The author of an artistic work has the right to be identified as the author of the work whenever:

- his work is published commercially;
- his work is exhibited in public;
- a visual image of his work is communicated to the public;

- a film including a visual image of his work is shown in public or copies of such a film are issued to the public;
- (in the case of a work of architecture in the form of a building or model for a building, a sculpture or work of artistic craftsmanship) copies of a graphic work representing it, or a photograph of it, are issued to the public[1].

1   CDPA s 77(4).

Paternity rights: commercial publication

10.07 'Commercial publication' for these purposes means, so far as literary, dramatic, musical or artistic works are concerned:

'(a) issuing copies of the work to the public at a time when copies made in advance of the receipt of orders, are generally available to the public, or

(b) making the work available to the public by means of an electronic retrieval system.'[1]

This excludes works which are published only after subscriptions have been received for the work (which is often the case, for example, in respect of academic works).

The reference to electronic retrieval systems makes it clear that commercial publication will occur if copies are never distributed to the public but the work is instead made available on, say, an online database.

1   CDPA s 175(2).

Paternity right: the need for assertion

10.08 There is no infringement of the right of paternity unless the right has been asserted by a statement to that effect by the author or director in an assignment of the copyright in a work, or by an 'instrument in writing signed by the author or director'[1].

For artistic works, the right may be asserted in relation to the public exhibition of the work:

'by securing that, when the author or other first owner of copyright parts with possession of the original, or of a copy made by him or under his direction or control, the author is identified on the original or copy, or on a frame, mount or other thing to which it is attached'[2].

In relation to copies of a work, the right may be asserted by a statement signed by the person granting the licence to make copies to the effect that the author asserts his right to be identified if the copy is exhibited in public. This is useful to artists who make prints, for example, rather than paintings or drawings[3].

1   CDPA s 78(2).
2   CDPA s 78(3)(a); see **paragraph 25.21**.
3   CDPA s 78(3)(b).

Paternity right: the persons bound by an assertion

10.09 Where an assertion of paternity is made in an assignment, the assignee and anyone claiming through him is bound by it, whether or not he has notice of the assertion[1]. Anyone acquiring the copyright in literary, dramatic, musical or artistic works or films should make enquiries as to whether or not the right has been asserted. The purchaser may want to examine the original assignment of copyright from the author, or at least take appropriate warranties that no rights have been asserted.

Where the right is claimed by an instrument in writing, only those people to whose attention the assertion has been brought are bound[2].

In the case of works of art, where the assertion is made on parting with possession of the original, or a copy made under the control of the author or first owner of copyright, then anyone into whose hands that original or copy comes is bound, whether or not the identification is still present or visible[3].

Where the assertion is made by inclusion in a licence to make copies of an artistic work, then the licensee is bound. Moreover, anyone into whose hands a copy made pursuant to the licence comes, is bound, whether or not he has notice of the assertion[4].

The right of paternity should always be asserted promptly, because in an action for infringement the court must take into account any delay in asserting the right[5].

1   CDPA s 78(4)(a).
2   CDPA s 78(4)(b).
3   CDPA s 78(4)(c).
4   CDPA s 78(4)(d).
5   CDPA s 78(5).

Paternity right: exceptions

10.10 The right to be identified as the author of a work does not apply to:

- computer programs, the design of typefaces or any computer-generated work[1];
- anything done by or with the authority of the copyright owner, where the copyright in the work originally vested in the author's (or director's) employer (ie done in the course of employment)[2];
- a number of acts which, by virtue of other provisions of the CDPA, do not infringe copyright[3], including:
  - (a) fair dealing for the purpose of reporting current events by means of sound recordings, films or broadcasts[4];
  - (b) incidental inclusion of work in an artistic work, sound recording, film or broadcast[5];

- (c) use in connection with setting, communication or answering examination questions[6];
- (d) use in connection with parliamentary and judicial proceedings, Royal Commissions and statutory inquiries[7];
- (e) use of design documents or model recordings for anything other than artistic works and typefaces to make an article to the design[8];
- (f) use in connection with acts permitted when copyright may be assumed to be expired in anonymous or pseudonymous works and other specific permitted acts[9];

- works made for the purpose of reporting current events[10];
- publication of literary, dramatic, musical or artistic works in a newspaper, magazine or similar periodical, and encyclopaedia, dictionary, yearbook or other collective work of reference if the work is made for the purpose of the publication or is authorised for inclusion by the author[11];
- Crown copyright or Parliamentary copyright works, or works in which copyright originally vested in an international organisation, except where the author or director has been identified on published copies[12].

1   CDPA s 79(2).
2   CDPA s 79(3).
3   See **Chapter 8**.
4   CDPA s 79(4)(a); see **paragraphs 8.03** ff.
5   CDPA s 79(4)(b); see **paragraph 8.08**.
6   CDPA s 32(3); see **paragraph 8.10**.
7   CDPA s 79(4)(d) and (e); see **paragraph 8.12**.
8   CDPA s 79(4)(f); see **paragraph 8.15**.
9   CDPA s 79(4)(h); and **paragraph 8.19**.
10   CDPA s 79(5).
11   CDPA s 79(6).
12   CDPA s 79(7).

Duration of right of paternity

10.11   The right of paternity subsists so long as copyright subsists in the work[1].

1   CDPA s 86(1). Reference should be made to **Chapter 5** to ascertain the period of copyright attributable to the type of work concerned.

Right to object to derogatory treatment (the 'integrity right')

10.12   Authors or directors of relevant works[1] have the right in certain circumstances not to have their work or any part of it subjected to derogatory treatment[2].

For these purposes, 'treatment' means an addition to, deletion from or alteration to or adaptation of the work. However, translations of literary or dramatic works, or arrangements or transcriptions of musical works which involve no more than a change of key or register do not constitute 'treatment'[3].

A 'treatment' is derogatory if it amounts to distortion or mutilation of the work, or is otherwise prejudicial to the honour or reputation of the author or director[4].

In *Tidy v Trustees of the Natural History Museum*[5], in considering whether the reduction in size of the claimant's cartoons by the museum established a derogatory treatment, the court treated the question as being whether this was a distortion or was otherwise prejudicial to the author's honour or reputation.

1   As described in **paragraph 10.13**.
2   CDPA s 80(1)(a).
3   CDPA s 80(2)(a).
4   CDPA s 80(2)(b).
5   [1996] 39 IPR 501.

Integrity right: who is protected?

10.13 The integrity right protects authors of literary, dramatic, musical or artistic works and the directors of films. As with the paternity right, the producers of sound recordings, authors of broadcasts and typographical arrangements are not protected by this right[1].

1   See **paragraph 10.03**.

Integrity right: literary, dramatic and musical works

10.14 In the case of literary, dramatic and musical works, the author has the right to object to a derogatory treatment when that treatment is:

- published commercially[1];
- performed in public;
- communicated to the public;
- included in copies of a film or sound recording issued to the public[2].

1   See **paragraph 10.07**.
2   CDPA s 80(3).

Integrity right: artistic works

10.15 The integrity in an artistic work is infringed whenever:

- a derogatory treatment of the work is published commercially or exhibited in public[1];
- a visual image of a derogatory treatment of the work is communicated to the public;

- a visual image of a derogatory treatment of the work is included in a film which is shown in public, or when copies of the film are issued to the public;
- (in the case of works of architecture in the form of a model for a building, a sculpture or a work of artistic craftsmanship) copies of a graphic work representing or a photograph of the derogatory treatment of the work are issued to the public[2].

It should be noted that the right does not arise where a building is erected which would constitute a derogatory treatment of the work if it had been issued to the public in the form of a graphic work or a photograph. However, in these cases the architect, if he is identified on the building, may require the identification to be removed[3].

1   See **paragraph 25.21**.
2   CDPA s 80(4).
3   CDPA s 80(5).

Integrity right: films

10.16   The integrity right is infringed whenever a film which constitutes a derogatory treatment of the work is:

- shown in public;
- communicated to the public;
- issued to the public[1].

A film soundtrack is both part of a film and a sound recording[2]. Authors of sound recordings and of film soundtracks do not have the right to object to a derogatory treatment of work. It is worth noting that only the director of the film or the authors of the literary, dramatic, musical or artistic copyrights in the film soundtrack would have the right to object to the derogatory treatment of a soundtrack.

1   CDPA s 80(6); see **paragraph 22.05**.
2   See **paragraph 2.08**.

Integrity right: no need for assertion

10.17   Unlike the paternity right, authors of copyright, literary, dramatic, musical or artistic works and directors of copyright films are not required to assert the integrity right. It is binding on all third parties, unless it falls within one of the exceptions or exclusions discussed below[1].

1   See **paragraph 10.18**.

Integrity right: exceptions

10.18   The right to object to a derogatory treatment of a work does not apply:

- to computer programs or any computer-generated work[1];
- to works made for the purpose of reporting current events[2];
- to the publication of literary, dramatic, musical or artistic works in a newspaper, magazine or similar periodical, or an encyclopaedia, dictionary, yearbook or other collective work of reference (or a subsequent edition of such works) if the work is made for the purpose of the publication or is authorised for inclusion by the author[3];
- to a number of acts which, by virtue of other provisions of ss 57 or 66A of the CDPA, do not infringe copyright (namely use in connection with acts permitted when copyright may be assumed to be expired in anonymous or pseudonymous works and films)[4];
- to acts done to avoid committing an offence, complying with a statutory duty and (in the case of the BBC) avoiding the inclusion in a broadcast of anything offending good taste or decency, or likely to encourage or incite crime or to lead to disorder or offend public feeling, provided that a sufficient disclaimer is included where the author or director of the work has been identified (either at the time of the act or previously)[5];
- to works in which copyright originally vested in the author's (or director's) employer (ie done in the course of employment), to Crown copyright or Parliamentary copyright works, or works in which copyright originally vested in an international organisation, provided that a sufficient disclaimer is added where the author or director has been identified either at the time of the act or previously on published copies[6].

1 CDPA s 81(2).
2 CDPA s 81(3).
3 CDPA s 81(4).
4 CDPA s 81(5).
5 CDPA s 81(6).
6 CDPA s 82.

Integrity right: secondary infringement

10.19 The right to object to a derogatory treatment can also be subject to 'secondary infringement'. Secondary infringement of copyright is considered in detail elsewhere in this *User's Guide*[1]. Briefly, the possession, sale, hire, offering for sale or hire, exhibition or distribution of an 'infringing article' in the course of business will constitute secondary infringement. Distribution other than in the course of business will also constitute a secondary infringement where that distribution is such as to 'affect prejudicially the honour or reputation of the author or director'[2]. For these purposes an 'infringing article' means a work, or copy of a work, which has been subjected to a derogatory treatment and which has, or is likely to be, subjected to one of the incidents giving rise to infringement referred to above[3].

1   See **paragraphs 6.10** ff.
2   CDPA s 89(1).
3   See **paragraph 10.12**.

Duration of right of integrity

10.20 Like the paternity right, the integrity right continues so long as copyright subsists in the work[1].

1   CDPA s 86(1); see **paragraph 10.11**.

False attribution of work

10.21 Of the moral rights set out in the CDPA, the right to prevent false attribution of work was the only right to be found in earlier UK legislation. The right consists of the right not to have a literary, dramatic, musical or artistic work falsely attributed to a person as being the author, or to have a film falsely attributed as having been directed by a person other than the director.

For these purposes 'attribution' means a statement (either express or implied) as to who is the author or director[1].

The right to prevent false attribution also applies where a literary, dramatic or musical work is falsely represented as being an adaptation of the work of another person. In the case of an artistic work, it applies where the work is falsely represented as being a copy made by the author of the artistic work[2].

It should be noted that the right does not apply to the authors of sound recordings, broadcasts, or typographical arrangements of published editions.

Section 84 was considered by Mr Justice Lightman in the *Alan Clark Diaries* case[3] which was primarily a passing off action relating to a 'spoof' column intended to misrepresent that it was written by Alan Clark MP in the style of his published political diaries.

1   CDPA s 84(1).
2   CDPA s 84(2).
3   *Clark v Associated Newspapers Ltd* [1998] 1 All ER 959.

Infringement of the right to prevent false attribution

10.22 The right to prevent false attribution will be infringed by a person who:

- issues copies of a literary, dramatic, musical or artistic work or a film in which there is a false attribution[1];
- exhibits an artistic work (or copy of such a work) containing a false attribution[2];
- either performs in public, or communicates to the public any literary, dramatic or musical work, or shows in public, broadcasts, as being

the work of, or directed by, a person, knowing or having reason to believe the attribution is false[3];

- issues or displays to the public material (such as advertising materials) containing a false attribution regarding any of the acts mentioned in the three paragraphs listed above[4];

- (in the course of business) possesses or deals with copies of a literary, dramatic, musical or artistic work or a film in which there is a false attribution (and in the case of artistic works possessing or dealing with a work which itself contains a false attribution) knowing or having reason to believe it contains an attribution and that the attribution is false[5];

- (in the course of business) deals with an artistic work as the unaltered work of the author, if the work has in fact been altered after the author parted with possession of it, or else deals with a copy of the altered work as being the unaltered work of the author, where he knows or has reason to believe this is not the case[6].

1 CDPA s 84(2)(a).
2 CDPA s 84(2)(b).
3 CDPA s 84(3).
4 CDPA s 84(4).
5 CDPA s 84(5).
6 CDPA s 84(6).

Duration of the right of false attribution

10.23 The right continues to subsist for 20 years after a person's death[1].

1 CDPA s 86(2).

Right to privacy of photographs and films

10.24 Under the CDPA the owner of the copyright in the photograph is the photographer. He is, therefore, able to sell copies of the photograph or to license newspapers and magazines to reproduce it, even though the person who had commissioned the photograph might not wish it to be seen publicly. The effect of the right to privacy is to mitigate against the inherent right of the copyright owner to deal with the photograph.

The right applies only to persons who have commissioned the taking of a photograph or the making of a film for private and domestic purposes[1] and conveys a right so long as copyright subsists in the work, to prevent copies of the photograph or film being issued to the public, being exhibited or shown in public or communicated to the public. Any person who does, or authorises the doing of, any of these acts without the permission of the person who commissioned the photograph, infringes only the right of privacy[2].

It should be noted that it is the commissioner who has the right to sue for the infringement of the right to privacy and not another person who may be in the photograph or film[3].

1   CDPA s 85(1).
2   Ibid.
3   CDPA s 85(1).

Exceptions to right to privacy

10.25 The right is not infringed in the following circumstances:

- the incidental inclusion of a photograph or film in an artistic work, film or broadcast[1];
- the use of a photograph or film for Parliamentary or judicial proceedings[2];
- the use of a photograph or film by Royal Commissions or statutory enquiries[3];
- any acts done in relation to a photograph or film under statutory authority[4]; and
- the use of photographs or films which are anonymous or pseudonymous works, where the acts are permitted on the basis of assumptions as to the expiry of the copyright on death of the author[5].

1   CDPA s 85(2)(a).
2   CDPA s 85(2)(b).
3   CDPA s 85(2)(c).
4   CDPA s 85(2)(d).
5   CDPA s 85(2)(e).

Duration of the right to privacy of photographs and films

10.26 The right subsists so long as copyright subsists in the work[1].

1   CDPA s 86(1).

Extended and revived copyright – exercise of moral rights

10.27 Moral rights continue to subsist as long as copyright subsists in a work. Moral rights are therefore exercisable during extended and revived copyright periods. Any waiver or assertion which existed immediately before the expiry of copyright continues to have effect during the revived copyright period.

If the author of a work or the director of a film died before 1 January 1996, the rights are exercisable by his or her personal representatives.

Assignment and transmission of moral rights

10.28 None of the moral rights are assignable. However, on the death of a person entitled to the paternity right, or the rights of integrity or privacy, the right will pass to such person as his will or other testamentary disposition specifically directs[1]. If there is no specific direction as to who is to inherit these moral rights, then, if the copyright was part of the author's estate (that is to say the copyright has not been disposed of before the death of the testator), the moral rights will pass to the person to whom the copyright passes. If neither of the first two situations are applicable, the personal representatives of the person entitled to the moral right have the right to exercise such right[2].

As regards the right to prevent false attribution, this is actionable after a person's death only by his personal representatives. The right cannot be transferred by will or other testamentary instrument[3].

We have seen elsewhere that copyright may be partially transferred (either by dividing the right to do different things with the work between different people, or by transferring rights for only part of the period of copyright[4]). Where on death, the right to undertake different acts are bequeathed to different people (eg where a novelist wills the publishing rights in his work to A and the film rights to B) the moral rights may be exercised by different people as follows:

- the paternity right may be asserted by any of them[5];
- the integrity right and the right to privacy can be exercised by any of them, and any consent or waiver issued by one right holder will not affect the position of any other[6];

It should be noted that not only can the author or director himself transmit the moral rights on death to such person as he sees fit by his will, but so also can that person who inherits the moral rights. Accordingly, it does not follow that the author's family will be entitled to exercise the moral rights on the death of the author.

1   CDPA s 95(1)(a).
2   CDPA s 95(1)(b) and (c).
3   CDPA s 95(5).
4   See **paragraph 9.22**.
5   CDPA s 95(3)(a).
6   CDPA s 95(3)(b) and (c).

Consents and waivers of moral rights

10.29 Although moral rights may not be assigned, there will not be an infringement if the person entitled to the right has consented to the doing of an act which would otherwise constitute an infringement[1].

Similarly, the rights may be waived by instrument in writing signed by the person giving up the right[2]. The waiver can relate to a specific work, to works of a specified description or to works generally, and may relate to existing or future works[3]. For example, a waiver might be given by an artist to an advertising agency which commissions him to create art works for advertisements, which relates to his works already in existence and those which he might make in the future.

The waiver may be conditional or unconditional, or be subject to revocation[4].

If the instrument in writing states that the waiver is made in favour of an owner or prospective owner of the copyright in a work or works to which it relates, then the waiver will be presumed to extend to the licensees and successors in title of the owner of copyright unless the instrument indicates a contrary interest[5]. So, if the author of a screenplay waives his moral right in favour of the film company to which he is assigning the copyright, that waiver will benefit any other companies who become licensees of that film company, or who purchase the rights in the screenplay from the film company.

Moral rights may also be waived informally, or as part of the general law of contract, as well as pursuant to an instrument in writing. If an artist sells a painting and tells the purchaser that he has the right to do anything with the picture that he sees fit, and this forms part of the contract of sale, the purchaser will be able to rely on the contract as a waiver of the moral right. The CDPA does not interfere with the operation of the general law of contract or estoppel in addition to such informal waivers[6].

1   CDPA s 87(1).
2   CDPA s 87(2).
3   CDPA s 87(3)(a).
4   CDPA s 87(3)(b).
5   CDPA s 87(3).
6   CDPA s 87(4).

Joint works

10.30 The meaning of the expression 'a work of joint authorship' is considered elsewhere[1]. In brief:

- the *paternity right* must be asserted by each joint author for himself[2];
- the *integrity right* is a right of each joint author, and any waiver issued by one joint author will not effect the position of any other[3];
- the *false attribution right* is infringed by any false statement as to authorship of a joint work, or by the attribution of a work by a single author as one of joint authorship[4]; and
- the *right of privacy* vests in each commissioner where the work was jointly commissioned, and the waiver by one commissioner will not affect the rights of any other[5].

In relation to films which are jointly directed, the position will be the same as for joint authors. For these purposes 'jointly directed' means 'made by the collaboration of two or more directors and the contribution of each director is not distinct from that of the other director or directors'[6].

1 See **paragraph 9.08**.
2 CDPA s 88(1).
3 CDPA s 88(2) and (3).
4 CDPA s 88(4).
5 CDPA s 88(6).
6 CDPA s 88(5).

Application of moral right to parts of works

10.31 The rights of paternity and privacy in photographs and films apply in relation to the whole or any *substantial* part of a work, whereas the rights to object to the derogatory treatment of a work and to false attribution apply in relation to the whole or any part of a work[1]. So, notwithstanding that the paternity right has been asserted, a short extract from a book can be quoted without identification. Similarly, a part of a photograph or a film, taken or made for private and domestic purposes, can be copied and issued to the public or exhibited etc without the commissioner's consent provided it is not a substantial part[2].

On the other hand, if even the smallest part of a work (other than a sound recording, broadcast or typographical arrangement of a published edition) is the subject of derogatory treatment or false attribution, there will be a breach of both those moral rights.

1 CDPA s 89.
2 What constitutes a 'substantial part' of a work as considered at **paragraph 7.06**.

Works made before 1 August 1989

10.32 The moral rights provisions of the CDPA apply only to acts which are done after the commencement of the CDPA. However, they apply to all works which were in copyright at the commencement of the CDPA, with certain important exceptions (see below). The provisions of the Copyright Act 1956 as to false attribution of authorship continue to apply in relation to acts done before commencement of the CDPA.

The exceptions are as follows:

- The paternity right and the integrity right do not apply to literary, dramatic, musical and artistic works the authors of which died before 1 August 1989. Nor do they apply to films made before commencement of the CDPA.
- As regards literary, dramatic, musical and artistic works, moral rights do not apply, in cases where the copyright first vested in the author, to anything done pursuant to an assignment of copyright or a licence which was made or granted before 1 August 1989 and the act done is pursuant to such assignment or licence. For example, the author of a screenplay of a film, who has assigned or licensed the right to make a film based on the screenplay, cannot object to any

changes made to his screenplay for the purpose of making a film under that assignment or licence.

- In cases where the copyright first vested in a person other than the author (of which the most common example is the work made in the course of employment where the copyright vests in the employer), there is no infringement of the paternity right or the integrity right if the act is done by or with the licence of the copyright owner.
- Under the 1956 Act a record could be made of a piece of music under what was known as a 'statutory licence' by serving an appropriate notice and paying a statutory licence fee. Moral rights do not apply to anything done in making a record of a piece of music pursuant to such a licence.
- The right of privacy of photographs and films[1] does not apply to photographs taken or films made before commencement of the CDPA.

1   **Paragraphs 10.24** ff.

Moral rights in performances

10.33 The WIPO Performances and Phonograms Treaty 1996 provided that, quite independent of the economic rights afforded to performers in respect of their performances[1], performers should also benefit from similar 'moral rights' protections to those already enjoyed by author's and described throughout this chapter.

Two rights are provided for in the Treaty:

(a)   a right to claim to be identified as the performer of a performance[2];
(b)   a right to object to any distortion, mutilation or other modification of his performance which would be prejudicial to his reputation[3].

The Treaty requires that these rights should apply to live aural performances, and their recorded performances ('fixed on phonograms'). There is no definition of the word 'aural' in the Treaty, but in the consultation documents circulated by the UK government, it has been taken to mean the 'sound element' of a performance.

These provisions are now embodied in the Performances (Moral Rights etc) Regulations 2006, SI 2006/18.

1   See **Chapter 11** for a full discussion of performers' rights.
2   Akin to the paternity right referred to at **paragraphs 10.02** ff.
3   Akin to the integrity right (ie the right to object to derogatory treatment) referred to at **paragraphs 10.12** ff.

The identification right

10.34 The *'identification right'* has been implemented by s 205C to the CDPA. When a performance is given in public or broadcast live, or a sound recording of the performance is communicated or issued to the public, the performer has a right to be identified[1]. For these purposes 'communication' means communication by electronic transmission.

The right may be satisfied (for live performances) by identifying the performer in the relevant programme and/or (for copies of any recording of the performance issued to the public) by identifying the performer in or on the copies.

For a live performance, the person who organises or promotes the performance who will have to give effect to the right to be identified. Guidance issued by the UK Patent Office indicates that this requirement will 'have to be met by those who regularly organise performances in concert halls or theatres, or those who only occasionally organise or promote a performance in a village or church hall or other venue'.

Section 205C(3) makes provision for performances given by groups[2]. There will be no right for performers to be individually identified where a performance is given a group performance[3], provided the group itself is identified. This reflects the perceived practical difficulties associated with dealing with large groups, and with live performances where not all performers are identified.

As in the case of authors' paternity rights, the identification right will need to be asserted[4].

Exceptions to the identification right are similar to those applicable to authors' and directors' moral rights[5] (eg performances given for reporting current events, incidental inclusion, for purposes of examination and for parliamentary proceedings). However, additional exceptions apply in respect of circumstances where it is not reasonably practicable to identify the performer[6] and/or where the performance is 'given for the purposes of advertising any goods or services'[7].

It is argued the latter right is necessary because listing performers featured in advertisements would be a substantial hindrance to advertisers and provide little benefit to performers. However, it is questionable whether, as drafted, s 205E(4) will achieve its desired effect: many cases recordings used in advertisements are commercial recordings. It will in most cases be difficult to argue that the original performance was rendered for advertising purposes.

1   The circumstances in which the right arises are set out in CDPA s 205C(1)(a) to (d) of the CDPA, and the rights are to be elaborated in CDPA s 205C(2)(a) to (d).
2   CDPA s 205C(3).
3   'Group' meaning two or more performers known by a particular collective name: CDPA s 205C(4).
4   CDPA s 205D.
5   See **paragraph 10.10**.
6   CDPA s 205E(2).
7   CDPA s 205E(4).

The integrity right (ie right to object to derogatory treatment)

10.35 This right is infringed where a performance is broadcast 'live', or if a sound recording of the performance is played or communicated to the public with any distortion, mutilation or modification which is 'prejudicial to the reputation of the performer'[1].

The right is similar to the integrity right afforded to authors and directors[2].

The exceptions to the integrity right allows modifications for the purpose of reporting current events, or which are consistent with 'normal editorial or production practice', or which are done to avoid committing an offence, complying with a duty under an enactment or, in the case of the BBC, to avoid offending good taste or decency, which is likely to encourage crime or lead to disorder, of which offends public feeling[3].

1 CDPA s 205F.
2 See **paragraphs 10.12** ff.
3 CDPA s 205G.

Other provisions in relation to performers moral rights

10.36 If implemented in their draft form, the Regulations will:

- provide that performers moral rights will subsist for the same duration as performers property rights[1];
- provide for similar provisions in relation to waiver and consent, non-assignability, transmission on death and remedies which are applicable to the moral rights applicable to authors and directors[2].

1 CDPA s 205I.
2 CDPA ss 205J, 205K, 205L, 205M and 205N.

Chapter 11

Rights in performances

Introduction

11.01 In addition to their moral rights[1], performers receive protection under two regimes in the CDPA:

* *performers' **non-property** rights and recording rights* comprise the right to consent to the recording or live broadcast or transmission of a performance, or to the use of the recording, or to the importation, possession or dealing with a recording[2];
* *performers' **property** rights* comprise the right to authorise the reproduction, distribution and rental and lending of copies of a recorded performance[3].

In addition, the performer is entitled to equitable remuneration from the playing, broadcast, cable transmission or rental of a commercially-produced sound recording[4], and to control the 'making available' to the public of a recording of a performance[5].

1   See **paragraphs 10.33** and **11.28**.
2   CDPA ss 182–184; see **paragraphs 11.06–11.10**.
3   CDPA ss 182A–182C; see **paragraphs 11.11–11.13**.
4   CDPA ss 191A and 191M.
5   CDPA s 182CA; see **paragraph 11.14**.

Relevant performances

11.02 For these purposes, 'performance' means:

'(a)   a dramatic performance (which includes dance and mime),
(b)   a musical performance,
(c)   a reading or recitation of a literary work, or
(d)   a performance of a variety act or any similar presentation,

which is, or so far as it is, a live performance given by one or more individuals'[1].

The ambit of these categories has been subject to debate in recent years. In the context of sporting performances, for example, the traditional view is that these are not capable of protection by way of a performance right. There may be an exception to this where activity is closely choreographed (eg an ice dance) so as to amount to a work of dance or mime. More difficult are some of the 'trade mark' movements and actions which have increasingly come to characterise, for example, the goal mouth celebrations of soccer players. In all but the most exceptional cases, these kinds of activities will not be of a character which are capable of being protected as a performance[2].

1   CDPA s 180(2).
2   See, generally, **Chapter 2**.

Persons entitled to rights in performances

11.03 Rights are conferred on a performer (who must give his or her consent to the exploitation of his or her performance) and the person who has recording rights in relation to a performance (who has rights in relation to recordings which are made without his or her consent or that of the performer)[1].

The definition of performer in the CDPA is not limited to a living performer: rights subsist in live performances by performers who died before the commencement of the CDPA[2].

1   CDPA s 180(1).
2   *Experience Hendrix LLC v Purple Haze Records Ltd [2007] EWCA Civ 501.*

Recordings of performances

11.04 A 'recording' in relation to a performance is a film or sound recording which is:

'(a)   made directly from the live performance,
 (b)   made from a broadcast of the performance, or
 (c)   made, directly or indirectly, from another recording of the performance'[1].

1   CDPA s 180(2).

Qualifying performances

11.05 A performance will not qualify for protection unless it is given by 'a qualifying individual ... or takes place in a qualifying country...'[1]. For this purpose, a 'qualifying country' means the UK, another Member State of the EEA, the Channel Islands, the Isle of Man, Gibraltar, a country which is party to the Rome Convention, or a country to which the protection has been extended by an order made pursuant to the

CDPA[2]. Such an order will only be made in respect of countries which provide reciprocal protection.

A 'qualifying individual' means 'a citizen or subject of, or an individual resident in, a qualifying country'[3].

1   CDPA s 181.
2   CDPA s 206(1).
3   CDPA s 206(1).

Non-property rights

Recording and broadcasting of performances

11.06 A performer's non-property rights are infringed by a person who, without his or her consent:

'(a) makes a recording of the whole or any substantial part of a qualifying performance directly from the live performance,

(b) broadcasts live the whole or any substantial part of a live performance, [or]

(c) makes a recording of the whole or any substantial part of a qualifying performance directly from a broadcast of the live performance'[1].

Although 'substantial part' is not defined, the expression is used in the same context in relation to copyright works[2].

1   CDPA s 182(1).
2   See **paragraph 7.06**.

Use of recordings made without consent

11.07 A performer's non-property rights are also infringed by a person who, without his or her consent:

'(a) shows or plays in public the whole or any substantial part of a qualifying performance, or

(b) communicates to the public the whole or any substantial part of a qualifying performance,

by means of a recording which was, and which that person knows or has reason to believe was, made without the performer's consent'[1].

1   CDPA s 183.

Importing, possessing or dealing with illicit recordings

11.08 It is an infringement of a performer's non-property rights to (amongst other things) possess for business purposes or deal with illicit recordings without his or her consent. Being a form of secondary infringement, it is necessary to show that the person against whom the infringement was alleged neither knew, nor had reason to believe, that the recording was illicit[1].

Again, any claim for damages for infringement will be limited to a reasonable payment for the act complained of where the infringer can show that the illicit recording was innocently acquired by him or her, or his or her predecessor in title[2]. For these purposes, a recording is 'innocently acquired' where the acquirer did not know and had no reason to believe that it was an illicit recording[3].

1   CDPA s 184(1).
2   CDPA s 184(2).
3   CDPA s 184(3).

Persons having recording rights

11.09 What the CDPA defines as the 'recording rights' apply only to persons who have the benefit of an 'exclusive recording contract', meaning a contract made between a performer and another person under which that person is entitled, to the exclusion of all other persons (including the performer), to make recordings of one or more of his or her performances with a view to their commercial exploitation[1].

Only qualifying persons are entitled to exercise the recording right. A person to whom the benefit of an exclusive recording contract is assigned or licensed will also benefit from the right, provided that he or she also is a qualifying person. For these purposes a 'qualifying person' means:

'a qualifying individual or a body corporate or other body having legal personality which –

(a)   is formed under the law of a part of the United Kingdom or another qualifying country, and
(b)   has in any qualifying country a place of business at which substantial business activity is carried on'[2].

For example, an American record company (assuming that the USA is not a qualifying country) which has an exclusive recording contract will not itself have the benefit of the protection of this part of the CDPA. But such benefit will be acquired by persons licensed by the record company to make recordings with a view to their commercial exploitation. This could equally apply to an assignee of a company which was not a qualifying person, if such assignee itself was a qualifying person. So, the UK subsidiary company of an American recording company could enforce the rights under an exclusive recording contract assigned to it by its American parent.

1   CDPA s 185(1).
2   CDPA s 206(1).

Infringement of recording rights

11.10 The rights of a person holding 'recording rights' in a performance will be infringed by a person who, without his or her consent or the consent of the performer (amongst other things), 'makes a recording of the whole or any substantial part of the performance'[1]. It is worth emphasising that a performer can give consent to the recording of his or her performance even though the effect of so doing would be to put him or her in breach of his or her exclusive recording contract.

1   CDPA s 186(1).

Property rights

The reproduction right

11.11 A performer's property rights are infringed by a person who, without his or her consent, makes a copy of a recording of a whole or any substantial part of a qualified performance[1]. It is irrelevant for these purposes whether the copy is made directly or indirectly[2].

1   CDPA s 182A(1).
2   CDPA s 182A(2).

The distribution right

11.12 A performer's property rights are also infringed by a person who, without his or her consent, issues to the public copies of a recording of the whole or any substantial part of a qualifying performance[1].

This restricted act has the same ambit as the restricted copyright act of 'issuing copies to the public'[2].

It should be noted that references to the issue of copies of a recording of a performance include the issue of the original recording of a live performance[3].

1   CDPA s 182B(1).
2   See **paragraph 6.05**.
3   CDPA s 182B(4).

Rental or lending of copies to the public

11.13 Performers are accorded a rental and lending right in relation to recordings of their qualifying performances in the same way as copyright owners[1].

There is a presumption of the transfer of this rental right, in the case of film production agreements:

'Where an agreement concerning film production is concluded between a performer and film producer, the performer shall be presumed, unless the agreement provides to the contrary, to have transferred to the film producer any rental right in relation to the film arising from the inclusion of a recording of his performance in the film'[2].

This presumption can be implied even where the agreement between the performer and the film producer is made by intermediaries such as agents or unions[3].

1 CDPA s 182C; see **paragraph 6.06**.
2 CDPA s 191F(1).
3 CDPA s 191F(3).

The making available right

11.14 A performer's rights are infringed:

'by a person who, without his consent, makes available to the public a recording of the whole or any substantial part of a qualifying performance by electronic transmission in such a way that members of the public may access the recording from a place and at a time individually chosen by them.'[1]

This is the so-called 'making available' right and its purpose is to allow performers to exercise control over the making available of their work over 'on demand' electronic systems.

It enables performers to control the making of recordings of their performances available to the public. It also means that, in commercial contracts such as recording agreements, companies will require an assignment of the exclusive right.

1 CDPA s 182CA(1).

Equitable remuneration

11.15 The CDPA provides that:

'Where a commercially published sound recording of the whole or any substantial part of a qualifying performance –

(a) is played in public, or
(b) is communicated to the public otherwise than being made available to the public in the way mentioned in section 182CA(1);

the performer is entitled to equitable remuneration from the owner of the copyright in the sound recording'[1].

This means that *no* equitable remuneration right exists in relation to the making available of such sound recordings by 'on demand' systems. However, a remuneration right is preserved for all other communications to the public.

The performer of a qualifying performance also has a right to receive 'equitable remuneration' from the rental of sound recordings or films in respect of which he or she has transferred his or her property right[2]. As with authors' rental rights[3] this right cannot be assigned except to a collecting society (for the purposes of collecting it for the author)[4]. Any attempt in an agreement to exclude or restrict the right to equitable remuneration will be void[5].

The level of equitable remuneration is to be set by the parties and, in the absence of agreement, the Copyright Tribunal may settle the amount[6]. As with the authors of copyright works, this provision is particularly significant in the film industry, where producers tend to adopt contractual devices intended to absolve themselves and those taking title from them from any obligation to pay further amounts in respect of such rights[7].

1   CDPA s 182D(1).
2   CDPA s 191G(1).
3   See **paragraph 6.06**.
4   CDPA s 191G(2).
5   CDPA s 191G(5).
6   CDPA s 191G(4).
7   See **paragraphs 6.06** and **9.27**.

Exceptions to rights in performances

11.16 The exceptions which are applicable to copyright infringement also broadly apply to rights in performances[1].

1   CDPA s 189; see **Chapter 8** above.

Duration of rights in performances taking place after 1 January 1996

11.17 The rights conferred by Part II of the CDPA as amended by the Duration of Copyright and Rights in Performances Regulations 1995 ('the 1995 Regulations'), and subsequent regulations, expire:

'(a) at the end of the period of 50 years from the end of the calendar year in which the performance takes place, or

(b) if during that period a recording of the performance, other than a sound recording, is released, 50 years from the end of the calendar year in which it is released, or

(c) if during that period a sound recording of the performance is released, 70 years from the end of the calendar year in which it is released.[1]'

A recording is 'released' when it is first published, played or shown in public, broadcast or communicated to the public, but no unauthorised act is to be taken into account in determining whether a recording has been released[2].

Where a performer is not a national of an EEA state, the duration of the rights in relation to his or her performance is that to which the performer is entitled in the country of which s/he is a national, provided that does not exceed the period set out above[3]. Therefore, nationals of those countries where the period of protection for a performance is

25 years will only receive a 25-year protection in the UK, unless this is overridden by an international agreement to which the UK is a party.

1   CDPA s 191(2).
2   CDPA s 191(3).
3   CDPA s 191(4).

Duration of rights in performances given before 1 January 1996

11.18   Although the CDPA also provided for a 50-year term of protection for performances, the introduction by the 1995 Regulations of a period of 50 years from the end of the calendar year in which a recording is released[1] had the effect of extending the period of protection for certain unpublished performances or recently-published performances. The new period applies not only to performances which take place on or after 1 January 1996, but also to:

* existing performances which first qualified for protection after 31 December 1995 by virtue of the new provisions[2];
* existing performances which qualified for protection under the provisions of the CDPA before it was amended by the 1995 Regulations[3];
* existing performances in which protection has expired in the UK but which would have been protected in another EEA state on 1 July 1995[4].

It follows that there are extended performance rights for a large majority of recordings, since the only recordings in which there will not be any extension are those where the recording was released in the same calendar year as the live performance took place.

Where the 50-year period from the end of the calendar year in which the performance took place has expired, but a record has been released during that period, there will be revived performance rights.

1   1995 Regulations, reg 10; CDPA s 191(2).
2   1995 Regulations, reg 10; CDPA s 191.
3   1995 Regulations, reg 16.
4   1995 Regulations, reg 16.

Assignability of performers' non-property rights

11.19   These rights are not assignable or transmissible[1], although when the person entitled to the performer's rights dies, the rights will be exercisable by the person to whom s/he wills them, or in the absence of any will, by his or her personal representatives[2].

1   CDPA s 192A(1).
2   CDPA s 192A(2).

Assignability of recording rights

11.20 These rights are not assignable or transmissible[1], although they are exercisable by the licensee or assignee of an exclusive recording agreement if s/he is a 'qualifying person'[2].

1   CDPA s 192B(1).
2   CDPA s 192B(2); see **paragraph 11.09**.

Assignability of performers' property rights

11.21 Performers' property rights can be transferred by assignment, testamentary disposition, or by operation of law, as personal or moveable property[1].

Like a copyright assignment, an assignment of performer's property right is not effective unless it is signed in writing by or on behalf of the assignor[2]. An assignment may be partial or limited, as in the case of a copyright assignment[3].

As in the case of a copyright licence, a licence of a performers' property rights is binding on successors in title to them, except a purchaser in good faith for value without actual or constructive notice of the licence, or a person taking rights from such a purchaser[4].

Where a performer has by an agreement assigned to the producer of a sound recording the reproduction, distribution and making available rights, or performers' property rights, then special rules apply[5] as follows. If at or after the end of a specified period the producer has failed to meet one or both of the following conditions – namely, to issue to the public copies of the sound recording in such quantity as to satisfy the reasonable requirements of the public for copies of it, or to make the sound recording available to the public by electronic transmission in such a way that a member of the public may access it from a place and at a time chosen by him or her – the performer may terminate the agreement by notice in writing. If the sound recording has been published within 50 years from the end of the calendar year in which it was made, the specified period referred to above means the period of 50 years from the end of the calendar year in which the sound recording was first published, or made available to the public by being played in public or communicated to it.

1   CDPA s 191B(1).
2   CDPA s 191B(3); see **paragraph 9.23**.
3   CDPA s 191B(2).
4   CDPA s 191B(4).
5   CDPA s 191HA.

Entitlement to extended and revived performers' rights

11.22 Because parties to agreements made before the period of protection of performance rights was extended or revived did not anticipate the survival of these rights beyond the original 50-year period, the 1995 Regulations legislate as to who may exercise these rights during the extended or revived period. In brief:

- *extended performers' rights* are exercisable by the person who was entitled to exercise them immediately before 1 January 1996, that is to say the performer, or (if he/she has died) the person entitled to exercise those rights, being either a beneficiary or a personal representative[1];
- *revived performers' rights* are exercisable:
  - (a) in the case of rights which expired after 1 August 1989, by the person who was entitled to exercise them immediately before they expired;
  - (b) in the case of revived pre-1988 performers' rights, by the performer or his or her personal representative[2].

1 1995 Regulations, reg 31(1).
2 1995 Regulations, reg 31(2).

Consents

11.23 In relation to performers' non-property rights and recording rights, consents may be given in connection with a specific performance, a specified description of performance, or performances generally, and in connection with past or future performances[1].

The consent must be given (in the case of performer's non-property rights) by the performer or (in the case of the recording rights) by the person entitled to the recording rights. In the case of recording rights, however, consent can also be given by the performer (even if that leaves the performer in breach of an exclusive recording contract)[2]. A consent given by the person entitled to recording rights will bind any successor in title or licensee to the exclusive recording contract[3], and a consent given by a performer will bind any person to whom the right to consent may at any time pass[4].

There is an implication that consents can be given by properly-authorised persons on behalf of performers or persons having exclusive recording rights[5], but if it is decided for convenience to rely on a consent from a person other than the performer, then a copy of the written authority to give such consent should be obtained.

The Copyright Tribunal can give consent in a case where the identity or whereabouts of the person entitled to the reproduction right in a performance cannot be ascertained by reasonable enquiry[6].

1 CDPA s 193(1).
2 See **paragraph 11.10**.
3 CDPA s 193(2).
4 See **paragraph 11.21**.

5   CDPA s 201(1).
6   CDPA s 190(1).

Civil remedies for infringement of performers' non-property rights

11.24 The right of action for infringement of a performer's non-property right is to sue for breach of statutory duty. The remedies, therefore, include damages, orders for the delivery of illicit recordings and the right to seize illicit recordings[1].

A right to seize illicit recordings was introduced into the CDPA to deal with the problem of street traders selling pirated or bootlegged audio cassettes and videos from mobile barrows, who may be untraceable before formal proceedings can be instituted or the police have had an opportunity to make an arrest under the criminal provisions contained in Part II of the CDPA. A person having performers' rights or recording rights can himself or herself authorise other people to seize and detain illicit recordings which are found exposed, or otherwise immediately available, for sale or hire[2]. Before anything is seized, however, notice of the time and place of the seizure has to be given to the local police station in a prescribed form[3]. The person exercising the right can enter premises to which the public have access, but nothing may be seized which is in the possession, custody or control of a person at a permanent or regular place of business, and no force may be used[4]. So, for example, a rights holder could enter a covered market and seize goods, but not from a trader who trades regularly in that market.

At the time when anything is seized, a notice in a prescribed form detailing the person by or on whose authority the seizure is made and the grounds for making the seizure, must be left at the place where it was seized[5].

1   CDPA ss 194–196.
2   CDPA s 196(1).
3   CDPA s 196(2).
4   CDPA s 196(3).
5   CDPA s 196(4).

Civil remedies for infringement of performers' property rights

11.25 The remedies for infringement of performers' property rights are the same as those for infringement of other intellectual property rights (ie damages, injunction, account of the profits gained by the defendant from the infringement, etc)[1].

As in the case of copyright infringement, an award of damages for infringement of performers' property rights will be affected by the circumstances. So, a claimant will not be entitled to damages where it is shown that at the time of the infringement the infringer did not know or have reason to believe that the rights subsisted in the recording to which the action relates[2]. On the other hand, the court may award additional damages taking into account the flagrancy of the infringement and any benefit accruing to the infringer from the infringement[3].

1   CDPA s 191I; see **paragraphs 7.11** ff. See for example *Henderson v All Around the World Recordings Ltd [2014] EWHC 3087 (IPEC)*, and *Experience Hendrix LLC v Times Newspapers Ltd [2010] EWHC 1986 (Ch)*.
2   CDPA s 191J(1); see **paragraph 7.12**.
3   CDPA s 191J(2); see **paragraph 7.13**.

Infringement of revived performers' rights

11.26   No act done before 1 January 1996 is to be regarded as infringing revived performance rights in a performance[1]. With regard to acts done after that date, it is not an infringement of revived performers' rights:

- to do anything pursuant to arrangements made before 1 January 1995 at a time when the performance was not protected[2]; or
- to issue to the public a recording of a performance made before 1 July 1995 at a time when the performance was not protected[3];
- if the name and address of a person entitled to authorise the act cannot by reasonable enquiry be ascertained[4].

For these purposes, 'arrangements' means 'arrangements for the exploitation of the performance in question'[5].

1   1995 Regulations, reg 33(1).
2   1995 Regulations, reg 33(2)(a).
3   1995 Regulations, reg 33(2)(b), (6).
4   1995 Regulations, reg 33(4).
5   1995 Regulations, reg 33(5).

Criminal liability

11.27   In addition to civil liability, criminal liability attaches to a person who, without sufficient consent, makes for sale or hire, imports other than for private and domestic use, possesses in the course of business with a view to committing an infringing act, or (in the course of business) sells, lets for hire, offers or exposes for sale or hire or distributes a recording which he or she knows or has reason to believe is an 'illicit recording'[1].

For these purposes, 'illicit recording' means a recording of the whole or any substantial part of a performance made otherwise than for private purposes (in the case of performers' rights) without the consent of the performer, and (in the case of recording rights) without the consent of the person holding the recording right, or the performer[2].

Similarly a person will commit an offence by causing the showing or playing in public or communicating to the public, of a recording of a performance made without sufficient consent, where the person knows or has reason to believe the rights have been infringed[3].

1   CDPA s 198(1).
2   CDPA s 197.
3   CDPA s 198(2).

Performers' moral rights

11.28 The regime of moral rights for performers is considered elsewhere in this *User's Guide*[1].

1   See **paragraph 10.33**.

Chapter 12

Collective management and licensing of copyright: Collecting societies, copyright licensing schemes and the Copyright Tribunal

Collecting societies (collective management bodies)

12.01 Copyright confers on its owner exclusive rights to exploit a copyright work. However, in some instances, individual licensing of rights may not be feasible: the difficulty of clearing rights in a large number of works from individual copyright owners may be so arduous that it deters users from seeking clearance for the use of particular works. Sometimes it may not be in the public interest for individual licensing to be the only option; for instance, in the education sector, it is important that there is easy access to a wide range of works. Often collective licensing is also in the interests of the copyright owner such as in circumstances where an individual copyright owner is likely to have an inferior bargaining position when negotiating with a major user of copyright works, such as a broadcaster. Collective licensing also benefits copyright owners by providing a licensing framework – and some remuneration – where users would have been deterred by the difficulties involved in seeking individual clearance.

The undoubted benefits of collective licensing in some circumstances have led to the creation, throughout the world, of organisations with the specialist function of licensing particular rights in copyright works on behalf of their members and/or the copyright owners. They collect the revenues received from users, and then distribute those revenues to their members and/or the copyright owners after deduction of their administration costs. These bodies, historically called 'collecting societies', are now often also referred to as collective management organisations ('CMOs'), the term used in the EU Directive on collective management of copyright (the 'CRM Directive')[1] which sets EU-wide standards for the control and regulation of CMOs and similar bodies (see **paragraph 12.16**).

Members either transfer the rights to be licensed on their behalf to the society, or appoint the society as their agent to enter into licences on their behalf. Since a number of collecting societies consequently control rights in huge numbers of works, they provide both an efficient method of negotiating acceptable licence terms and fees for the member, and a convenient source of rights clearances for users. Many societies negotiate 'blanket' agreements which allow use of works for a fixed fee or tariffs for classes of use.

Collective licensing began with the licensing of music in the nineteenth century but over time has extended to include other sectors such as printed material, artistic works and images, the rental and cable retransmission of audio-visual works and the recording of television programmes by educational institutions.

In the UK the principal societies[2] and their functions are, in brief:

- *The Performing Right Society (PRS)*: which takes an assignment of and administers for its members the public performance rights, broadcasting and cable re-transmission rights in musical works, the right to include such works in cable programme services, the right (in certain cases) to record musical works onto the soundtrack of films (ie 'synchronisation rights') and the right to authorise third parties to do the above[3];
- *The Mechanical Copyright Protection Society (MCPS)*: which acts as agent for its members in licensing rights to make sound recordings of musical works, issue copies of those recordings to the public, importing those copies, or authorise third parties to do the above[4];
- *Phonographic Performance Limited (PPL)*, including *Video Performance Ltd (VPL)*: which takes an assignment or acts as exclusive agent for its members in licensing public performance rights and broadcasting and cable transmission rights and the 'dubbing' right in recorded music and music videos (ie the right to copy, produce, reproduce or make records embodying sound recordings for the purpose of exercising the performance right) and authorising third parties to do the above[5];
- *The Copyright Licensing Agency Ltd (CLA)*: which acts on behalf of the Publishers Licensing Society, the Authors' Licensing & Collecting Society, the Design and Artists Collecting Society, Picsel Ltd, and (in certain cases) other organisations in granting licences to

photocopy, scan or re-use content from magazines, books, journals and electronic and online publications (see **Chapter 19**);

- *NLA Media Access Ltd (formerly The Newspaper Licensing Agency Ltd)*: offers licences to make copies of articles published in newspapers and magazines (either in print or online) and to use these copies in leaflets, websites and as part of media monitoring services (see **Chapter 19**).

Other collecting societies operating in the UK include: the Authors' Licensing and Collecting Society Ltd (ALCS); the Publishers Licensing Society; the British Equity Collecting Society Ltd (BECS); the Design and Artists Copyright Society Ltd (DACS); Artists Collecting Society (ACS); Picture Industry Collecting Society (Picsel); Printed Music Licensing Ltd (PMLL); Directors UK and the Educational Recording Agency Ltd (ERA), all of which administer different rights on behalf of the various members. The function of these societies will be considered in further detail in the various chapters focusing on copyright use[6].

There has been increasing speculation as to the future of collecting societies in the digital environment which increasingly facilitates complex, automated individual rights clearance. So far collecting societies have adapted to provide a complementary offering to individual clearance by the copyright owners themselves. Collecting societies have been seen by the regulatory authorities, both in the UK and the EU, as playing an important role as part of a well-ordered copyright regime in enabling access to content by users, whilst protecting the rights of copyright owners and ensuring the payment to them of some remuneration for the use of their works.

1   Directive 2014/26/EU on collective management of copyright and related rights and multi-territorial licensing of rights in musical works for online use in the internal market.
2   This list includes licensing bodies loosely known as collecting societies which may be CMOs, bodies known as Independent Management Entities (IMEs) or other types of organisations involved in copyright licensing. For a fuller list see the Intellectual Property Office website at https://www.gov.uk/guidance/licensing-bodies-and-collective-management-organisations.
3   See **paragraph 20.07**.
4   See **paragraph 20.08**.
5   See **paragraph 20.22**.
6   See **Part 2**.

Extended Collective Licensing

12.02 Typically collecting societies issue licences to cover works where they have received an authority to do so from the copyright owner. But this potentially leaves a gap in the repertoire coverage available to licensees for those copyright works where the collecting society has no form of authority. The education sector in particular needs to be able to copy from as broad a range of copyright works as possible. 'Extended Collective Licensing' (ECL) is an approach intended to address this need by extending the coverage of a copyright licence that can be offered by a collecting society.

The CDPA was amended[1] to allow licensing bodies (see **paragraph 12.08**) to be granted an authorisation (limited to five years but renewable after three years) to grant copyright licences in respect of works (including any embedded works such as photographs or drawings) in which copyright is not owned by a person on whose behalf the licensing body acts. The effect is that both the grant of a licence, provided it is done in accordance with the authorisation, and the doing of any acts permitted by that licence, do not constitute an infringement of copyright.

Detailed regulations[2] provide for the procedure to be followed for the application and authorisation of an ECL scheme, including the terms of the licence and the fees to be charged. Fees must be distributed as soon as practicable and, in any event, within nine months of the relevant year end where the rights holder is identified. Undistributed funds are to be held in a separate designated account pending discovery of the rights holder. After three years the licensing body must, unless otherwise directed, pay undistributed funds to the government who holds these for a further period of eight years from the date of the initial authorisation. The government must then determine the use to which any fees still undistributed must be put which may include appropriate social, cultural and educational activities.

The licensing body must show evidence that it has obtained the informed consent of its members and show that its members are truly representative of the class of rights owners whose works are to be included in the ECL scheme. The licensing body must be owned or controlled by the copyright owners themselves or by bodies organised on a not-for-profit basis; this addition to the definition of licensing body for ECL purposes brings it into line with that of CMOs under the UK regulations implementing the CRM Directive (see **paragraph 12.15**). The licensing body must also operate in accordance with the requirements of the Collective Management of Copyright (EU Directive) Regulations 2016 (the 'CMO Regulations')[3].

An important protection for copyright owners is that the ECL scheme must allow copyright owners to 'opt out' so that no copyright owner is forced to participate in the scheme: it does not amount to a compulsory licence. Proposals for ECL schemes must be widely publicised so that rights holders are aware of the existence of the scheme and of the possibility to opt out of it.

1   CDPA s 116B.

2   Copyright and Rights in Performances (Extended Collective Licensing) Regulations
     2014, SI 2014/2588.
3   SI 2016/221.

Compulsory licences for the inclusion of sound recordings in broadcasts

12.03 The CDPA (as amended by the Broadcasting Act 1990) now provides a statutory right to use sound recordings in broadcasts. The right relates to 'needletime' (meaning the proportionate time in any period in which recordings may be included in a broadcast). If a licensing body refuses to grant a licence for unlimited needletime (or such lesser amount of needletime requested by the user) on payment terms acceptable to the user, or refuses to alter a current licence to provide unlimited needletime (or the amount requested by the user), that person will be treated as if he has a licence from the copyright owner provided that he:

- gives the licensing body sufficient advance notice of his intention to exercise his statutory right and his proposals for payment;
- complies with any reasonable conditions of the licensing body;
- provides the licensing body with information regarding his use as reasonably required by the body;
- gives notice to the Tribunal of his intention to exercise his statutory right and then applies to the Tribunal to settle the terms of payment;
- and pays to the licensing body either the amount set out in any Order of the Copyright Tribunal or the amount required by the licensing body. If there is no Order of the Tribunal or the fee proposed by the licensing body is unreasonable, the amount notified by the user in his proposal must be paid pending settlement by the Tribunal.

Collective administration of cable retransmission right

12.04 The CDPA provides a system of compulsory collective administration for cable retransmissions of broadcasts from within other Member States of the European Economic Area (the EEA).

The CDPA (s 144A) implemented the EU Cable and Satellite Directive 1993 to provide owners of literary, dramatic, musical or artistic works, sound recordings or films with a new 'cable retransmission right' which can only be exercised 'as against a cable operator' through a licensing body. The cable retransmission right only applies to cable retransmissions in the UK of wireless broadcasts in which the work is included where the broadcast originates in another EEA Member State. The reason for the collective administration of these rights is that it was felt counterproductive to the development of the European market for cable retransmission to allow rights holders an effective veto over this form of exploitation, and to facilitate rights clearance for cable operators.

If an owner of one of these rights has not transferred management of such rights to a licensing body, the licensing body managing rights of the same category is deemed to be mandated to exercise his right. The copyright owner in such cases will have the same rights and obligations as a copyright owner who has transferred management of retransmission rights to the licensing body. However, these rights must be exercised within three years from the date of the cable retransmission concerned.

Significantly, the requirement to license collectively does not extend to broadcasters. The maker of a broadcast is entitled to license individually any rights exercised by him (whether in relation to the broadcast and any works included in it).

Control and regulation of collecting societies

12.05 Notwithstanding the public benefits that collecting societies deliver, their collective control of copyright works represents a potential monopolistic threat which has the potential to distort the market. In addition to the possible application of competition law, there have always been provisions in the CDPA designed to address the problem. The CDPA provides a regulatory framework for 'licensing schemes' and 'licensing bodies' subject to the jurisdiction of the Copyright Tribunal (originally the Performing Rights Tribunal) whose primary purpose is to resolve disputes between collecting societies and users. But in recent years there has been an increasing focus, both in the UK and the EU, on the control of collecting societies.

In the EU this resulted in the CRM Directive of 2014[1]. The UK government, anticipating the CRM Directive, decided to introduce domestic legislation (the Copyright (Regulation of Relevant Licensing Bodies) Regulations[2]) to address the problem. But once the CRM Directive came into force in the UK in April 2016, these Regulations had to be largely replaced by the CMO Regulations[3] in order for the UK to comply with the CRM Directive.

There are therefore three types of control of collecting societies in the UK – the original provisions of the CDPA, the CMO Regulations under the CRM Directive and competition law.

1   See **paragraph 12.16**.
2   SI 2014/898.
3   See **paragraph 12.15**.

UK Regulation under the CDPA

12.06 Chapter 7 of the CDPA regulates copyright licensing and is mainly concerned with copyright licences (being licences to do, or authorise the doing of, any of the acts restricted by copyright) issued by licensing bodies or as part of a licensing scheme.

Licensing schemes

12.07 Under the CDPA, a 'licensing scheme'[1] means:

'a scheme setting out:

(a) the classes of case in which the operator of the scheme, or the person on whose behalf he acts, is willing to grant copyright licences; and

(b) the terms on which licences will be granted in those classes of case'.

A scheme will include anything in the nature of a scheme whether it is described as a scheme or as a tariff or by any other name. If licences are not available 'off the shelf' but have to be tailored individually to particular circumstances there may not be a 'licensing scheme' for the purposes of the CDPA (although each such licence may be the subject of a reference to the Copyright Tribunal if issued by a 'licensing body').

1   CDPA s 116.

Licensing bodies

12.08 For the purposes of the CDPA, a 'licensing body'[1] means a 'society or other organisation which has its main object, or one of its main objects, the negotiation or granting of copyright licences and where those objects include the granting of licences covering works of more than one author'. This provision is designed to capture licences which are individually negotiated and which would not otherwise be subject to the jurisdiction of the Copyright Tribunal as part of a licensing scheme. A copyright user may, for example, need a licence from a licensing body for a use which does not come within any licensing scheme and therefore requires a tailor-made licence. Licences to television broadcasters which are negotiated on an ad hoc basis are examples of such individual licences.

1   CDPA s 116.

Referral of licensing schemes to the Copyright Tribunal

12.09 The jurisdiction of the Copyright Tribunal covers licensing schemes[1] and licences issued by a licensing body which cover works by more than one author: individual licences and licensing schemes covering works made by a single individual or by employees of, or commissioned by, a company (or group of companies) are excluded from the remit of the Copyright Tribunal; equally a licence for a collective work (a work with multiple authors) would not be covered unless offered as part of a licence covering other works.

The licensing schemes that can be referred to the Copyright Tribunal are those which relate to licences for:

• copying the work;

- rental or lending of copies of the work to the public;
- performing, showing or playing the work in public; or
- broadcasting the work or including it in a cable programme service.

Any dispute on the terms of an existing licensing scheme may be referred to the Copyright Tribunal either by a person requiring a licence under the scheme or by an organisation claiming to be representative of such persons. The terms of a proposed licence can also be referred by a representative body unless the Copyright Tribunal decides that the reference is premature.

However the reference arises, the Copyright Tribunal can either confirm or vary the terms of the scheme on such terms as it considers to be reasonable in the circumstances. The order can specify that the scheme should last indefinitely or for a specified period.

Schemes that the Copyright Tribunal has already adjudicated upon can be referred back to the Copyright Tribunal (although not in the first year unless there are exceptional circumstances) not only by a person wanting a licence or a representative body but also by the scheme operator. Again the Copyright Tribunal can make such order, either confirming or further varying the terms of the scheme, as it considers reasonable in the circumstances.

Applications may also be made to the Copyright Tribunal by persons who claim to have been refused, or refused within a reasonable time, a licence covered by a scheme or, in cases not covered by a scheme, by persons who claim to have been unreasonably refused a licence, or refused one within a reasonable time, or offered a licence only on unreasonable terms. The Copyright Tribunal can, if it considers appropriate, make an order that the applicant is entitled to a licence on terms according with the scheme or as the Copyright Tribunal considers reasonable.

1   CDPA ss 117–123.

Referral of individual licences offered by licensing bodies to the Copyright Tribunal

12.10 As with licensing schemes, references may be made regarding licences which authorise copying, rental or lending of copies to the public, performing, showing or playing the work in public, or broadcasting the work.

A prospective licensee (note but not a representative body) may refer the terms on which a licensing body proposes to grant a licence to the Copyright Tribunal[1]. Again, unless the Copyright Tribunal thinks the application is premature, it can consider the application and make such order confirming or varying the terms as it considers reasonable.

A licensee can also apply to the Copyright Tribunal when an existing licence is due to expire (whether the expiry is as a result of a notice given by the licensing body or simply through the passage of time) on the ground that it is unreasonable in the circumstances that the licence should cease to be in force. The Copyright Tribunal has the power to order that the licensee should continue to benefit from the licence on such terms as the Copyright Tribunal considers to be reasonable.

Licensing bodies and licensees may apply to have an order reviewed (again not in the first year unless there are exceptional circumstances) and the Copyright Tribunal can make such order, either confirming or further varying the terms of the scheme, as it considers reasonable in the circumstances.

1   CDPA ss 124–128.

Factors to be taken into account by the Copyright Tribunal

12.11 The CDPA sets out some general factors, and some factors specific to particular cases, that should be taken into account by the Tribunal in reaching a determination. These factors do not however affect the obligation to have regard to all relevant circumstances.

GENERAL FACTOR – UNREASONABLE DISCRIMINATION
12.12 In all cases, in deciding what is 'reasonable', the Copyright Tribunal must have regard to the availability and terms of other schemes, or the granting (and terms) of other licences in similar circumstances. The overriding aim is to ensure that there is no unreasonable discrimination between licensees or potential licensees.

SPECIFIC FACTORS FOR PARTICULAR LICENSING SCHEMES
12.13 The CDPA contains special rules with regard to certain types of copyright licences[1]. These rules deal with the matters to which the Copyright Tribunal must have regard when an application or reference has been made to it in such cases. These cases and a brief description of the factors to be considered are:

- *licences for reprographic copying (see below) of published literary, dramatic, musical or artistic works*: the availability of the work, the proportion to be copied and the use to which the copies are likely to be put;
- *licences for educational establishments in respect of works included in broadcasts*: the extent to which copyright owners have already received, or are entitled to receive, payment for the use of their works included in broadcasts being recorded (so as to avoid double payment);
- *licences to reflect conditions imposed by promoters of events*: to encourage promoters of entertainment events to permit the making of a recording, a film or a broadcast of the event, any contractual terms (other than those relating to fees and charges) imposed on

the maker of the recording, film or broadcast must be considered in determining the licence fee payable by a user to that maker;

- *licences to reflect payments in respect of underlying rights*: as with the recording of broadcasts by educational establishments, the extent to which copyright owners have already received, or are entitled to receive, payment for the use of their works (the underlying rights) included in a sound recording, film or broadcast or within another work being rented out;
- *compulsory licences for the inclusion of sound recordings in broadcasts*[2]: the terms of any orders the Tribunal has made in similar cases; and
- *licences in respect of works included in cable re-transmissions of broadcasts*[3]: the extent to which copyright owners have already received, or are entitled to receive payment for the first transmission, again intended to avoid double payment.

1 CDPA ss 130–135D.
2 See **paragraph 12.03**.
3 See **paragraph 12.04**.

Implied indemnity in licences for reprographic copying

12.14 Special provision is made for licences and licensing schemes for 'reprographic copying' that 'do not specify the works to which the licence or scheme apply with such particularity as to enable licensees to determine whether a work falls within the scheme or licence by inspection of the scheme or licence and the work'[1]. A 'reprographic process' is defined[2] as a process for making facsimile (ie identical) copies or involving the use of an appliance for making multiple copies. In such cases an indemnity is implied into the licence or scheme against any liability incurred by the licensee by reason of his having infringed copyright by making or authorising the making of reprographic copies of a work in circumstances where it is not apparent from inspection of the licence and the work that it does not fall within the scope of the licence.

1 CDPA s 136.
2 CDPA s 178.

UK regulation under the CMO Regulations

12.15 The definition of a CMO under the CMO Regulations is similar to that of 'licensing bodies' but with the addition that the licensing body must be owned or controlled by the copyright owners themselves or by bodies organised on a not-for-profit basis.

The CMO Regulations require a CMO to act in the best interest of the right holders they represent and must not impose on them any obligations which are not objectively necessary for the protection or the effective management of their rights.

The CMO Regulations place extensive obligations on both CMOs and their managers particularly as regards governance, the distribution of fees collected and on the running of the business. There is a requirement to provide an annual transparency report with an extensive list of matters to be disclosed; this is in addition to the annual report and accounts required under company law although some of the obligations overlap. Management fees must not exceed justified and documented costs and any other deductions must be reasonable in relation to the services provided by the CMO and established on the basis of objective criteria.

There are duties also to licensees such as a requirement to negotiate in good faith and to provide necessary information (including details on how licence fees are calculated) and to provide a complaints procedure. There are reciprocal obligations on users to provide necessary information and to negotiate in good faith.

Managers at CMOs are now under a formal legal duty to manage the business in a sound, prudent and appropriate manner, using appropriate administrative and accounting procedures and ensuring there are suitable internal control mechanisms and staff training procedures for employees. These obligations are backed up by financial penalties for non-compliance of up to £50,000 (or £5,000 plus a daily default fine of £500) which can be imposed on managers as well as on the CMO.

There are further obligations on dealings with other CMOs on whose behalf a CMO manages rights under a representation agreement and a new regime on multi-territorial licensing of musical works for online uses (see **Chapter 20**) aimed at reducing the number of licences that need to be obtained to operate a multi-territorial online music service.

EU regulation of CMOs

12.16 The CRM Directive is part of the European Commission's 'Digital Agenda for Europe' and is one of the measures aimed at improving the licensing of rights and access to digital content, particularly across borders within the EU.

The CRM Directive was prompted by the growing concerns regarding the transparency and the governance of CMOs and the handling of revenues collected on behalf of their members. The Commission highlighted the lack of influence and oversight of copyright owners over CMOs which it believed had contributed to irregularities in financial management and investment decisions, as well as instances of risky investments, by several continental CMOs.

The CRM Directive addresses these concerns by imposing an overriding general principle that CMOs must act in the best interests of the copyright owners they represent.

It aims to modernise and improve standards of governance, financial management and transparency of CMOs and sets out the standards CMOs must meet to ensure that they do act in the best interests of their members. It enshrines protections for copyright owners, in particular as to the collection and distribution of licence fees and deductions for administrative and other costs.

The detailed way in which these aims are to be achieved are beyond the scope of this book but are reflected in the UK's CMO Regulations discussed above.

Competition law

12.17 Chapter 13 deals in more detail with the potential impact of both EU and UK competition law on copyright but it is worth noting here a specific provision (s 144) of the CDPA on copyright licensing. This addresses the position where there is a finding by the Secretary of State or the Competition and Markets Authority under the Enterprise Act 2002 (as amended) dealing, broadly, with activities which operate against the public interest and where that finding relates to:

- conditions in copyright licences restricting the use of a work or the right of a copyright owner to grant licences;
- a refusal of a copyright owner to grant licences on reasonable terms.

In such cases there is a power to modify or even cancel the offending restrictions or to provide a copyright licence as of right. The terms of such a licence are, in default of agreement, to be determined by the Tribunal.

Chapter 13

EU law, competition and copyright

Introduction

13.01 Most of the impetus for the changes to UK copyright law over the last two decades has its origins in the European Union ('EU'), and at the root of all EU legislation is the treaty that is now called the Treaty on the Functioning of the European Union ('TFEU')[1] whose main objective is to establish a common market and other common policies. EU law most noticeably has affected copyright in the following ways:

- directives which have the effect of harmonising copyright law throughout the EU[2];
- regulations which have the effect of direct law in all Member States of the EU ('Member States');
- the provisions of Arts 34–36 of the TFEU, which seek to eliminate restrictions on the free movement of goods;
- the provisions of Arts 56–62 of the TFEU, which seek to eliminate restrictions on the free movement of services;
- the provisions of Art 101 of the TFEU, which prohibit agreements that restrict, prevent or distort competition; and
- the provisions of Art 102 of the TFEU, which prohibit abuse by private enterprises that have a dominant position in a particular market.

This chapter will consider selected aspects of EU law as they impact on copyright.

1   OJ C326/47.
2   See **paragraph 1.08**.

EU legislation and strategies

13.02 Various EU directives impacting on copyright, including the following, have been transposed into the national laws of the UK:

- Directive on semi-conductor topographies[1];
- Directives on the legal protection of computer programs[2];
- Directives on rental, lending and neighbouring rights[3];
- Directive on satellite broadcasting and cable transmission[4];
- Directives on copyright duration[5];
- Directive on the legal protection of databases[6];
- Directive on the legal protection of services based on, or consisting of, conditional access[7];
- Directive on copyright and related rights in the information society[8];
- Directive on the resale right for the benefit of the author of an original work of art[9];
- Directive on the enforcement of intellectual property rights[10];
- Directive on orphan works[11]; and
- Directive on collective management of copyright and related rights[12].

Furthermore, various EU regulations impacting on copyright have been adopted, including the regulation concerning customs enforcement of intellectual property rights[13], and the regulation on cross-border portability of online content services in the internal market[14].

EU policies and strategies announced in recent years with an impact on copyright law have included, amongst others, its strategy for intellectual property rights dated May 2011, and its communication on a digital single market strategy for Europe dated May 2015.

1   87/54/EEC.
2   91/250/EC, consolidated by 2009/24/EC.
3   92/100/EEC, replaced and codified by 2006/115/EC.
4   93/83/EEC.
5   93/98/EEC, as consolidated and amended by 2006/116/EC and 2011/77/EU respectively.
6   96/9/EC.
7   98/84/EC.
8   2001/29/EC.
9   2001/84/EC; see **paragraph 25.22**.
10   2004/48/EC.
11   2012/28/EU.
12   2014/26/EU.
13   Regulation (EU) No 608/2013.
14   Regulation (EU) No 2017/1128.

Freedom of movement of copyright material

13.03 Articles 34 and 35 of the TFEU prohibit quantitative restrictions on imports and exports respectively between Member States, and measures which have an equivalent effect. Once goods protected by copyright have been placed on the market in a Member State by or with the consent of the copyright owner, they must be allowed to circulate freely, without national copyright being invoked to prevent them from entering into the territory of another Member State.

Article 36 contains an exception to Arts 34 and 35 for (amongst other things) measures 'justified on grounds of...the protection of industrial and commercial property'. Copyright falls within this category.

One of the earliest leading cases on the application of Art 34 was *Deutsche Grammophon GmbH v Metro*[1] in which it was held that a German company could not prevent the re-importation into Germany of goods marketed in France by its French subsidiary, for such a restriction on importation went beyond the specific object of the copyright.

1   Case 78/70: [1971] CMLR 631, ECJ.

Exhaustion of rights

13.04 It follows that the principles of Arts 34 and 35 of the TFEU, and the territorial rights afforded by copyright, are in a sense in conflict. In part, that conflict is resolved by the harmonisation initiatives of the EU[1], but the issue has also been specifically addressed by the development of the doctrine of 'exhaustion of rights' by the Court of Justice of the EU ('CJEU').

The essence of the principle of European exhaustion of rights is considered elsewhere in the context of its implementation into the CDPA[2]. However, it is worth noting here that the exhaustion of one right in a copyright work does not exhaust all rights in respect of that work. As we have noted in other parts of this *User's Guide*, copyright is a bundle of rights. Particular rights can be separately licensed or assigned. So, for example, whilst the issue of copies of a CD or DVD into the EU market with the authorisation of the owner will exhaust its right to sell etc those copies within the EU, it will not exhaust, say, the right to authorise the performance, playing or showing of the work embodied on those copies in public, or the rental of those copies[3].

In *Art & Allposters International BV v Stichting Pictoright*[4] the CJEU ruled that, if a physical object into which a protected work has been incorporated is marketed with the consent of the copyright owner, the distribution right will thereby be exhausted.

1   See **paragraph 13.01**.
2   See **paragraph 6.05**.
3   For example *Metronome Musik GmbH v Music Point Hokamp GmbH (C-200/96)*. And for the application of exhaustion principles to the online distribution of software, see *UsedSoft GmbH v Oracle International Court (C-128/11)* and *Ranks and Vasilevics (Case C-166/5)*.
4   Case C-419/13.

Freedom of movement of services

13.05 Article 56 of the TFEU prohibits restrictions on the freedom to provide services within the EU in respect of nationals of Member States who are established in a state other than that of the person for whom the services are intended. The exception provisions of Art 36[1] do not apply to Art 56.

In *Coditel SA v Ciné Vog Films SA*[2] the owner of the film *Le Boucher* granted a licence to the German television channel ARD to broadcast the film. At the same time, Ciné Vog had an exclusive licence in the theatrical distribution and television broadcast rights in the film for Belgium. The Coditel companies were cable television operators in Belgium. They retransmitted the German broadcast to their cable subscribers.

Ciné Vog sued Coditel on the grounds that the cable retransmission infringed Ciné Vog's exclusive rights. Coditel claimed that Arts 56–62, providing for the free movement of services, constituted a defence to Ciné Vog's claim since if Ciné Vog succeeded there would be a restriction on the movement of services, television having been established to be a service for the purposes of Art 56. The CJEU held, however, that the performance of the film was an essential element in the copyright in the film which went to the 'specific subject matter' or 'object' of the copyright and in the circumstances could be protected by a geographically-limited licence. What *Coditel* established was that copyrights which depend on performance such as broadcasts may be licensed on a geographical basis within the EU without infringing Art 56. In other words, although the distribution right in goods may be exhausted by the first distribution of the goods within the EU which is authorised by the owner, the same does not apply to performances.

In a much later leading case, *FAPL v QC Leisure*[3], the CJEU held that rules in the CDPA prohibiting the importation into the UK of satellite decoding devices from overseas that would otherwise allow broadcasts transmitted from another Member State to be received amounted to a contravention of Art 56, in that they restricted the freedom to provide services. One of the consequences of this ruling was that the English High Court subsequently held that Ms Murphy had been wrongly convicted under the criminal provisions of the CDPA[4]. But in *FAPL v Luxton*[5] the Court of Appeal confirmed that the defendant had infringed the claimant's copyright by means of his commercial use of domestic TV decoder cards that had been purchased abroad, rejecting his contention that he had a defence under Art 56.

1   See **paragraph 13.03**.
2   (Case 262/81). In a subsequent case, the CJEU considered the compatibility of an exclusive licence with Art 101: see **paragraph 13.12**.
3   *Football Association Premier League Ltd v QC Leisure; Karen Murphy v Media Protection Services Ltd (Cases C-403/08 and C-429/08)*.

4   *Karen Murphy v Media Protection Services Ltd [2012] EWHC 466.*
5   *Football Association Premier League Ltd v Luxton [2014] EWHC 253 (Ch).*

EU competition law and copyright: Arts 101 and 102 of the TFEU

13.06 Article 101[1] prohibits (amongst other things) agreements between undertakings that have as their object or effect the prevention, restriction or distortion of competition within the internal market. Article 102[2] prohibits the abuse by one or more undertakings of a dominant position within the internal market or a substantial part of it. The said prohibitions only apply where trade between Member States may be affected.

1   See **paragraphs 13.08–13.13** below.
2   See **paragraphs 13.14–13.19** below.

Parallel provisions in UK law

13.07 In the UK, the Competition Act 1998 introduced two main prohibitions, which are closely modelled on Arts 101 and 102 of the TFEU. The first, the Chapter I prohibition, prohibits (amongst other things) agreements which have as their object or effect the prevention, restriction or distortion of competition within the UK and which may affect trade within the UK. Provisions which have such an effect will be void, unless they are exempted under certain EU or UK block exemptions or individual exemption. The second, the Chapter II prohibition, prohibits any conduct on the part of one or more undertakings which amounts to the abuse of a dominant position in the UK in a market if it may affect trade within the UK. Under s 60 of the Competition Act 1998, the UK courts and authorities are obliged, where possible, to interpret questions arising under it in a manner which is consistent with EU jurisprudence.

Article 101(1) – agreements restricting competition

13.08 Article 101(1) contains the following examples of the prohibited agreements referred to in **paragraph 13.07**, namely those which:

'(a)   directly or indirectly fix purchase or selling prices or any other trading conditions;

(b)   limit or control production, markets, technical development or investment;

(c)   share markets or sources of supply;

(d)   apply dissimilar conditions to equivalent transactions with other trading parties, thereby placing them at a competitive disadvantage; or

(e)   make the conclusion of contracts subject to acceptance by the other parties of supplementary obligations which, by their nature, or according to commercial usage, have no connection with the subject of such contracts'.

In addition to 'agreements' between undertakings, Art 101(1) also prohibits decisions by associations of undertakings and concerted practices, if they 'have as their object or effect the prevention, restriction or distortion of competition within the internal market'.

Appreciable effect

13.09 The CJEU has held that an agreement will only infringe Art 101(1) where the effect on trade between Member States and the restriction of competition is appreciable. The European Commission ('the Commission') has declared that agreements involving undertakings operating at the same level of trade (ie horizontal agreements) and having an aggregate market share of no more than 10%, and agreements between parties at different levels of trade (vertical agreements) and having an aggregate market share of no more than 15%, will not generally be considered as having an appreciable effect on trade between Member States[1].

1   Commission, Notice on Agreements of Minor Importance: 2014/C291/01.

Effect of infringing Art 101(1)

13.10 Provisions of agreements which infringe Art 101(1) will be void and unenforceable by virtue of Art 101(2). Such unenforceable provisions might render the entire agreement unenforceable, if the provisions in question are fundamental to the agreement as a whole. In other cases, the unenforceable provisions may be severable. Whether the provisions are fundamental or can be severed will usually be a matter for a court having jurisdiction in respect of the agreement and will be decided under the governing law of the agreement.

Parties to an agreement that infringes Art 101(1) may be subject to fines imposed by the Commission. The fines imposed on each party can amount to up to 10% of its total annual worldwide turnover (including the turnover of any parents or subsidiaries)[1].

Any third party who suffers loss as a result of the infringing provisions may be entitled to sue for, and recover, damages in the national courts.

1   In practice, fines are imposed in respect of serious infringements of Art 101(1), such as market partitioning or price fixing.

The possibility of exemption

13.11 Before 1 May 2004, the parties to commercial agreements that infringed Art 101(1) could notify them for an exemption to the Commission, which was empowered to grant exemptions if the criteria in Art 101(3) were met. The key advantage for parties to agreements of notifying their agreements was that for the period from the date of notification they could not be fined (unless the Commission took the unusual step of withdrawing the immunity), although the other consequences of infringing Art 101(1) – including fines and actions in local courts by adversely-affected third parties – were unaffected.

Since 1 May 2004, the procedure described above has no longer been possible and the parties must assess for themselves whether their agreement is caught by the prohibition contained in Art 101(1) and, if so, whether it satisfies the criteria for an individual exemption under Art 101(3). In order to meet the latter, it is necessary that the agreement:

> 'contributes to improving the production or distribution of goods or to promoting technical or economic progress, while allowing consumers a fair share of the resulting benefit'[1].

However, the exemption criteria are not met if the agreement imposes on the undertakings concerned restrictions which are not indispensable to the achievement of these objectives or affords 'such undertakings the possibility of eliminating competition in respect of a substantial part of the products in question.'[2]

Guidelines have been published by the Commission to assist with the application of Art 101(3)[3] to agreements, and the Commission has also published a number of block exemptions which exempt entire classes of contractual arrangements, provided that they fall entirely within the scope of the block exemptions. There is no applicable block exemption that is dedicated to agreements concerning copyright. However, the Vertical Agreements Block Exemption[4] may apply to exempt various provisions relating to (amongst other things) copyright from falling within Art 101(1). And the Technology Transfer Block Exemption[5] applies to (amongst other things) bilateral software copyright licensing agreements and ancillary provisions relating to copyright, provided that the market share thresholds[6] are met. It does not cover non-software copyright; however, the Commission explains in the accompanying Guidelines that it will apply the principles set out in the block exemption to licences of copyright for the production of contract products (but not to the licensing of rights in performances and other related rights)[7].

1   Article 101(3).
2   Ibid.
3   Commission Notice *Guidelines on the Application of Article 101(3) of the Treaty* (2004/C 101/08).
4   Regulation 330/2010.
5   Regulation 316/2014.
6   For agreements between competitors, one of the conditions for the block exemption to apply is if the combined market share of the parties does not exceed 20% on the relevant market(s). For agreements between non-competitors, one of the conditions for the block exemption to apply is that the market share of each of the parties does not exceed 30% on the relevant market(s).
7   *Guidelines on the application of Art 101 of the TFEU to technology transfer arrangements* (2014/C89/03) paras 48–49.

Exclusive copyright licences and Art 101

13.12 A key question in the case of copyright licences is the extent to which exclusivity can be granted without infringing Art 101(1), or, if it is infringed, the circumstances in which an exemption is justified.

In determining the application of Art 101(1) to licence agreements, the Commission considers:

- whether the agreement restricts competition that would have existed in the absence of the agreement; and
- whether any individual provisions of the agreement are more restrictive than would appear to be objectively necessary.

The position under Art 101(1) was considered in the *Coditel (No 2)* case[1]. The CJEU held that although an exclusive licence to exhibit a film in the territory of a Member State did not per se infringe Art 101(1), it would do where it created 'artificial and unjustifiable' economic barriers or generally restricted competition. For example, Art 101(1) would be likely to be infringed where the agreement, assessed in the context of other similar agreements in the industry, substantially foreclosed the market, for example by materially affecting the ability of third parties to enter or expand their activities in the market.

In one case, exclusive 15-year licences to broadcast a large number of films in the MGM/United Artists film library were granted to a group of public German television broadcasting organisations (ARD). The Commission granted an exemption to the agreements, but only after ARD agreed to modify its licence to permit the licensor to grant licences in respect of its films to other broadcasters within the same geographical area during fixed periods varying from two to six years (known as 'windows')[2]. The Commission expressed its concern that an exclusive licence of large quantities of content, such as, in this case, an entire library, would amount to an artificial barrier to competition. Other television stations would be unable to obtain the rights to a large pool of titles, including those which the licensee elected not to show.

Where exclusivity is granted for particular windows and the licensor remains free to license the particular programmes to third parties outside such windows, and where the exclusivity only applies to a particular distribution platform, the risk of interference by the authorities will be less likely, especially where there are competing suppliers of programming.

This was applied in *Telenor/Canal+/Canal Digital*[3], in which Canal+ sold its 50% shareholding in the satellite pay TV distribution platform Canal Digital to the other shareholder, Telenor and, to ensure the continuity of the service, the parties entered a long-term exclusive agreement for the DTH satellite distribution of Canal+'s premium pay

TV and pay-per-view services. The Commission was able to exempt the agreement after the parties agreed to reduce the duration of the exclusivity rights. The Commission also required the parties to eliminate restrictions which were not related to the pay TV market, particularly rights of first refusal concerning the acquisition and marketing of premium content through new media platforms.

The grant of exclusive rights has been extensively examined in the context of premium sports rights and, prior to 1 May 2004, the Commission granted several exemptions under Art 101(3). In this context, in reviewing the effect of exclusivity in licences of premium content licences, the Commission was concerned about the effect of those rights on downstream markets, and particularly new media rights. In the cases examined by the Commission, the restrictions found by it were a result of joint selling or the pooling of rights by sellers, resulting in the concentration of rights and the risk that a single buyer could acquire all the rights.

For example, in the UEFA exemption[4], the Commission's concerns were that the rights were licensed in each national market to a single broadcaster for three years (with only limited sublicensing), clubs were prevented from licensing their own rights in many cases, and new media rights were not exploited. In order to satisfy the requirements of Art 101(3), the Commission required the licences granted to be limited in scope and duration. UEFA agreed to offer 15 different packages for a period of three years (including three live packages), and provided for the co-exploitation of new media rights by the clubs and the leagues for certain rights to be exploited by the clubs alone.

The leading cases in recent years on the interface between Art 101 and exclusive broadcasting licences in the context of premium sports have involved restrictions imposed by the Football Association Premier League on its broadcasting licensees designed to prevent members of the public from accessing the broadcasts outside the licensed territories. These restrictions have been found by the CJEU[5] to infringe Art 101 by virtue of partitioning national markets and eliminating competition, and were found not to qualify for an exemption under Art 101(3). Applying this ruling, the English High Court allowed a high profile appeal by a publican, Karen Murphy, against her previous criminal conviction for having screened broadcasts of Premier League football matches by the use of a foreign decoder[6].

1   *Coditel SA v Ciné Vog Films SA (No 2) (Coditel (No2)) Case 262/81.*
2   Film purchases by German television stations IV31.734 (89/536/EEC) Official Journal L284, 03.10.1989, pp 36–44.
3   Case COMP/C2/38.287.
4   UEFA COMP 37.398, Joint selling of the commercial rights of the UEFA Champions League.
5   See **paragraph 13.05**, n 3.
6   See **paragraph 13.05**, n 4.

Co-operative joint ventures and Art 101

13.13 In part because of the cost of establishing and operating television services, there has been a significant number of mergers and joint ventures in the media sector. Although a discussion of mergers law is beyond the scope of this *User's Guide*, it is worth noting that joint ventures which are of a co-operative nature rather than a form of merger may infringe Art 101(1) where the joint venture parties are actual or potential competitors who would otherwise be competing, and/or the agreement contains restrictions on the parties' commercial freedom which are not ancillary to the creation or operation of the joint venture's actual or potential competitors.

Article 102 – abuse of a dominant position

13.14 Any abuse by one or more undertakings of a dominant position within the internal market or in a substantial part of it is prohibited to the extent that it may affect trade between Member States. Such abuses are not exhaustively defined, but Art 102 specifies a number of examples of abuse:

'(a) directly or indirectly imposing unfair purchase or selling prices or unfair trading conditions;

(b) limiting production, markets or technical development to the prejudice of consumers;

(c) applying dissimilar conditions to equivalent transactions with other trading parties, thereby placing them at a competitive disadvantage;

(d) making the conclusion of contracts subject to acceptance by the other parties or supplementary obligations which, by their nature or according to commercial usage, have no connection with the subject of such contracts'.

Like Art 101, Art 102 has been subject to a large number of decisions before the CJEU and of the Commission, and a detailed review is beyond the scope of this *User's Guide*.

Meaning of 'dominance'

13.15 Dominance is considered to exist where an undertaking has the ability to act independently of competitors, customers and consumers[1]. It is not assessed purely in terms of market share, although market shares of 30% and over may be indicative of dominance. This largely depends on the structure of the market, the position of key participants within the market and the existence of barriers to entry. To assess market share it is necessary to define the relevant product market. Regard should be had, when assessing the definition of the market, to other products which are substantially interchangeable with the relevant products in question.

In one case, the CJEU considered the circumstances in which a record producer would be considered as dominant:

'the manufacturer should have the power to impede the maintenance of effective competition over a considerable part of the relevant market, having regard in particular to the existence of any producers marketing similar products and to their position on the market. If recording artists are tied to the manufacturer by exclusive contracts consideration should be given, inter alia, to their popularity on the market, to the duration and extent of the obligations undertaken and to the opportunities available to other manufacturers of sound recordings to obtain the services of comparable performers.'[2]

1   *Hoffmann-La Roche & Co AG v EC Commission (Case 85/76) [1979] ECR 461.*
2   *Deutsche Grammophon Gesellschaft mbH v Metro SB-Großmärkte GmbH & Co KG, [1971] ECR 487, paras 17–18 (Case 78-70).*

Meaning of 'abuse'

13.16 It is the *abuse* of the dominant position, rather than the dominant position itself, which is prohibited by Art 102. The CJEU has held that the concept of abuse 'is an objective concept relating to the behaviour of an undertaking in a dominant position which is such as to influence the structure of a market'[1]. Yet the distinction between conduct which is permissible and conduct which amounts to abuse can be a difficult one to make. It will be a question of fact and degree in each case, and will depend on such factors as normal industry practice, the effect on competitors, and customers, the intention of the dominant firm and the proportionality of the conduct.

1   *Hoffmann-La Roche & Co AG v EC Commission (Case 85/76) [1979] ECR 461 at 541.*

Examples of 'abuse'

13.17 Examples of behaviour which has in the past been held to be abusive include:

* imposing unfair prices (eg, excessive, predatory or discriminatory prices);
* imposing unfair trading conditions;
* discriminatory treatment of equivalent transactions and/or persons;
* refusal to supply;
* bundling of goods and/or services.

Collective licensing societies raise specific issues under Art 102. These are considered in **Chapter 12**.

Refusal to license

13.18 One of the leading cases on the circumstances in which a refusal to license copyright will infringe Art 102 is the *Magill TV Guide* case[1]. The case arose out of the refusal in the 1980s of the BBC, RTE and ITP (the owners of copyright in TV listing information for terrestrial television in UK and the Republic of Ireland respectively) to license their TV programme schedules for publication to Magill TV Guides other than on a restrictive basis. At the time each broadcaster produced a guide based on its own television information, and therefore no comprehensive guide existed. Magill wanted to produce a comprehensive weekly television guide covering the services of all broadcasters, and complained to the Commission that the refusal to license meant that it was unable to do so.

The Commission found that there had been an abuse of a dominant position under Art 102, and this was confirmed on appeal by the General Court and, on a subsequent appeal, by the CJEU. The latter held that a dominant firm's refusal to grant a licence did not in itself constitute an abuse of a dominant position, but that a refusal to grant a licence may amount to abusive conduct where:

- the refusal to license prevents the creation of a new product for which there is potential customer demand;
- there is no objective justification for the refusal; and
- the effect of the refusal is to reserve a secondary market to the dominant firm.

In *Magill*, the TV companies were reserving to themselves the secondary market of weekly television guides by excluding all competition in the market. This was denying access to the information essential for the compilation of a comprehensive weekly guide.

At the time of the *Magill* judgment, it was suggested that the principles established by the court were an application of the 'essential facilities' principle which was developed in the context of access to port facilities to the effect that a company in a dominant position which also controls access to infrastructure that is essential to competing in the market must have a valid reason ('objective justification') for refusing access to the infrastructure. However, when the issue was reconsidered in the *IMS Health* case[2], the CJEU did not base its judgment on essential facilities principles.

The *IMS Health* case concerned a refusal by IMS to grant a licence to a competitor, NDC, to use the copyright in a database known as the '1,860 brick structure' which had become the standard way of analysing sales of pharmaceutical products in Germany. NDC used a similar structure for the market studies that it sold. IMS successfully sued NDC for copyright infringement, and thereafter NDC sought, and was refused, a licence of IMS's copyright. NDC complained to the Commission that IMS was abusing its dominant position.

In ruling on the question of whether the refusal was an abuse of a dominant position, the CJEU found that the following circumstances would be considered sufficient to justify a compulsory licence:

- there must be no objective justification for the refusal to license;
- the use of the intellectual property rights in question must be indispensable to operating on the relevant market and the refusal of a licence must eliminate all competition on that market;
- the person seeking the licence must have intended to produce new goods and services that would have met specific consumer requirements not met by the copyright owner's goods and services;
- there must be at least potential consumer demand for the new goods and services.

In other words, the refusal to license must prevent the introduction to the market of a new and innovative product for which there is demand from consumers.

More recently, Microsoft has been held to have abused its dominant position by refusing to provide information needed by third party providers of operating systems to achieve interoperability with Microsoft PC operating systems. The initial decision was made by the Commission in 2004[3]; it was subsequently upheld on appeal by the General Court[4], in which it was held that enough information needed to be provided to make sure that competitors could properly compete on the market on the same footing as the dominant undertaking.

1 *P Radio Telefis Eireann (RTE) and Independent Television Publications Ltd (ITP) v Commission of the European Communities (Joint Cases C-241/91 P and C-242/91).*
2 *IMS Health GmbH v NDC Health GmbH (Case C-418/01).*
3 *Microsoft: COMP 37.792.*
4 T-201/04.

Tying

13.19 The decisions in the *Microsoft* case[1] also found that Microsoft had been acting abusively by 'tying', the first time that this abuse had been found in a case concerning intellectual property rights. The decisions relied on principles enunciated by the Commission in other decisions[2] based on Art 102(d). It was found that as the Windows operating system is all-pervasive in the market for PC operating systems, Microsoft had been able to abuse its super-dominant position by 'tying' the sale of Windows Media Player with the Windows operating system as a single package. Essentially, the dominant nature of the 'tying' product (Windows) meant that the 'tied' product (Windows Media

Player) would foreclose the market in media players and software to competition.

1 See **paragraph 13.18**.
2 *Tetra Pak (Case C-333/94)* and *Hilti AG v Commission of the European Communities (C-53/92 P)*.

Chapter 14

The protection of databases

Introduction

14.01 A database is simply a collection of information which is organised in a particular way. The word 'database' was not even mentioned in UK copyright legislation until 1997, although English courts have historically been more inclined to afford copyright protection to works which may be described as 'databases' than some of their other European counterparts[1]. In the UK the courts usually protected such works as 'tables or compilations'[2]. The disparity in the legal protection afforded to databases in different EU Member States was the primary reason for Directive 96/9/EC of the European Parliament and of the Council on the Legal Protection of Databases ('the Database Directive'), which was implemented in the UK by the Copyright and Rights in Databases Regulations 1997[3] ('the 1997 Regulations'). In brief, the 1997 Regulations protected databases as a new category of literary work protected by copyright, and also introduced an additional *sui generis* property right in databases, 'database right'. The provisions dealing with databases as literary works were added to the CDPA by way of amendments; the provisions dealing with the *sui generis* right, on the other hand, are only to be found in the 1997 Regulations.

The owner of a database may therefore look to at least two possible tiers of protection (ie copyright and the database right) for his or her work. Compilations and tables receive yet another tier of protection. This is over and above any copyrights which exist in any material included on the database. Unfortunately the result is a fairly complex framework.

1 See **paragraph 2.02**.
2 Ibid.
3 SI 1997/3032.

Definition of a 'database'

14.02 For the purpose of the CDPA (as amended) a 'database' means 'a collection of independent works, data or other materials which: (a) are arranged in a systematic or methodical way, and (b) are individually accessible by electronic or other means'[1]. This closely follows the definition in the Database Directive. In this context the phrase 'or other means' indicates that databases are protected notwithstanding that they do not use electronic storage methods. So, a paper filing system or a newspaper may be capable of protection as a database.

The wording of the Database Directive recites a number of categories of work which are intended to be excluded from the definition, including computer programs used for making or operating electronic databases, recordings, films, literary and music works[2]. Under the Database Directive, a music compilation is also expressed to be outside the meaning of database[3].

1   CDPA s 3A(1).
2   Recitals 17 and 23.
3   Recital 19.

Databases as literary works

14.03 The fact that English courts have traditionally adopted a lower test for originality than other European jurisdictions is discussed in detail elsewhere in this *User's Guide*[1].

However, reflecting the EU sensibilities guiding the Database Directive, the amended CDPA imposes a requirement that a database can only be considered an original literary work if (by reason of the selection or arrangement of its contents) it 'constitutes the author's own intellectual creation'[2]. No similar criteria apply to the test of establishing whether a table or compilation should receive copyright protection. So, one of the effects of the 1997 Regulations was to increase the burden on a person seeking to establish that a database (as opposed to a table or compilation) qualifies for copyright protection. The requirement of 'intellectual creation' is therefore an additional hurdle for rightholders. A database which is entirely the production of mechanical processes or a software program will not be protected by 'database copyright'.

In *Infopaq International a/s v Danske Dagblades Forening*[3], the CJEU said that the intellectual creation of the author could be evidenced 'from the form, the manner in which the subject is presented and the linguistic expression', and could be expressed through the author's 'choice, sequence and combination of those words'. It found that an extract of as little as 11 words could be enough to embody the author's own intellectual creation.

The CJEU returned to this issue in *Football Dataco Ltd v Yahoo! UK Ltd*[4], a case that involved the defendant's unauthorised exploitation of the claimant's football fixture lists of English and Scottish leagues. It was held that databases could only be protected by copyright if the selection or arrangement of their contents was 'original' in the sense of being the result of the author's own intellectual creation. Without such originality the labour and skill required to set up the database would not justify copyright; and, in assessing the subsistence of copyright, the intellectual effort and skill of creating the data was irrelevant.

As with other literary works (except computer-generated works), the author will be the person who creates the database. If the database is computer-generated, its author is the person by whom the arrangements necessary for the creation of the database are undertaken[5].

Broadly, a database which receives copyright protection may be infringed in all the ways that a literary work may be infringed[6]. However, several special provisions also exist in relation to copyright databases as a consequence of the 1997 Regulations:

- *Infringing acts*: as with computer programs, the restricted act of adaptation in the context of a copyright database means an 'arrangement or altered version of the database, or a translation of it'[7].
- *Fair dealing:* use of a copyright database for research for a non-commercial purpose may only be 'fair dealing' if it is accompanied by a sufficient acknowledgement[8].
- *Permitted acts*: copyright in a database is not infringed if a person who has the right, by licence or otherwise, to use the database (or any part of it) does any act in exercising his or her rights which is necessary for the purpose of accessing and using the content of the database (or part). Significantly, this permitted act cannot be prohibited or restricted by a contract between the owner and the user. Any term that purports to do so will be deemed void[9].

1　See **paragraph 3.01**.
2　CDPA s 3A(2).
3　Case C-5/08.
4　Case C-604/10.
5　CDPA s 9(3); see **paragraph 9.03**.
6　See **Chapter 7**.
7　CDPA s 21(3)(ac); see **paragraph 6.09**.
8　See **paragraph 8.02**.
9　CDPA ss 50D and 296B.

Database right

14.04 Regardless of whether a database is capable of receiving copyright protection as a literary work, it will be protected in principle by the *sui generis* database right if 'there has been a substantial investment in obtaining, verifying or presenting the contents of the database'[1]. This formulation emphasises the nature of the protection offered by database right, which is intended to protect the economic rather than the intellectual investment in its creation. Since database right is a separate intellectual property right that is different from and independent of copyright, it falls outside the main scope of this *User's Guide*, and the discussion of it in the remainder of this chapter is therefore abbreviated.

The meanings of the expressions 'obtaining', 'verifying' and 'substantial investment' were considered in the case of *British Horseracing Board Ltd v William Hill Organisation Ltd*[2], in which the CJEU held that to qualify for protection under the Database Directive, there must be a 'substantial investment' (qualitative and/or quantitative) in creating the database. The relevant investment, it held, was restricted to that involved in 'the obtaining, verification or presentation of the contents', that is 'seek[ing] out existing independent materials and collect[ing] them in the database'. It did *not* include the actual 'creation as such of independent materials'.

In subsequent rulings relating to football fixtures[3] the CJEU refused to accept that the *sui generis* database right could exist in football fixtures, followed by the English Court of Appeal in *Football Dataco Ltd v Yahoo! UK Ltd*[4], though subsequent attempts by defendants in English litigation to rely on the above principles in order to argue that claimants were not entitled to database right have been unsuccessful[5].

1   1997 Regulations, reg 13(1).
2   *Reference for a preliminary hearing under Article 234 EC, from the Court of Appeal on the case of British Horseracing Board Ltd v the William Hill Organisation Ltd (Case C-203/002).*
3   The football fixtures references were: *Fixtures Marketing v OPAP (Case C-444/02) [2005] IPLT 453, Fixtures Marketing v Oy Veikkaus (Case C-46/02) [2005] IPLT 490* and *Fixtures Marketing v Svenska Spel (Case C-338/02) [2005] IPLT 520.*
4   [2010] EWCA Civ 1380.
5   *British Sky Broadcasting Group Plc v Digital Satellite Warranty Cover Ltd [2011] EWHC 2662 (Ch)*, and the joined cases *Football Dataco Ltd v Stan James Plc, and Sportradar GmbH [2013] EWCA Civ 27.*

Database right: ownership

14.05   The first owner of a database right is the 'maker' of the database[1]. Again, in line with the aim of protecting the 'risk taker' behind the database, 'maker' is defined for these purposes as the 'person who takes the initiative in obtaining, verifying or presenting the contents of a database and assumes the risks of investing in that obtaining, verification or presentation'[2]. If all these functions are undertaken by more than one person, then the database will be considered a work of joint authorship so that the database right will vest jointly in all those persons[3].

As with copyright works, the first owner of the database right in work undertaken by an employee in the course of his or her employment will (in the absence of an agreement to the contrary) be the employer[4]. The case law considering the ambit of the analogous copyright principle will also be relevant here[5]. The Crown is deemed to be the maker of a database where the database is made by an officer or servant of the Crown in the course of his or her duties[6]. Similarly, if a database is made by or under the direction of the House of Commons or the House of Lords, the owner will be deemed to be the relevant House. If both, the Houses of Parliament will be joint makers[7].

1   1997 Regulations, reg 15.
2   1997 Regulations, reg 14(1).
3   1997 Regulations, reg 14(5).
4   1997 Regulations, reg 14(2).
5   See **paragraph 9.11**.
6   1997 Regulations, reg 14(3).
7   1997 Regulations, reg 14(4).

Database right: qualification

14.06 The qualification criteria for the database right differ significantly from copyright works. Database right is a creature of EU law and thus protection is only afforded to works which, in essence, qualify as of EU origin. To qualify for database right, the maker (or one of the joint makers) of the database must, at the material time, be a natural person who is a national of or resident in an EEA state, a body (eg a limited company) incorporated under the laws of an EEA state, or a partnership or other unincorporated body formed under the laws of an EEA state[1]. Where the maker is an incorporated body, or a partnership or other unincorporated body, there is an additional requirement that it has its 'central administration or principal place of business' in the EEA, or that its registered office is in the EEA and its operations 'are linked on an ongoing basis with the economy of an EEA state'[2].

1   1997 Regulations, reg 18(1), which contains corresponding provisions relating to the Isle of Man.
2   1997 Regulations, reg 18(2), which contains corresponding provisions relating to the Isle of Man.

Database right: duration

14.07 Database right continues until expiry of the later of 15 years after the end of the year of its completion, or 15 years after the end of the year in which it is first made available to the public (provided that that period starts within 15 years after the end of the year of its completion)[1]. So if, for example, a database was completed on 30 December 2000, but not made available to the public until 30 December 2015, any database right in it will survive until 31 December 2030. It is in the nature of most databases that they are periodically reviewed and updated. If the revision is substantial enough to qualify for protection in its own right[2] then it will receive a database right of itself for its own period of protection[3].

1   1997 Regulations, reg 17.
2   Ie there is sufficient investment; see **paragraph 14.04**.
3   1997 Regulations, reg 17(3).

Database right: restricted acts and infringement

14.08 Database right is infringed if a person *extracts* or *re-utilises* all or a substantial part of the contents of a database without the owner's consent[1], and the exclusive licensee of a database is entitled to commence and maintain proceedings for database right infringement in its own name[2]. Furthermore, the repeated and systematic extraction or re-utilisation of insubstantial parts of the contents of the database may amount to the extraction or re-utilisation of a substantial part of those contents[3].

For these purposes, 'extraction' is defined as 'the permanent or temporary transfer of those contents to another medium by any means or in any form', and 're-utilisation' means 'making those contents available to the public by any means'[4].

So, for example, copying a substantial part of a qualifying electronic database of telephone numbers onto a computer hard disk, or printing out hard copies of it, or converting, say, a database of addresses into labels to be attached to envelopes, would or could amount to 'extraction' and infringe the database right if undertaken without the owner's consent. Similarly, including a substantial extract in a broadcast or distributing copies to the public would or could constitute '*re-utilisation*' and so infringe the database right in the absence of consent.

In *British Horseracing Board Ltd v William Hill Organisation Ltd*[5] and in subsequent cases[6] the CJEU has ruled on what constituted 'extraction', 're-utilisation', transfer and 'substantial part'. English cases[7] have examined, amongst other things, the test of substantiality.

1   1997 Regulations, reg 16.
2   1997 Regulations, reg 23.
3   1997 Regulations, reg 16(2).
4   1997 Regulations, reg 12(1). For examples of English court rulings that extraction and/or re-utilisation had occurred, see *Magical Marking Ltd v Holly [2008] EWHC (Ch) 2428*, *Forensic Telecommunications Services Ltd v West Yorkshire Police [2011] EWHC 2892 (Ch)*, and *Technomed Ltd v Bluecrest Health Screening Ltd [2017] EWHC 2142 (Ch)*.
5   See **paragraph 14.04**.
6   *Directmedia Publishing GmbH v Albert-Ludwigs-Universität Freiburg (Case C-304/07)*; *Apis-Hristovich EOOD v Lakorda AD (Case C-545/07)*; *Innoweb BV v Wegener ICT Media BV, Wegener Mediaventions BV (Case C-202/12)*.

7   *Football Dataco* (see **paragraph 14.04** above); *Beechwood v Guardian [2010] EWPCC 12.*

Database right: avoiding contractual limitations

14.09 A term which purports to limit the extraction or re-utilisation of a database by a 'lawful user' (ie a person having a right to use the database, either because of licence or otherwise) is void[1].

1   1997 Regulations, reg 19(2).

Database right: exceptions to infringement and permitted acts

14.10 Fewer exceptions to database right infringement are provided by the 1997 Regulations than are provided in relation to copyright infringement. There is, for example, no exception for 'fair dealing' for the purpose of criticism, review or news reporting, or in relation to libraries[1] and archives. However, extraction of a substantial part of a database that has already been made available to the public is permitted if the person making that extraction is otherwise a lawful user of the database (eg it has a licence from the owner), the source is indicated, and the extraction takes place for the purpose of providing an illustration for teaching or research (other than for commercial purposes)[2]. A number of other exceptions to database infringement are set out in the 1997 Regulations[3]. Essentially, these relate to public administration. So, database right is not infringed by things done in relation to Parliamentary or judicial proceedings, Royal Commissions and statutory inquiries, or by extraction from databases open for public inspection or on official registers. Similarly, there are limited rights enabling the Crown to extract and re-utilise substantial parts of databases communicated to it by the owner for a public purpose, if that use could reasonably have been anticipated by the owner, enabling the use of public records and undertaking acts for which statutory authority has been granted.

1   Except for deposit libraries: 1997 Regulations, reg 20A(1).
2   1997 Regulations, reg 20(1).
3   1997 Regulations, Sch 1.

Database right: assumptions and presumptions

14.11 Database right will not be infringed by an extraction or re-utilisation of substantial parts of a database if:

'(a) it is not possible by reasonable inquiry to ascertain the identity of the maker, and
(b) it is reasonable to assume that the database right has expired'[1].

Also, there is a rebuttable presumption that where a name purporting to be the maker's name, or a year of first publication, is recorded on copies of a database, it will be correct, and that (in essence) the author has not created the database during the course of one of a number of specific relationships (such as employment) by which a third party is the first owner of the database right[2].

1   1997 Regulations, reg 21(1).
2   1997 Regulations, reg 22.

Database right: remedies

14.12 With the exception of the lack of any right to require delivery up or seizure, the remedies available for infringement are the same as copyright infringement, as are the rights of exclusive licensees[1]. There are no express criminal remedies.

1   1997 Regulations, reg 23; see **paragraphs 7.11** ff.

Database right: licensing

14.13 Licensing schemes and bodies are considered in detail elsewhere in this *User's Guide*[1]. The 1997 Regulations provide for licensing bodies to conduct schemes in relation to the database right, which will be subject to the jurisdiction of the Copyright Tribunal[2].

1   See **Chapter 12**.
2   1997 Regulations, regs 24 and 25.

Database right: transitional provisions

14.14 The 1997 Regulations apply to all databases, whenever created[1], although acts done prior to commencement on 1 January 1998, or afterwards pursuant to pre-existing agreements, will not infringe database right[2]. Also, copyright databases which were created on or before 27 March 1996 and were still in copyright immediately prior to 1 January 1998 will continue to receive copyright protection during the full copyright term[3]. For databases completed on or after 1 January 1983, which receive a database right as of 1 January 1998, that right will have continued for 15 years following 1 January 1998[4].

1   1997 Regulations, reg 27.
2   1997 Regulations, reg 28.
3   1997 Regulations, reg 29.
4   1997 Regulations, reg 30.

Part 2
Copyright in use

Chapter 15

Publishers and printers

Introduction

15.01 Publishers and printers deal mainly with literary and artistic works and, to a lesser degree, with dramatic and musical works. This chapter highlights some of the special copyright problems that they encounter. However, much of **Part 1** of this *User's Guide* is applicable to publishers[1]. Issues regarding newspapers, magazines and periodicals are dealt with separately[2]. Electronic publishing is also dealt with separately[3].

1   References to those paragraphs particularly applicable to publishers and printers are listed in **paragraph 15.16**.
2   See **Chapter 16**.
3   See **Chapter 24**.

Definitions

15.02 'Literary work' is defined by the CDPA as meaning:

'any work, other than a dramatic or musical work, which is written, spoken or sung, and accordingly includes –

(a)   a table or compilation other than a database,
(b)   a computer program,
(c)   preparatory design material for a computer program, and
(d)   a database'[1].

'Writing' is defined as including 'any form of notation or code, whether by hand or otherwise and regardless of the method by which, or medium in or on which, it is recorded, and "written" shall be construed accordingly'[2].

Other significant activities include 'adaptation'[3] and 'publication'[4].

Definitions applicable to 'artistic works' (relevant in the case of book illustrations) are considered in detail elsewhere in this *User's Guide*[5].

1   CDPA s 3(1).
2   CDPA s 178.
3   CDPA s 21(3)(a).
4   See **paragraphs 4.05** and **4.06**.
5   See **paragraph 2.06**.

Ownership

15.03 The owner of copyright in a book is prima facie the author, even if the book has been specially commissioned[1]. If the publisher wishes to be the first owner (and this has certain advantages for it) of a book that it has commissioned, then the commissioning agreement must provide that copyright is assigned to the publisher[2]. Future copyright can be assigned even though it is not in existence at the time when the assignment is made[3].

In practice, books often contain contributions from several people, including illustrators, photographers, editors, designers and typesetters, as well as a primary author. In the book publishing industry it is, in most cases (the educational sector is a common exception) unusual for the publisher to acquire more than an exclusive licence from authors who are not staff writers. In the case of contributions by staff members, the copyright in any literary, dramatic or artistic work which is produced in the course of employment will belong to the employer without requiring any special assignment[4]. Nevertheless, publishers should have written contracts of employment with staff writers, illustrators and editors who make contributions to avoid disputes as to whether their work was in fact done in the course of employment.

In some cases, the use of artistic works as illustrations may be cleared on a collective licensing basis through the Design and Artists Copyright Society[5].

1   See **paragraph 9.02**.
2   See **paragraph 9.22**.
3   See **paragraph 9.24**.
4   See **paragraphs 9.11** ff.
5   See **Appendix 1**.

Quotations and acknowledgements

15.04 When including a quotation in a book, the questions for the publisher are 'Would the unauthorised reproduction of the quotation constitute prima facie infringement of the original work?', and, if so, 'Is one of the statutory fair dealing defences available?'[1]. If not, a licence should be sought from the owner of the copyright in the original work.

The common (but not uniform) practice is for the publisher and not the author to decide whether an acknowledgement for a quotation from another work is required. If so, the publisher will often seek consent for the use of the quotation from the publisher of the work quoted, even though, as a matter of law, it may not consider any consent or even any acknowledgement is necessary.

1   See **paragraph 7.07**.

Foreign authors

15.05 Where there is any doubt as to the ownership of a work written by a foreign author, legal advice should be sought in the country concerned. In the case of works written by authors resident in, or citizens of, the USA, or which have first been published in the USA, it is advisable to arrange for a search to be made at the Library of Congress in Washington. There are a number of firms in Washington specialising in this service[1].

1   See **Appendix 1** for details.

Assignments and licences

15.06 An assignment of copyright from an author invariably offers better protection for a publisher of a copyright work than a mere licence[1]. However, when a publisher takes rights from an author it is unlikely that, unless there are unusual circumstances, or in certain sectors such as educational publishing, it will require (or in any event obtain from a well-advised author) more than an exclusive licence.

When a publisher takes rights from another publisher, it is advisable for the former to undertake 'due diligence' to ensure that the latter has the rights which it purports to own (eg requiring it to provide a copy of its agreement with the author). If it is intended to make any use of the work in the USA, a search at the Library of Congress should also be made[2].

In most cases an assignment from one publisher to another will apply only to some of the restricted acts applicable to the book.

When an assignment or licence comes to an end (remembering that an assignment can be limited in point of time)[3] there may be an issue as to what happens with any stock remaining unsold. If the publisher continues to sell copies after the expiry of its assignment or licence, it may infringe the restricted act of issuing copies to the public[4]. It is therefore vital that any limited term licence or assignment deals adequately with the need for a 'sell-off' period after the end of the term.

If a publisher takes an assignment or licence of publishing rights, it will not necessarily be obliged to publish the book, but an obligation to publish may be inferred under certain circumstances. If a publisher enters into a contract with an author under which it is given the exclusive rights to the author's works over a period of time and the publisher does not accept any obligation to publish the works during that period but only to pay a royalty in the event of publication, then the court may hold that such a contract is unenforceable as being 'a restriction of trade' or oppressive against public policy. The reason for this is that such a contract, if enforced against an author, would prevent him or her from earning his or her living by writing books for other publishers, even though the publisher with whom he or she had entered into a contract was refusing to publish his or her works.

It is therefore vital for both parties to a publishing agreement to express the extent of the publisher's obligation to publish (or otherwise to exploit) the author's work.

1   See **paragraph 9.21**.
2   See **paragraph 15.05**.
3   See **paragraph 9.22**.
4   See **paragraph 6.05**.

Ownership of manuscripts

15.07 The manuscript of a work will belong prima facie to its author, unless there is an agreement to the contrary. Ownership of the manuscript is unrelated to ownership of copyright[1] in the work embodied in the manuscript. Even if there is an outright assignment of the publishing rights to that work, the publisher will have no rights over the manuscript, although leaving the manuscript with another person may eventually result in a deemed abandonment of the personal property in the manuscript.

If an author fails, or refuses, to deliver a manuscript in accordance with the terms of a publishing agreement, the publisher may be entitled to sue him or her for damages or, if it can be shown that the author in fact completed the book, to seek an order of the court requiring the author to deliver the manuscript. If the author has not yet written the book, the rights of the publisher are likely to be limited to damages. A court will not order an author to write a book. Today publishers normally require manuscripts to be delivered in electronic form, and often require the author to maintain a back-up copy.

1   See **paragraph 9.01**.

Reversionary copyright

15.08 Assignments and licences of copyright made by authors before 1 July 1957 become ineffective on the expiration of 25 years from the date of the death of the author even if the author did not die until after June 1957[1]. At that point in time the rights in the work revert to the estate of the author, irrespective of the existence of any assignments made in the author's lifetime. Publishers, therefore, should always obtain confirmatory assignments from the executors or administrators of the estates of those deceased authors who had assigned works to them before 1 July 1957. Alternatively, if the author is still living they can now obtain such a grant from the author himself or herself[2].

1   Copyright Act 1911 s 5.
2   CDPA Sch 1, para 27.

Publishing agreements not considered

15.09 It is beyond the scope of this *User's Guide* to consider the terms of publishing agreements generally, although in any event, many if not most problems arising under publishing agreements are likely to be matters of contract rather than copyright. A common difficulty with both new and existing contracts is determining how far traditional 'volume form' grants of rights for print on paper extend into new forms of digital exploitation[1].

1   See **paragraph 9.30**.

National libraries: obligation to deposit

15.10 The publisher of every book published in the UK is required to deliver, within one month after the date of publication, at its own expense, a copy of the book to the British Library Board. In addition if it receives a written demand before the expiration of 12 months from the date of publication, the publisher is required within one month after the receipt of the written demand to deliver at its own expense a copy of the book to each of the following libraries: the Bodleian Library, Oxford; University Library, Cambridge; the National Library of Scotland; the Library of Trinity College, Dublin; and the National Library of Wales[1]. The British Library Board requires that until a publisher (who publishes the same content both in print and in digital media) has successfully registered for depositing content digitally, it should continue to deposit the content in print.

Copies of trade publications do not have to be delivered to national libraries.

Foreign books printed abroad and published in England are not usually required to be delivered, unless the British publisher has its name printed in the book as a publisher.

A publisher that fails to comply with these requirements is liable to a fine.

1   See the Legal Deposit Libraries Act 2003, whose provisions were extended to non-print media as well by the Legal Deposit Libraries (Non-Print Works) Regulations 2013 (SI 2013/777). The latter (inter alia) entitle the deposit libraries listed above to request the delivery of works published online, and permit them to copy prescribed works from the internet.

Importation of books

15.11 A book that has been published outside the UK may not be imported (except for private or domestic use) if the importer knows or has reason to believe that it is an 'infringing copy' (ie a copy the printing of which in the UK would have infringed the copyright of the copyright owner or an exclusive licensee of the right to make copies of the work in the UK). This is a 'secondary infringement' of copyright, the details of which are considered in detail elsewhere[1]. It should be noted that this principle is subject to the important qualification that importation of copies from another EEA state where they have been distributed with the authorisation of the owner, will not infringe copyright due to the operation of the doctrine of 'exhaustion of rights' in Europe[2].

1   See **paragraph 6.10**.
2   See **paragraphs 6.05** and **13.04**.

International copyright protection

15.12 It is most important to include the © symbol followed by the name of the copyright owner and the date of first publication on all books.

Firstly, this will assist in securing the widest possible copyright protection for the work in those countries which have adhered to the Universal Copyright Convention. The notice must be placed in such manner and location as to give reasonable notice of claim of copyright. In effect this means proximate to the title page. It is not considered advisable to place the notice at the end of the work, although no precise position is stipulated in the Convention[1].

Secondly, such a notice assists in proving in an infringement action that the alleged infringer knew that the work was in copyright (it is a defence in secondary infringement actions to show that the defendant did not know that the work was in copyright)[2].

1   See **paragraph 4.16**.
2   See **paragraph 7.23**.

Published editions of works

15.13 The copyright in a published edition of a book is quite distinct from the copyright in the work itself. See the Table of Incidence of Copyright in **Appendix 2** for the period of copyright, the restricted acts, general exceptions and first owner of published editions. The publisher is deemed to be the author of the typographical arrangement, not the printer[1].

1   CDPA s 9(2)(d), and see **paragraphs 2.11** and **5.11**.

Typefaces: exception for use of typefaces in printing

15.14 The design of a typeface is in principle entitled to copyright protection as an artistic work[1]. However, the CDPA permits the use of typefaces which are in copyright if the typeface is used in the ordinary course of typing, composing text, typesetting or printing[2]. Nor is it an infringement of copyright to possess an article for the purposes of such use or to do anything in relation to material produced by such use[3].

However, where persons make, import, possess or deal with equipment for printing in a particular typeface, then notwithstanding this general exception, the copyright owner of the typeface can obtain remedies under the 'secondary infringement' provisions of the CDPA[4]. Where articles specifically designed or adapted for producing material in a typeface entitled to copyright protection have been marketed by or with the licence of the copyright owner, the copyright in the typeface expires 25 years from the end of the calendar year in which the first such articles were marketed[5].

1 **Paragraph 2.06.** Software used to display electronic fonts will also usually be protected by copyright. Users should apply such software in compliance with the relevant licence agreement. See **paragraph 16.11.**
2 CDPA s 54(1)(a).
3 CDPA s 54(1)(b) and (c).
4 See **paragraph 6.10**.
5 CDPA s 55.

Moral rights

15.15 Authors will almost certainly wish to assert their right to be identified (the *paternity right*)[1]. This should be stated in the contract with the publisher[2]. Contracts by publishers with their sub-licensees should oblige the sub-licensees to comply with the obligation to identify the author in the same terms as those contained in the contract with the author.

The author will also usually have the right to object to the derogatory treatment of his or her work (the *integrity right*)[3]. Unlike the paternity right, this right does not need to be asserted[4]. A lurid and unsuitable cover to a book may be regarded by its author as a derogatory treatment. Similarly, inappropriate artistic works in the form of photographs or illustrations to a book may be subject to the same objections. Unless the author specifically waives the integrity right in the contract with the publisher, his or her consent should be obtained to the covers, artwork and to any editing of the work. A publisher may seek a waiver but agree specific contractual approvals.

It is worth noting that the rights of paternity and integrity do not apply to publications in encyclopaedias, dictionaries and other collective works, which are specifically excluded from the application of these rights[5].

The moral right of privacy of photographs may also be relevant where publishers are including photographs in a book[6]. It is not the subject of the photograph who can object to the inclusion of a photograph on the grounds of the moral right of privacy, but the person who commissioned the taking of it. It may not always be easy to find out beyond doubt whether a photograph was specially commissioned. Therefore, publishers should seek warranties from the author, photographer or other person who is providing the photograph to the publisher to the effect that it was not commissioned, other than by the person providing the photograph himself or herself. If the photograph was commissioned by a third party, then a waiver should be sought from the latter for the use of the photograph in the book. It should be remembered that the right to privacy of photographs only arises in the case of photographs which have been commissioned for private and domestic purposes, which will narrow the field considerably. Moreover, it does not apply to photographs taken before 1 August 1989.

1   See **paragraphs 10.02** ff.
2   See **paragraph 10.08**.
3   See **paragraphs 10.12** ff.
4   See **paragraph 10.17**.
5   See **paragraph 10.18**.
6   See **paragraph 10.24**.

General

15.16 Reference should be made to the Table of Incidence of Copyright in **Appendix 2** for the period of copyright, restricted acts, general exceptions, and rules as to first owners applicable to literary works, artistic works, photographs, engravings and published editions of works[1].

The special problems faced by publishers in the field of copyright arise mainly in connection with assignments and licences. The problems of infringement and plagiarism which have to be faced by publishers every time they consider publishing a book are not special to publishers, and reference should be made to **Part 1** for a general discussion of infringement[2].

Some of the high-profile copyright infringement cases decided within the last 15 years, as discussed elsewhere in this *User's Guide*[3] involved book publishers. For cases relating to the publication of newspapers, magazines and periodicals, see **Chapter 16**.

The major challenges to copyright posed by the growth in 3D printing are outside the scope of this *User's Guide*.

1   The following paragraphs in **Part 1** of this *User's Guide* are also particularly relevant when dealing with literary works in the context of publishing:
Definition of literary works – **2.02**;
Fixation – **2.05**;
Definition of artistic works – **2.06**;
Definition of graphic work – **2.06**;
Copyright in published editions – **2.11**;
Qualification for copyright protection – **4.01–4.06**;
Publication – **4.05**;
Term of copyright and publication right – **Chapter 5**;
Restricted acts in literary, dramatic, and musical works – **6.02** ff;
Principal exceptions and defences – **8.01**;
Fair dealing and sufficient acknowledgement – **8.03** ff;
Ownership in literary, dramatic, musical and artistic works – **9.03**;
Ownership in published editions – **9.07**;
Ownership in works by joint authors and co-owners – **9.08**;
Assignments and licences – **9.21** ff;
Moral rights and false attribution of authorship – **10.01** ff.

2   See **Chapters 6** and **7**. In addition, reference should be made to **Chapter 3** as to originality.

3   For example, *Michael Baigent and Richard Leigh v The Random House Group Ltd [2007] EWCA Civ 247*; and *Paul Gregory Allen (acting as trustee of Adrian Jacobs (deceased)) v Bloomsbury Publishing plc (2) Joanne Kathleen Murray (professionally known as JK Rowling) [2010] EWHC 2560 (Ch)*.

Chapter 16

Newspapers, magazines and periodicals

Introduction

16.01 The main copyright issues which face the editors, journalists and other persons involved with newspapers, magazines and periodicals, concern the ownership of the copyright in the separate contributions and the quotation or re-use of copyright material from elsewhere. Most 'print media' publishers have developed significant digital products (both 'online' and 'offline'), and consequently the importance of ensuring the copyright has been adequately dealt with in publishers' arrangements with contributors has never been greater. Newspapers, magazines and periodicals can be 'compilations' of other works and such compilations attract copyright independent of the copyright in their contents[1]. If the separate contributions which make up the whole qualify for copyright protection they too will each be entitled to their own separate copyright. A newspaper will also constitute a 'published edition'. The typographical arrangement of the newspaper will be entitled to copyright protection[2]. Typographical content is unlikely to exist in less than a page. When considering what constitutes a 'published edition' for these purposes, it is necessary to consider the newspaper as a whole, not as individual articles[3].

1 See **paragraph 2.02**.
2 See *Newspaper Licensing Agency v Marks & Spencer plc [2001] UKHL 38*.
3 See **paragraph 2.11**.

Definition

16.02 There is no definition of 'newspaper', 'magazine', or 'periodical' in the CDPA. In practice, it is unlikely that there will be much difficulty in determining whether or not a particular publication falls within the expression. If a journal, for example, was published on an occasional, rather than a regular basis, with an identical format, it might be a periodical. But such a publication, published without any regularity, and without similarity as to format (even though having the same title) may well not be a periodical for the purposes of copyright law.

Contributor's copyright

16.03 The Copyright Act 1956 contained a provision as to the ownership of copyright in contributions to newspapers, magazines and similar periodicals. It provided that in the case of a literary, dramatic or artistic work made by an author in the course of his employment under a contract of employment or apprenticeship by the proprietor of a newspaper, magazine or similar periodical, and made for the purpose of publication in a newspaper, magazine or similar periodical, the proprietor of the newspaper, etc, was entitled to the copyright in the work – but only in so far as the copyright related to publication in *any* newspaper etc.

The CDPA removed this provision. The rules regarding the ownership of copyright in material produced by newspaper employees are now the same as for any other literary, dramatic, musical or artistic works produced by employees. The copyright in works produced by such employees in the course of their employment under a contract of employment vests in the employer, in the absence of any agreement to the contrary[1].

It is matter of fact in every case whether a person providing services is an independent contractor or is working under a contract of employment. A writer who contributes one article a week to a newspaper, who works from home and who has reasonable choice as to the form and content of the article, may well not be working under a contract of employment[2].

The ownership of the copyright in photographs is considered in detail elsewhere[3].

The principle is the same as for text: the copyright in a photograph by a staff photographer working under a contract of employment for a newspaper will usually belong to the newspaper. But copyright in photographs submitted by outsiders will vest in the person who 'created' the photograph. In the absence of special arrangements, it will not belong to the person who commissioned it[4]. Attention should also be given by publishers to the right of privacy in certain photographs[5].

Increasingly, the power of individuals to negotiate special terms, and the complexity of benefits packages made available to both employees and independent contractors, can make the question as to which category the arrangement falls into difficult to determine.

1   See **paragraphs 9.11** ff.
2   See **paragraph 9.12**.
3   See **paragraphs 25.03** and **25.19**.
4   See **paragraphs 9.02** and **9.16**.
5   See **paragraphs 10.24** ff.

Freelance and unsolicited contributions

16.04 Freelance material is frequently delivered under short deadlines. In these circumstances, imposing assignments or express licences of copyright may be impracticable. If there is no express agreement, it may be possible to imply a licence to use the material. The publisher, however, must be cautious about relying on implied licences. A court will only uphold an implied licence to the extent that it is necessary to give business efficacy to the initial arrangement[1].

In *Banier v News Group Newspapers Ltd*[2], a newspaper relied unsuccessfully upon industry practice as a defence to a damages claim where it used a photograph without an express licence, on the basis that the photograph was needed urgently and the licence fee would be paid subsequently. An implied licence may be inadequate for the publisher wishing to make additional use of material over and above its initial inclusion in a print publication (such as including it on an archival database or adding it to an online news service). A publisher may issue 'standard terms of acceptance' to contributors who have no written contract. The National Union of Journalists and bodies representing photographers have, however, led vocal campaigns against 'digital rights grabs'.

When an unsolicited contribution (such as a letter to the editor) is received by a newspaper, it is again a matter of construction as to whether or not the author intends the letter to be published. If there is an intention to publish, then a licence giving the newspaper the right to publish the work may be implied, but this implied licence will be narrow in scope, its extent depending upon the circumstances.

1   See **paragraph 9.29** and *Ray v Classic FM plc [1998] FSR 622*, which involved the creation of a database of classical music selected for broadcast.
2   [1997] FSR 812.

The news

16.05 Copyright arises not because of originality of an idea or item of news, but because it is reduced to a material form and qualifies as a literary work. Copyright attaches to the form rather than to the idea[1]. It follows that there is no copyright in unwritten news and the only copyright which attaches to the news is the manner in which it is presented. The courts have given protection in certain cases to news agencies which sell news, but on grounds of breach of contract, or of breach of confidence or privacy, rather than copyright.

It is common for news publishers to receive input from news and photo agencies, which form a valuable source of information and copyright material. This material will be provided under the terms of licence arrangements allowing specified uses. For the publisher, the extent of his reproduction and distribution rights under the licence will be of key concern[2], as will its ability to edit the material at its discretion. Given the general issues which arise in relation to the licensing of copyright material, a well-advised publisher will seek appropriate protection from the licensor, such as warranties that he has the right to make the material available, and suitable indemnification against breach.

It is also common practice for journalists to rewrite news stories from the information contained in other articles. In these cases, the question will be whether a 'substantial part' has been copied, or whether a defence to copyright infringement may be established on the basis of fair dealing[3].

1   See **paragraphs 1.03** and **2.13**.
2   See **paragraphs 6.02** ff.
3   See **paragraphs 7.06** and **8.03** ff.

Quotations

16.06 Newspapers often quote or otherwise use other copyright material. The fact that a newspaper, having used its best endeavours to trace the owner of the copyright in the quotation, is unable so to do, does not give that newspaper the right to publish a copyright work. Copyright will be infringed if a substantial part of the original work is published. 'Substantial' does not necessarily mean substantial in proportion to total length. If it is the most important part of the original work, then a relatively short extract could be a substantial part[1].

If a substantial part is published, no effort having been made to trace the copyright owner, a newspaper can be subject to heavy damages. On the other hand, if the newspaper proprietor, having made reasonable enquiries, is unable to ascertain the identity of the author, the copyright in the work which is being quoted will not be infringed, provided that:

•   copyright has expired; or
•   the author died 70 years or more before the beginning of the year of publication of the relevant issue of the newspaper etc[2].

This exception does not apply to Crown copyright, nor to a work of joint authorship which is still in copyright where it would have been possible to identify one of the authors.

1   See **paragraph 7.06**.
2   CDPA s 57; see **paragraph 8.19**.

Fair dealing: reporting current events

16.07 Fair dealing with a literary, dramatic or musical work is not an infringement of the copyright in the work if it is for the purpose of reporting current events in a newspaper, magazine or similar periodical, provided it is accompanied by a sufficient acknowledgement[1].

A 'sufficient acknowledgement' means an acknowledgement identifying the work in question by its title, or other description, and also identifying the author. However, it is not necessary to identify the author if the work was published anonymously, or if in the case of an unpublished work it would not be possible to identify the author by reasonable enquiry[2].

The fair dealing provisions in the CDPA, regarding the reporting of current events, do not extend to photograph, so newspapers may not publish a photograph of some current event taken by another newspaper and then attempt to avoid a breach of copyright action by claiming the benefit of the fair dealing provisions[3].

1 See **paragraph 8.07**.
2 See **paragraph 8.19**.
3 See **Chapter 8** for a fuller discussion of these issues.

Fair dealing: criticism and review

16.08 The fair dealing provisions of the CDPA also extend to the use of all kinds of copyright works for the purpose of criticism or review provided that the work has been 'lawfully made available to the public' (following the implementation of the Copyright and Related Rights Regulations 2003[1]). Again it is necessary that the work be accompanied by a sufficient acknowledgement unless this turns out to be impossible[2].

1 SI 2003/2498 ('2003 Regulations').
2 See **paragraph 8.07**, and see Information Society Directive (2001/29/EC), Art 5(3)(c)

Use of notes or recordings of spoken words

16.09 The copyright in the words of an interviewee will vest in the interviewee, notwithstanding that they may be recorded by the interviewer. However, the CDPA contains a specific provision to the effect that it is not an infringement of the copyright in spoken words, as a literary work, to use a record of them for the purpose of reporting current events provided that certain conditions are met[1].

Where the contribution of the interviewer qualifies for copyright protection, its use will also require proper authorisation.

1 See **paragraph 8.20**.

Pseudonyms

16.10 Although there is no copyright in a title[1], if a contributor to a newspaper uses a nom de plume, on leaving that newspaper he can take the nom de plume with him. Therefore, newspaper proprietors sometimes provide in contracts of service that the contributor shall have no right to use the nom de plume, except for articles written for the commissioning employer's paper.

1   See **paragraph 3.02**.

Digital issues and newspapers, magazines and periodicals

16.11 Newspapers, magazine and periodicals commonly employ digital methods for transmitting information in the process of producing and exploiting their publications[1]. All significant newspaper publishers in the UK now have an on line presence. The significance for the publisher is to ensure that the arrangements by which he has acquired content are sufficient to enable him to include and exploit that content as part of his 'online' service[2], and to allow him to use the content to the extent necessary for him to include it on the online service. Increasingly this may require the interpolation of the material with other material as part of an interactive presentation. Paying close attention to the wording of licence agreements is more necessary than ever[3].

Inevitably, the ability to exploit newspaper and similar formats 'online' also enables the publishers to use films and sound recordings in his service in a way previously unavailable. Issues regarding the use of films and sound recordings in online services are considered in detail elsewhere[4].

Publishers should note that not merely the content, but also any software element of its electronic publication is properly cleared (eg search engines, screen displays, software enabling manipulation etc).

Particular problems also arise in the context of the use of software for generating fonts. The CDPA provides that no copyright infringement occurs where a typeface is used in the ordinary course of typing, composing text, typesetting or printing. Nor is it an infringement to do anything in relation to material produced by such use, or to possess articles for the purpose of such use. It follows that an electronic copy which is typeset using font software will not, per se, render the publisher liable for infringement.

However if, say, the electronic transmission of material involves the transfer of font software itself, this may result in an infringement. So, for example an infringement may arise where software for generating fonts is transferred to a publisher by a person transferring a copy digitally. The publisher should therefore seek assurances from any persons making digital transfer of copy that (where font software is to be transferred) an appropriate authorisation has been obtained from the owner to allow such transfer to take place.

1   For a view of the issues see *PRCA v Newspaper Licensing Agency Ltd* [2013] UKSC 18.
2   As to licensing and assigning copyright, see **Chapter 9**.
3   For a further analysis of the moral right of integrity, see **paragraphs 10.12** ff.
4   See **Chapter 24**.

Chapter 17

Schools, universities and other educational establishments

Introduction

17.01 Schools, universities and colleges make extensive use of copyright material. Literary, dramatic, musical and artistic works, recordings, films and broadcasts (both television and radio) are all used in educational establishments.

The use of copyright material in educational establishments involves doing many of the acts subject to the copyright owner's exclusive right (the 'restricted acts') and so generally requires permission. In particular, copying works, performing works in public, making adaptations (for example, translations), causing recordings to be heard in public and showing films in public are all activities regularly undertaken in educational establishments. The term 'public' here includes a subset of the public such as staff and students.

However, the CDPA recognises that educational establishments are a special case and accordingly makes special provision for them, both in the exceptions to copyright and in the copyright licensing rules of Chapter 7 of the CDPA giving the government power to extend existing schemes or to order that a new scheme be instituted.

Definitions

17.02 The CDPA defines an 'educational establishment' as:

- any school; and
- any other description of educational establishment specified by statutory instrument[1].

Schools are themselves defined by reference to various Education Acts in such a way that virtually all schools in the UK are covered. Similarly, the classes of educational establishment specified in the relevant statutory instrument[2] cover almost all universities and colleges in the higher education sector, colleges of further education and theological colleges.

1 CDPA s 174(1).
2 Copyright (Educational Establishments) Order 2005, SI 2005/223.

Copying of literary, dramatic, musical and artistic works and published editions

17.03 The exclusive rights of copyright owners – the restricted acts – are subject to various copyright exceptions of general application as discussed in **Chapter 8**. There are also several exceptions specific to educational establishments. These specific exceptions were subject to considerable change in 2014, implemented by the Copyright and Rights in Performances (Research, Education, Libraries and Archives) Regulations 2014[1] ('the 2014 Regulations') passed as part of the government's reform of copyright. The general exceptions of particular relevance to educational establishments are briefly discussed first and then the education-specific exceptions are dealt with.

The 2014 Regulations also introduced a provision to protect some of the exceptions from being excluded or restricted by contractual terms. Thus in many exceptions any contractual term is unenforceable 'to the extent that it purports to prevent or restrict the doing of an act permitted' by the relevant exception (the 'no contract override' provision).

1 SI 2014/1372.

General exceptions

Research and private study

17.04 It is not generally appreciated that there is no exception in UK law for personal copies. An intended amendment to the CDPA to introduce a 'personal copies for private use' exception as part of the government's 2014 copyright reforms was subject to a judicial review of the provision[1]. The verdict was that the government's decision not to provide fair compensation to copyright owners for the harm they might suffer as a consequence, as required by EU law, was based on 'wholly inadequate' evidence. Given that the private copying exception could cause significant harm to copyright owners, the lack of any provision for fair compensation paid meant that the government's decision to introduce such an exception was unlawful. As a result the new exception was quashed.

1 [2015] EWHC 1723.

17.05 The only exception, therefore, that deals with personal or private copies is one that relates to 'fair dealing' with a copyright work for the purposes of research for a non-commercial purpose, provided that it is accompanied, if practicable, by an acknowledgement of the title and author (a 'sufficient acknowledgement') or for private study[1]. This exception was amended by the 2014 Regulations which extended the exception to cover all forms of copyright works and not just literary, dramatic, musical or artistic works (and the typographical arrangement in such works). It therefore now applies also to films, sound recordings and broadcasts. It is also now subject to the 'no contract override' provision.

The CDPA defines 'private study' as excluding any study which is either directly or indirectly for a commercial purpose[2]. Therefore the making by an individual person of single copies may, depending on the extent of the amount copied, amount to a 'fair dealing' under the exception. But the making of multiple copies is highly unlikely ever to amount to a 'fair dealing' as it will probably either conflict with the author's normal exploitation of the work or prejudice unreasonably the author's legitimate interest which are some of the principles contained in the international copyright treaties[3] to which the UK is party and which therefore underpin the concept of 'fairness' in UK law. Furthermore, the CDPA[4] provides that where a person making the copies is someone other than the researcher or student himself and that person knows, or has reason to believe, that the copying will result in copies of substantially the same material being provided to more than one person at the same time and for substantially the same purpose (ie classroom copying) it is not 'fair dealing'. There are similar provisions for librarians making copies[5].

1   See **paragraphs 8.03–8.07**.
2   CDPA s 178.
3   Berne Convention 1886.
4   CDPA s 29(3).
5   See **Chapter 18**.

Criticism, review, quotation and news reporting

17.06 The 2014 Regulations also added 'quotations' to the 'fair dealing' exception for criticism, review and news reporting[1] so that the use of a short quotation necessary and relevant to an essay or academic paper is not an infringement of copyright. This is also now subject to the 'no contract override' provision.

1   CDPA s 30.

Education-specific exceptions

17.07 The education-specific exceptions, prior to the 2014 Regulations, covered three broad areas: (a) reprography (the making of multiple copies of literary, dramatic or musical works by mechanical or electronic means); (b) the performance of literary, dramatic or musical works; and (c) the recording of broadcasts. These exceptions were substantially amended by the 2014 Regulations and the reprography exceptions in particular were extended to a wider class of copyright works and to cover, or to cover more clearly, the use of digital technology such as interactive whiteboards so that the significance of the term 'reprography' is now much reduced.

Illustration for teaching

17.08 This exception[1] had previously applied only to literary, dramatic, musical or artistic works being copied 'in the course of instruction' by a teacher *provided* it was not done by a 'reprographic process'[2]. Colloquially known as the 'chalk and talk' exception aimed at inadvertent copyright infringement caused, for example, by writing something up on a blackboard or a whiteboard, it has now been extended to provide a more general 'fair dealing' exception for education, albeit now limited to 'illustration for teaching purposes'.

The exception now applies to all forms of copyright work and covers acts of copying done for the sole purpose of illustration for instruction, provided it is for a non-commercial purpose and done by a person giving or receiving instruction (or preparing to give or receive instruction). 'Giving or receiving instruction' includes setting, communicating and answering exam questions.

The copying must amount to a 'fair dealing' and contain a sufficient acknowledgement. There is no longer any requirement that the copying must be done by a reprographic process and, as above, films and sound recordings are covered provided that the use is a fair dealing and limited to illustration for teaching. The exception does not now apply only to educational establishments but covers any form of teaching that complies with these requirements. The exception is subject to the 'no contract override' provision.

1 CDPA s 32.
2 A 'reprographic process' is defined by the CDPA s 178 as a process for making facsimile (ie identical) copies or involving the use of an appliance for making multiple copies.

Copying and use of extracts by educational establishments

17.09 This exception[1] had previously applied to reprographic copying (see above) by educational establishments of passages from published literary, dramatic or musical works. Following the 2014 Regulations it now applies also to copying of films and sound recordings, although it still excludes broadcasts (see below) and artistic works *unless* an artistic work (such as a photograph or illustration) is incorporated into another work. The exception covers copying:

- by, or on behalf of, an educational establishment;
- for a non-commercial purpose;
- of less than 5% of any one work in a 12-month period (it had previously been limited to 1% per quarter).

The copies must be accompanied by a sufficient acknowledgement, unless it is impossible for reasons of practicality or otherwise.

The exception is also expressed to apply to any electronic communication to pupils and staff (again if for the purposes of instruction). Therefore delivering copyright content digitally eg via Virtual Learning Environments (VLEs), and interactive whiteboards and receiving it on laptops are not infringements. The copyright content communicated in this way may even be received outside the premises of the establishment provided it is done by means of a secure electronic network accessible only by staff and pupils.

The exception does not apply if, or to the extent that, licences are available which would authorise the copying in question and the educational establishment responsible for the copies knew or ought to have been aware of that fact. The exception has been tightened in one respect, as previously the test was limited to the knowledge of the person making the copies rather than the presumably wider institutional knowledge of the educational establishment in question.

1   CDPA s 36.

17.10 It is not just collective licensing schemes, such as that operated by the Copyright Licensing Agency (CLA), that disapply the exception; any relevant individual licences that are available also have that effect, But any such licence cannot restrict the amount of copying permitted to below the statutory 5% permission.

Apart from the CLA licence, collective licences can also be obtained from NLA media access (for newspapers and magazines); Printed Music Licensing Ltd for printed music in schools; and Christian Copyright Licensing International Ltd for hymns and other Christian music.

Making works available through dedicated terminals

17.11 Educational establishments also benefit from the new exception to the communication right introduced by the 2014 Regulations (taken directly from the EU Copyright Directive) for libraries, archives and museums to make copies of works available electronically to the public for the purposes of research or private study by means of dedicated terminals situated on their premises. This is discussed in more detail in **Chapter 18**.

Use of sound recordings, films and broadcasts

17.12 Virtually all educational establishments are equipped to record and play or show, films and broadcasts and sound recordings. These are all copyright works protected in their own right (as distinct from the rights in the underlying musical, dramatic and literary works which they record or contain). As for the restricted acts applicable to films, sound recordings and broadcasts, see the Table of Incidence of Copyright in **Appendix 2**.

Again there are a number of general and education-specific exceptions. The general exception for a 'fair dealing' with a work for the purposes of non-commercial research and private study was extended by the 2014 Regulations to include sound recordings, films and broadcasts as has been discussed above; the exceptions specific to education for performing, playing or showing a copyright work and the recording of broadcasts are now addressed.

Recording of broadcasts

17.13 A recording of a broadcast or a copy of such a recording may be made by an educational establishment (or on its behalf) for the non-commercial educational purposes of that establishment without infringing the copyright in the broadcast, or in any works included within the broadcast provided that it is accompanied by a sufficient acknowledgement[1]. The communication of such a recording, or a copy of it, to pupils or staff, is likewise not an infringement of copyright provided it is for the non-commercial educational purposes of that establishment. The 2014 Regulations widened the exception by allowing any such communication to be received outside the premises of the establishment provided it is via a secure electronic network accessible only by the establishment's pupils and staff. But the previous permission to communicate such recordings to 'the public', provided they were within the establishment's premises, has been removed.

The exception does not apply if, or to the extent that, licences are available authorising the recording or copying and the establishment knew, or ought to have known of the existence of those licences. The Educational Recording Agency Limited (ERA)[2] offers a collective licensing scheme which reflects the wider scope of the exception. The requirement that, for the exception to be displaced, any such licensing scheme must be certified in accordance with the CDPA s 143 was removed in the 2014 Regulations.

1   CDPA s 35(1).
2   See http://www.era.org.uk.

Performing, playing or showing of works in the course of educational activities

17.14 It is not a 'public performance' (for the purposes of copyright infringement) for a literary, dramatic or musical work to be performed before an audience which consists only of teachers and pupils and others directly connected with the activities of an educational establishment, provided that the performance is given either:

'(a) by the teacher or pupil in the course of the activities of the establishment; or

(b) at the establishment by any person for the purpose of instruction'[1].

Similarly, the copyright in a sound recording, film or broadcast will not be infringed by playing or showing it before such an audience at an educational establishment for the purpose of instruction.

The CDPA provides that a person is not for this purpose 'directly connected' with the activities of the establishment simply because he or she is a parent (or a guardian) of a pupil at the establishment. If, however, a parent has some other link to the establishment or its activities (eg as a member of the board of governors), he or she could be regarded as being 'directly connected' with the activities of the establishment.

The performance of a play for the benefit of the parents of pupils does not fall within the exception and would therefore constitute an infringement of copyright. Accordingly, when a school wishes to perform a play otherwise than in accordance with the conditions set out above, it must obtain a licence from the owner of the rights.

It is worth emphasising that the exception only applies 'for the purposes of instruction' so extracurricular uses (such as film clubs and after-school activities) are still subject to copyright and will require permission of the copyright owner or a collective 'blanket' licence – see for example the Performing Rights Society (PRS), Phonographic Performance Limited (PPL) and Mechanical Copyright Protection Society (MCPS) for playing and recording music, Filmbank and Motion Picture Licensing Company for showing of films[2].

1   CDPA s 34.
2   A useful website listing the organisations and licences available for schools is: http://www.copyrightandschools.org/.

Performers' rights

17.15 If an educational establishment wishes to make a film or a sound recording of a live performance of a play or musical work or of the reading of a literary work, the right of performers, as well the rights in any copyright literary, dramatic or musical work which is performed, will need to be properly cleared[1].

1   See **Chapter 11**.

Ownership of copyright by teachers

17.16 Teachers at all educational establishments produce a considerable amount of material which is entitled to copyright protection. This includes examination papers, teaching notes, lecture papers and the like. The author of a literary, dramatic, musical or artistic work is the first owner of the copyright unless the work was created under a contract of service, in which case the employer will generally own the copyright[1]. So, when a teacher prepares an examination paper in the course of his employment and he is an employee working under a contract of service, the copyright in that examination paper will usually belong to his employer without any formal assignment. If however, the teacher works outside his normal working hours to prepare lectures and notes for an entirely new course of study which he is subsequently invited to give to the school, the position will be less clear-cut. The teacher may well have an argument that the copyright material was not produced in the course of employment – unless of course his contract of employment specifically covered out of hours produced material. Each case would need to be considered on its merits.

1   See **Chapter 9**.

Lending by educational establishments

17.17 Lending a work is a restricted act but the CDPA provides an exception for education so that copyright is not infringed by the lending of copies of a work by an educational establishment[1].

1   CDPA s 36A.

Copyright licensing

17.18 The provisions of the CDPA dealing with licensing schemes and licences issued by licensing bodies were dealt with in **Chapter 12** but there are two further provisions on licensing schemes specific to education worth noting:

- the coverage of licensing schemes and licences to educational establishments authorising the making of reprographic copies may be extended, by order of the Secretary of State, to include works of a description similar to those covered by the scheme or licence. The compulsory inclusion of these works must not conflict, however, with the normal exploitation of those works or unreasonably prejudice the legitimate interests of the author;
- the Secretary of State can appoint a person to inquire into the question whether a new licensing scheme, or a general licence, is required to authorise the making by educational establishments of

reprographic copies of literary, dramatic, musical or artistic works not covered by an existing scheme or licence. If this results in a recommendation that a new licensing scheme or a general licence is required, and the recommendation is not implemented by copyright owners within one year, he can order that the making by or on behalf of an educational establishment of such reprographic copies shall be treated as licensed by the copyright owner.

Chapter 18

Libraries, archives and museums

Introduction

18.01 Cultural institutions such as libraries, archives and museums enjoy special status under copyright law allowing them to undertake a range of activities which would otherwise represent copyright infringement. In addition to providing a place to read and research books and other publications, libraries (and to a lesser extent, archives and museums) may lend or make copies of copyright works. The exceptions to copyright relevant to these institutions were amended in 2014 as part of the UK government's reform of copyright. The purpose was to simplify the law in this area and to widen both the types of copyright work to which the exceptions applied and the class of institutions that could benefit from the exceptions. Legislation dealing with 'orphan works' (copyright works where the owner cannot be identified or traced) was also introduced.

Definitions

18.02 A 'library' is defined[1] as a library which is either publically accessible or is a library of an educational establishment and a 'museum' includes a gallery. References to a librarian, archivist or curator include a person acting on their behalf.

The expression 'conducted for profit' in relation to a library, archive or museum, means a library, archive or museum which is established or conducted for profit or which forms part of, or is administered by, a body established or conducted for profit[2]. Therefore, the libraries of solicitors' and accountants' offices, pharmaceutical companies and the like, will be libraries 'conducted for profit' and unable to benefit from many of the exceptions.

A 'public library', which is relevant to the provisions on lending by libraries, is defined by the CDPA to mean a library administered by or on behalf of:

- in England and Wales, a library authority within the meaning of the Public Libraries and Museums Act 1964;
- in Scotland, a statutory library authority within the meaning of the Public Libraries (Scotland) Act 1955;
- in Northern Ireland, an Educational Library Board within the meaning of the Education and Libraries (Northern Ireland) Order 1986[3].

An 'orphan work'[4] is a 'relevant work' which, following a 'diligent search' (see **paragraph 18.12**), the copyright owner of the work (which includes an exclusive licensee) has not been identified or, if identified, has not been located. Where there are multiple copyright owners in the work, it is an orphan work if one or more of the copyright owners has not been identified following a diligent search or, if identified, has not been located. A 'relevant work' is broadly any copyright work first published in an EU Member State but notably not an artistic work such as a photograph (except to the extent that it is included in another copyright work).

1   CDPA s 43A.
2   CDPA s 43A.
3   CDPA s 178.
4   Copyright and Rights in Performances (Certain Permitted Uses of Orphan Works) Regulations 2014, SI 2014/2861.

Copying by libraries – generally

18.03 The CDPA provides a number of exceptions specific to libraries and similar cultural institutions often known as the 'library privileges'. These permit the copying, and sometimes the supply of copies, of copyright material. Many of the relevant provisions in the CDPA were considerably altered in 2014 by the Copyright and Rights in Performances (Research, Education, Libraries and Archives) Regulations 2014[1] ('the 2014 Regulations'). The previous law was a complex mix of detailed wording in the CDPA amplified, but often duplicated, by overlapping provisions in a separate statutory instrument. The provisions have been simplified and have now been incorporated into the CDPA. The main changes are to:

- extend the exceptions to include museums (including galleries) and archives as well as libraries;
- include all forms of copyright work, not just literary, dramatic or musical works, within the scope of the exceptions;
- simplify the procedure relating to the declarations that have to be given by users to whom copies are supplied under these exceptions. Declarations may be given electronically and no longer have to be personally signed by the individual;

- remove the restriction in many of the exceptions limiting their application to 'prescribed libraries' (being libraries designated by an Order of the Secretary of State). This has been replaced, where appropriate, by a reference to bodies (libraries, archives and museums) 'not conducted for profit';
- introduce an exception for making works available to the public through dedicated terminals.

Some of the acts permitted by these exceptions to copyright may also be undertaken by libraries which are conducted for profit. These are the supply of a single copy to another library, the making of a replacement copy in a permanent collection and the supply of a single copy of an unpublished work.

Another change which applies to many of the exceptions (and also to the exceptions for educational institutions) is that any contractual term is unenforceable to the extent that it purports to prevent or restrict the doing of an act permitted by the exceptions (the 'no contract override' provision).

1   SI 2014/1372.

Single copies of published works

18.04 This exception[1], permits librarians of libraries that are not conducted for profit to make and supply a single copy, for non-commercial research or private study, of one article in a periodical (that is a magazine, journal or newspaper) or a 'reasonable proportion' of any other *published*[2] copyright work provided that certain conditions are complied with (as to which see below). What is a 'reasonable proportion' is not defined but the accompanying government guidance[3] to the 2014 Regulations states that it means 'only a limited part necessary for the research project'. It should be borne in mind that while a book is a single literary work, so is a poem, short story or even a letter so care should be taken to identify the 'work' in question to ensure that only a 'reasonable proportion' of it is copied.

It is worth noting that the 2014 Regulations extended the scope of the exception to apply to all copyright works, not just literary, dramatic and musical works. It therefore now includes pictures, photographs and other artistic works, films, sound recordings and broadcasts.

The conditions that must be complied with for the exception to apply are that:

- the copy is supplied in response to a request from a person who has provided the librarian with a declaration in writing containing the information set out below;
- the librarian is not aware that the declaration is false in a material particular.

The declaration must include, in addition to the name of the person requiring the copy ('the requester') and the identity of the required material, a statement that:

- the requester has not previously been supplied with a copy of that material by any library;
- the requester requires the copy for a non-commercial purpose or private study (which also has to be non-commercial), will use it only for those purposes and will not supply a copy to any other person;
- to the best of the requester's knowledge, no other person with whom the requester works or studies has made, or intends to make, at or about the same time, a request for substantially the same material for substantially the same purpose.

These conditions reflect the provisions applying under the fair dealing exceptions (see **paragraph 17.05**) for students making copies for themselves, the rationale being that a librarian ought to be able to make copies lawfully for students (and others) where those students would have been permitted by the law to make the copies for themselves. Equally librarians cannot make multiple copies (eg for classroom use) just as students cannot themselves use the fair dealing exception for private study to make multiple copies for classmates.

There is no longer a requirement for the declaration to have a personal handwritten signature, so it may be signed electronically[4]. Nor is there now any *obligation* for the librarian to charge the requester for the copy, but if he or she does make a charge, the sum must be calculated by reference to the costs attributable to the production of the copy.

Any copy supplied consequent upon a declaration that is false in a material particular will be an infringing copy and the requester liable as such. The librarian would only be liable if he or she was actually aware that the declaration was false.

1   CDPA s 42A.
2   'Published' means that copies have been issued (or made available by an electronic retrieval system) to the public in sufficient quantity as to meet reasonable demand.
3   See   https://www.gov.uk/government/uploads/system/uploads/attachment_data/file/375956/Libraries_Archives_and_Museums.pdf.
4   'Writing' is defined to include any form of notation whether by hand or otherwise (CDPA s 178).

Copying by librarians or archivists of certain unpublished works

18.05 Libraries, whether or not conducted for profit, and also now archives, may make and supply a single copy of the whole or part of an *unpublished* copyright work[1]. In this case the whole, not just a reasonable proportion, of the work may be copied provided certain conditions are met. The conditions are that the copy is supplied in response to a request from a person who has provided the librarian with a declaration in writing containing certain information and the librarian is not aware that the declaration is false in a material particular.

The information the declaration must contain is the same as for the exception for single copies of parts of published material (described above) other than that there is no requirement for the requester to state that, to the best of the requester's knowledge, no other person with whom the requester works or studies has made, or intends to make, at or about the same time, a request for substantially the same material for substantially the same purpose.

If the work had been published before the document was deposited in the library or archive and the librarian or archivist is, or ought to be, aware of that fact, the exception does not apply and the library or archive would infringe copyright in supplying the copy.

Similarly, no copy of an unpublished work may be supplied if the copyright owner has prohibited copying of the work and the librarian or archivist is, or ought to be, aware of the prohibition.

1   CDPA s 43.

Supply of single copies for other libraries

18.06 A library, again whether or not conducted for profit, may make a single copy of part or even the whole of a published copyright work and supply it to another library, provided the library requesting the copy is conducted not for profit[1].

The exception does not apply, however, if the librarian making the copy did not at the time of making the copy know (and could not reasonably find out) the name and address of a person entitled to authorise the making of a copy, unless the copy requested is of an article in a periodical in which case the librarian may make a copy in any event. Again there is no obligation for the librarian to charge for the copy, but any sum that is charged must be calculated by reference to the costs attributable to the production of the copy.

1   CDPA s 41.

Replacement copies of works for libraries, archives and museums

18.07 A librarian, archivist or curator of any library, archive or museum (an 'institution') may make a copy from any item in its permanent collection either to preserve or replace that item in the collection or to replace an item in the permanent collection of another institution which has been lost, damaged or destroyed[1]. However, the following conditions must be complied with:

- the item in question must be: (a) included in the part of the collection kept wholly or mainly for the purposes of reference on the institution's premises; (b) included in a part of the collection not accessible to the public; or (c) an item which is available on loan only to other institutions;
- it must not be reasonably practicable for the librarian or archivist to purchase a copy of that item for replacement purposes. Note the slight difference here from the related condition applying to the exception for the supply of a single copy to another library[2] which requires that the librarian did not know, and could not reasonably find out, the name and address of a person entitled to authorise the making of a copy;
- the institution making a copy for its permanent collection can be any library, archive or museum, whether or not conducted for profit; likewise any institution can supply a copy under this exception but the recipient institution must be one conducted not for profit;
- where the copy is being supplied to other libraries a charge may be made but any such charge must be calculated by reference to the costs attributable to its production.

1   CDPA s 42.
2   See **paragraph 18.06**.

Copies of work required to be made as a condition of export

18.08 Under certain circumstances, the grant of an export licence for an article of cultural or historical importance or interest may only be granted subject to the condition that a copy of the article is made and deposited in an appropriate library or archive[1]. Where such a condition is imposed on export, then it is not an infringement of copyright to make that copy.

1   CDPA s 44.

Making works available through dedicated terminals

18.09 The 2014 Regulations introduced a brand new exception[1] to the communication right taken directly from the list of permitted exceptions in the EU Copyright Directive[2]. It permits libraries, archives and museums (and educational establishments) to communicate a work to the public or to make it available[3] to the public by mean of dedicated terminals situated on their premises.

This allows individual members of the public to access copyright works owned by the institution on computers in that institution's premises, provided it is for the purposes of research or private study. Note that here, unlike elsewhere, the term 'research' (reproducing exactly the words of the EU Copyright Directive) is not specifically qualified by the requirement that it be for non-commercial purposes even though the term 'private study', as defined by the CDPA[4], excludes any study which is directly or indirectly for a commercial purpose. This inconsistency appears to be an oversight. It is likely that the term 'research' would be construed narrowly given the need for the exception to comply with the requirements of the EU Copyright Directive that any exception should not conflict with a normal exploitation of the work or unreasonably prejudice the legitimate interests of the author.

A further, important, restriction is that the communication is made in compliance with any purchase or licensing terms to which the work is subject. It is not clear what this wording, again copied directly from the EU Copyright Directive, means in practice. Works acquired electronically will always come with their own purchase and licensing terms and most hard copy books, journals and magazines will have some form of copyright notice which may be relevant. On one interpretation this might mean that any work where the purchase or licensing terms prohibit further copying (as most are likely to) cannot be communicated under the exception – and there is no provision here preventing any 'contract override'. An alternative interpretation is that contractual terms cannot prevent the exception applying but any other contractual or licensing terms, so long as not in conflict with the exception, have to be observed.

There has been one decided case in the Court of Justice of the European Union ('CJEU') on the identical provision in the EU Copyright Directive (the *Darmstadt* case[5]) which seemed to suggest that only terms specifically concluded between the copyright owner and the institution for the purpose of the exception were relevant and that the terms of standard form sale or licensing agreements might not be applicable. It might be that this had more to do with the way the provision of the Directive was incorporated into German law and where the possibility of 'fair compensation' to the copyright owner may also have been relevant. A court in the UK would have to decide what Parliament intended. As this is not a mandatory exception that the UK had to implement, the exception could be interpreted more narrowly (although it could not be construed more widely) than the corresponding EU provision.

1   CDPA s 40B.
2   Directive 2001/29/EC.
3   Confusingly the wording in the exception refers both to 'communication' and 'making available' of the copyright work. But the CDPA s 20 defines 'communication' (meaning electronic transmission) to include making available (as well as broadcasting).
      Furthermore, the term 'making available' is itself described as being electronic transmission in such a way that members of the public can access the work 'in a place and at a time individually chosen by them'. This would conflict with the requirement of the exception (and of the permitted exception in the EU Copyright Directive) that

the transmission must be via a dedicated terminal on the establishment's premises. It is assumed that the reference to 'making available' is a mistake.

4 CDPA s 178.

5 *Technische Universität Darmstadt v Eugen Ulmer KG (Case C-117/13).*

Copying for archival purposes of sound recordings and broadcasts

18.10 Prior to the 2014 Regulations many of the above exceptions did not apply to sound recordings, films and broadcasts. As noted above the exceptions have been extended to cover all copyright works (and similar amendments have been made to performers' rights). There are two special provisions which permit the making and copying of sound recordings of folk songs and recordings of broadcasts for archival purposes:

- *Recordings of folk songs*: the words and music of a song may be recorded for the archive of a body conducted not for profit, provided that the song is unpublished and of unknown authorship at the time the recording is made[1]. The recording must not infringe any other copyright (eg another sound recording) and must not have been prohibited by any performer.

  Copies of such recordings may also be made and supplied by archivists in response to a request from a person (the 'requester') who has provided the archivist with a declaration in writing containing the information set out below and the archivist is not aware that the declaration is false in a material particular. The declaration must include, in addition to the name of the requester and of the relevant sound recording, a statement that:

  (a) the requester has not previously been supplied with a copy of that sound recording by any archivist;

  (b) the requester requires the copy for a non-commercial purpose or private study (which also has to be non-commercial), will use it only for those purposes and will not supply a copy to any other person.

- *Recording of broadcasts for archival purposes*: recordings of broadcasts, and copies of such recordings, may be made for the purpose of being placed in an archive of a body conducted not for profit[2].

1 CDPA s 61.

2 CDPA s 75.

Legal deposit

18.11 The provisions of the CDPA regarding the delivery of copies of books and other printed publications, and of non-print publications such as electronic journals and copies of websites, to the British Library and other national libraries are dealt with elsewhere in this *User's Guide*[1].

1   See **paragraph 15.10**.

Orphan works

The EU Orphan Works Directive

18.12 The government implemented the EU Directive on Certain Permitted Uses of Orphan Works[1] in 2014 as part of its package of copyright reforms[2]. This allows publicly accessible libraries, educational establishments, museums, archives, film or audio heritage institutions, and public service broadcasting organisations ('relevant bodies') to make certain permitted uses of orphan works.

The permitted uses are making the orphan work available to the public or reproducing it for the purposes of digitisation, making available, indexing, cataloguing, preservation or restoration. Before any use may be made of an orphan work, a 'diligent search' must have been carried out by the relevant body and recorded in the Office for Harmonisation in the Internal Market ('OHIM'). Such a search must as a minimum include:

- the relevant databases maintained by OHIM; and
- where there is no record that the relevant work is an orphan work in the OHIM databases, various other relevant sources are identified by the legislation. These include the databases of legal deposit libraries and other libraries, and the databases of publishers' and authors' associations, and collecting societies. The full list of sources to be searched by type of copyright work are listed in Part 2 of Schedule ZA1 introduced into the CDPA by the implementing Regulations.

Any revenues generated in the course of use of an orphan work must be exclusively used in covering the costs of digitising the orphan work and making it available to the public. The orphan work must be used solely in order to achieve the relevant body's 'public interest mission' such as the preservation or restoration of works in its collection or providing cultural or educational access to them. There must also be an acknowledgement of any author or other right holder who has been identified. Any breach of these requirements would remove the protection of the exception thus exposing the relevant body to civil and potentially criminal risk for copyright infringement.

1   Directive 2012/28/EU.
2   See the Copyright and Rights in Performances (Certain Permitted Uses of Orphan Works) Regulations 2014, SI 2014/2861.

The UK orphan works licensing scheme

18.13 At the same time as implementing the EU Orphan Works Directive, the UK government introduced its own orphan works legislation[1] pursuant to powers contained in ss 116A–116D of the CDPA[2]. The terms and conditions of the scheme are broadly similar to those in the EU Orphan Works Directive, although artistic works are covered and it allows anyone (not just libraries or similar cultural institutions) to apply online to the Intellectual Property Office (the 'IPO') for a licence to use orphan works.

An orphan works licence can be for commercial or non-commercial uses and can be granted for up to seven years (renewable).

Licences for non-commercial uses attract a nominal licence fee in addition to the application fee. Licence fees for commercial use are calculated to take account of market rates. The licence fee is held on behalf of the missing copyright owner for eight years by the UK's IPO so that the licence fee can be paid to the missing copyright owner should they come forward to claim within this period. After the eight-year period, the unclaimed licence fee can be used to cover the set-up and running costs of the orphan works scheme, with any surplus used to fund social, cultural and educational activities.

In the first year of operation, 27 orphan works licences were granted covering 247 works with a value over £8,000. Further details on the orphan works scheme and the application process can be found on the IPO's website[3].

1 Copyright and Rights in Performances (Licensing of Orphan Works) Regulations 2014, SI 2014/2863.
2 As inserted by the Enterprise and Regulatory Reform Act 2013 s 77.
3 See https://www.gov.uk/government/collections/orphan-works-guidance.

Lending of books by libraries

18.14 The CDPA, as amended to implement the Rental and Lending Right Directive[1], makes the rental and lending of most types of copyright work a restricted act so that the copyright owner has the exclusive right to rent or lend the work to the public[2]. But copyright is not infringed by the lending of a book by a *public library* if the book is in the public lending right scheme[3]. The CDPA was further amended by the Digital Economy Act 2010[4] to include audiobooks and e-books[5] within the scope of the exception (see **paragraph 18.16**). Other libraries or archives, provided they are not conducted for profit, can also lend any kind of copyright work without infringing copyright[6]. Making a copyright work available for on-the-spot reference use does not constitute 'lending' and so is not an infringement of copyright.

1 Directive 2006/115/EC.
2 See **paragraph 6.06**.

3   CDPA s 40A(1).
4   Digital Economy Act 2010 s 43(7).
5   As those terms are defined in the Public Lending Right Act 1979 (as amended).
6   CDPA s 40A(2).

The statutory lending right

18.15 Although the introduction of the lending right to the CDPA had the effect of removing the right of public libraries to lend sound recordings and films without infringing copyright, the CDPA contains a provision[1] which entitles the Secretary of State to make an Order to provide that the lending of copies of sound recordings or films (as well as copies of literary, dramatic, musical or artistic works) to the public shall be treated as licensed by the copyright owner subject only to payment for such reasonable royalty or other payment as may be agreed or determined in default of agreement by the Copyright Tribunal. No such Order can be made if, or to the extent that, there is a certified licensing scheme[2] providing for the grant of licences. There is as yet neither any Order creating a statutory licence nor any such certified licensing scheme.

1   CDPA s 66.
2   See CDPA s 143.

The public lending right

18.16 The Public Lending Right Act 1979 conferred on authors (note not the copyright owners) of books which have an ISBN a right, known as the 'public lending right' ('PLR'), to receive payment for the free lending of their books by public libraries.

The Digital Economy Act 2010 extended the public lending right to cover audiobooks and e-books and added narrators and producers to writers and illustrators (if named on the title page) as 'authors' who may be eligible to benefit from the scheme. It also determined the respective shares of each of these types of creator to any entitlement under PLR.

These provisions came into force in 2014[1] but insofar as e-books were concerned only applied to those 'lent' on the library's premises either as the lending of a physical item (such as a CD) or downloaded to a fixed terminal on the library's premises and then taken away on loan on portable devices to be read elsewhere (although there is little evidence this actually happens).

Remote e-lending to a borrower *not* on the library's premises was not covered by the exception. The concern was that remote electronic lending would infringe another exclusive right of the copyright owner, the communication right. This restricts communication to the public by electronic transmission without the copyright owner's authorisation and it was unclear whether a new exception to the communication right to allow the inclusion of remote e-lending within the PLR scheme would be compatible with EU law. A decision of the CJEU[2] in November 2016 seemingly clarified that the Rental and Lending Right Directive permits e-lending on a 'one copy per user' model and as a result the UK government included a provision in the Digital Economy Act 2017 amending the definition of 'lent out' in the Public Lending Right Act 1979 to include the making available of a copyright work to a member of the public for use away from library premises for a limited time. This includes communication by means of electronic transmission to a place other than library premises. This is subject to two conditions, namely that:

- the book has been lawfully acquired by the library; and
- the lending is in compliance with any purchase or licensing terms to which the book is subject. The meaning of this wording has been discussed above at **paragraph 18.09**[3].

PLR is not a copyright, rather it is the right of authors to receive remuneration from a fund established under the Act ('the Central Fund'), in respect of such of their books as are lent out to the public by local library authorities in the UK. The scheme is administered in accordance with the rules set out in the Public Lending Right Scheme 1982 (as amended). Responsibility for administering the scheme was transferred from the Registrar of Public Lending Right (whose role was abolished) to the British Library Board in 2013[4]. The Central Fund does not receive money obtained from the public by a charge or levy exacted by libraries; it is instead funded by a grant from the Treasury.

The duration of the PLR is the life of the author plus 70 years.

The scheme provides for the PLR:

- to be established by registration (a significant distinction from copyright);
- to be assignable to up to four persons or otherwise capable of being dealt with by testamentary disposition (as is copyright);
- to be capable of renunciation.

The right applies only to collections of books held by local authority libraries for the purpose of being borrowed by the public (including mobile local authority libraries).

The author's entitlement to PLR is dependent on, and the amount payable to each author calculated by reference to, the number of occasions on which books are lent out. This is ascertained by the returns from a sample selection of a minimum of 30 libraries in various parts of the UK. There is a maximum payment threshold, currently, of £6,600. To be eligible, authors must reside in the EEA. The division of PLR between the co-authors of a book is a matter for negotiation and agreement between them although there are fixed shares for translators and adapters/retellers. Each separate editor of a book is entitled to PLR payments. Each volume in a series is treated as a separate book.

In order to be eligible for PLR registration a book must:

- be written by an eligible author (one eligible author among the co-authors is sufficient);
- have not more than three co-authors on the title page (two in the case of an encyclopaedia, dictionary or comparable publication);
- not be wholly or principally a musical score;
- be printed and bound (paperbacks are regarded as bound volumes);
- not be a serial publication such as a newspaper, magazine, journal or periodical;
- be published by copies having been issued for sale to the public;
- not be Crown copyright; and
- show on its title page an author who is an individual and not a company or association.

Registration is effected by completing a form, deposing to it as a statutory declaration and sending it to the PLR office of the British Library Board.

1   Digital Economy Act 2010 (Appointed Day No 4) Order 2014, SI 2014/1659.
2   *Vereniging Openbare Bibliotheken v Stichting Leenrecht (C-174/15) ECJ 2016.*
3   The provisions to include e-lending within the PLR scheme need to be brought into force by a Statutory Instrument expected in July 2018. See the PLR website for further news: https://www.plr.uk.com/.
4   Public Bodies (Abolition of the Registrar of Public Lending Right) Order 2013, SI 2013/2352.

Chapter 19

Businesses and the professions

Introduction and definitions

19.01 The CDPA lists certain acts 'restricted by copyright' which may only be done by or with the permission of the copyright owner who therefore has an exclusive right as regards that act. The first exclusive right that the CDPA lists is the right to 'copy the work'[1]. This is often referred to as the reproduction right (the name given to it by the EU Copyright Directive). The reproduction right obviously covers traditional analogue copying where a hard copy is made of printed material but the CDPA extends this to cover 'reproducing the work in any material form' which is expressed to include 'storing the work in an electronic medium'.

This means that the CDPA has always been framed in a way that covers electronic copying and some changes in 2014 to the CDPA, particularly in relation to educational copying activities (see **Chapter 17**), have reinforced this.

In addition to copyright works such as literary, dramatic and artistic works, copyright also subsists in the typographical arrangement (ie the lay out) of a 'published edition'[2]. A 'published edition' simply means a published edition of the whole or a part of a literary, dramatic or musical work. Copying in relation to the typographical arrangement means making a facsimile copy; a 'facsimile copy' is an identical copy but includes a copy which is reduced or enlarged in scale[3].

1   CDPA s 17.
2   CDPA s 1(1)(c).
3   CDPA s 178.

Infringement of copyright by copying

19.02 When a copy is made, whether it is of printed or electronic material, this will involve copying both the content and the typographical arrangement. It follows that in addition to infringing the copyright in the literary, dramatic or artistic work that is copied, the copyright in the typographical arrangement of that work will also be infringed[1].

The growth of electronic networks and devices such as PCs, tablets, e-readers and smart phones introduced a whole raft of possibilities for making digital copies. Scanning a hard copy of a copyright work into digital form constitutes making a copy for the purposes of the CDPA as does saving or storing it, as well as emailing or otherwise transmitting it; printing out a hard copy obviously creates yet another copy. Each time a document is viewed another technical copy is created. For ease of reference in this chapter all these acts of 'digital copying' are covered by the terms 'copy' and 'copying'.

1   See **paragraph 6.04**.

Liability

19.03 A person who, without the licence of the copyright owner (or his agent), makes, or authorises another to make, a copy is liable for copyright infringement to the owner of the work copied, unless one of the exceptions to copyright applies[1].

Companies and professional firms (such as solicitors and accountants) making or circulating unauthorised copies within their organisations are exposed to the risk of copyright infringement. Companies are vicariously liable for the acts of their employees and those employees can themselves be personally liable for copyright infringement. Similarly using electronic publications beyond the terms of an access or subscription contract and putting extracts of published articles on corporate websites are other examples of where 'ordinary' business activities may constitute copyright infringement. Indeed posting copies of extracts of copyright works onto a corporate website may infringe another 'restricted act' namely the exclusive right of the copyright owner to communicate the work to the public[2]. Although aimed primarily at broadcasting and cable retransmission this restricted act covers 'any communication to the public by electronic transmission'. This has implications for the risk attached to the infringement, with the possibility of criminal sanctions (see **paragraph 19.12**).

Finally companies using media monitoring services and web aggregators (who will need their own licence) may well need an end-user licence to circulate or make available press cuttings within their organisation.

1   See **paragraph 7.03**.
2   CDPA s 20.

19.04 The acts of infringement described above do not require knowledge that the act in question constitutes copyright infringement:

the mere fact of making the copy constitutes the infringement regardless of knowledge or intention[1].

But there are also some acts that can constitute what is known as 'secondary infringement' of copyright: 'secondary' because they require the primary act of infringement described above to have happened first. These acts do require a degree of knowledge of the likely infringement and the one most relevant to businesses is the possession or distribution, in the course of a business, of an article which a person (this term includes a company or a firm) knows, or has reason to believe, is an infringing copy[2].

Ownership of a machine that can be used for making copies generally does not, of itself, constitute secondary copyright infringement, unless the machine has been designed or adapted specifically for making copies of a particular copyright work[3], although, depending on the facts, allowing a machine to be used for making an infringing copy may amount to authorisation. A copy shop making copies of copyright works on behalf a commercial customer will be as liable for copyright infringement as the organisation ordering the copies.

1   Although note the limited defence offered by the CDPA s 97(1) where the defendant did not know, and had no reason to believe, that copyright subsisted in the work. This is not the same as saying that ignorance of copyright law is a defence since any person must assume that a literary work might well be protected by copyright. It is perhaps aimed at cases where it might be thought that the work was no longer in copyright or did not qualify for copyright protection in the UK. In such a case the defendant would not be liable for damages but without prejudice to any other remedy such as injunction, delivery up and account of profits.
2   CDPA s 23.
3   CDPA s 24(1).

Copyright ownership distinct from material ownership

19.05 The ownership of copyright in a copyright work is quite independent of the ownership of the material upon which, or the medium on which, the copyright work is recorded – whether it be paper, film, etc[1]. If the person who is seeking to have a copy made owns the physical paper or book which he requires to be copied, it does not automatically entitle him to have that work copied without infringing the copyright in it (although see the new exception for text and data analysis discussed at **paragraph 19.10**).

Whether any rights to copy are acquired by the person buying the physical material will depend upon the circumstances. In the absence of any express agreement on the issue, a copyright licence may sometimes be implied. If a book contains standard forms and precedents for example, for use in the preparation of commercial agreements, then it seems clear that the forms are intended to be used as a source and that some licence to copy may be implied by the sale of the book. However the licence will be limited (it may not for example extend to creating alternative forms and precedents based upon those supplied for resale as part of another book). The issues surrounding implied licences are considered elsewhere in this *User's Guide*². The position is generally clearer with digital material which is always accessed under some form of licence whose terms and conditions will specify what rights are granted to the user.

1   See **paragraph 9.01**.
2   See **paragraph 9.29**.

Exceptions to copyright

19.06 Those copyright exceptions that *may* be relevant to businesses are briefly discussed below. Many are subject to the requirement that they must be a 'fair dealing' with the copyright work, a term which is not statutorily defined but which has been the subject of much case law. It embraces the UK's implementation of its EU and International treaty obligations that exceptions to copyright should not conflict with a normal exploitation of the work or unreasonably prejudice the legitimate interests of the author. It is something that has to be determined on the facts of each case (a 'matter of impression and degree') and balances fairness to the author (in terms of the act of copying competing with the author's exploitation of the copyright or depriving him or her of royalty revenue) with the public interest regarding access to works and freedom of expression.

Copyright exceptions and 'fair dealing' are covered in more detail in **Chapter 8**.

Research and private study

19.07 The CDPA provides that 'fair dealing' with a work (this includes the typographical arrangement) for the purposes of research for a non-commercial purpose or private study will not constitute an infringement of the copyright in the work, provided that it is accompanied by an acknowledgement, where practicable, of the title of the work and its author (a 'sufficient acknowledgment'). The use of the term 'research' limits the ambit of the exception as it does not cover copying just for the purposes of sharing information. The further requirement that, for any copying to benefit from this exception, it has to be for a non-commercial purpose or for private study (which itself has to be of a non-commercial nature) means that, together with the overriding requirement for it to be a 'fair dealing', the exception is of limited application to commercial companies and professional firms.

Criticism, review, quotation and news reporting

19.08 This group of exceptions[1] is also subject to the fundamental test of whether the copying amounts to a 'fair dealing'. If the copying does not pass this initial hurdle the exceptions cannot apply. All require there to be a sufficient acknowledgement. The exceptions are:

- *use for criticism and review*: aimed at critical reviews of literary and artistic works;
- *the use of quotations*: whether for criticism or review or otherwise and subject to the requirement that the extent of the quote is no more than is strictly necessary for the specific purpose for which it is used;
- *reporting of current events*: aimed at news reporting.

These exceptions may occasionally apply but are framed so narrowly that they are unlikely to apply to much, if any, of the routine copying undertaken by companies and firms.

1   CDPA s 30.

Judicial proceedings

19.09 Copying for the purposes of judicial proceedings is not an infringement of copyright[1]. The wording of the CDPA might suggest that, for the exception to apply, the judicial proceedings must already be under way when the copying is done, but it is possible that it extends to cover also copying done in contemplation of proceedings yet to be initiated. What is clear is that this is not an exception for all copying undertaken by or on behalf of law firms. Many such firms will have subscription agreements with legal publishers and/or an appropriate copyright licence from a collecting society (see **paragraphs 19.15** and **19.16**) to authorise their copying and re-use of copyright works. Outside copying agencies undertaking copying work for law firms should ensure that the firms of solicitors for whom the copies are being made confirm in writing that, as appropriate, the works are not in copyright, the permission of the copyright owner has been received for the making of the copies, the copies are being made for the purposes of judicial proceedings or that an appropriate copyright licence is in place.

1   CDPA s 45(1).

Text and data mining

19.10 A new exception was introduced in 2014[1] allowing a person with lawful access to a work to carry out computational analysis of anything recorded in the work for research, provided it is done for a non-commercial purpose. Researchers wishing to text or data mine copyright works within a commercial context will need to seek clearance from the copyright owner. Many large publishers have schemes allowing this and the Publishers Licensing Society offer a digital clearing house service[2] for researchers' requests.

1 Copyright and Rights in Performances (Research, Education, Libraries and Archives) Regulations 2014, SI 2014/1372.
2 See https://www.pls.org.uk/services/text-and-data-mining.

Abstracts of scientific or technical articles

19.11 Copies may be made of abstracts indicating the contents of articles on a scientific or technical subject published in a periodical without infringing copyright, unless a certified licensing scheme is in existence (no such scheme exists at the present time)[1].

1 CDPA s 60.

Damages for making unauthorised copies

19.12 A claim for damages for copyright infringement is subject to the same rules of assessment as apply in other legal actions. It has to be shown that the infringement caused the loss claimed and that it was reasonably foreseeable that the infringement would cause the loss. In the case of an organisation making infringing copies for internal use only, the infringement consists of doing an act without the permission of the copyright owner and so the damages are likely to be measured by reference to the amount that would have been charged by way of royalty had the permission of the copyright owner been sought and a licence granted.

Where the infringement involves making copies available in some way to the public it is likely that the damages could be higher. If a person charges a fee to the public at large for making copies, and takes no care to ensure that the copies are being made with the licence of the copyright owners, he may be liable for significant damages. Furthermore the court is given power by the CDPA to award such additional damages as it may consider appropriate in the circumstances having regard in particular to the flagrancy of the infringement and any benefit shown to have accrued to the defendant by reason of the infringement[1].

1 CDPA s 97.

19.13 For more serious cases involving secondary infringement there is also the possibility of criminal liability under the CDPA s 107. This provides that a person (again including a company or firm) who distributes in the course of a business what he knows, or has reason to believe, is an infringing copy commits an offence liable on summary conviction to imprisonment for a term of up to six months or a fine or both. The previous limit on the fine of £50,000 was removed in 2015. It is also an offence for a person to communicate a copyright work to the public in the course of a business (see **paragraph 19.03**) if he knows or has reason to believe it is an infringing copy. A director, manager, secretary or similar officer of a company shown to have connived at or consented to an offence committed by that company is also guilty of the offence[1].

1   CDPA s 110.

Avoidance of liability

19.14 Liability for copyright infringement can only be avoided by a company by ensuring that no copying takes place outside of the statutory exceptions or by obtaining the permission of the copyright owner for every instance of copying:

- occasionally 'no copy' policies have been instituted by organisations wishing to avoid the risk. Apart from the self-defeating nature of depriving staff access to information and the ability to share it, these policies are rarely effective. As above the statutory exceptions are so narrow that commercial organisations are unlikely to find them of much use and 'no copy' policies are unlikely to prevent all copying of copyright works. The institution of such a policy is no defence to a claim for infringement and is unlikely to reduce any damages award, especially if the policy had not been monitored or enforced;
- obtaining individual permissions is likely to prove an expensive, time-consuming and uncertain business with no guarantee that a permission will be forthcoming. It is likely to be feasible only where there are just a few isolated instances of copying. Of more use will be subscription agreements with publishers for electronic resources that can cover some of a company's copying needs.

Ultimately a collective licence (see **paragraphs 19.15** and **19.16**) is the only sure way to ensure compliance with copyright law.

How should a company which is in the business of offering the service of making copies protect itself? It could ask persons seeking to make copies to sign a declaration to the effect that the person submitting the document has a licence or the consent of the copyright owner to make the copy or, alternatively, that the copy is for the purposes of research or private study[1].

Such a declaration would not of itself provide a defence to a claim for copyright infringement but would give the copy shop a right of action against that person and it would assist in ensuring that the court does not award additional damages under the provisions of the CDPA as per **paragraph 19.12**. The declaration should therefore contain an indemnity in favour of the owner of the copying machine against any proceedings or damages incurred by the owner in case of any breach of copyright being proven in respect of the copy. The copy shop would need to satisfy itself that the indemnity was worth having and that they could trace the person giving the indemnity and successfully enforce it.

1   See **paragraph 19.07**.

Licences

Copyright Licensing Agency Ltd

19.15 The Copyright Licensing Agency is a collecting society established by publishers and authors as a not-for-profit company and limited by guarantee. Its purpose is to collect and distribute revenue from copyright licences granted for the right to copy and re-use digital content from books, journals, magazines and periodicals published in print and in digital format. It was founded in 1983 by the Authors' Licensing Collecting Society Ltd and the Publishers Licensing Society Ltd who represent UK authors and publishers. CLA has signed over 30 reciprocal representation agreements with similar organisations throughout the world which means that its collective licences cover a vast number of overseas publications. These various international organisations (including the CLA) are also members of the International Federation of Reproduction Rights Organisation, an international non-governmental organisation. This is the main international network of collective management organisations and creators' and publishers' associations in the text and image spheres, established to protect and enable easy legal access to copyright material[1].

The division of the licence fees collected by CLA between authors, publishers and visual artists is calculated in accordance with an independent valuation process. CLA has distributed over £600m to copyright owners since it commenced operations.

CLA grants licences to organisations in all sectors of the economy: schools, colleges, universities and charities as well as to businesses and the public sector. CLA has developed licences tailored to the needs of particular sectors such as law firms, pharmaceutical companies, media monitoring organisations and for document supply organisations such as the British Library.

Typically CLA licences permit up to 5% or, if greater, one complete chapter of a book, or one article from a journal, magazine or periodical to be copied. The precise terms of the licences should be referred to as they vary slightly and are subject to periodic renegotiation[2].

1   See www.ifrro.org for further information.
2   See https://www.cla.co.uk.

NLA Media Access Ltd

19.16 NLA Media Access is a publisher owned rights licensing and database business. It provides access to, and licenses the re-use of, publishers' content in printed and online national and regional newspapers, magazines and newspaper websites. Like CLA it has a network of reciprocal representation agreements with similar organisations throughout the world that allows it to offer extensive coverage of international titles as well. It has distributed over £196m to copyright owners since it commenced operations.

NLA offers a basic licence to business to cover 'occasional copying and distribution' (that is copying on an ad hoc basis and not for distribution to a pre-determined set of recipients) within organisations which can be extended to cover additional regional newspapers, magazines, specialist publications and foreign newspapers. Its frequent copying licence is for regular copying and distribution of articles within the organisation. Both licences can be extended to cover content supplied by a third party such as a public relations consultancy or media monitoring organisation. It also offers a web end-user licence that allows companies without a business licence to receive and use for commercial purposes material received from media monitoring organisations on a paid-for basis.

Other licences

19.17 If an organisation plays music for its staff or customers in an office or workplace, or for customers in a reception or sales area or has recorded 'music on hold' on its telephone system, it will need to consider taking a music licence probably from both PPL and PRS (as to whom see **Chapter 20**).

Chapter 20

The music industry: publishers and composers, artists and record companies

Introduction

20.01 The commercial music industry exploits copyright works of all descriptions, but in this chapter we will focus in particular on the two primary categories of work involved, namely *musical compositions* (ie music, and any lyrics with the music, each of which are separately protected by the CDPA as *musical* and *literary* works respectively), and *sound recordings* (ie the recorded versions of musical compositions). Musical compositions and sound recordings are sold in their own right, and are also included in films, games and videos, and in broadcasts and internet and mobile transmissions, and where physical copies are sold to the public the packaging will also usually carry artistic and literary material[1]. Issues which arise in connection with the exploitation of public performances, such as concerts, are considered elsewhere[2].

Copyright issues raised by the exploitation of music are consistently the most puzzling to those who do not work within the industry. There are several reasons for this, including the following:

- *Conceptual issues*: users often have difficulty at first with the conceptual problem that, when considering the exploitation of a music product, there will almost always be a number of independent copyrights to deal with: the copyright in the musical composition as a musical work; the copyright in any accompanying lyrics as a literary work; and the copyright in the sound recording. These copyrights are more than likely to be owned or controlled by different entities, each with separate concerns.
- *Collective licensing*: of all media industries, the music industry remains the one most dependent upon the use of blanket licensing

schemes and collective rights management bodies to administer copyrights on behalf of owners. Without those schemes, the task of clearing rights from a myriad of separate owners would be prohibitively time-consuming for the major users of music (such as broadcasters). These bodies have separate constitutions, rules and practices. The three most significant to the UK music industry are Performing Right Society (PRS), Mechanical Copyright Protection Society (MCPS) and Phonographic Performance Limited (PPL)[3].

- *Industry dynamics*: the relationship between major talent and industry is volatile. Record companies are fond of referring to the rule of thumb that of ten artists they sign, only one will ever recoup for the company the costs invested in developing, recording and promoting that artist, and hopefully the other nine as well. Historically, therefore, artist recording contracts contained exclusivity and product delivery options in favour of the record company which sometimes tied up an artist's services for the best part of their likely career. Increasingly, these contracts have been challenged in the courts as a 'restraint of trade'[4]. Although a detailed discussion of this issue is beyond the scope of this *User's Guide*, it is worth noting that such decisions have thrown doubt on longer-term contracts, and the norm now is for a record company to have rights and options for a limited number of albums only. A record company is still likely, however, to own the copyright in recordings delivered by the artist for the full term of copyright. More recently the 'artist services' model has developed, under which a company provides production, marketing and distribution services to the artist as a service provider, rather than engaging the artist's services and owning the results.

- *Digitisation*: the position of the industry is not static. Since sound recordings lend themselves easily to use in the context of digital media, the industry has been forced to deal head on with the challenges posed by digitisation. The difficulty of tracking uses, the ease of piracy, and the replacement of traditional distribution methods by new industry models have all led to considerable soul searching in the sector in recent years. The rise in popularity of music streaming has to a significant extent replaced not only the traditional CD market but the download market as well, and the revenues from streaming services are now distributable far more widely and therefore far more thinly around the industry, challenging its structure, its priorities and above all its bottom line. Meanwhile the live industry continues to gather in strength, a part of the industry from which record labels, the most significant investors in the industry, do not directly benefit.

In developing an understanding of how copyright affects the industry, we must first distinguish between the issues arising in exploitation of musical works (usually called 'the publishing rights') on the one hand and those affecting sound recordings (usually called 'the recording rights') on the other.

The publishing rights are generally controlled by music publishers who acquire the rights from songwriters and composers, and they are also controlled to some extent by collective rights management organisations (traditionally known as 'collecting societies'). The performing right in compositions and the right to include those compositions in broadcasts and online services are usually vested in PRS by the author/composer, and the so-called 'mechanical' rights are usually managed by MCPS for the publisher[5]. It is rare for any publishing rights to be retained by the composer of a musical work (except the right to receive royalties from the work, and the so-called 'grand rights').

Similarly the recording rights are traditionally controlled by record companies, who will generally either be the first owner of the copyright in the sound recordings (as producer), or will acquire ownership from the artist by way of an assignment[6]. The record company will therefore have the right to exploit the copyright in the sound recording by authorising the 'restricted acts'[7]. Again, certain of the recording rights will be administered on behalf of the record company by the collecting society PPL[8].

Broadly, then, the principal commercial players in the recorded music industry are the music publishers and the record companies.

The performing and broadcasting rights in a significant proportion of all music videos are managed for record companies by Video Performance Ltd (VPL), a branch of PPL, although the major record companies will do direct deals with broadcasters and significant digital service providers for their videos.

1   As to these categories of copyright work generally, see **Chapter 2**.
2   See **Chapter 23**.
3   These are described in more detail at **paragraph 12.01**.
4   For example the George Michael case *Panayiotou v Sony Music Entertainment (UK) Ltd [1994] EMLR 229*.
5   See **paragraphs 12.01** and **20.02**.
6   See **Chapter 9**.
7   Generally, see **Chapter 6**.
8   The performing right is usually administered by PPL, see **paragraphs 12.01** and **20.22**.

20.02 The term 'publisher' is not defined in the CDPA. However, in the music industry the expression commonly means the company in which the copyright in a musical composition (except the performing rights) is vested, or the company which administers the rights in the composition. Although to the layman publishing may imply publishing sheet music and other printed material, that activity is only a small part of the business of a music publisher. The major part lies in promoting their songwriters and composers, issuing synchronisation licences for the use of music in films and other productions, and collecting and distributing income from record companies and from PRS and MCPS. Sheet music *is* published, but in the case of popular music usually only after the music has been successful in another medium (such as by way of sales).

A number of other definitions from the CDPA are relevant in relation to the exploitation of music and are considered in detail elsewhere in this *User's Guide*. These include the definitions of the works in question (ie literary works, musical works, and sound recordings)[1], and of the acts restricted by copyright in relation to those works (ie copying, issuing copies to the public, rental or lending, performing, communicating to the public etc)[2].

Although the expression 'mechanical rights' is not used in the CDPA, it is used extensively by the industry. It means the right to make copies of a musical composition in *any* medium, both physical and digital.

Similarly, the expression 'synchronisation rights' is not defined in the CDPA but is extensively used by the music industry to refer to the right to synchronise sound recordings and musical compositions (including songs) into the soundtracks of films and other audiovisual productions.

1 See **paragraphs 2.02, 2.04,** and **2.07**.
2 See **paragraphs 6.02** ff.

Part I: Publishers and composers
The copyright owner's rights: restricted acts in musical works

20.03 The acts restricted by copyright (that is to say, the rights which only the owner of the music or persons licensed by him can exercise) in a musical work are:

- *copying the work* (ie reproducing the work in any material form, including in writing, by printing, recording on disc, tape or film, or storing the work in any medium by electronic means);
- *issuing copies of the work to the public* (which is usually taken to mean physical copies);
- *renting or lending copies of the works to the public* (again, usually taken to mean physical copies);
- *performing in public* (including both public performance of a musical work given by a live performer, and performance effected by some mechanical means, such as by playing a recording, showing a film or placing a radio or television screen in a public place);
- *communicating the work to the public* (by radio or television or by way of online and mobile services);
- *adapting the work* (which includes making arrangements or transcriptions)[1].

As we have seen, in the case of a musical composition, the lyric is not a part of the composition in legal terms, but is a literary work, with its own separate copyright[2]. The restricted acts applicable to a literary work are essentially the same as those for musical works, but see the Table of Incidence of Copyright in **Appendix 2** for the copyright attributes of musical and literary works. Essentially the lyrics of a song receive the same copyright treatment as the music, and for commercial purposes the two are usually licensed as if they are one single copyright work.

It is customary for a composer (and in this chapter, for convenience, the term 'composer' includes a lyricist, unless there is an express reference to the lyricist) to assign or license the entire copyright in his music to a publishing company, with the exception of the right to perform the music in public and the right to communicate the music to the public, both of which he assigns to PRS by virtue of his membership of PRS. The publisher usually delegates control over the right to make recordings of the music (the 'mechanical' right) and the collection of mechanical royalties to MCPS as agent. The publisher is left with the administration of the synchronisation and sheet music rights as its directly managed functions.

1   See **paragraphs 6.02** ff.
2   See **paragraph 2.04**.

Quality and originality

20.04 The CDPA does not require that a work should be of any minimum standard or quality in order for it to be entitled to copyright. In *Sawkins v Hyperion Records Ltd*[1] it was held that:

'A work may be complete rubbish and utterly worthless, but copyright protection may be available for it, just as it is for the great masterpieces of imaginative literature, art and music. A work need only be "original" in the limited sense that the author originated it by his efforts rather than slavishly copying it from the work produced by the efforts of another person.'

So originality is a key requirement for copyright protection[2], whereas artistic merit is not. The extent of originality is a problem which sometimes arises in connection with music. If only five bars out of 50 in a work are original, and the remainder are taken from an existing tune, it is unlikely (but not impossible) that the work will be regarded as an original work as a whole unless those five bars contain a key melody of an unusual nature which demonstrates some skill and/or labour on the part of the composer and which converts what is otherwise a common tune into a new variation.

The work in the example above, assuming it has the status of a new copyright work, may also be an infringement of the original tune, if the original tune is in copyright. Many infringement claims are made in the popular music industry, although few get as far as the courtroom. Claims usually relate to either sampling, which is the incorporation by A into A's sound recording of an extract of B's sound recording, or copying, in other words the creation by A of a musical composition which is (or parts of which are) similar to B's musical composition (and which therefore may amount to copying). In the few cases that do get to court the expert evidence of musicologists is usually required to assist the court in determining whether or not unauthorised sampling or copying has taken place.

There can also be copyright in the arrangement of a piece of music, but it must be shown that labour and skill have been applied to the production of the arrangement. In *Sawkins v Hyperion Records Ltd* it was held that a claim to copyright in a new version of a musical work is not to be rejected simply because the editorial composer had made no significant changes to the notes, whether by correction or addition. That is too rigid a test, and not one which properly respected the reality of what music is (music is the sounds one hears, not simply the notes on the stave). Where the material produced is based on an existing score, the test is whether the new work is sufficiently original in terms of the skill and labour used to produce it.

So a new arrangement of an old composition which is out of copyright may be entitled to copyright in its own right. Similarly, arrangements for one instrument of a piece of music written for a different instrument may have a new copyright. In one case, for example, the court was satisfied that the composition of the piano score of an opera involved such skill and labour as to justify the creation of a new copyright work[3].

If the arrangement is of a piece of music which is still in copyright, although the arrangement may itself be a new work with its own copyright, there will still be the need to acquire a licence from the owner of the original work before the new arrangement can be used, since the arrangement is an adaptation, and as noted in **paragraph 20.03** adapting a copyright work is a restricted act.

1   *Sawkins v Hyperion Records Ltd (2004) EWHC 1530 (Ch)*.
2   See **paragraphs 3.01** ff. The *Infopaq* case is also relevant to the question of originality: see **paragraph 3.04** and *Infopaq International A/S v Danske Dagblades Forening (C-5/08) [2010] FSR 20, CJEU*.
3   *Wood v Boosey (1868) LR 3 QB 223, Exch.*

Material form

20.05   Until it has been recorded or written down, there is no copyright in a piece of music. In order for copyright to subsist in a musical work, it is necessary for the work to be recorded, in writing or otherwise[1]. The making of a sound recording of a musical work is a sufficient process to confer copyright on the musical work, and so is setting it in musical notation. It is immaterial for this purpose whether the work is recorded or notated by the composer or by a third party. Even an unauthorised recording of a musical work has the effect of giving copyright protection to the work, if it has not previously been recorded in some form. But it does not follow that the person making the recording of the work is the owner of the work. The owner is the *author* (ie the person who creates the work), and the person making the recording cannot claim to be anything more than the author of the *recording*.

1   See **paragraph 2.05**.

Ownership

20.06   The first owner of a musical work is the author (ie the composer), unless the work is composed in the course of employment under a contract of service, in which case his employer will be deemed the first owner of any copyright material the author creates in the course of his employment, in the absence of any agreement to the contrary.

Because a song is two separate works in copyright law – the words are a literary work and the music is a musical work – a song is not a work of joint authorship between the composer and the lyricist in legal terms. However, there can be joint authors of the lyrics and joint authors of the music[1]. In *Godfrey v Lees*[2] it was held that a claimant to joint authorship must establish that he had made a significant and original contribution to the creation of the work and that he had done so pursuant to a common design. A case involving the band *Spandau Ballet*[3] considered in detail the question as to whether the work of 'jamming' musicians can be said to amount to an original contribution to a song, meriting copyright protection as joint authors (in that case it did not).

Music is often commissioned for stage musicals, for films, for television, for radio etc. Assuming the composer is not in the employment of the person who commissioned the work, which is usually the case, the copyright will at the outset be owned by the composer, and the person commissioning must obtain either a licence or an assignment of the work from the composer in order to use it[4].

Since it is possible to assign copyright in work which has not yet been created, it is common for agreements with composers to assign the rights in the composer's work before the music is composed[5].

In practice, many composers who accept commissions are in the full-time employment of single purpose companies which are owned or controlled by the composer. These 'loan out' companies are usually established for tax planning purposes rather than for copyright reasons. When acquiring rights from a 'loan out' company, the acquirer should make sure that he also secures a relationship which is legally enforceable directly against the composer. Traditionally this has been achieved by obtaining a separate 'inducement letter' in favour of the acquirer, signed by the composer, in which the composer undertakes to ensure the fulfilment of the contract by his loan out company.

It is the practice of many music publishing companies to engage composers whenever possible on an exclusive contract for a given term, so that the copyright in everything the composer writes during the term belongs to the publisher. The courts have held that such contracts are unenforceable if the publishing company has no obligation to exploit the works of the composer, and so all such contracts now include (or should include) an undertaking by the publisher to use reasonable endeavours to exploit the music, and a reversion right in favour of the composer in respect of any unexploited titles. Other rights and reversion issues in the contract will need to be negotiated, and therefore contracts under which composers are to write exclusively for a publisher over a period should always be the subject of legal advice, on both sides.

All these publishing contracts and arrangements will be subject to the rights owned by PRS, as to which see the following section.

1   See **paragraph 9.08**.
2   Ibid.
3   *Hadley v Kemp [1999] EMLR 589*, and see **paragraph 9.08**.
4   See **paragraphs 9.22** ff.
5   See **paragraph 9.24**.

Performing rights: the Performing Right Society (PRS)

20.07   The Performing Right Society now trades as PRS for Music, but is referred to as 'PRS' in this book. Composers and publishers enter into a membership contract when they join PRS under which the performing right in all works already composed and published by them, and in all works composed (or published) by them in the future while they are a member of PRS, is in effect automatically assigned to PRS. For PRS purposes the 'performing right' means the right to perform the works in public and the right to communicate the works to the public, and all rights of a similar nature in other jurisdictions[1]. Having taken this assignment, PRS is able to license others to exercise the performing right on a 'blanket' ie all-repertoire basis. PRS works in close association with similar collective rights management organisations outside the UK (for example SACEM in France and GEMA in Germany), both in licensing those bodies to collect royalties in respect of the works administered by PRS when they are performed outside the UK, and also in collecting performing right royalties in respect of works performed in the UK, but which are administered by the foreign organisations. Taking into account also the music licensed to PRS by the overseas performing right organisations under reciprocal agreements with those organisations, PRS repertoire consists of virtually every significant piece of published music in copyright worldwide, or at least in the Western world[2].

PRS grants blanket licences authorising:

*   radio and television cable and satellite broadcasters to broadcast music, and to simulcast it from their websites;
*   digital services to transmit streams (live and on demand) and downloads;

- concert venues to stage live performances or the public playing of music on premises (the licence is normally granted to the proprietor of the premises at which the music is to be publicly performed, or to the promoters of the musical entertainment. It is not usually granted to performers, as such[3]);
- shops, bars, clubs and similar venues to perform or play music on the premises (eg live, DJ, jukebox);
- many other sites, businesses and activities involving the performing or playing of music.

Certain of these licences take the form of licensing schemes, which are standard 'rate card' arrangements which apply equally to all licensees of a particular description. Larger businesses, particularly major broadcasters and major online services, are under negotiated deals.

PRS currently administers the rights of MCPS under contract from MCPS, which is a separate legal entity, and as a result it licenses broadcasters, digital services and others who require both mechanical and public performance rights on a joint rights basis under a single licence agreement. The range of venue licences issued by PRS mostly grant PRS-only rights, since no copying is taking place at the venue, only public performance. By contrast the licences issued by PRS to broadcasters and digital online services are joint PRS/MCPS licences granting both mechanical and public performance rights.

Like broadcast licences, the digital service licences are available on a licensing scheme basis for smaller businesses, while the larger music service providers such as Apple and Spotify are under individually negotiated deals. But unlike broadcast licences which are always granted on a national basis and permit all-repertoire use, online music service licences are granted on a pan-European basis but with limited repertoire. PRS currently only represents certain music publishers' catalogues in the online world, and some of the major publishers have placed their Anglo-American catalogues exclusively with overseas PRS equivalents which they believe provide a preferred service. To get blanket rights to all repertoire therefore, an international music service operator needs to obtain licences from a number of different collecting societies.

PRS also licenses the use of music in films and TV programmes offered by video on demand services, and these licences are generally granted on a national all-repertoire basis in the same way as broadcast licences are granted.

PRS does not currently license certain uses which are informally regarded as exempt from licence, and those uses include (among other uses) certain healthcare premises and residential homes; divine worship; weddings, funerals and other ceremonies; and certain educational uses. Also, PRS does not license the performance of musicals, operas, ballets, etc when performed on stage in their entirety or in excerpts, or the dramatic performance of other so-called 'dramatico-musical works'. These latter two rights must be cleared directly from the owner (usually a publisher). When it is not being 'dramatically' performed in the context as part of a musical, opera, ballets or other dramatico-musical work, PRS will control the performance rights in the music written for such productions (eg where the music is interpolated into another production)[4].

PRS licences are granted in return for the payment of royalties which (following the deduction of administrative expenses) PRS then distributes to its composer and publisher members in accordance with PRS distribution rules. It has long been the rule of PRS to divide fees on the basis of fractions of 12 or multiples of 12, although the equivalent in percentage terms is now more often used in practice. Where there is a publisher, then the composer(s) is/are entitled to 6/12ths and the publisher 6/12ths of the distributable royalties, known as the 'writer's share' and the 'publisher's share' respectively. Where there is *no* publisher, PRS royalties are distributed entirely to the composer(s). In each case the share going to the songwriters/ composers is split in the proportion they agree. PRS's rules do not permit it to allocate to composer(s)/songwriter(s) jointly less than half of the net royalties available for distribution in respect of a work. But PRS will honour publishing agreements under which the publisher agrees that the composer(s)/songwriter(s) will receive a larger share than 6/12ths.

1   See PRS Rule 1(l).
2   Although PRS repertoire also includes unpublished works.
3   See **Chapter 23**.
4   For a full account of rights administered and licences available, please see the PRS website at www.prsformusic.com.

Mechanical rights: the Mechanical Copyright Protection Society (MCPS)

20.08 The mechanical right is the right to make copies of a musical work (the composition, *not* the sound recording). The right is exercised when a record company makes a CD, when a TV producer copies music into a programme, when a digital service provider copies music onto a server, when music is incorporated into a computer game, and when any other form of copying is done in any form or medium. Unlike PRS, which takes an assignment of its rights, MCPS acts as an agent for the licensing of the mechanical rights, and it represents writers and publishers in the UK and, through its overseas reciprocal agreements, copyright owners overseas. MCPS also licenses the sound recording rights in production music on behalf of library (or production) music publishers.

MCPS licenses all audio-only products (CDs and vinyl) as well as video products (DVDs), and it also licenses digital service providers (jointly with PRS). Although the MCPS agency agreement is an exclusive agreement it is subject to certain optional exclusions. The major publishers and larger independent publishers usually license TV and radio adverts and film and game synchronisation (which is a form of copying) directly.

A significant proportion of MCPS revenue is derived from licensing record companies to make CDs and DVDs. There are essentially two alternative types of licence available to record companies:

- a sales agreement (AP1), under which the record company accounts to MCPS on shipments; and
- a manufacturing agreement (AP2), under which the record company accounts to MCPS on pressings.

Provided the works to be licensed are in the MCPS repertoire, a record company will receive a licence for the manufacture of CDs from MCPS without the need to seek the music copyright owner's consent, except in the case of a first recording, where the copyright owner has the right to prevent such a recording being distributed (in other words, to approve who first records the work). In these cases, the record company will be notified by MCPS that the work is subject to 'first licence refusal'.

The rates at which MCPS licenses CD and music video DVD manufacture/shipping are the result of extended negotiations with the British Phonographic Industry (for the recorded music industry), and are available on the PRS website. The rates are inclusive of both the mechanical and (in the case of DVD) synchronisation rights. The DVD1 music video licence scheme gives to record companies automatic access to all the MCPS repertoire without the need for prior approval from copyright owners for the use of each individual musical work. Other types of DVD (for example film DVDs) also require an MCPS licence if there is music in the film, and if the mechanical rights to the music have not already been pre-cleared.

MCPS enters into blanket licences with radio and television broadcasters and digital services, and as noted above these licences are granted under joint PRS/MCPS licence agreements administered by PRS. The scope of the licences to broadcasters is usually limited to 'convenience copying' by the broadcaster allowing it to retain copies for longer than the period allowed under 'ephemeral copying' exceptions set out in the CDPA. The licences to digital services enable them to make a master copy of their servers and include the copies made in the course of transmission (to the extent not excluded by the transient copies exception) and any copies made by the end user. Licences may also be obtained by broadcasters from MCPS for the synchronisation of MCPS library music and recordings in broadcaster produced programming (such as promotional materials), and for the broadcast of library recordings.

Sheet music

20.09 Royalties earned from the performance of music and from the making of recordings of music are collected by the relevant collective rights management organisations[1], but there is no collection society for sheet music royalties (except for PMLL (Printed Music Licensing Ltd) the organisation recently set up to license the use of sheet music by schools). Instead, the publisher receives a percentage of the sales direct from the retailer and accounts to the composer in accordance with the agreement between the composer and the publisher. The standard industry royalty payable by the publisher to the composer in respect of sales of sheet music is 10–12.5% of the recommended retail sales price, although sometimes the royalty is based on wholesale prices.

1   See **paragraphs 20.07** and **20.08**.

Publication of music overseas

20.10 Publishing arrangements overseas are usually undertaken by foreign affiliates of UK publishers, or, if the UK publisher has no overseas affiliates, by third party overseas publishers under licence (who are known as 'sub-publishers' under such arrangements). Where this is the case, the composer should seek the maximum transparency in the publishing arrangements to ensure that he is aware of, and approves, the arrangements by which revenue will flow back to him.

As a separate matter, and as discussed above, the rights administered by collective management organisations in the UK are administered by their overseas equivalents when exploited outside the UK, and are initially paid through to the UK organisations before being remitted to UK composers and publishers. Some publishers and composers arrange direct membership of overseas collective management organisations to speed up the receipt of royalties and cut out the overseas sub-publisher.

In order to ensure ease of enforcement and in some cases to ensure that music does not lose its copyright when published overseas, all copies of the music (including CDs) should bear the © symbol followed by the name of the copyright owner and the year of first publication[1]. Note that on a CD or other physical product the © symbol refers only to the musical composition (or to the artwork). The ownership of copyright in the recording is denoted by similar use of the ℗ symbol, and the two notices should not be combined.

When music is published in the USA, it should be borne in mind that, unlike in the UK and many other jurisdictions, there is a system for the registration of copyright, although registration is not necessary in order to obtain basic copyright protection[2]. Registration of copyright works at the US Copyright Office is advisable in order to bring the benefits in the USA that registration affords.

1   See **paragraph 4.16**.
2   See **paragraph 4.14**.

Term of copyright

20.11 Copyright in musical works subsists for the life of the composer and a period of 70 years from the end of the calendar year in which he died. In the case of joint composers the last to die is the relevant life. In the rare case of computer-generated musical works the copyright expires 50 years from the end of the calendar year in which the work was made[1].

In the case of works composed before 1 August 1989 (the date on which the CDPA came into force) care should be taken, since depending on the date of composition, some works enjoyed extended copyright protection under the CPDA and some did not.

In the case of assignments or licences of music effected before 1 June 1957 (the date upon which the Copyright Act 1956 came into force) the rights granted will revert to the estate of the composer at the expiry of 25 years after his death, irrespective of any assignments or licences of the copyright made by the composer in his lifetime. However, if the composer has assigned or assigns the reversionary right after 1 August 1989 the reversion will no longer apply.

There are certain important exceptions from these provisions and the rules are complex, so when dealing with copyright works which were written by composers who are now deceased, legal advice should be taken to ensure that the person purporting to sell the rights is in fact the true owner.

1   See **paragraphs 5.02** and **5.04**.

Infringement – the substantial part rule

20.12 Infringement is the act of carrying out an act in respect of a work protected by copyright without the permission of the copyright owner(s) of the work. There can be no infringement of copyright unless a 'substantial part' of the work has been reproduced, adapted, copied, etc. The test of what amounts to a 'substantial part' is qualitative, not quantitative. If from a very long piece of music (a Wagner opera, perhaps) a composer makes use of, for example, 15 bars, being not particularly important or significant bars, such use may not constitute the use of a substantial part of that work. On the other hand, copying as little as three notes of a popular song, for example, if those three notes are the 'hook' of the song, could amount to copying a substantial part[1].

1   See **paragraph 7.06**.

Exceptions to the copyright owner's exclusive rights

20.13 If a substantial part of a work has been used, it is then necessary to see if any other exceptions could apply to the use. The mandatory exceptions in relation to the 'making of temporary copies' and fair dealing are discussed in detail elsewhere in this *User's Guide*[1]. A number of other exceptions apply to musical works and these are also considered elsewhere[2]. In summary, the CDPA provides that 'fair dealing' with a musical or literary work for the purposes of:

- non-commercial research and private study; or
- data mining if undertaken for non-commercial research purposes; or
- criticism or review, whether of that work or another work (provided that the work has been made available to the public); or
- quotation (introduced as a new exception in 2016 and still of uncertain application); or
- parody, caricature and pastiche (introduced as a new exception in 2016 and still of uncertain application, although the Intellectual Property Office ('IPO') has given its view that the parody of an entire composition would not be fair dealing); or
- reporting current events,

will not amount to an infringement of the work[3], provided that sufficient acknowledgment is given (although not required in case of temporary copies and parody).

1   See **paragraphs 8.02–8.06**.
2   See generally **Chapter 8**.
3   See **paragraphs 8.03** ff.

Incidental inclusion of musical works in other works

20.14 Copyright in a work is not infringed by its incidental inclusion in an artistic work, sound recording, film or broadcast. But a musical work or lyrics are not to be regarded as incidentally included in another work if they are deliberately included[1].

1   See **paragraph 8.08**.

Moral rights in musical works

20.15 The author of a musical work or lyrics has a right to be identified (the so-called 'paternity right') whenever:

- the work is published commercially; or

- copies of a sound recording of the work are issued to the public; or
- a film, the soundtrack of which includes the work, is shown in public or copies of such a film are issued to the public[1].

The paternity right includes the right to be identified whenever a musical work has been adapted. The right must be asserted[2].

The author also has the right to object to a derogatory treatment of his musical work. 'Treatment' in relation to a musical work means any addition to, deletion from or alteration to or adaptation of a work, other than an arrangement or transcription of a musical work involving no more than a change of key or register. Moral rights cases are rare, but in the case of *Morrison Leahy Music Ltd v Lightbond Ltd*[3] the court held that taking parts of five different George Michael songs and putting them together amounted to 'treatment'[4].

1   CDPA s 77(3), see **paragraph 10.05**.
2   See **paragraph 10.08**.
3   [1993] EMLR 144.
4   See **paragraph 10.12**.

Part II: Artists, records and the recording business
Copyright in recordings distinguished from copyright in underlying material

20.16 In Part I of this chapter it was emphasised that in order to understand the relationship between copyright and the exploitation of music, it is important to understand that there are separate copyrights in the sound recording, and in the material which is 'fixed' on the recording[1]. A sound recording is a copyright work in its own right[2], but if a producer captures the performance of a musical composition on his sound recording, he will be copying that composition. That process of copying will require authorisation from the owner(s) of the composition[3] because copying is a restricted act in relation to musical (and all other varieties of copyright) works[4]. So, if a composer records a performance of a new composition which he has composed but not yet written down, two copyrights will simultaneously come into existence: the copyright in the sound recording, and the musical composition fixed on the recording.

The recording of a musical composition will also inevitably involve a performance of the work. A performer has rights in his performance which are analogous to copyright. These rights are very significant to the music industry, but they are equally important to other industries (such as the film and television industry) which involve the recording of performances, and in this *User's Guide* performances are therefore dealt with in a separate chapter[5].

1   See **Paragraph 20.01**.
2   See **paragraph 2.07**.
3   Usually a music publisher, see **paragraphs 20.01** ff.
4   See **paragraph 6.02**.
5   **Chapter 11.**

The copyright owner's rights: restricted acts in sound recordings

20.17 The acts restricted by the copyright in a sound recording are the same as for other copyright works[1] with the exception of the adaptation right:

- copying the sound recording;
- issuing copies of the sound recording to the public;
- renting or lending copies of the sound recording to the public;
- playing the sound recording in public[2]; and
- communicating the sound recording to the public.

1 See **paragraph 20.03** for more detail on these rights.
2 Although note that exceptions are applicable to the public performance of broadcasts; see **paragraph 6.07**.

Ownership

20.18 The author and the first owner of a sound recording is the producer of the recording, and the producer is defined by the CDPA as the person by whom the arrangements necessary for the making of the sound recording are undertaken[1].The courts have in the past interpreted this to mean that the entity that pays the recording bill is the producer for legal purposes, rather than the individual producer who is usually engaged to produce a recording in a technical sense. This is a default provision, which applies absent any other agreement.

However, in some circumstances it could be argued that the producer of a sound recording is the individual organising the recording, rather than the company paying the bills. To avoid doubt, all individuals who are involved with the recording should be required to enter into agreements at an early stage assigning all present and future copyright in relation to the recording to the appropriate entity.

It should be noted that the provisions regarding ownership in relation to copyright works, whereby the employer of the author is the owner of the copyright from the outset, do not apply to sound recordings[2].

The copyright in sound recordings can be assigned and licensed like other copyright works[3].

1 CDPA s 9(2) and s 178; see **paragraph 9.04**.
2 See **paragraph 9.12**.
3 See **paragraphs 9.21** ff.

Term of copyright

20.19 The copyright in a sound recording produced by a national of an EEA state now subsists for a period of 70-years from the end of the calendar year in which it was first released[1]. The 70 year term was introduced on 1 November 2013, following much lobbying from the recorded music industry and musician organisations. Before 1 November 2013 the term was only 50 years, and if under the 50-year rule a sound recording had fallen out of copyright by 1 November 2013 then it remains out of copyright, and so several early Beatles and Elvis Presley hits are now out of copyright in the UK and are freely usable. If a recording has never been released the 50-year term still applies as from the date of recording. A sound recording is released when it is first published, played in public or communicated to the public. In this context, publication means the issue to the public of physical products embodying the recording[2].

As part of the term extension rules recorded performers and musicians will also benefit, after 50 years following publication of the sound recording, from additional measures including:

- a 'session fund' paying session players and backing singers 20% of revenues from sales, downloads and streams of their recordings[3];
- a 'clean slate' provision, whereby a producer may no longer recoup any unrecouped advances or expenses from royalties payable to featured performers[4];
- a 'use it or lose it' clause – which allows any performer to claim back their rights in sound recordings if they are not being commercially exploited (either physically or digitally)[5].

Record companies these days are increasingly remastering recordings that are nearing the end of their copyright term in an attempt to create a new copyright term in the remastered recording. This remastering raises an issue as to whether the producer of the remastered recording is entitled to a new period of copyright protection in respect of the remastered recording. As explained in the following paragraph, originality is not necessary in order to receive protection for a sound recording, but copyright will not subsist in a new sound recording (including a digitally remastered recording) which is, or to the extent that it is, a copy of a previous sound recording[6]. On that basis it seems unlikely that a remaster could acquire a new period of copyright protection, although views differ on this point.

1   Assuming the release occurred or occurs within 50 years of the date of recording.
2   See **paragraph 5.05**.
3   CPDA s 191HB.
4   CPDA s 191HB.
5   CPDA s 191HA.
6   CDPA s 5A(2).

Originality

20.20 There is no requirement for a sound recording to be original in order to gain copyright protection. Copyright arises automatically in respect of any recording of any sound, musical or otherwise, by virtue of the fact that it is made. However, to avoid the direct copying of sound recordings giving rise to new copyrights the CDPA provides that, as noted above, copyright does not subsist in a sound recording which is, or to the extent that it is, a copy taken from a previous sound recording[1]. So there is no infringement of an existing sound recording of a musical composition if a band 'copies' that recording by making a new recording of the same composition so as to sound identical to the original recording. However, if that band were to attempt to market the new recording as if it were the original, the owner of the original would probably be able to bring an action in 'passing off' against the band.

1   CDPA s 5A(2).

Mechanical royalties

20.21 Record labels must pay mechanical royalties to MCPS on all copies of sound recordings that they manufacture or ship[1]. Over the years there has been much debate between the record industry and the publishing industry as to the appropriate royalty rate. Following a reference to the Copyright Tribunal by the British Phonograph Industry (BPI) on behalf of record companies, which was heard in 1991 and 1992, a rate of 8.5% of the dealer price of CDs was determined by the Copyright Tribunal and is now payable[2]. The Copyright Tribunal has jurisdiction in cases where the parties are unable to agree upon the terms of a licensing scheme or an appropriate royalty rate. All MCPS licences are subject to the jurisdiction of the Copyright Tribunal (as are all other collective rights management organisation licences): not only the mechanical recording licences, but also all other licences including the blanket broadcast licences which include mechanicals.

1   Labels have the option to choose, subject to terms, see **paragraph 20.08**.
2   See **Chapter 12** for an analysis of the Copyright Tribunal.

Phonographic Performance Limited (PPL)

20.22 PPL, the record labels' and performers' collective rights management organisation, performs the equivalent functions of both MCPS and PRS as regards the public performance and broadcasting of sound recordings. It licenses its members' broadcasting rights and the right to copy recordings for the purposes of broadcasting. PPL operates (like PRS) by taking a mandatory assignment of the relevant elements of the copyright in sound recordings owned by members of PPL for broadcasting purposes, which enables PPL to authorise the public performance and broadcasting of those sound recordings. For online use members appoint PPL, if they wish, as their non-exclusive agent, with an opt-out for certain uses.

PPL issues blanket licences to broadcasters (both television and radio). These licences cover most forms of television and radio, and simulcasts of UK radio broadcasts by means of the internet. However, in general PPL does not have the mandate to license the use of sound recordings on internet or mobile services apart from such simulcasts, so licences for internet and mobile services must be obtained directly from the record companies concerned.

PPL also licenses discotheques, night clubs, public houses, hotels, cafés, restaurants, clubs, halls, keep-fit and dancing classes, football, greyhound and speedway tracks, sports clubs, shops, stores, shopping precincts, amusement parks, amusement arcades, theatres, cinemas, leisure centres, swimming pools and local authority properties. Because these venues are also licensed by PRS for the use of the musical compositions incorporated in the music they play, PPL and PRS set up a joint licensing initiative in 2016 to license both PPL and PRS rights jointly to certain venues, so as to save licensing costs and to make the licensing process easier for venue owners.

The members of PPL are record companies and other owners of sound recording copyrights (which includes many artists) on the one hand, and performers who have performed on sound recordings on the other hand. PPL operates by dividing up between its members the licence fees it receives in accordance with the reporting on usage made by its licensees. Prior to the coming into force of regulations on 1 December 1996 which, amongst other things, gave rental and lending rights to performers[1], PPL paid 12.5% of the revenue it collected to the Musicians Union on an ex gratia basis. Both performers and sound recording copyright owners are now entitled to 'equitable remuneration' whenever their recordings are played in public or broadcast[2], and PPL therefore divides the licence fees it receives (the equitable remuneration in question) on a 50/50 basis between the sound recordings copyright owners on the one hand and the performers on the other. Currently, the 50% payable to performers is divided on a default basis as to 65% to featured performers and as to 35% to session musicians, although the performers on a recording are free to agree a different split if they wish.

As with PRS, the fees which PPL charges for the licences it issues depend on a number of factors, including the size of the premises, and the likely size and type of audience.

Unlike PRS, PPL has a very limited mandate in the online and mobile licensing environment, where usage is largely on demand. One reason is that copyright in a recording is typically wholly owned by one owner – the record label – and so the label can more easily manage its catalogue licensing alone, whereas musical compositions are often co-owned by two, three or more co-publishers, and an intermediary body (PRS) is required to collect licence fees and make the necessary revenue share allocations. It is also the case that, unlike PRS, PPL does not take an assignment of communication to the public rights from its performer members, so that the record label that owns the copyright in the recordings can directly license to the digital service provider all the rights in the recordings, including the performers' rights, that the provider requires. Finally, record labels prefer to individually negotiate all their online and mobile deals rather than apply a rate card approach at any level. It is therefore the case that almost all digital music services require direct label licences, with the limited exception of some online radio services with restricted pause and skip facilities for which PPL retains the mandate. These digital licences can sometimes require significant advances from the digital service provider and the biggest streaming services are now responsible for a significant part – in some cases a majority – of the typical record label's income.

1   See **Chapter 11**.
2   See **paragraph 20.26**.

Video Performance Limited (VPL)

20.23 VPL is the UK collective management organisation set up by the music industry in 1984 to administer the broadcast and public performance rights in short form music videos, and the right to copy (or 'dub') videos for such purposes. It is a branch of PPL. VPL represents the copyright owners of music videos and currently has some 800 members comprising mainly, but not exclusively, record companies.

VPL takes an assignment from its members of the public performance right in their videos and the right to copy for the purpose of public performance, subject in some cases to a licence back to the member to enable it to grant rights itself direct in some cases. It grants to users the right to publicly perform videos (eg in video juke boxes), include videos in broadcasts and some on demand services, and copy videos for the purpose of exercising the above rights. VPL issues blanket licence agreements and its charges are based on a rate card for most uses.

Rental and lending of sound recordings

20.24 The CDPA provides that the Secretary of State may, by Order, provide for a compulsory licensing scheme for the lending to the public of sound recordings, subject only to the payment of such reasonable royalty or other payment as may be agreed or determined in default of agreement by the Copyright Tribunal. A likely instance where such an Order would be made would be the refusal of record companies to allow public libraries to loan out their output of sound recordings[1].

1   **Paragraph 6.06** deals with rental and lending.

Agreements with recording artists

20.25 Contracts between record companies and recording artists are very complex, providing for different royalties for different types of sales. Thus, different royalties may be paid according to whether the sale is at full price, mid-price, overseas, on a compilation, as a single etc. As in the case of contracts between composers and publishers, the contracts between artists and record companies may be unenforceable if they operate as an unreasonable restraint of trade (eg because the term is too long, the artist cannot terminate if the company does nothing to exploit the rights or the payment provisions for the artist are unreasonably low, etc). Equally, contracts between artists and their managers may be unenforceable[1]. If, for example, the artist is not separately advised, the management contract may be held to be unenforceable on the grounds that the record company or manager exercised undue influence over the artist. Professional advice should always be sought on such arrangements.

1   For example, *O'Sullivan v Management Agency and Music Ltd [1985] QB 428, CA.*

Performers' equitable remuneration – public performance and broadcasting of sound recordings

20.26 The CDPA provides that:

'where a commercially published sound recording of the whole or any substantial part of a qualifying performance:

(a)   is played in public, or

(b)   is communicated to the public otherwise than by its being made available to the public [on demand][1],

the performer is entitled to equitable remuneration from the owner of the copyright in the sound recording ...'[2].

The provision above has the effect of placing the obligation to pay the equitable remuneration on the record label in typical circumstances (where the record label owns the copyright in the recording). The labels delegate this obligation to PPL, as seen above, and the 50/50 split of relevant broadcast revenue between labels and performers (the remuneration in question) has always been agreed to be equitable, so no negotiation on that point between labels and performers is necessary.

The right to receive equitable remuneration can be assigned by the performer only to a collective management organisation, and then only for the purpose of collecting it on his behalf. PPL fulfils this purpose on behalf of the performer. However, it can be transmitted under the performer's will or on his intestacy to his heirs or passed to his trustee in bankruptcy.

Any provision in a contract which excludes or restricts the performer's right to equitable remuneration is void, as is a provision designed to prevent him from questioning the amount of equitable remuneration payable or from taking the matter to the Copyright Tribunal[3].

1 CDPA s 182CA gives a performer the exclusive right to authorise or prohibit the making available of recordings by electronic transmission, so no equitable remuneration is payable for such usage. Considered further at **paragraph 11.14**.
2 CDPA s 182D.
3 Equitable remuneration is considered further at **paragraph 11.15**.

Performers' equitable remuneration – rental of sound recordings

20.27 Where a performer has transferred his rental right concerning a sound recording to the producer of the sound recording, he retains the right to equitable remuneration for the rental. 'Rental' in this case is generally taken to mean the rental of physical copies on the basis that they will be returned to the lender. The right may not be assigned by the performer, except to a collecting society for the purpose of enabling it to enforce the right on a performer's behalf. It can be transmitted by will or by operation of law (for example, bankruptcy). The person into whose hands it passes can further assign or transmit it. The equitable remuneration is payable by the person for the time being entitled to the rental right, that is, the person to whom the right was transferred or any successor in title. This will normally be the record company.

Due to the infrequency with which recordings are lent in the UK this right is of negligible commercial value to performers.

Exceptions to the copyright owner's exclusive rights

20.28 The requirement that there must be use of a substantial part of a recording before there is an infringement of copyright applies equally to sound recordings as it does to musical works[1].

The mandatory temporary copies exception under the CPDA applies to sound recordings, as do the 'fair dealing' exceptions under the CDPA[2]. No acknowledgement is required in the case of the use of a sound recording for the purposes of reporting current events[3].

The 'incidental inclusion' exception also applies to sound recordings[4], and the CDPA also contains specific exceptions dealing with Parliamentary and judicial proceedings[5].

1 See **paragraphs 7.06** and **20.12**.
2 See **paragraph 20.13**.
3 See **paragraph 8.07**.
4 See **paragraph 8.08**.
5 See **paragraph 8.12**.

Labelling

20.29 It is essential that the cover of records, when issued, shows the name of the copyright owner and the year in which the recording was first published. The information should be preceded by the ℗ symbol, which denotes copyright ownership in a sound recording. The labelling or marking of sound recordings in this way enables the copyright owner to gain the benefit of the presumption as to copyright ownership[1], and ensures that the recording and the performers are properly protected in the countries which are parties to the Rome Convention and to the Phonograms Convention.

Records should also and separately show the © symbol together with the date of first publication to denote the copyright owner of the cover artwork. This will ensure that the copyright in the artwork is protected in those few countries which are parties to the Universal Copyright Convention but not also parties to the Berne Convention and which require formalities as a prerequisite to copyright protection[2].

The placing of the copyright notices on the packaging of the actual disc also assists in civil and criminal infringement suits where it is necessary to prove that the defendant knew that the material infringed was in copyright[3].

1   See **paragraph 4.16**.
2   See **paragraph 4.16**.
3   See **paragraph 7.21**.

Infringement of copyright in sound recordings

20.30 It is an infringement to copy by any sort of recording process the sound made when a sound recording is played. It is not an infringement, however, to copy a sound recording in the sense of creating a new recording of a new performance that mimics (and therefore sounds the same as) the original performance on the original recording.

To sell, hire or offer for sale or even exhibit for sale in public, a recording which has been made without the licence of the owner of the copyright in the recording, constitutes an infringement of the copyright in the recording. Where a pirated recording is imported into the UK, the company importing it is liable for infringement of copyright[1]. Similarly, where a pirated record is offered for sale, the shop or website offering it for sale is liable for breach of copyright. If the person against whom the breach of copyright is alleged can show that he did not know and had no reason to believe that the recording concerned had been made in infringement of the copyright in the original recording, he will not be liable for infringement of copyright. In other words, genuine ignorance of the original piracy is a complete defence[2].

1   See **paragraph 6.10**.
2   A full analysis of 'secondary infringements' is considered in **paragraphs 6.10** ff.

Parallel importation of sound recordings

20.31 If copies of a recording made outside the UK (for example, in the USA) by or with the licence of the owners of the sound recording and musical composition copyrights in the USA, are imported into the UK, the UK licensee of the copyright owner can take action against the importer.

This does not apply within the EEA. Due to the EU rule on the freedom of movement of goods and services, a record which has been lawfully imported into or manufactured in one EEA country can be freely sold in all other EEA countries irrespective of the fact that the copyright owner may have granted exclusive licences to different companies in different EEA countries[1].

1   See also **paragraphs 6.05** and **13.05**.

Use of recordings by other media

20.32 The use of recordings in sound and television broadcasts and films are considered in detail elsewhere in this *User's Guide*[1].

1   See **paragraphs 22.03** and **22.11**.

Moral rights for performers in sound recordings

20.33 Since 2006 performers have had the benefit of moral rights in their performances. These rights are:

- the right to be credited wherever the performer performs in public, or his performance is broadcast live, or communicated to the public otherwise than by way of broadcast, or distributed in physical copies; and
- the right not have such a broadcast made, or a recording of his performance played in public, with any distortion, mutilation or other modification that is prejudicial to the reputation of the performer.

Where the performer is part of a group (for example a band or an orchestra) it is sufficient that the group is named (except in the case of physical distribution). There are a number of exceptions to these rights, and performers are very often required to waive their moral rights when entering into performer contracts[1].

1   Moral rights are discussed in **Chapter 10**.

Private copying

20.34 Anyone who copies a sound recording embodying a musical composition at home in the UK, for private use, is infringing the copyright in both the recording and the composition, unless a disabled exception applies, or one of the other (very limited) copyright exceptions applies. This breach of copyright commonly takes place and it is not practically possible to take proceedings against infringers when the infringement is on such a massive scale. In recognition of this fact, other European jurisdictions compensate lost revenue to the recording industry by raising a levy on blank tape sales, although no levy is in operation in the UK.

The UK government managed to introduce a limited personal copying exception into law in 2014 to deal with the typical 'format shifting' copying that many people undertake to move recordings between home devices. The introduction, however, was challenged by the music industry on the grounds that no compensatory levy was introduced at the same time, and that the government had not adequately assessed whether such a levy was necessary. The industry won its argument and the exception was repealed some ten months after its introduction. It is still therefore illegal to carry out any home copying (unless done within the functionality and rules of a fully licensed music service that expressly permits such copying, or an exception applies).

Chapter 21

Drama, ballet and opera production

Introduction

21.01 The works entitled to copyright protection which are incorporated in ballet, opera and live theatre productions (plays, revues, musicals, pantomimes and the like) are many and various and the following is a non-exhaustive list:

- *Artistic works*: set designs, back projection of slides, photographs, and potentially costumes and properties;
- *Dramatic works*: plays, sketches, pantomimes, revues, mime, libretti, choreography;
- *Musical works*: musical score, songs;
- *Sound recordings*;
- *Films.*

Various other elements of the production, such as lighting design, also may arguably be capable of protection, subject to the general prerequisite to copyright protection[1].

Reference should be made to the Table of Incidence of Copyright in **Appendix 2** to ascertain the period of copyright, the restricted acts and the rules for identifying the first owner, applicable to each of these types of works.

1 See **Chapters 2** and **3**.

Definitions

21.02 What constitutes a 'dramatic work' is considered in detail elsewhere in this *User's Guide*[1].

As to what amounts to a 'performance', the CDPA contains two definitions. In relation to issues regarding rights in performances per se, 'performance' means:

'(a) a dramatic performance (which includes dance and mime), or

(b) a musical performance,

(c) a reading or recitation of a literary work, or

(d) a performance of a variety act or any similar presentation, which is, or so far as it is, a live performance given by one or more individuals'[2].

When discussing the *restricted act* of performance in relation to copyright works, *performance* includes delivery in the case of lectures, addresses, speeches and sermons and in general any mode of visual or acoustic presentation including presentation by means of a sound recording, film, or broadcast of the work[3].

This latter definition is not an exhaustive list. Consequently, when considering the *restricted act* of performance, the word has its natural meaning, provided that the above categories of delivery are considered.

1   See **paragraph 2.03**.
2   CDPA s 180(2); see also **paragraph 11.02**.
3   CDPA s 19(2); see **paragraph 6.07**.

Set designs, costumes, properties and the like

21.03 All these works are in principle capable of being protected as artistic works. The first owner of copyright in an artistic work is the author, unless the work is made by an employee in the course of his employment[1]. So if a theatre company employs a set designer to work full-time at designing its sets and costumes, the copyright in the materials will belong to the company, in the absence of any agreement to the contrary. If, on the other hand, the set designer is engaged on a freelance basis or commissioned for the purpose of preparing the designs for one production only, the copyright in the designs will belong to the designer, although (absent any other agreement) there will be an implied licence permitting the company to use the designs for the purposes of its production.

As a general rule, in order to avoid the potential pitfalls of relying on the employer/employee rules or implied licences, it is wise to enter into a written contract with the designer clearly expressing how the copyright is to be owned and dealt with[2]. There is a fundamental difference between an assignment and a licence of copyright[3]. In short, an assignment is the outright sale of the copyright, whilst a licence is a limited contractual grant of rights to use the work for a defined period.

If the entire copyright for all purposes is to pass to the commissioning company, this should be stated and put in writing, signed by both parties. However, many designers seek to retain copyright in their designs.

It should be noted that copyright ownership is quite distinct from the ownership of the physical record of the designs themselves, and of the sets, costumes, etc made from the designs. Whilst the theatre companies may own the physical sets and costumes, the use to which they may be put will depend upon the copyright position[4].

When anything less than an outright assignment of copyright is taken, care should be taken to spell out clearly the rights which are granted by the designer. For example, it should be stated clearly whether or not the theatre company has the right to use the designs, not only for the original production, but also for other productions of the same play; or, possibly, any other productions whatsoever; whether it may assign the designs to any other company to use in their productions of the play; whether the rights include the right to use the designs in television or film versions of the production; whether the production may be presented outside the UK without additional payment. The period during which the company will be entitled to use the sets and costumes should also be set out.

If it is intended that the rights to be granted to the company are to be limited to the one production for which the designer has been commissioned to prepare designs, and further limited so that they can only be used by the company itself, then consideration should be given as to whether the company should be given options to use the designs in other contexts (in a revival of the production or in films or television versions of the production) on payment of an additional sum.

1   See **paragraph 9.11**.
2   Issues regarding implied licences are dealt with at **paragraph 9.29**.
3   See **paragraphs 9.21** ff.
4   See **paragraph 9.01**.

Use of existing artistic works in the theatre

21.04 If a painting, photograph, sculpture or other artistic work is used as part of the set, there will be no breach of copyright, because such a use is not an infringement of any of the restricted acts applicable to artistic works[1]. However, if it is necessary to *reproduce* the artistic work for the purposes of the production, for example by preparing a slide for projection or enlarging a photograph, then this will involve making a copy of the artistic work, which is a restricted act[2]. Accordingly, in such circumstances it is necessary to obtain a licence from the owner of the copyright in the photograph or other artistic work which is to be copied. But if a slide is obtained or a photograph is projected without having been reprinted, no authorisation is required.

If it is necessary to adapt (in the ordinary sense of the word) an artistic work for the purposes of designing a set, the adaptation will not constitute an infringement of the copyright in the artistic work. However, the adaptation may amount to a 'derogatory treatment' for moral rights purposes[3]. If there is any doubt whether a use will infringe another's moral rights, a waiver should be sought from the owner of the moral rights in question[4].

The adaptation of any other type of copyright work for use on the stage, for example a literary, dramatic or musical work (and note that films can be dramatic works) requires the consent of the copyright owner. If a film, for example, is projected as part of the scenic effects of the production, a licence will be required from the owner of the film, since the adaptation will amount to a restricted act, as will the performance of the film[5].

1   See **paragraph 6.02**.
2   See **paragraph 6.04**.
3   See **paragraph 10.29**.
4   See **paragraph 6.07**.
5   This issue is considered in further detail in **Chapter 10**.

Rights of the director

21.05 Unlike the director of a film, the director of a play, opera or ballet acquires no copyright interest in the production as a result only of his direction[1]. Obviously, if he creates dialogue he will own the copyright in the resulting 'literary work'[2] (always depending on the nature of his agreement with the producers).

If the director writes down his stage directions, he will have copyright in the wording and it cannot be copied into a new written version of the play without his licence.

If the production is filmed, an adaptation of the play (or relevant work) is likely to be created ie the play or work as interpreted by the stage directions, and if another stage director then copies the stage directions from the film (such as the movement of actors) then this may infringe copyright in the stage directions and/or the adapted work[3].

1   See **paragraph 9.05**.
2   See **paragraph 2.02**.
3   See **paragraph 6.04**.

Lighting designs

21.06 The lighting designer's plots are drawings, and are entitled to copyright protection as artistic works[1]. To the extent that they consist of written instructions, they are entitled to protection as literary works in themselves[2].

The making of copies is a restricted act applicable to literary, artistic and dramatic works. It follows that copies of the lighting designs cannot be made without the consent of the copyright owner. However the actual use of lighting designs for the purpose of a production in a theatre does not in itself constitute copyright infringement, because the CDPA provides that it is not an infringement of copyright to make an 'article' from the design, in this case the article being a lighting rig, and it is not an infringement of copyright to perform an artistic work in public[3].

Therefore, a person who obtains a copy of a lighting design and uses it for the purposes of his own production without authorisation will not be infringing the copyright in the designs. It follows that if a lighting designer does not restrict the use of his designs in the contract under which he is engaged to prepare them, even though he may retain the copyright in them, he is unlikely to be able to sue for unauthorised copying of the designs themselves, nor for unauthorised use. Ideally, a lighting designer should carefully spell out in any contract of engagement the limits of the uses of his designs permitted to the theatre company engaging him. He should state clearly on all copies that any copying of the designs requires his written consent. All copies should be numbered and they should be circulated to as few people as possible.

In some cases the lighting design, like the stage directions, may form part of the dramatic work itself, depending on their originality and whether they become 'merged' as part of the production process. A 'merger' of this type usually only happens when the lighting/direction or other merger element takes on a defining and permanent role in the piece and appears in every production, and when the producer takes ownership or control of the merged package as a whole.

1 See **paragraph 2.06**.
2 See **paragraphs 2.02** and **2.03**.
3 See **paragraphs 6.04** and **25.05**.

Expressions, not ideas, have copyright

21.07 Copyright protects the expression of ideas, not ideas themselves[1]. So, using the idea or concept of a designer but reconstructing completely new designs from new drawings is not of itself breach of copyright. If a production is set entirely in white, for example, another designer might also produce designs in white for the same play. Provided the new designs are different from the old ones, there would be no copyright infringement.

1 See **paragraphs 1.03** and **7.04**.

Plays, sketches and other live theatrical entertainments (except ballet and opera)

21.08 All these works are dramatic works and reference should be made to the Table of Incidence of Copyright in **Appendix 2** as to the attributes of copyright appropriate to dramatic works.

Mimes, choreography and choreology

21.09 Works of dance or mime are 'dramatic works'[1] and reference should be made to the Table of Incidence of Copyright[2] in order to ascertain the copyright incidents of choreographic works. In order to receive protection, these types of works must be recorded, in writing or otherwise.

If recorded in writing, the form of the writing is immaterial. The CDPA defines writing as including 'any form of notation or code, whether by hand or otherwise'[3]. Thus, choreology (which is the reduction of choreography to writing) is protected as a dramatic work. It does not matter what type of choreology is used: the shorthand notation of Benesch; the longer, more academic and elaborate Laban system; or even a choreographer's personal notes in his own invented system.

However, a simple way of ensuring that a dance, mime or other form of dramatic work (that is not easily reduced to writing) acquires copyright is to film it.

1   See **paragraph 2.03**.
2   See **Appendix 2**.
3   CDPA s 178; see **paragraph 2.05**.

Ownership of dramatic works

21.10 The first owner of a dramatic work is the author, unless he is an employee who creates the dramatic work in the course of his employment, in which case the employer will be the first owner in the absence of any agreement to the contrary[1].

1   See **paragraph 9.11**.

Adaptations of dramatic works

21.11 For the purposes of the CDPA, an adaptation of a dramatic work is:

- creating a non-dramatic version of the work, so for example writing a novel based on the play[1];
- creating a dramatic version of a non-dramatic work, so for example turning a novel into a play[2];
- creating a version in which 'the story or action is conveyed wholly or mainly by means of pictures in a form suitable for reproduction in a book, or in a newspaper, magazine or similar periodical'[3];
- a translation of the work[4].

It is a breach of copyright in relation to a dramatic work to make an unauthorised adaptation, so that a licence is required from the copyright owner of an original play before a translation of the play can be made. There will be a separate copyright in the translation, but it cannot be used unless the owner of the copyright in the original play grants a licence.

1   CDPA s 21(3)(a)(ii).
2   CDPA s 21(3)(a)(ii).
3   CDPA s 21(3)(a)(ii).
4   CDPA s 21(3)(a)(i).

Plots

21.12 Plots themselves are not per se entitled to copyright. However, if a producer were to borrow the basic plot, the dramatic incidents, the order of incidents and characters of another play without authorisation there may well be a breach of copyright[1].

1   See **paragraph 7.04**.

Use of real life incidents in the theatre

21.13 If a play is based upon real life incidents or upon an unwritten story told to the author by some other person, there is no question of breach of copyright in those incidents or that story[1]. However, the playwright who uses information which has been told to him by another person should always bear in mind the laws relating to breach of confidence.

1   See **paragraph 2.13**.

Exceptions

21.14 There is a 'fair dealing' provision in the CDPA that makes it possible to quote from other works in a play without the need for a licence if the usage in question amounts to fair dealing. The exception was introduced not long before the publication of this latest edition of the *User's Guide* and there is no case law as yet to help determine the permitted extent of the exception, but it would be unwise to rely on it for more than a borrowed line or perhaps two, and the use would have to be by way of quotation within the dramatic context, with suitable acknowledgement. It is likely that the 'substantial part' rule probably permits the same extent of usage, although under the substantial part rule no acknowledgment is required[1].

Reading in public by one person of any reasonable extract from a published literary or dramatic work, if accompanied by a suitable acknowledgement, does not constitute an infringement of the copyright[2]. However it is unlikely that a court would hold that the performance of part of another dramatic or literary work in the course of a play amounts to a reasonable extract. It would be unwise to rely on this provision for the usual varieties to dramatic performance. A licence should always be obtained from the copyright owner when part of another copyright work is incorporated in a play[3].

1   For what constitutes a 'substantial part' see **paragraph 7.06**.
2   CDPA s 59(1); see **paragraph 8.21**.
3   The exceptions to copyright infringement (including 'incidental inclusion') are considered in detail in **Chapter 8**.

Moral rights

21.15 Moral rights generally are discussed in **Chapter 10** of this *User's Guide*.

Improvisations

21.16 An improvisation is a play which is not written down, although there may be written guidelines for the actors. There will be no copyright protection for such an improvisation unless and until it is recorded by some means. Upon being recorded, the copyright in the words will vest in the creator, not the recorder[1], although the recorder will have the copyright in the recording, absent any agreement to the contrary. Also, if it is clearly stated on tickets and programmes that recording a performance would be a breach of confidence and that admission is conditional upon no unauthorised reproduction, there will be a right of action for breach of confidence and breach of contract against anyone who tries to make an unauthorised use of the production.

1 See **paragraph 9.03**.

Deposit requirements – Theatres Act 1968

21.17 The Theatres Act 1968 states that a copy of every play must be deposited with the British Museum not later than one month after the date of the performance of the play. No charge may be made to the British Museum for the copy so delivered. It is a criminal offence to fail to deposit copies at the British Museum[1].

1 Theatres Act 1968 s 11.

Opera, ballet and original musicals – grand rights

21.18 These types of entertainment constitute dramatic works[1]. The comments made above regarding plays apply equally to opera and ballet[2]. In the industry the dramatic staging rights in these works are commonly known as 'grand rights'.

Music forms an essential feature of these works; however there is an important difference between performances of opera, ballet and original musicals on the one hand, and other presentations including music on the other. Although in general the performing rights in music are vested with the Performing Right Society (PRS)[3], this is not usually the case with grand rights works, in respect of which the performing rights are retained by the composer. Therefore, when a company wishes to present an opera or ballet or musical, it is necessary to obtain not only a licence to perform the choreography and the libretto, but also an individual licence from the composer or his publisher to perform the music.

1   See **paragraph 2.03**.
2   See **paragraph 21.09** as to choreography.
3   As to which, see **paragraphs 12.01** and **20.07**.

Filming or broadcasting opera, ballet and live theatre

21.19 Including a dramatic work in a broadcast without authorisation infringes the copyright in the dramatic work, since broadcasting is a restricted act in relation to copyright works[1].

To make a film or sound recording of a dramatic work without permission is an infringement of any copyright in the work[2]. In addition, when the film is shown to the public, this will constitute performing the work in public[3]. Therefore, it is essential to check the original grant from the author of the play before the theatre company permits any television or sound broadcast or feature film or video tape or similar audio/visual record to be made of its production of the play.

1   See **paragraph 6.08**.
2   See **paragraph 6.04**.
3   See **paragraph 6.07**.

Music incorporated in live theatre productions (except ballet, opera and original musicals)

21.20 The performance of music in a play requires authorisation from the copyright owner. Where the performance is of 'pre-existing' music (ie music not specifically written for the production), rights should be cleared through PRS. Where the music was specifically written for that play or production, the likelihood is that the performing rights in the music form part of the licence of the work as a whole.

If a recording of music is used, a licence will also be required from the owner of the copyright in the sound recording itself (as distinct from the owner of the copyright in the music). If a sound recording of music is to be made especially for the production, the company should approach the Mechanical Copyright Protection Society (MCPS) for a licence[1].

1   See **paragraph 20.08**.

Contracts with theatre owners

21.21 Copyright is relevant to the contract with the theatre owner, because the CDPA specifically provides that the copyright in a dramatic or musical work is infringed by any person who permits a place of public performance to be used for a performance in public of a work where the performance constitutes an infringement of the copyright[1]. It follows that the owners of theatres and other places used for public performances should insist upon a warranty by the production producer that they have a licence granted by the owner(s) of the copyright to perform the dramatic or musical work in public.

1   See **paragraph 6.12**.

Dealing with dramatic works

21.22 In summary, agreements for the right to perform dramatic works are usually licences, since the authors prefer to retain their copyright. Licence fees will often be based on the producer's gross weekly box office receipts, so it is incumbent on the producer to ensure that there is sufficient profit to keep the show going. Having obtained the licence to produce and stage a work, the producer will engage the talent and the creative team necessary to put on the show.

The exception to the licence occurs in the case of producing theatres and individual producers who create new dramatic works themselves by a combination of commissioning talent to write for them and licensing in other copyright elements that the production requires. Often the producer will 'merge' these rights together in a package that it can own and license on to others so as to enjoy the revenue not simply from its own production. Naturally the producer will account to any third party licensor involved for a share of licence revenue, and there may well be contractual royalty participants as well, such as music composers, the original director and lighting designer, and perhaps the original choreographer if it is a musical.

Points to be covered in licences of dramatic works

21.23 A grant of rights in a dramatic work should deal specifically with the following points:

- *The date by which the first performance must take place*: it is usual to provide that unless the first performance takes place by a certain date the licence will lapse.
- *The precise rights granted*: if it is intended that the play is to be performed by professional actors only in the West End of London, with a right to tour before and afterwards, the licence should say so. Sometimes any rights to overseas tours or foreign presentations, or the right to license presentations of the production overseas, are expressed to arise only after a qualifying number of performances have taken place in the UK.
- *Sub-licences*: if it is intended that the producer licensee is to have the right to grant sub-licences either in the UK or abroad to other companies to perform its production of the play, this again should be clearly stated.

- *The period of the grant*: it is common to provide for a fixed period subject to extension if the work is performed for a minimum number of performances.
- *Royalty provisions*: there should be a clear statement as to what happens in the event of any failure to pay royalties. That is to say, are the unpaid royalties to be treated simply as a recoverable debt, or are all the rights in the play granted to the producer liable to revert to the copyright owner in such circumstances?
- *The right to arrange for film, television or radio performances of the work*: normally the producer is not given any such rights, except those necessary to enable it to advertise the work. It is nevertheless not uncommon to include a provision, in the case of new works, that after a certain number of performances the producer is entitled to a share of the proceeds of any grant of the film and television rights that the owner of the copyright might make (since the producer's efforts and investment will enhance the opportunity for the sale of film and television rights).
- *The right of the producer to make any changes in the text or title of the play*: in most cases a new play is changed in varying degrees during the course of rehearsals. Sometimes these changes are made by the director, or even by members of the cast. If they are written down by the director, then the copyright in them will vest in the director. Accordingly, the agreement should provide that the copyright in all changes should belong to the author or owner.

  Even if the right to make changes is granted, if such changes amount to a derogatory treatment of the work, the author (or other person to whom the moral rights in the play have been transmitted if the author is deceased) will have the right to sue for infringement of the moral right to object to derogatory treatment of the work[1]. A specific waiver or approval should therefore be sought.
- *Holdbacks*: if the author reserves rights to himself (and it is common for agreements granting the right to create a stage play to reserve, for example, film and television rights), the producer may seek restrictions upon how these are exercised. The nature of these restrictions will depend upon the negotiating positions of the parties. At one end of the spectrum, the author may agree not to exploit these rights at all whilst the stage play is being exploited. This kind of holdback is becoming less common, and may be counterproductive since the theatrical production might well benefit from the promotional opportunities created by, say, a film of the work. On the other hand, the producer has a legitimate concern to ensure that exploitation of these rights harmonises with his own plans, and for that reason consultation rights with regard to the exploitation of such rights are common.

1   See **Chapter 10**.

Chapter 22

Film and television production

Introduction

22.01 In this chapter, we consider copyright issues arising in the process of producing films. The CDPA defines 'film' very broadly, as 'a recording on any medium from which a moving image may by any means be produced'[1]. For this reason, most of the comments made in this chapter will apply equally to the production of feature films, television productions (other than live transmissions) and the creation of original video content for, say, the internet.

Although quite distinct industries, there are many similarities between the production process of television and film projects. In essence, in each case 'production' consists of three broad phases:

- *Development*: initially, the producer[2] will acquire control in the copyright (if any) of the work he wishes to use as a basis for his project (eg a novel, play, original screenplay, treatment or format) and will find a suitable cast, director and other personnel, locations and facilities, funding and distribution. Frequently, the producer will seek funding for this initial stage from a third party financier, and in exchange will usually enter into some limited assignment of the rights he has acquired in order to secure this loan investment. In the case of the film industry this finance will often come from a public funding body or from a broadcaster with interests in the film industry, and more rarely, given the perceived risky nature of development, by private investment.

- *Production*: next, *pre-production* consists of those steps necessary immediately before filming can begin (including set design and building, final casting, hiring crew, securing locations, equipment and facilities etc). If all goes well, pre-production should end with the commencement of the production phases proper, in which performances of the principal cast will be recorded ('principal photography'). After the completion of the photography of the shooting script, production will give way to *post-production* during which, broadly, the film which has been recorded will be edited, effects added in the studios, sound effects dubbed, and music added to the soundtrack (both in terms of original music commissioned for the film and 'licensed in' tracks). In the case of television projects the production process may well take a different shape, in particular where a series of programmes is commissioned by a broadcaster.

•   *Exploitation*: the production stage will end on delivery of the finished film or programme to its distributor (or broadcaster). Where the project is a television programme, its exploitation life may consist of single or repeat showings on television. On the other hand the project may be intended for the fullest possible international exploitation in all media. In the latter case, it will be common for the producer to appoint a 'sales agent' or intermediate distributor to handle the sale of rights internationally, who will commonly sell rights on to distributors on a territorial basis.

1   See **paragraph 2.08** and CDPA s 5B(1).
2   Whilst reference is made to 'the producer' throughout for ease of understanding, note that a company, an 'SPV' (special purpose vehicle), will almost certainly be established at the outset of a project to enter into all film-related agreements, ensuring the clean acquisition of all film-related rights and ring-fencing liability.

Definitions

22.02 Copyright works of all kinds are relevant to film production[1]. The definition of 'film' under the CDPA itself is very wide and also protects the soundtrack of the film as part of the film itself[2].

Although the practical steps necessary to create a feature film, a television series, a one-off television special or a music video may be very different, as stated above, for copyright purposes they will all be films and most of the comments in this chapter will apply to all these works.

The restricted acts, with the exception of adaptation, are all relevant when considering the infringement of copyright in films[3]. In particular, the reader should note the technical meaning of 'broadcast' and 'communication to the public' in this context[4].

The authors of a film are the producer and the principal director[5]. For these purposes, the producer is 'the person by whom the arrangements necessary for the making of the film are undertaken'[6]. That person can be either an individual, or a corporate entity, or both.

1   See **paragraph 1.02**.
2   See **paragraph 2.08**.
3   See **Chapter 6**.
4   See **paragraphs 2.09–2.10**.
5   See **paragraph 9.05**.
6   CDPA s 178; see **paragraph 9.05**.

The elements of production

22.03 The feature film producer must acquire sufficient rights to enable him to create and exploit his film in any and all media[1] by any manner or means worldwide. Except in the context of licensed music and sound recordings, it is customary for the producer to acquire these rights by way of assignment[2]. The basic elements of a film are as follows:

- *Underlying works* (eg the novel, play, biography, story board, treatment, format, original screenplay, research etc): it is customary for the producer to take an irrevocable assignment of the underlying works used for the film. However, in some cases, a full assignment of all rights will not be available (eg print publication rights, with certain limitations, are usually reserved to the author, and in the case of a novel, will be a primary means of exploitation for the writer) or certain unexploited rights may be negotiated as retained by the author as a potential alternative source of income (eg publishing rights, stage and radio rights, subject to hold backs). In any event, to make and exploit his film, the producer will need to acquire the right to:
  - (a) *adapt* the work (eg from a novel into a screenplay for film or television, or possibly to create a novelisation of a screenplay);
  - (b) *copy* the work (eg by creating the film and trailers, and possibly prequels, sequels remakes, spin-off's etc);
  - (c) *issue copies to the public* (eg physical or downloaded copies containing the film embodying the work, for sale to the public, or by the publication of screenplay, or a 'book of the film', synopses etc);
  - (d) *rent or lend copies of the work to the public* (eg by video rental);
  - (e) *perform, play or show the work in public* (eg by performing it as part of the films or other works created by the producer in front of audiences in cinemas, or alternatively on stage);
  - (f) *communicate to the public* the film or films he creates (by all forms of transmission media, although stage and radio rights in the underlying work are commonly reserved and may be subject to some form of hold back or other limitation on exploitation). It will be important to ensure the assignment is clearly drafted to include all forms of transmission)[3];
  - (g) *make alterations to or manipulate the work* (ie a waiver of the author's moral right of integrity)[4].

  The agreement will also deal with issues such as credit, fees (including standard wording dealing with equitable remuneration for rental and lending[5]) and other entitlements of the owner (eg premieres).

  If the owner is not the author, it will be necessary to establish a complete 'chain of title' by which the present owner demonstrates how he acquired the rights. This chain will need to track dealings with the rights from the first owner of copyright through to the current owner. The owner will be expected to provide copies of all relevant documentation, and provide warranties and indemnities as to its completeness and his ownership of the rights.

At an early stage, the producer will commonly seek to reduce his costs by taking an exclusive option to acquire the necessary rights from the owner within a period (usually one year, with a right to extend for at least one and usually two or more similar period(s)) against payment of a fee. The fee may vary widely, but one rule of thumb is 10% of the projected purchase price of the work for the initial option fee. It will be vital to the producer to ensure that having paid his option fee, he can ensure that a mechanism is in place whereby the owner must transfer the rights to him on pre-agreed terms if and when the option is exercised. Consequently the full terms of the assignment are usually negotiated simultaneously and the option and the agreed wording is appended to or forms part of the option agreement itself.

If the underlying work is 'in the public domain', either because copyright protection in it has expired or because the work was not of a kind which was capable of attracting protection[6], there will be no legal reason to acquire any rights in the underlying works. In the case of copyright works it will be necessary to assess carefully whether the copyright has expired in all intended countries of exploitation[7].

- *The screenplay*: except in the unlikely circumstance that the producer acquires rights to an original screenplay which requires no rewriting, it will be necessary to hire the services of a writer. Again, the producer must ensure that he has all the rights he requires in the screenplay. If the writer is an employee of the producer pursuant to a contract of service, the producer will be the first owner of copyright in the writer's work, provided that it was created during the course of his employment and provided that there is no agreement to the contrary[8]. Nevertheless, the writer's agreement should contain a confirmatory assignment for absolute clarity and to avoid the possibility of arguments later on[9]. Since the agreement will (hopefully) be entered into prior to delivery of the work, such assignments will include all 'present and future copyright' created by the writer in relation to the screenplay[10].

The same agreement will need to address the issue of moral rights (to which the writer will be entitled unless he worked as an employee[11], and in respect of which a waiver should be obtained[12]), credit, remuneration, and service obligations and entitlements (eg premieres, transportation and expenses). In the case of writers, an agreement, the Screenwriting Credits Agreement 1974, between the Writers Guild of Great Britain and the Film Production Association of Great Britain (the predecessor to the Producers' Alliance for Cinema and Television (PACT)) will provide a mechanism for establishing the credit to be applied in any particular instance[13] where the agreement so provides or otherwise, in the event of dispute.

- *Musical compositions – copying the music as part of the film*: the use of music in film is a complex area, but in brief, the inclusion on the soundtrack of each composition (ie synchronisation) will need to be authorised, as will the subsequent exploitation in the compositions. The extent to which the producer clears those exploitation rights at production stage depends on the type of production. Film producers will usually need to clear all rights in all media. TV producers usually clear more limited TV rights, and if working on commission may have the advantage of a blanket licence. Video producers will similarly clear more limited rights. In all cases the exception is the rights owned by PRS, which will be cleared by the cinema, broadcaster, online service or other business that is the last link in the chain of supply to the consumer[14].

- *Sound recordings – copying sound recordings as part of a film*: again, if a film is to include previously recorded versions of musical compositions, the producer will need to obtain authorisations to dub these sound recordings in addition to a grant of rights from the owners of the musical compositions, and this clearance process is in general the same as for musical compositions, but with important differences[15].

- *Sets designs, costume designs, locations etc*: various copyright works will be created or used during the course of making a film. Many of these will be protectable as original artistic works[16]. Similarly, the producer may make use of pre-existing footage, photographs etc. Again, the producer must ensure that he has taken all the rights he needs to exploit these works to enable him to make his film, usually by way of assignment or licence. Commonly, artistic and other copyright works of various descriptions will be caught on film (for example the artistic works embodied in buildings passed during a street scene), and where they are 'incidentally included' there will be no breach of copyright[17]. In some circumstances it may be permissible to include copyright works without infringing copyright (eg fair dealing); the issues associated with making such uses of works are considered elsewhere in this *User's Guide*[18].

- *Performances*: performers such as actors and musicians have 'property rights' akin to copyright and 'non-property rights' in their performances and additionally, have a right to be identified as a performer (on condition of assertion) and a right to object to derogatory treatment. In brief, a performer's engagement terms should contain the fullest possible grant or assignment of these rights (and waiver, in the case of moral rights) and confirm the consent of the performer to the recording and exploitation of his performance in all media[19].

- *The director*: the principal director is an author and (unless he produces the work in the course of his employment[20]) will be a first owner of the copyright of the film together with the producer[21]. Additionally the director may contribute to any of a number of other creative elements of the film (including the screenplay). Consequently, the producer must ensure that an adequate transfer of copyright, and waiver of moral rights[22], in the film (and all other products of the director's services on the film) is properly effected.

1   To enable the fullest possible exploitation in a world of constantly evolving technology and means of viewing content, any assignment of rights should allow for exploitation in any and all media now existing or invented in the future. Any reservation of rights by the owner or other restriction to the rights acquired by the producer will have to be very carefully negotiated on a case-by-case basis, having regard to various commercial factors, such as the bargaining power of the parties and commercial value of the work.
2   See **paragraph 9.21**.
3   The above rights correspond to the restricted acts referred to at **paragraph 6.02**.
4   See **paragraph 10.29**.
5   See **paragraph 6.06**.
6   See **paragraph 2.12**.
7   As to which see **Chapter 5**.
8   See **paragraph 9.11**.
9   Additionally, for the purposes of a clean chain of title clearly showing the passage of all relevant rights to the producer, which will be required by any financier and/or distributor of the film. See **paragraph 10.13**.
10 See **paragraph 9.24**.
11 See **paragraph 10.10**.
12 See **paragraph 10.29**.
13 For further information contact the WGGB, whose address is set out in **Appendix 1**.
14 These issues are considered in detail in **paragraph 22.10** and the paragraphs referred to in that paragraph.
15 These issues are considered in detail in **paragraph 22.11** and the paragraphs referred to in that paragraph.
16 See **paragraph 2.06**.
17 One important qualification to this principle being that a musical work or such other work as includes a music work will not be held 'incidentally included' if it is deliberately included, see **paragraph 8.08**.
18 See **Chapter 8**.
19 See CDPA, Part II and **Chapter 11**.
20 See **paragraphs 9.11** ff.
21 See **paragraph 9.05**.
22 See **paragraph 10.29**.

Issues when acquiring rights – ancillary rights

22.04 Commonly, ancillary rights will mean merchandise, comics, books, clothes and the like of all kinds and in all languages etc, namely rights which are supplementary and subordinate to the principal right of exploiting the film in its original format. Even if the producer does not acquire all ancillary rights in the work, he will always require the right to distribute and translate synopses of the work to assist sales etc. It will not always be clear whether these will infringe the copyright in underlying works, but since these may feature substantial parts of copyright works included in the film (such as drawings or stills of characters, or extracts or adaptations of the screenplay) the producer will want to ensure that he has the fullest rights to exploit 'ancillaries' based on the project. For major projects the producer will be anxious to protect its interest in such works by registering trade and service marks, although a detailed consideration of this issue is beyond the scope of this *User's Guide*.

Issues when acquiring rights – moral rights

22.05 Moral rights are discussed in detail elsewhere in this *User's Guide*[1].

The paternity right, the integrity right, and the right to object to false attribution are all available to the authors of literary, dramatic, musical or artistic works, and film directors[2]. Since the film-making process involves manipulating and adapting the content provided by all the various creative people involved (eg by editing, applying effects, reducing the duration of the film, removing or altering material for censorship purposes, modifying the aspect ratio of the image for television exploitation, etc), it is customary to obtain a waiver from the owner of all their moral rights. It is worth noting that the integrity right of an author in respect of works created by him as an employee in the course of his employment, where the act is done with the authority of the copyright owner, is not infringed unless the author or director has been identified at the time of the act or has previously been identified in or on published copies of the work. Even then, a claim of infringement can be avoided if 'sufficient disclaimer' is given[3].

In France, it has been held[4] that the colourisation of a black and white film may constitute derogatory treatment. The cutting of a film into a shorter version to fit a television slot may well constitute a derogatory treatment, although in most cases, this will be expressly permitted by the terms of the director's contract with the producer.

If an author or director wishes to assert his paternity right, he must do so in writing at the time of the assignment (not afterwards)[5]. It is advantageous for the author or director to make the assertion in the assignment of copyright, since otherwise it will only be binding on those to whose attention it is brought[6]. The right will not in any event apply where the work is made by an employee during the course of his employment[7].

The right to prevent false attribution of a work applies equally to the director of a film as to the authors of literary, dramatic, musical and artistic works. So, if a producer re-cuts a film such that the director no longer regards it as his own work, he may argue an infringement of this moral right[8].

If a producer wishes to make use of a film or photograph made for private and domestic purposes he will require authorisation not only from the copyright owner, but also from any third party who commissioned it[9]. It should be noted that moral rights do not apply to films made before 1 August 1989[10]. However, they do apply to acts done to literary, dramatic, musical and artistic works which were in existence before that date, provided their authors were still alive as at that date. An act undertaken pursuant to a licence or assignment entered into prior to 1 August 1989 will not infringe moral rights[11]. In short, if a producer acquired rights prior to 1 August 1989, he need not worry about moral rights under the CDPA in relation to the exercise of his right under the licence or assignment, although false attribution provisions under the Copyright Act 1956 would continue to be relevant[12].

1   See **Chapter 10**.
2   **Paragraphs 10.03** and **10.13**. Note also certain moral rights (the right to be identified and the right to object to derogatory treatment) are conferred upon performers by CDPA, Part II Chapter 3 (see **paragraph 22.06**).
3   See **paragraph 10.18**.
4   In 1991, by the Supreme Court of France, re 'The Asphalt Jungle' by John Huston.
5   See **paragraph 10.08**.
6   See **paragraph 10.09**.
7   See **paragraph 10.10**.
8   See **paragraph 10.21**.
9   See **paragraph 10.24**.
10 Ie commencement of the CDPA.
11 See **paragraph 10.32**.
12 See **paragraph 10.32**.

Issues when acquiring rights – performers' rights

22.06 Performers' rights are dealt with in **Chapter 11**. Essentially, performers are entitled to *performers' non-property rights and recording rights*[1] and *performers' property rights*. The former include the right to consent to the recording or live broadcast or transmission of a performance, or to the use of the recording, or to the importation, possession or dealing with a recording[2], and the latter comprise the right to authorise the reproduction, distribution, rental and lending and making available of copies of a recorded performance[3]. Furthermore, a performer is accorded certain moral rights, namely, the right to be identified and the right to object to derogatory treatment, subject to certain exceptions[4]. Significantly, the Copyright Tribunal may grant consent on behalf of a performer whose whereabouts cannot be ascertained by reasonable inquiry[5], although the new orphan works clearance regime will now take precedence as the preferred process by which rights to works of unknown authorship can be cleared[6].

Although no permission is required to record on film the actions of people which do not amount to protectable performances, there is a clear danger that filming in such circumstances may amount to a breach of confidence (depending on the circumstances). Commonly, producers will obtain wide releases, or 'quitclaims', from persons they film confirming that use of their appearance will not infringe their rights.

1   Recording rights are held by a person or entity (eg a film production company or recording company) with the exclusive right to record performances of a performer.
2   See **paragraphs 11.06–11.10**.
3   See **paragraphs 11.11–11.13**.
4   See CDPA, Part II Chapter 3.
5   See **paragraph 11.23**.
6   See the government website at https://www.gov.uk/guidance/copyright-orphan-works#overview for more detail of this clearance regime.

Issues when acquiring rights – rental rights and equitable remuneration

22.07 Rental rights of authors and qualifying performers are dealt with in detail elsewhere in this *User's Guide*[1]. Briefly, these rights are presumed to be transferred in film production agreements (except for the author of a screenplay, dialogue or music created for the film). The authors of literary, dramatic, musical and artistic works, and film directors, and qualifying performers, also have an inalienable (other than to a collecting society acting on his behalf) right to receive equitable remuneration from the rental of their works notwithstanding that the rental right itself is transferred by the author or performer to, say, the producer of a film. The level of equitable remuneration is to be set by the parties and in the absence of agreement, the Copyright Tribunal may intervene. In the film industry, producers usually attempt to pre-estimate the 'equitable remuneration'[2] or, more commonly, will include acknowledgement by the author or qualifying performer that the fee payable under the agreement includes full, equitable and adequate consideration for the rental and lending rights assigned to the producer and the exploitation of such rights by the producer.

1   See **paragraphs 6.06, 9.27** and **11.13**.
2   See **paragraphs 6.06** and **9.27**.

Issues when acquiring rights – films as dramatic works

22.08 In 2000, the Court of Appeal held that a film[1] may itself be capable of enjoying protection as a 'dramatic work' in its own right[2]. It follows that if a producer wishes substantially to duplicate the scenes and content of an earlier film but without copying the footage itself, he should consider the need not only to acquire necessary rights in the underlying material from its owners, but also in the earlier film.

1 As distinct from any dramatic work which may have been recorded in the film.
2 See **paragraph 2.03**.

Issues when acquiring rights – works of joint authorship

22.09 The producer will need to be cautious where he wishes to acquire rights in works in which there have been contributions from other people, such as story collaborators or script editors, to ensure that all potential authors have assigned their rights, or entered into binding agreements confirming they have no rights (including moral rights) over the material to be acquired. Although it will be unusual for such persons to acquire copyright, they may do if their contributions to the protectable parts of the resulting work are sufficiently distinct and original[1]. Such contributions are a common source of copyright claims in the film and television industry.

1 See **paragraphs 3.01, 9.03** and **9.08**.

Issues when acquiring rights – musical compositions

22.10 Music used in films may either be used in the background, or as 'featured' music (ie it is played by the actors, or it is evidently audible to the actors in the scene). It may be pre-existing music which is licensed in for the film, or it may be specifically commissioned by the producer from a composer. It may be library music (particularly the case for TV programmes). It may be performed live (eg where the film features a concert performance) or taken from recordings. In any event, the producer will need to obtain the right to synchronise the musical compositions to the soundtrack of the film and to any trailers which it may produce to promote the film[1]. This synchronisation right will need to be obtained from the relevant music publisher(s), although TV broadcasters and certain TV production companies can synchronise music in the MCPS repertoire under their licences from MCPS, which allow for limited use of that repertoire on named TV channels, but these licences are not blanket licences and exclude the rights of significant publishers.

The synchronisation rights to specially commissioned music are legally owned by PRS, as provided by the PRS membership agreement (assuming the composer is a PRS member)[2]. However, the widespread practice is for composers to assign the synchronisation right direct to the commissioning producer. This assignment is legally possible under an arrangement by which PRS agrees that the composer may enjoy a reversion of the film synchronisation right for a given production (so that he may then give a valid assignment of the right to the producer) provided that the producer pays to PRS a fee in respect of public performance of the relevant production in US cinemas in return for a licence of that right, for which public performance royalties are not otherwise payable. In practice the composer is often required to grant such US public performance rights to the producer direct under the commission agreement, in which case the reversion does not take place, and this means the composer's grant of rights to the producer is invalid. This is a peculiarity of the industry where law and practice do not necessarily match up.

The mechanical right (ie the right to copy the musical composition onto carriers such as DVD and on the servers of video on demand services) will also need to be cleared by the producer, and depending on the circumstances this right may in some respects and to some extent be included in the synchronisation licence, and it is otherwise administered and licensed on behalf of the publisher by MCPS[3].

The exploitation of the film including musical compositions will also involve engaging in other acts restricted by copyright in relation to the musical compositions: namely the public performance of the work (ie by exhibition of the film in cinemas etc) and its inclusion in broadcasts and in video on demand services. These rights must also be cleared, although such clearance is done by the broadcasters and exhibitors of the film, not the producer. It is important for the producer to ensure that his agreements with distributors clearly set out the rights to be cleared by parties other than the producer[4].

1   Ie to authorise the restricted act of copying, see **paragraph 6.03**.
2   See **Appendix 1**.
3   See **paragraph 20.08**.
4   The right to perform compositions and include them in broadcasts and other public communications are considered in **paragraphs 20.07** and **23.13**.

Issues when acquiring rights – sound recordings

22.11 Unless the musical compositions to be included in a film are performed 'live' on the soundtrack for the film (such as, for example, in the case of a concert), it will be necessary to obtain the right to synchronise the sound recordings featuring the musical compositions onto the film soundtrack, and, again, the right to copy the recordings onto carriers such as DVDs on which copies of the film will be sold to the public. Where the music is specially commissioned for the film (ie from a composer) it is usual for the producer to take an assignment of the copyright and all other rights in the recordings the composer makes, and that assignment will include the synchronisation right. Where the producer wants to use pre-existing commercially released recordings, or library music, the producer will have to license the synchronisation right from the relevant record company or music library. Synchronisation licences of recordings are often called 'master use' licences.

Whether the score is specially commissioned by the producer, or pre-existing recordings are licensed in for the film, it will be necessary to ensure that all performers' rights are properly cleared. In a composer commission agreement the composer's performers' rights (which arise when the composer records his score) are invariably 'bought out' by payment of the commission fee. Any session musicians or orchestra players engaged to perform on the score recordings are usually engaged on standard industry terms agreed between the Musicians' Union and PACT (the Producers' Alliance for Cinema and Television)[1]. When recordings are licensed in from a record company the licences will usually require the producer to clear and pay any so-called 're-use fees' to the non-featured performers who performed on the recording; those re-use fees for film and TV use are set out in the Musicians' Union/PACT agreement. Library music licences are generally clear of all performers' rights.

The exploitation of a film whose soundtrack includes sound recordings of musical compositions will also involve engaging in other acts restricted by copyright in relation to those sound recordings: namely playing the works in public (ie by exhibition of the film in cinemas etc[2]) and their inclusion in broadcasts and video on demand services. Unlike for musical compositions, this public performance right is usually included on a buy-out basis in master use licences granted to film producers, so the producer can pass this right on down the distribution chain. TV use licences, on the other hand, exclude the public performance right, so that TV broadcasters pay for the public performance under their blanket licences with PPL (Phonographic Performance Limited). Library music licences often include the public performance rights on a buy-out basis. As with the musical compositions embodied in sound recordings, it is important for the producer to ensure that its agreements with distributors clearly set out the rights to be cleared by parties other than the producer.

1   The latest version of this standard industry agreement is dated 1 January 2016.
2   See **paragraph 6.07**.

Sequels, prequels and remakes

22.12   We have mentioned elsewhere that there is no copyright in an idea[1], although it is possible that copyright infringement may occur as a consequence of the appropriation of plot or characters. In any event, the owner of an earlier work may well have a legitimate claim for passing off. The producer will want to ensure that the position regarding derivative works based on the work he acquires is clearly dealt with in his contract with an author. Usually the producer will take the right to create his own sequels, prequels and remakes of his film (although may agree to the author being entitled to certain passive payments from revenues generated from the exploitation of such rights), and will want to have some right to acquire, or at least to have a favourable opportunity to negotiate for, any author-written sequel to a novel for which he acquires film rights.

1   See **paragraph 7.04**.

Co-productions

22.13 Many European films are created as 'co-productions', where two or more producers divide responsibilities for the development, financing, production and distribution of the film. If structured as an official co-production under the terms of a bi-lateral treaty entered into by the UK or under the European Convention on Cinematographic Co-Production, each co-producer will be entitled to access to certain national benefits, which may otherwise not be available. Since the authors of a film are the producer and the director[1], the producer for these purposes meaning 'the person by whom the arrangements necessary for the making of the film are undertaken'[2], it will be necessary to carefully distinguish in the co-production arrangements how ownership will be shared between the producers. It is common for co-producers to divide exploitation of the film between them along territorial lines. If this is the case, particular attention should be paid in any contract to those transmissions which are not territorially limited[3].

1   See **paragraph 9.05**.
2   See **paragraph 22.03**.
3   For example, satellite transmissions, as to which see **paragraphs 24.21** ff.

Infringement

22.14 The acts restricted by copyright in relation to films are:

- *Copying*: this will include taking a photograph of the whole or a substantial part of a frame (ie 'video grab')[1].
- *Issuing of copies to the public*: this applies to the first act of putting particular copies of the work into circulation within the EEA or putting into circulation outside the EEA copies not previously put into circulation in the EEA or elsewhere[2].
- *Rental and lending*[3].
- *Performing, showing or playing in public.*
- *Communicating to the public*[4].

It is worth noting that the restricted act of adaptation is not applicable to films[5].

An infringement will only take place if a 'substantial part' of a work is copied, although the test is qualitative not quantitative[6].

1   See **paragraph 6.04**.
2   See **paragraph 6.05**.
3   See **paragraph 6.06**.
4   See **paragraph 6.08**.
5   The acts which may only be undertaken with the authority of the copyright owner are considered in detail in **Chapter 6**.
6   See **paragraph 7.06**.

Permitted acts

22.15 A number of acts may be undertaken in relation to films without infringing copyright, and broadly, these are the same as those applicable to other categories of copyright work[1]. It is worth noting that special provision is made to deal with acts undertaken when it is reasonable to assume the copyright in the film has expired[2].

1   See **Chapter 8**.
2   See **paragraph 8.29**.

Duration

22.16 The basic rules for establishing the author and period of copyright of copyright works are set out in **paragraphs 9.05** ff and **5.07–5.09**. It should be noted that the copyright treatment given to film will vary significantly depending upon when it was made. Films made before 1 June 1957, for example, did not receive copyright protection in their own right at all.

International issues – local formalities and foreign registrations

22.17 Producers should ensure that in order to receive the widest possible international protection for their films, the '©' symbol, the name of the copyright owner and the year of first publication appear on all film prints and negatives[1].

It is worth noting that although compliance with local formalities is not required under the terms of the Berne Convention[2], it is common (given the significance of the US market) for producers to ensure that the underlying work and screenplay are registered at the US Copyright Office[3], since registration acts as effective notice to third parties of the rights of the producer. Options and assignments may also be registered, and where US exploitation is potentially anticipated, it is customary for the writer's agreement and option/assignment agreements to attach a short form confirmatory document which is supplied to the US Copyright Office for registration. Searches of the Register by title may reveal existing interests recorded against the title, and will enable the producer (and financiers) to become aware of other projects with similar titles. Such a search is usually an item required for the financing and delivery of the film and is also required by film insurers. A registry of titles is also operated by the Motion Picture Association, although other companies are available to carry out specialised title and copyright searches. Registration does not confer copyright or other protection on a title, although a search may assist the producer in bringing his product to the market without causing confusion. As we have considered elsewhere, a title is unlikely to be sufficiently original to receive protection as a literary work[4].

1   Issues of international copyright are considered in detail in **Chapter 4**.
2   See **paragraph 4.12**.
3   See **Appendix 1**.
4   See **paragraph 3.02**.

Chapter 23

Public performance: discotheques, concert halls, cinemas, theatres, clubs, hotels, etc

Introduction

23.01 The owners, occupiers and managers of places where public performance takes place are concerned with copyright because the performance of a literary, dramatic or musical work in public and the playing or showing of a sound recording, film or broadcast in public may infringe the copyright in such works unless licensed[1]. So we are concerned here not just with live performances in front of an audience, but any kind of playing of a performance, both live and from recordings. In each case a licence is usually required from the respective copyright owners for the public performance of the works. There are no material exceptions to this rule.

1   See **paragraph 6.07**.

Definitions

23.02 The CDPA gives the owner of a literary, dramatic or musical work the exclusive right to authorise or prevent the performance in public of their work. The CDPA defines 'performance' as including: 'delivery in the case of lectures, addresses, speeches and sermons'. It also includes 'any mode of visual or acoustic presentation, including presentation by means of a sound recording, film, or broadcast of the work'[1].

It also includes, specifically, 'delivery, in the case of lectures, addresses, speeches and sermons'.

'In public' is not defined. However, the Gregory Committee Report on Copyright said:

'So far as we can see, the courts have generally interpreted the term "performance in public" as a term in contradistinction to a performance which takes place within the domestic circle'[2].

The English courts have largely upheld this view, with the effect that even if the public in general are not admitted to an event or a venue, the performance will still be 'in public' if people are present, or potentially present, who are not strictly within the domestic circle. It is an infringement of copyright to do acts in relation to a work which are designated as restricted acts, and it also an infringement of copyright to authorise restricted acts. As has been seen, public performance is designated as a restricted act in relation to certain works[3].

The expression *'to authorise'* is not defined in the CDPA, but the courts have held it to mean to 'sanction, approve and countenance', in other words it is not enough to simply enable someone to do the act in question; there must be a purported grant (express or implied) of the authority to do the act[4].

1   CDPA s 19(2).
2   See **paragraph 11.28** for a further consideration of 'public' in this context.
3   See **paragraph 6.07**.
4   The question of authorising infringement was considered in detail in *CBS Songs Ltd v Amstrad Consumer Electronics plc [1988] 2 All ER 484, HL.*

The public performance of music and sound recordings

23.03 In considering any question involving the performance of music, it is essential to distinguish between the performance of a sound recording and the performance of the musical composition (and any associated lyrics) embodied in that sound recording.

In the case of a live performance, the only licence required is from the owner (or owners) of the relevant copyright in the musical compositions (and any separate lyrics) that are performed. Lyricists and composers in the UK, almost without exception, assign the performing right in their music to the Performing Right Society (PRS) which trades under the name PRS for Music[1]. Moreover, foreign composers and lyricists usually have similar arrangements with their national performing right organisation, which itself will have reciprocal collection arrangements that include PRS. Consequently, PRS licences include the right to play music controlled by all other performing right organisations in the world with which PRS has reciprocal arrangements (which is the vast majority).

When a sound recording is played in public, two consents are required: one from the owner(s) of the copyright in the musical composition and the other from the owner of the copyright in the sound recording. In the great majority of cases, the owners of the copyright in sound recordings which are issued for sale to the public assign the right to perform such recordings to their collective management organisation Phonographic Performance Limited (PPL)[2]. So, in the case of a performance of a record on, say, a jukebox in a public house, two licences are required: a PRS licence to perform the *musical composition* in public and a licence from PPL to play the *recording* of the music in public. At the time of writing, PRS and PPL are beginning to offer joint PRS/PPL licences for certain types of public performance to ease the licensing process for certain smaller venues.

1　See **paragraphs 12.01** and **20.07**.
2　See **paragraphs 12.01** and **20.22**.

Musical compositions – PRS public performance licences

23.04 The general practice of PRS is not normally to grant the public performance licence to the persons actually performing the music or to the people who actually play the recordings, but to the business or person who controls the premises where the music is performed or played. In law, both the performer and the premises owner are liable for the acts of public performance, but the premises licence will cover the performer's liability[1].

PRS issues music licences to almost every place where it is conceivable that music could be performed in public, ranging from aircraft to roller-skating rinks and pop festivals to football grounds, speedway stadia, retail shops, ice rinks, holiday centres etc. If music is played to the public (whether or not they pay for admission), there will be a breach of copyright unless a licence has been granted by PRS (and, if applicable, PPL[2]). As we have seen above, the word 'public' includes members of private clubs. What constitutes the public is a question of law depending on the facts of each case, but it is only when a performance takes place in a truly domestic context that it can safely be regarded as not being a public performance. Whenever there is any doubt, an application should be made to PRS for a licence.

1　Further detail with regard to PRS can be found in **paragraph 20.07**. Its licence fees are available on the PRS for Music website: www.prsformusic.com.
2　See **paragraph 23.08**.

Exceptional cases where no PRS licence is required

23.05 PRS makes voluntary exemptions as a matter of policy from the general rule that a licence is required for a public performance. The exceptions are available on the PRS for Music website, and include (among other uses): certain healthcare premises and residential homes; divine worship; weddings, funerals and other ceremonies; and certain educational uses.

Opera, ballet and other 'grand rights'

23.06 Performances of opera, operetta, musicals, revues, pantomime and ballet, insofar as they consist of words and music written expressly for such works (ie 'dramatico-musical works'), similarly require licences from the copyright owner(s), but in most cases PRS is not the owner of the performing rights for dramatically staged works such as these (also known as 'grand rights') – the rights are retained by the authors/composers. Accordingly, in the case of opera, operetta, musicals, revues and ballets etc it is likely to be necessary to negotiate directly with the composer, or more likely his/her publisher or agent, in order to stage the work.

Division of PRS fees and royalties

23.07 The revenue collected by PRS, after deduction of its administration costs, is split up between its writer and publisher members, and where applicable it is paid to the writers and publishers who are members of similar societies in foreign countries to which PRS is affiliated.

The division of PRS royalties between composers, lyricists and publishers is determined by reference to the PRS rules and to the relevant publishing and sub-publishing contracts[1].

In order to enable PRS to make as equitable a distribution as possible between all the interested parties, it is a condition of many of its licences that lists of the works actually performed or broadcast are supplied to it by licensees at regular intervals. PRS divides its revenue among the interested parties by reference to these returns and to other playout information to which it has access. Major terrestrial radio and television broadcasters are required to submit complete returns of each day's playout. Smaller broadcasters' usage is analysed on a sample basis. As regards premises where public performances take place, returns are required in respect of certain live performances, and PRS has the right to request returns from any licensed venue.

Managers of premises which have PRS licences should ensure that the performers assist them in completing the programme forms so that they accurately reflect the set list.

1   See **paragraph 20.07**.

Recorded music – PPL public performance licences

23.08 Whilst a PRS licence is required for both live and recorded performances (because the licence is given in respect of the use of the musical compositions), a PPL licence is required only in respect of performances of recordings, so live events generally require no PPL licence. PPL has different rates and licensing schemes for different types of venue, as does PRS. The same considerations as regards the meaning of 'in public' apply as for PRS licensing.

PPL grants licences in much the same way as PRS and application should be made to PPL for a quotation for their fee in each case[1].

1   See **Appendix 1** for PPL's contact details.

Jukeboxes

23.09 In the majority of cases PRS and PPL grant public performance licences to the occupier of the premises on which the jukebox is sited. However, the operator of online jukeboxes (ie the person who rents out the jukebox and supplies it with content) is also likely to require separate PRS and PPL licences for the elements of the service that go on 'behind the scenes'.

Video jukeboxes are licensed by Video Performance Ltd[1] instead of PPL.

1   See **paragraph 20.23**.

Public performances of broadcasts

23.10 There is copyright in a broadcast, and this copyright is quite distinct from and additional to the copyright in any TV programme, music, film etc, which is featured in the broadcast. The acts restricted by the copyright in a broadcast include playing or showing the broadcast in public[1]. So the playing or showing of a broadcast in public will amount to the public performance of both the broadcast and of the various copyright works featured within the broadcast.

The CDPA contains a limited exception to this right of 'playing or showing' a broadcast in public as it relates to the broadcast itself, and to certain sound recordings in the broadcast[2]. The copyright in any sound recording created by the broadcaster is not infringed by the public performance of the broadcast to an audience who have not paid for admission to the venue in question, but there will be an infringement of any other sound recordings featured in the broadcast unless an appropriate public performance licence is obtained. PPL offers relevant licences. The rights in any literary, dramatic or musical works included in a public performance of a broadcast are infringed, whether or not the audience is a paying audience, unless an applicable public performance licence has been obtained from PRS. The copyright in any films included in the broadcast will also be infringed unless the public performance right has been pre-cleared by the broadcaster.

To take an example, where a piece of recorded music is contained in a broadcast which is played or shown in public, for example on a TV or radio in a public place, there will be at least three copyrights involved, and possibly four:

- *First, the copyright in the musical composition*: since the public performance of the composition is a restricted act in relation to that composition, a licence is required from PRS. The definition of performance in the CDPA includes *presentation* of a work by means of a broadcast[3].

- *Second, the copyright in the sound recording:* which is infringed if there is no licence for the playing of the recording in public (whether or not the audience is a paying audience) from the owner of the performing right in the recording (PPL, in most cases). If the sound recording is included in a broadcast which is played or shown to a paying audience, then a PPL licence will be required. However, as has been seen, copyright in a sound recording created by the broadcaster is not infringed by the public performance of the broadcast to a non-paying audience[4].

- *Third, the copyright in any film*: if the broadcast involved is a TV broadcast and it includes any pre-recorded material, that pre-recorded material will be a 'film' for copyright purposes and the right to perform in the film in public will be required. In practice, this right is very difficult to clear unless pre-cleared by the broadcaster. Note that if a film in the broadcast contains a recording of a musical composition, that recording is not a sound recording for copyright purposes and will not require clearance unless such clearance is required on a contractual level by the owner of the recording.

- *Fourth, the copyright in the broadcast itself*: if the broadcast is to be seen or heard in public by a *paying audience*, then a licence is required from the broadcaster. However, no licence is required in respect of the public performance of the broadcast to a non-paying audience. In the case, for example, of a pub where the audience is *not a paying audience*, a licence will be required from PPL for the performance of the sound recordings and from PRS for the performance of the musical compositions in the broadcast, and the rights in any films will need to be cleared, but not rights in the broadcast itself.

In summary, the practical effect of all this is that:

- A PRS licence is always required in respect of public performances of a musical composition in broadcasts so far as the copyright in the composition itself is concerned.

- A PPL licence is always required in respect of the public playing of sound recordings of musical compositions in broadcasts (except those owned by the broadcaster).

- A licence is always required in respect of the public playing of films in broadcasts (although there is no practical means of clearing such rights other than by way of broadcaster pre-clearance).

- A licence is required from the broadcaster provider when television broadcasts are seen and/or heard in public by paying audiences, but not if there is no paying audience.

1 CDPA s 19(3); see **paragraphs 2.09, 2.10** and **6.07**.
2 See **paragraph 6.07**.
3 CDPA s 19(2).
4 See **paragraphs 6.07** and **23.11**.

Meaning of paying audience

23.11 Payment of a general admission charge does not necessarily trigger the liability – it seems likely that for the liability to arise, the charge must be specifically made in respect of the provision of the broadcasts. An audience is treated as having paid for admission to a place if they have paid for admission to a place of which that place forms part[1].

1 CDPA s 72(2)(a).

Plays and dramatico-musical works

23.12 The copyright in a play, opera or ballet is infringed by performance without a licence from the copyright owner[1]. There is no industry collection body for the performing rights in plays as such. Yet, whenever a play, opera or ballet is performed in public (except in schools as part of an educational curriculum), a licence from the copyright owner is required. In the case of the exercise of amateur performances there are commercial companies which license the performing rights to amateur bodies for most plays[2].

If it is desired to perform a play which is in copyright, but the copyright owner cannot be traced, the performance of the work will, nevertheless, be an infringement of copyright. It can be prevented by injunction or can be the subject of a suit for damages. In the case of plays (unlike music) it is the company performing the play which is licensed and not the occupier of the premises.

The music in dramatico-musical works (eg stage musicals) must be the subject of a performing right licence, and although such rights may be vested in PRS, the licence is normally granted by the publisher of the music[3].

1 See **paragraph 23.06**.
2 For example Samuel French and Warner Chappell.
3 PRS Rule 9 states that PRS will not administer performance rights in musical works performed in the context of dramatico-musical works. These rights are effectively retained by the publisher (or author if unpublished).

Cinemas

23.13 The showing of a film in a cinema is a public performance of all relevant copyrights. There is copyright in the screenplay, in any music in the soundtrack (both sound recordings and underlying musical compositions), and in the film itself as a copyright work quite distinct from the rights in the 'ingredients' which make up the film. It is customary for the producer of a film to obtain from the owners of the basic literary or dramatic work and of the screenplay all rights necessary to enable the film in which they will be incorporated, to be performed[1]. Furthermore, the distributor takes from the producer a licence or an assignment of the performing rights in the film. However, the right to perform *musical compositions* which are included in the soundtrack of the film is vested in PRS or overseas equivalent, so it cannot be granted by the composer of those compositions or his/her music publisher. PRS does not grant a licence of the right to perform the music to the owner of the film, or to the distributor, because they themselves are not performing it. Instead, PRS grants a licence to the operator of the cinema or other venue in which the film is shown.

A PRS and PPL licence will also be required by the cinema operator in respect of any music which is performed before and after the exhibition of the films, or during any interval, or in the foyer of the cinema[2]. PPL does not currently license cinema screenings because in general the public performance right in sound recordings synchronised into films is pre-cleared in the synchronisation licence.

1 See **paragraph 22.03**.
2 Ibid.

Owners' and occupiers' liability

23.14 The CDPA provides that the copyright in a literary, dramatic or musical work is infringed by any person who permits a place of public entertainment to be used for a performance in public of the work, where the performance constitutes an infringement of the copyright of the work[1].

A 'place of public entertainment' is defined as including any:

> 'premises which are occupied mainly for other purposes but are from time to time made available for hire for the purposes of public entertainment'[2].

However, the person who gives permission for the place to be used for the infringing performance will not be liable if, at the time permission is given, he believes on reasonable grounds that the performance would not infringe copyright[3].

There is an additional liability in respect of infringing public performances which are given by use of equipment for playing sound recordings, for showing films, or for 'receiving visual images or sounds by electronic means' – an expression which includes the use of television screens to receive broadcasts. In such cases the supplier of the equipment is liable for the infringement if he knows or has reason to suspect that it will be used for unauthorised public performance. The occupier of premises who gives permission for the apparatus to be brought onto the premises with the same knowledge or belief is also liable for the infringement. He can avoid liability if he can show that, when he gave permission, he did not know and had no reason to believe that the equipment was likely to be used to infringe copyright[4].

The person giving permission for the premises to be used for a performance or the occupier permitting performing equipment to be used on the premises should check whether there are current PRS and PPL licences and that they are applicable. If there is no appropriate licence, then one should be obtained.

1   See CDPA s 25(1) and **paragraph 6.12**.
2   CDPA s 25(2).
3   See **paragraph 6.12**.
4   See **paragraph 6.13**.

Copyright Tribunal

23.15 PRS and PPL have powerful positions by virtue of the fact that they control the performing rights in almost all the compositions and sound recordings which are currently in copyright and for which there is any public demand, at least in the Western world. Accordingly, under the CDPA the Copyright Tribunal has the ability to determine disputes arising between licensing bodies and the persons requiring performing right licences. It is beyond the scope of this *User's Guide* to discuss the mechanics of the Tribunal in detail, suffice it to say that if any person or company seeking a performing right licence from PRS or PPL considers that the terms being asked are excessive, or unfair, then the matter can be referred to the Copyright Tribunal[1].

1   See **Chapter 12**.

Performers' rights

23.16 Performers are accorded rights in their performances by the CDPA. Although these are not technically rights in copyright, they are in many respects the equivalent of copyright. Infringement of these rights can give rise to claims in both civil and criminal law[1].

To summarise (although these are detailed provisions which we would recommend be read in full):

• *Performers' non-property rights and recording rights* comprise the right to prevent the unauthorised recording or live broadcast of a performance, and the right to prevent the importation, possession or dealing with an unauthorised recording of a performance[2].

- *Performers' property rights* comprise the right to prevent the reproduction, distribution, rental and lending or making available of copies of a recorded performance[3].

It follows that anyone wishing to exploit rights in a recorded performance should obtain the necessary consents required under the CDPA[4], and obtain an assignment or licence of performer's property rights (the performer cannot assign his non-property rights)[5].

A simple consent and form of assignment, directly referring to the CDPA, should be included in any letter, agreement or formal contract with performers when it is intended to record, film, broadcast or communicate to the public their performance. If there is no such contract, then the consent and assignment wording could be incorporated in the receipt given for payment of fees, which the performer should sign, but this approach is not advised.

If it is intended to record or film a performance by an orchestra or group, the conductor of the orchestra or leader of the group can give a consent and assignment under the CDPA on behalf of other members of the orchestra or group only if he is duly authorised to do so. Evidence of such authority should *always* be obtained before accepting the signature of anyone claiming to be authorised to sign a consent or assignment on behalf of other performers.

In addition, if a record label or other entity has exclusive recording rights over a performer's performances, it would be sensible in practice to obtain the written consent of the label or other entity for the making of the recording, although strictly speaking in law only the consent of the performer is necessary[6].

The kinds of performance to which the CDPA applies are considered in further detail elsewhere in this *User's Guide*[7].

It is not necessary to obtain a performer's consent or assignment (and indeed there is no breach of the provisions of the CDPA) if the recorded performance is only 'incidentally included' in the film or recording, or if the recording is only to be used for the purpose of reporting current events[8]. For example, a television news item on a pop music festival which incidentally included some film of a performance at the festival would not require a consent from the performers (subject to the usual limitations on fair dealing discussed in detail elsewhere in this *User's Guide*)[9]. Similarly if, for example, someone is being interviewed and the performance is being conducted in the background, or if a film is made about the building or design of a theatre which incorporates some shots of a performance, there may not be any infringement of copyright[10].

Performers have two moral rights in their performances: the right to be identified as a performer (so all performers must be named, although a group credit is sufficient in the case of bands and other collective performing groups), and the right to object to derogatory treatment of the performances[11]. These are discussed elsewhere in the *User's Guide*[12].

1   These rights are considered in detail in **Chapter 11**.
2   CDPA ss 182–184; see **paragraphs 11.06–11.10**.
3   CDPA ss 182A–182C; see **paragraphs 11.11–11.13**.
4   See **paragraph 11.20**.
5   See **paragraph 11.21**.
6   See **paragraph 11.10**.
7   See **Chapter 11**.
8   See **Chapter 11**.
9   See **paragraphs 8.03** ff.
10 See **paragraph 8.08**.
11 CDPA s 205C–205F.
12 See **paragraph 10.33**.

Chapter 24

Networked communications: broadcasting, cable, internet and mobile transmissions

Introduction

24.01 The owner of the copyright in a work has the exclusive right to 'communicate the work to the public'[1]. Under the CDPA, 'communication to the public' means a communication to the public by electronic transmission, including broadcasting and on demand transmissions[2]. This is a non-exhaustive definition and, as technology develops and innovates, the scope of relevant communications grows (and the applicable law becomes increasingly complex).

Whilst these communications are a 'right' of the copyright owner they do not typically attract copyright in their own right, whereas a 'broadcast' (ie the programme-carrying signal) may qualify for copyright protection in its own right as the only *transmission* capable of constituting a copyright work.

Under the CDPA a 'broadcast'[3] is an electronic transmission of content that must either be a scheduled transmission at a time determined solely by the broadcaster, or a transmission for simultaneous reception by members of the public that they can lawfully receive. This encompasses both wired and wireless transmissions and therefore covers both satellite and cable broadcasting[4]. However, it will not include encrypted transmissions unless authorised decryption equipment has been provided.

Internet transmissions will not constitute broadcasts unless such transmissions are analogous to, or simulcasts of, traditional broadcasting. However, whether or not a broadcast, an internet transmission may still be deemed a communication to the public.

A single 'communication to the public' may involve a range of copyright works and therefore engage the rights of a number of separate copyright owners. By way of example, if a broadcast of a film which has a commercial sound recording included on its soundtrack is made, there are at least five copyright works involved:

- the screenplay on which the film is based (a dramatic work);
- the music on the soundtrack (a musical work and, where there are lyrics, also a literary work);
- the recording of the music on the soundtrack (a sound recording);
- the film (a film); and
- the broadcast by which the film is transmitted (a broadcast).

If the film is included on an 'on demand' service, the transmission signal carrying the work will not be protected as a separate copyright work (although the operator of the service will be entitled to other rights designed to inhibit the fraudulent reception of its services and the circumvention of protection measures)[5].

This chapter considers these electronic transmissions and their composite copyright works, and explores some of the common issues affecting their exploitation and protection.

The question of whether a work enjoys copyright protection is in part dependent on establishing that the work falls within one of those categories of work for which copyright protection is available. A typical television programme will receive sui generis protection under the CDPA as a 'film'. However, more complex interactive 'digital products' which may be communicated to the public do not sit easily within any of the defined protectable copyright 'works' referred to in the CDPA. The word 'digital' cannot be found in the CDPA, but in this chapter the expression 'digital product' will be used to refer to any product which is an amalgam of copyright works designed for exploitation by means of digital media (such as a multimedia presentation on a website).

1   See **paragraph 6.08**.
2   CDPA s 20(2).
3   CDPA s 6.
4   The CDPA was amended by the Copyright and Related Rights Regulations 2003, SI 2003/2498 ('2003 Regulations') to remove the concept of a 'cable programme' as a distinct protectable copyright work, and to expand the concept of a 'broadcast' to include wired as well as wireless transmissions. See **paragraphs 2.09** and **2.10**.
5   See **paragraphs 24.38 ff**.

Definitions

24.02 Numerous terms of art are used in the broadcasting industry and in the context of other digital transmission media. Whilst it is impossible in the context of this *User's Guide* to attempt a comprehensive list, it is worth clarifying some common industry terms:

- *A la Carte* means the ability of a television viewer to choose to subscribe to individual television channels rather than having to take packages or 'tiers' of channels.
- *Analogue* means the direct electrical representation of pictures or sound by means of waves of differing amplitude, as opposed to digital technology which is a binary coded electrical representation.
- *Analogue Television* means a television system, or a television receiver, which makes use of signals transmitted as analogue waveforms.
- *Bandwidth* means the range of frequencies occupied by a signal or the range of frequencies over which a signal receiver operates.
- *Basic Tier* means the programmes/channels which are supplied to a subscriber as part of the basic periodic rental (effectively the advertising supported independent channels and any community or similar programmes originated by the distribution platform).
- *Broadband* means a service or a connection which enables the movement of sufficient information to enable the conveyance of very complex data (such as that required to generate moving audio visual pictures) at speed.
- *Browser* means software which allows computer based displays of web pages and other HTML text.
- *Bundling* means the tying of one service or product to the supply of others, including some situations where the supply of services is linked through the use of discounts.
- *Cable Operator* means a person providing a cable retransmission of a wireless broadcast[1].
- *Cable Retransmission* means the reception and immediate retransmission by cable, including the transmission of microwave energy between terrestrial fixed points, of a wireless broadcast[2].
- *Cable Television System* means an end-to-end proprietary television system (and therefore excludes the internet and IPTV) which uses coaxial cables or fibre optic cables to deliver audio-visual content from a head-end to a subscriber's premises.
- *Cache* means, commonly, the temporary storage of information for the purpose of speeding up the operation of network communications (as in cache copying).
- *Carriage Agreement* means the agreement between a distribution platform and a programme provider/broadcaster.
- *Connected TV* means a television which is able to receive and display audio-visual content transmitted via the internet (also called a 'Smart TV').
- *Content Scramble System (CSS)* means an encryption code designed to protect DVDs against unauthorised copying.
- *Copper Line* is the 'narrowband' medium commonly used in telecommunications networks to connect telephone equipment to

the local exchange. A copper line is unable to convey broadband type services unless used in conjunction with enabling technology such as DSL.

- *Cord Cutting* means the movement away from traditional pay television subscription services in favour of OTT offerings.
- *Crawler software* means software applications which are designed to search the internet for particular types of data.
- *DBS* means direct broadcast satellite.
- *DeCSS* means software designed to circumvent copy protection afforded by CSS systems.
- *Digital* means a method of representing information (such as text, audio or video) as a series of computerised signals (binary data bits) rather than in analogue form.
- *Digital Audio Broadcasting (DAB)* means a radio signal which is transmitted in digital rather than analogue form.
- *Digital Compression* means a process using techniques to reduce the amount of information transmitted while still allowing reconstruction of a picture, sound or data in the receiver.
- *Digital Rights Management (DRM)* means the process of managing rights in the digital environment, via the implementation of systems designed to track and/or limit access to copyright works in accordance with pre-determined systems of rules.
- *Digital Subscriber Line (DSL)* means the technology which allows ordinary copper line to be used to send large quantities of information (such as the information necessary to convey moving audio visual pictures) to the user whilst also enabling a 'return path' (consisting, for example, of the kind of control channels necessary to establish interactive services) to be established.
- *Digital Terrestrial Television (DTT)* means terrestrial broadcasting services by which channels are carried via Multiplexes.
- *Digital Video Broadcasting (DVB)* means an industry-led consortium of broadcasters, manufacturers, network operators, software developers, regulatory bodies and others committed to designing global standards for the delivery of digital television and data services.
- *Digital Video Disc (DVD) (aka 'Digital Versatile Disc')* means a family of optical disc standards that have much greater capacity and flexibility than the Compact Disc (CD). They are typically used to store movies and use digital image compression technology.
- *Direct to Home (DTH)* means a satellite delivery method where digital content is delivered directly from a satellite to the end user's receiving equipment.
- *Downlink* means the signal sent from the transponder to earth.
- *Downloading* means the process of copying a file onto a user's device following reception from another source via a communication network.

- *E-commerce* means the buying and selling of goods by electronic means eg the internet, interactive TV.
- *Electronic Sell Through (EST)* means a method by which an individual may purchase content in a digital format on a permanent basis thus owning a copy of the content and obtaining all rights necessary to view the content (often also called 'DTO' or 'download-to-own').
- *Encryption* means scrambling a television signal in such a way that it can be received only by those who have the appropriate decoders.
- *EPG* means 'electronic programme guide', a navigational aid allowing subscribers to view programme listings data and which may act as a gateway to other services, such as VOD, pay-per-view services, interactive services etc.
- *Footprint* means the area of the earth's surface where the signal of the satellite can be received.
- *Framing* means the actuation of a link from site (A) to site (B), such that content from site B is displayed on the viewers screen, 'framed' by content (e.g. advertising) on site A.
- *Free-to-Air* means a television service which is not encrypted and can be received without paying a fee.
- *Free-to-View* means a television service which can be received without paying a fee, although transmissions may be encrypted and require use of a decoder and smart card. Reception may be deliberately restricted to certain geographical areas only.
- *Headend* means the physical place from which a cable operator transmits its signal to its subscribers.
- *Host* means to provide a storage facility, typically a computer server, on which information is held.
- *Hyperlink* means the functionality of linking between pages via the internet, by use of HTML code.
- *Hypertext Markup language (HTML)* means the computer language used in the creation of web pages.
- *Information Society Service* means a service 'normally provided for remuneration, at a distance, by electronic means and at the individual request of a recipient of services'[3].
- *Integrated Services Digital Network (ISDN)* means an international communications standard for sending voice, video and data over digital telephone lines or normal telephone wires. ISDN lines offer high-speed access to the internet.
- *Interactive Service* means any service or system (or any part of any service or system) which distributes transmits and/or exhibits audio and/or audiovisual programming and which allows the recipient to interrupt the linear reception of such programming and/or manipulate or interact with the content of the service or system but excluding NVOD and VOD.

- *Interactive Television* means TV programming with interactive content and enhancements, blending traditional TV viewing with the interactivity of a personal computer.
- *Internet Protocol Television (IPTV)* means digital television services (usually MPEG2 or 4 based) where the transport stream is encapsulated within IP packets for delivery across an IP network to IPTV receivers.
- *Internet Service Provider (ISP)* means a company that provides individuals and organisations access to the internet.
- *Linking* means the process whereby a web page (B) may be accessed from another web page (A) by means of the inclusion of HTML in page (A) code citing the relevant URL for page (B). 'Deep linking' occurs where a link is made directly to content held on a third party site, bypassing any home page on that site.
- *Metatag* means a 'tag' used to identify and order web pages.
- *MHEG-5* means a standardised method of providing digital text and simple interactive applications for digital television. Used in the UK for digital terrestrial television.
- *Microwave Distribution Video System (MVDS)* means a television distribution service using microwave transmissions.
- *Microwave Frequencies* means radio frequencies at the higher end of the radio spectrum, generally above 1 GHz (1,000 MHz).
- *MMDS* means multichannel multipoint distribution system.
- *Mobile Telecommunications Technology* means a number of technologies with radio frequency spectrum in any band which may be used to enable or facilitate transmission of audiovisual content to mobile devices.
- *Modem* means a device for connecting a computer or other device (eg a set-top box) to a network (usually a phone line). The modem converts the digital information that a computer uses into audio signals which can be sent along a phone line.
- *MPEG* means an audio and video standard used to encode video and audio for broadcast over digital TV networks.
- *Multichannel Multipoint Distribution System (MMDS)* means a system for broadcasting programme transmission using the UHF/SHF frequency bands. It provides low power, line-of-sight coverage to relatively small areas (sometimes referred to as a 'wireless cable network').
- *Multiplex* means a single digital transmission comprising several programme services and sometimes additional data services.
- *Narrowband* means an old cable television system with a limited channel capacity, usually four or seven channels, or more frequently slower internet connectors (eg internet services utilised via a 56 kbps connection).
- *Near Video On Demand (NVOD)* means a service which allows users to access the same piece of content which is being transmitted

on a multi-scheduled basis throughout a certain time period. With NVOD, multiple broadcasts of a programme are scheduled by the broadcaster with staggered start times.

- *Non Theatrical Distribution* means distribution and exhibition to closed user groups, eg hotels, restaurants, bars, educational institutions (ie schools, public libraries, colleges, universities, dormitories and residence halls), churches, museums, summer camps, commercial premises, business and industry, the transportation industry (ie aeroplanes, ships and trains) and organisations of an educational, cultural, religious, charitable or social nature including drama groups, film societies and professional associations and to all other like entities.
- *Over-The-Top (OTT)* means distribution of audiovisual content over the internet without being tied to a primary subscription offering.
- *Pay-Per-View* or *Pay-Per-Period* means a service for which the viewer has to pay on a per programme or 'per period' (eg per day) basis.
- *Personal Video Recorder (PVR)* means a device which incorporates a digital TV receiver and which allows the user to store programmes on a hard drive to be watched at a later date.
- *Premium Channels* usually refers to more expensive channels which offer first run films or sports coverage where the programmes have a 'premium' over normal subscription channels (often à la carte). It can also be used to refer to pay-per-view channels.
- *Server* means an individual computer on, for example, a LAN (Local Area Network), that acts as a service or resource provider to client computers, by sharing the resources within the network infrastructure.
- *Set-Top Box (STB)* means a device which connects to a television or other display device which accepts an input usually containing digital television services.
- *Short Messaging Service (SMS)* means a text message service that enables short text messages of up to 160 characters in length to be sent and transmitted from a mobile phone.
- *SMATV* means satellite (or small) multiple antenna television – ie hotels, military camps, oil rigs, blocks of flats and other places of multiple occupancy which have antenna to receive satellite television for the benefit of their guests.
- *Streaming* means the delivery of content where such content may be viewed by the user at the time as it is delivered by the content provider, but not stored by the user.
- *Terrestrial* means a reception system where the signals are sent from a ground (terrestrial) transmitter to an aerial.
- *Thumbnail* means an image which is reduced in dimensions (usually to facilitate reproduction as part of, for example, a web page).

- *Transponder* means that part of a satellite which receives a signal from earth and relays it back to earth.
- *Uplink* means the signal sent from the ground transmitting station to the transponder.
- *Uplink Station* means the place from which programme-carrying signals are transmitted to a satellite.
- *Video on Demand (VOD)* means a service by which a particular programme may be sent to a single viewer (as distinct from, say, a group of subscribers) at the individual request of, and a time selected, by the viewer. This may occur on a streaming or download basis. It may also occur on a variety of different consumption models, eg subscription (SVOD), free (FVOD), advertising-funded (AVOD), pay-per-view (transactional VOD – TVOD).
- *Watermark* means data embedded into digital content identifying the owner.
- *Wireless Application Protocol (WAP)* means a standard for providing mobile phones, pagers and other handheld devices with secure access to e-mail and text-based web pages.
- *Wireless Broadcast* means a broadcast by means of wireless telegraphy[4].
- *Wireless Telegraphy* means the sending of electro-magnetic energy over paths not provided by a material substance constructed or arranged for that purpose but does not include the transmission of microwave energy between terrestrial fixed points[5].

1 See **paragraph 2.10**.
2 CDPA s 144A(7).
3 Directive 2000/31/EC (Directive on Electronic Commerce), Art 2(a).
4 CDPA s 178.
5 CDPA s 178.

Broadcasts and digital products – ownership of copyright

Broadcasts

24.03 Issues of copyright ownership are considered in detail in **Chapter 9** but, in summary, the author of a broadcast will be the person or entity making the broadcast. The criteria for establishing the maker are considered in detail elsewhere. In brief, the maker will be the entity transmitting the programme (if it is responsible for its content, which is unusual) and any person who provides the programme and makes the arrangements necessary for its transmission (which is usually the broadcast company).

Digital products

24.04 Where a digital product is a 'multimedia' work comprised of a number of different copyright elements (such as literary, dramatic, musical and artistic works, films and sound recordings), each of these elements will be entitled to copyright protection in its own right, and any computer software included in the product will be protected as a 'literary work'[1]. In other jurisdictions, visual components of some multimedia works have been construed as 'films' and that is also a possibility under UK law[2]. Taken as a whole, the collection of works will not have copyright protection as a collection unless it amounts to a compilation or a database (both categories of literary work) and/or as a database for the purpose of the database right[3]. In general terms, where the author of a digital product, consisting of a collection of other works, has invested skill and labour in its creation, so that it constitutes his own intellectual creation, his work will certainly be entitled to copyright protection. Additionally, if the collection is a 'qualifying' database it will attract database rights where there has been substantial investment in obtaining, verifying or presenting the contents of the database. The 'maker' of the database (ie the person who assumes the risk of relevant investments) is the person entitled to exercise the database right in the work[4].

In relation to the component copyright works, each of these will be created by an author, the identity of whom can be established according to normal copyright principles[5]. In essence, the author of any literary, dramatic, artistic or musical work will be the natural, qualifying, person who creates the protectable elements of the work[6], and that person will also as a general rule be the first owner of his work, an exception being where the author is an employee who creates the work during the course of his employment, in which event (in the absence of any agreement to the contrary) his employer will own the work[7]. Where the collection includes films and sound recordings, the author of those elements will be the producer, and in the case of a film the producer and director jointly[8]. Like a film producer, the creator of a digital product will need to ensure that he has obtained adequate assignments or licences of all the 'underlying' works he wishes to include in his product which will be necessary to enable him to make and fully exploit his creation[9].

Particular issues arise in the context of computer-generated works. Where a literary, dramatic, musical or artistic work is computer-generated (ie as distinct from the situation in which the computer is simply used as a tool to assist human creativity), the author will be the person by whom the arrangements necessary for the creation of the work were undertaken[10].

1   See **paragraph 2.02**.
2   *Galaxy Electronics Pty Ltd v Sega Enterprises Ltd [1997] 145 ALR 21*.
3   See **Chapter 14**.
4   See **paragraphs 9.03** and **Chapter 14**.
5   See **paragraphs 9.03** ff.
6   See **paragraph 9.02**.
7   See **paragraphs 9.11**.
8   See **Chapter 22** for a detailed analysis of the issues involved in this process.
9   See **paragraph 9.21**.
10 CDPA s 9(3).

Broadcasts and digital products – moral rights

24.05 Moral rights do not protect the authors of broadcasts. However, they do apply to the elements of a 'digital product' in the same way as, say, the elements of a film. Particular moral rights issues arise in the context of digital exploitation. In the context of digital media, where the rearrangement and re-purposing of copyright material is often of the essence of 'interactive' services, manipulation of content is common. Various acts take place which may be argued to infringe moral rights: a work may be 'cropped', reduced in size, or framed with or linked to other material. English courts have not been asked, on the whole, to assess whether these activities infringe moral rights (although in one English case simply reducing an image in size was not enough to find summary judgment for a claimant who claimed that that use infringed his moral rights[1]). However, given the multi-jurisdictional nature of the internet, it will also be necessary to give appropriate consideration to the laws of other jurisdictions (such as France) where moral rights protection is enforced perhaps more vigorously than in the UK.

An electronic publisher will, for example, infringe moral rights if:

- he manipulates an author's works in circumstances where a moral right in the work arises and the act is sufficient to amount to a derogatory treatment to the work[2]; so, for example, if he manipulates a work digitally in such a way as to change details or colours, he may infringe the author's moral rights;
- he fails to properly identify the author, or falsely attributes authorship of a work[3]. So, for example, if an online service makes available digital images of artistic works without crediting the artist, this may infringe the artist's right to be identified as author of a work (the 'paternity right').

It follows that publishers and other providers of such services must take care to ensure that they are free to manipulate the material they acquire without complaint from the author. In practice, this will require ensuring that suitable moral rights waivers are obtained from those involved[4].

The paternity right must be asserted by the person entitled to the right[5]. It follows that when acquiring rights from, say, a producer of material to be used by an electronic publisher or online producer, it will be necessary to take appropriate warranties that waivers of moral rights have been obtained from all relevant authors, and that no paternity rights have been asserted[6].

1   See **paragraphs 10.12** and **25.21**.
2   Ibid.
3   See **paragraphs 10.21** ff.
4   See **paragraph 10.29**.
5   See **paragraph 10.08**.
6   See **Chapter 10** for a full analysis of moral rights. Moral rights for performers are considered in detail at **paragraph 10.33**.

Broadcasts and digital rights – term of copyright and licensing

Duration of rights

24.06 The term of copyright in a broadcast (as distinct from any copyright work included in the broadcast) under the CDPA is 50 years from the end of the calendar year in which the broadcast is made. Repeating a broadcast does not extend the life of copyright[1]. It should be noted that this period may be shorter in relation to the protection afforded to broadcasts emanating from outside the EEA[2].

Where a 'digital product' is protected as a literary work (either as a compilation or a database), it will, when taken as a whole, receive the same period of protection afforded to other literary works, namely 70 years following the end of the year of the author's death[3]. Any database right which may subsist in the digital product will continue until expiry of the later of 15 years after the end of the year of its completion, or 15 years after it is first made available to the public (provided that period starts within 15 years after the end of the year of its completion)[4]. Ordinary principles of duration of term will apply to the period of copyright in the components to the digital products.

1   See **paragraph 5.10**.
2   See **Chapter 4**.
3   See **paragraphs 5.05** ff.
4   See **paragraph 14.07**.

Acquiring and licensing rights

24.07 Exploitation of any content is likely to include the exploitation of copyright works[1]. Such exploitation will probably also involve communicating such works to the public. Other exclusive rights of the copyright owner may also be engaged, for example, by any copying required to facilitate such exploitation.

In order to exploit these works without infringing copyright, the necessary rights must be acquired from the copyright owners.

Where a party intends to acquire the ownership of a work and its copyright (and all the exclusive rights this confers), this should take the form of an assignment. A producer, for example, may wish to ensure that it owns all copyright in its programming and all copyright works it comprises. Issues regarding the acquisition of rights in programmes intended for television broadcast are considered in more detail elsewhere in this *User's Guide*[2].

Where a party only wishes to exploit (or the copyright owner is only willing to permit such party to exploit) content for a particular purpose, the parties may look to enter into a licensing arrangement, eg a programme licence to a broadcaster for limited exhibition.

Where content contains a number of copyright works it is important to carefully consider these component elements, as they may require different treatment. For example, a copyright owner may wish to assign any bespoke elements of a digital product but may wish to retain ownership (and only grant a licence) of any underlying tools or software[3]. Similarly, where a digital product is licensed, the scope of usage and exclusivity of each element may differ.

The parties to a licence agreement may have very different objectives. Typically the licensee will seek as broad a grant as possible, whereas the licensor will look to define the grant of rights as precisely as it can.

The relevant considerations will hinge on the applicable circumstances. However, the following non-exhaustive list may be material in defining the scope of the licence:

- *Permitted means of distribution*: Whereas the licensee may wish to distribute via all media to all platforms, the licensor should carefully consider the permitted transmission means (eg satellite, cable etc) and authorised platforms (channels, websites, digital applications etc). These platforms may be limited in a number of ways, including specific reference, ownership/branding conditions and/or approval requirements. The licensor may even wish to take these limitations one step further and seek to limit the user devices which access these platforms. In seeking to ensure that the limits imposed do not prohibit its intended exploitation, the licensee should also consider any necessary 'future-proofing' to ensure that advances in technology and evolving platforms and devices do not nullify its rights.
- *Distribution basis*: In addition to the means of distribution, the licensor may wish to control the manner in which the content is made available. Is the content intended for linear distribution only or may it be made available on an on demand basis? May it be downloaded or only streamed? Are there any restrictions on the financial model that may be adopted (free, pay-subscription, pay-per-view etc)?
- *Scope of distribution*: The licensor may wish to limit availability of the content to a certain user group or territory. It may also wish to limit the applicable availability window.
- *Exclusivity*: Are the rights granted intended to be exclusive or non-exclusive? Where exclusive rights are granted, it is important to consider and specify the scope of such exclusivity and any required carve-outs. Is the exclusivity intended to only extend to the specific rights granted (eg the relevant permitted transmission means or platform) or will it exceed this grant?
- *Developments and created works*: Where, for example, a database is licensed, it may be necessary to consider whether the licence applies

to the form as at the date of the agreement or includes subsequent developments during the licence term. In some circumstances, a licence may also lead to the creation of new copyright works, eg the broadcasting of a programme will create a 'broadcast'. The licensor will need to consider whether it is happy for the licensee to own this copyright or whether it should be assigned back to the licensor.

- *Clearances*: The licensee should seek to ensure that all rights in the content are cleared by the licensor for its intended purpose. However, there may be some elements or specific uses that require additional consents or licences and should be specifically addressed in the licence agreement. For example, the inclusion of music in a transmission may involve the exploitation of music publishing rights or sound recording rights which do not sit with the licensor. Considerations relating to the exploitation of such rights are set out more fully elsewhere in this *User's Guide*[4].

- *Compliance obligations*: In order to ensure compliance with the usage limitations, it may be desirable to impose certain additional obligations such as technical restrictions (geo-targeting, DRM, encryption etc) or monitoring and enforcement conditions. The required measures may depend on the permitted transmission means, for example, in the absence of restriction, internet transmissions may be available on an international basis[5]. However, in agreeing such restrictions, regard must be had to applicable law and the enforceability of such measures.

- *Sublicensing*: If the licensee requires the ability to grant its rights to third parties, this should be expressly addressed in the licence. If the licensor is willing to permit such sublicensing, it should clearly set out the intended restrictions and parameters.

It is important to note that, in order to ensure an effective grant of rights, a valid agreement must exist between the parties. Although a detailed discussion of principles of contractual law is beyond the scope of this *User's Guide*, basic contract law requires that in order to establish a binding contract the elements of offer, acceptance and consideration (ie the exchange of value) must be satisfied. No further formalities are required, although any assignment or exclusive licence of copyright should be in writing[6].

1   Reference should be made to the *Table of Incidence of Copyright* which summarises the incidents of these works – see **Appendix 2**.
2   See **Chapter 22**.
3   Software is protected under the CDPA as a literary work; see **paragraph 2.02**. Computer software is considered in detail in **Chapter 28**.
4   See **paragraph 12.01**.
5   See **paragraph 24.38**.
6   See **paragraph 9.23**.

Shrink wrap licences

24.08 In the case of offline software purchases, it is common for licence terms to be enclosed within the sealed wrapping enclosing the purchased product on which the software is stored. A notice in the wrapping may instruct the user not to open the product unless he agrees to the licence terms. As mentioned above, on basic contract law principles, the time to incorporate terms into a contract is before the contract is accepted. It follows, therefore, that if a software product has already been purchased before an opportunity to read the licence terms has been offered, there is a clear argument that the terms are not incorporated into the contract such that the contract will not be enforceable. Although there is a Scots law case that supports the enforceability of shrink wrap licence agreements in the event that the user is subsequently provided with the opportunity to review and reject the terms[1], this approach has been criticised and, given the decline of the use of offline shrink wrap licences, it may be that the issue will not be resolved before shrink wrap licences effectively die out and are replaced with digital downloads[2]. For obvious reasons, shrink wrap licences are not an option in the context of online services, although such licences may accompany software etc purchased offline for use as part of online services (eg networked games).

There is an argument that, even where a contractual licence is not effective, an implied, non-contractual copyright licence may be deemed to have been granted, and as such a licence does not need to be 'accepted' in order to have effect[3]. However, the scope of any such implied licence is uncertain and relying on such a position is unlikely to benefit either party.

1   *Beta Computers (Europe) Ltd v Adobe Systems (Europe) Ltd 1996 SLT 604*, in which Lord Penrose held that the contract for a shrink wrapped software product was between the retailer and purchaser (as opposed to the rights holder and the purchaser), and was concluded on the opening by the purchaser of the wrapping.
2   Law Commission and Scottish Law Commission, *Unfair Terms in Consumer Contracts: a new approach?* Issues Paper, App C, para C39.
3   *Barrett v Universal-Island Records Ltd [2006] EWHC 1009 (Ch)* at para 362.

Click wrap licences

24.09 More commonly, particularly in the context of online services, the user will be presented with a button or icon, typically bearing words such as 'I accept', clicking on which denotes acceptance of the terms for use of the relevant material. Contractually speaking, as long as the user has been presented with the relevant terms in advance or at least provided with an opportunity to review them, this approach poses much less of an issue than shrink wrap licensing, because it supports the basic requirements for contract formation and requires the user to take an active step to indicate their agreement to the terms. There is no UK case law specifically relating to click wrap licence agreements to support this view. However, precedent may be found in the Irish High Court decision in *Ryanair Ltd v Billigfluege.de GMBH*[1]. In finding that a valid contract existed, the Irish High Court stated:

'It seems that the Terms of Use were clearly accessible by way of a hyperlink which was at all times clearly visible to users of the plaintiff's site. The Terms were not hidden in an awkward part of the screen or in any way concealed or difficult to find. The inclusion by Ryanair of their website terms of use via a hyperlink that the website user is required to view and assent to results in the user entering into what is known as "a click-wrap agreement" with Ryanair.'

1   [2010] IEHC 47.

Browse wrap licences

24.10   Commonly, website terms and conditions will include provisions stating that use of the website will be deemed to constitute acceptance of those terms, whether or not they have in fact been viewed. This approach poses similar issues from a contractual perspective as do shrink wrap licence agreements. In both instances, the user will not have had a chance to view the terms before they are deemed to apply. No UK case law exists regarding the validity of browse wrap licence agreements. However, a Discussion Paper published by the European Commission's Expert Group on Cloud Computing suggests that '[b]rowse-wrap agreements are per se not prohibited under EU consumer law' but that 'the acceptance of the terms and conditions by the mere use of the website might not allow consumers to become aware of the legal consequences of entering into a binding agreement. This is unfair under the (Annex I point i) of the Unfair Contract terms Directive'[1].

Case law in the US generally supports the view that browse wrap licences will not be contractually binding[2] although there have been some exceptions[3].

1   European Commission's Expert Group on Cloud Computing Contracts: 'Unfair Contract Terms in Cloud Computing Service Contracts' Discussion Paper (March 2014).
2   *Specht v Netscape Communications Corpn and AOL Inc, Case 00 Civ 4871 (AKH) US Dist Court, Southern NY.*
3   See for example *Register.com, Inc v Verio, Inc 356 F3d 393, 401–403 (2d Cir 2004)* and *Cairo, Inc v Crossmedia Services Inc 2005 WL 756610 (ND Cal, 1 April 2005).*

Implied licences

24.11   Where material is made available online in an unrestricted manner, in the knowledge that certain acts restricted by copyright will be undertaken by any person viewing the content, it may be argued that an implied licence exists to enable viewers to undertake those acts. By way of example, any person viewing content offered on a web page will make a copy of that content in his computer's memory. It follows that it may be implied that the person making the content available on that web page should be taken to have authorised that act of copying. However, in implying licence terms, the law will not go further than what is necessary to give 'business efficacy' to the relationship. It follows that it will be more difficult to argue, under English law principles, that simply making available content in this manner should be taken to have permitted other uses of the content (such as redistribution)[1].

Following the CJEU's decision in the long-running *Meltwater* case, it is clear that implied licences for on-screen browsing, and for local caching for the purposes of browsing, are no longer required, since these acts come within the temporary copies exception provided in the Copyright Directive[2].

Issues regarding the ownership and transfer of rights in copyright works are considered in further detail in **Chapter 9**.

1 See **paragraph 9.29** for a discussion of implied licences.
2 *Public Relations Consultants Association Ltd v The Newspaper Licensing Agency Ltd (Case C-360/13)*.

Broadcasts

Wireless broadcasts – overspill and the 'country of origin' principle

24.12 Terrestrial wireless broadcast signals intended for reception in a single country are often capable of reception in other jurisdictions. The concept is known as 'overspill'. So, for example, German television signals are received and relayed by cable stations in Holland, Belgium, Switzerland and Austria, and the signals of the UK broadcasters are capable of being received on the coast of mainland Europe. In the context of satellite signals the issue of overspill is much more significant. The 'footprint' of a satellite will cross many more borders than a terrestrial signal, to a much larger potential audience, although only a relatively small area of that footprint may be exploited. It is common for broadcasting agreements to acknowledge an acceptable degree of overspill and to provide for measures to limit its effect, usually by financially compensating the programme provider or by requiring that the signal is encrypted and decoders are not actively marketed other than in the territory of grant.

A foreign broadcast which is not protected in the UK will not be infringed by inclusion in, say, a communication to the public, although such inclusion may infringe any copyright material (eg literary, dramatic and musical works) included in the broadcast.

The CDPA contains provisions allowing the government to apply copyright protection to works and people from countries to which the CDPA does not otherwise extend[1]. This is achieved by an Order in Council, implemented by Statutory Instrument. The latest such Order[2] protects broadcasts originating from a number of listed countries. These include, for example, all EEA states.

For the purpose of ascertaining whether a wireless broadcast is entitled to copyright protection under the CDPA, the broadcast is treated as being made at:

'the place where, under the control and responsibility of the person making the broadcast, the programme-carrying signals are introduced into an uninterrupted chain of communication (including, in the case of a satellite transmission, the chain leading to the satellite and down towards the earth)'[3].

This 'country of origin' principle was introduced into the CDPA by the Copyright and Related Rights Regulations 1996, SI 1996/2967 ('1996 Regulations'), which implemented the Satellite and Cable Directive[4]. The position is varied in the case of certain satellite broadcasts, where the wireless broadcast is made from a country which is not an EEA state and where the law of that country fails to provide a specified level of copyright protection. In these circumstances, if the country in which the uplink station is an EEA state:

'(a) that place shall be treated as the place from which the broadcast is made, and

(b) the person operating the uplink station shall be treated as the person making the broadcast'[5].

If, on the other hand, the uplink station is not located in an EEA state, but a person who is established in an EEA state has *commissioned* the making of the broadcast:

'(a) that person shall be treated as the person making the broadcast, and

(b) the place in which he has his principal establishment in the European Economic Area shall be treated as the place from which the broadcast is made'[6].

For these purposes, the specified level of protection, below which the non-EEA originating state must at least afford a level of protection, is as follows:

'(a) exclusive rights in relation to the wireless broadcasting equivalent to those conferred by section 20 (infringement by communication to the public) on the authors of literary, dramatic, musical and artistic works, films and broadcasts;

(b) a right in relation to live wireless broadcasting equivalent to that conferred on a performer by section 182(1)(b)(consent required for live broadcast of performance); and

(c) a right for authors of sound recordings and performers to share in a single equitable remuneration in respect of the wireless broadcasting of sound recordings'[7].

So, by way of example, if a US television broadcaster, which makes its programmes in the US, uplinks its transmission from the US to a satellite which is downlinked to Europe and the signal is retransmitted by an uplink station located in the UK, then the UK will be treated as the place from which the broadcast is made.

Section 6A(2)(b) of the CDPA (which provides that the person operating the uplink station is to be treated as the person making the broadcast) seems also to have the effect of making the UK uplink company the owner of the broadcast because the owner of the broadcast is the person making the broadcast. In the debate in the House of Commons on the 1996 Regulations, a government spokesman stated that this was not intended to be the case and he did not believe that a UK court would so hold. However, on the face of the wording of the CDPA, this does seem to be the proper construction.

If the transmission from the US is not downlinked to an EEA uplink station for retransmission to the UK, but is downlinked for direct reception by the public as a single hop (ie there is an uplink from the USA and reception of the downlink from that satellite by the UK public), then it is necessary to establish whether the wireless broadcast has been 'commissioned'. If it was commissioned, then the commissioner is the person making the wireless broadcast and the place where the broadcast is made is that from which the commissioner has his principal establishment in the EEA.

'Commission' is not defined in the CDPA. An obvious case would be if the UK broadcaster requested an American broadcaster to transmit an NFL football game live from the US and paid for the transmission. There would be no doubt in such a case that the UK broadcaster commissioned the broadcast.

In the case of a US broadcaster who uses an Atlantic satellite for DTH transmissions in Europe, which he uplinks from the US, there could be no suggestion that the wireless broadcast had been commissioned by a person established in an EEA state. In such a case the only conclusion would be that the place of making the broadcast was the US and the person making the broadcast was indeed the broadcaster. In these circumstances one would have to look at the Copyright (Application to Other Countries) Order 1999[8] to determine if the CDPA extends. The US is not so listed and, therefore, the broadcast would have no copyright protection in the UK.

1 CDPA s 159.
2 Copyright (Application to Other Countries) Order 1999, SI 1999/1751. See **paragraph 4.09**.
3 CDPA s 6(4).
4 Directive 93/83; see **paragraph 13.02**.
5 CDPA s 6A(2).
6 CDPA s 6A(3).
7 CDPA s 6A(1).
8 SI 1999/1751.

Infringements[1]

24.13 To summarise, the acts restricted by copyright in relation to broadcasts are:

- *Copying*: this will include taking a photograph of the whole or a substantial part of an image forming part of a broadcast (ie a 'video grab')[2]. Copying includes the making of copies which are transient or incidental to some other use of the work. An infringement will only take place if a 'substantial part' of a work is copied. The test for what constitutes a 'substantial part' is qualitative, not quantitative[3]; see, however, the exceptions to copyright infringement considered at **Chapter 8** and below.

- *Issuing of copies to the public*: the territory within which the copies are circulated is relevant, as is whether they have previously been put into circulation by or with the consent of the copyright owner. If the work has not previously been put into circulation in the EEA[4] by or with the consent of the copyright owner, it will be an infringement to put a copy of the work into circulation (eg making a copy of a live broadcast and distributing it to the public) within the EEA. It is also an infringement to put into circulation outside the EEA copies of a work not previously put into circulation in the EEA or elsewhere by or with the authority of the copyright owner (ie distributing unreleased copies).

- *Playing or showing in public*: where a broadcast is shown or played in public to a non-paying audience (such as on a 'big screen' in a sports bar), copyright in a broadcast, or in a sound recording (other than an excepted sound recording) which is included in the broadcast, will not be infringed[5]. However, if the broadcast contains a film[6] or an excepted sound recording (ie a sound recording whose author is not the author of the broadcast in which it is included), the playing or showing of the broadcast is only permitted if doing so is necessary: (a) to repair equipment for receiving broadcasts; (b) to demonstrate that such a repair has been carried out; or (c) to demonstrate such equipment for sale or hire.

- *Communication to the public*[7]: this includes broadcasting and making available by other electronic transmission. Where the transmission is by wireless broadcast of any kind (ie by satellite or other wireless means) the so-called 'emission theory' will apply such that any act of infringement will occur at the place where the signals are transmitted[8]. In relation to the making available right, the UK courts have applied the CJEU's ruling in *Sportradar*[9] such that the infringement will occur at least in the Member State in which the recipient is located where there is evidence that the communication is targeted at the public in that Member State, and it is generally considered that the act occurs also at the point of reception.

It is worth noting that the restricted acts of rental and lending, and adaptation, are *not* applicable to broadcasts, although they may well be applicable to the content featured in such transmissions[10].

1   The acts which may only be undertaken with the authority of the copyright owner are considered in detail in **Chapter 6**.
2   See **paragraph 6.04**.
3   See **paragraph 7.06**.
4   See **paragraph 6.05**.
5   See **paragraph 6.07**.
6   CDPA s 72. This section was amended to exclude films following the Court of Appeal decision in *Football Association Premier League Ltd v QC Leisure [2012] EWCA Civ 1708*.
7   See **paragraph 6.08**.
8   See *Football Dataco Ltd v Sportradar GmbH [2010] EWHC 2911 (Ch)* at para 66.
9   *Football Dataco Ltd v Sportradar GmbH (Case C-173/11)*.
10 See **paragraphs 6.06** and **6.09**.

Broadcasts – acts permitted in relation to broadcasts

24.14 Most of the general exceptions to the acts restricted by copyright apply to broadcasts[1]. A number of specific permitted acts are also authorised in respect of these categories of work. These include:

* making a recording of a broadcast (or a copy of the recording) by or on behalf of an educational establishment for non-commercial educational purposes, provided the recording is accompanied by an acknowledgement[2];
* making incidental copies for the purposes of making broadcasts ('the ephemeral right')[3];
* making copies for the purposes of supervision and control of broadcasts[4];
* making copies for the purposes of time shifting for private use[5];
* taking photographs of television broadcasts for private use[6];
* making free public showings of broadcasts[7];
* reception and retransmission of wireless broadcasts by cable[8];
* making and issuing to the public sub-titled copies of broadcasts;
* making copies for archival purposes[9].

1   See **Chapter 8**.
2   See CDPA s 35.
3   See **paragraph 8.31**.
4   See **paragraph 8.32**.
5   See **paragraph 8.33**.
6   See **paragraph 8.34**.
7   See **paragraphs 6.07** and **8.35**.
8   See **paragraph 8.36**.
9   See **paragraph 8.36**.

Broadcasting live events

24.15 There is no copyright in a live event per se. So, if a communication to the public includes a live transmission of an event which is not protectable as a copyright work[1], and does not contain protectable performances[2], no licence will be required to transmit the event. A sporting event, for example, does not attract copyright, and sportsmen will not usually acquire performers' rights[3]. The fees paid by broadcasters to sports governing bodies for the 'broadcast rights' to sporting events are not paid to acquire copyright. What broadcasters pay for is the right to bring their cameras onto the premises to create live signals and films recording the event (the 'access right' – which is protected not by the law of copyright, but of trespass).

If an event contains copyright material or a protectable performance, these rights will need to be cleared. So, for example, a 'half-time show' featuring the display of a military band will require a licence in respect of the music being played, and appropriate performers' consents including an assignment of relevant performers' property rights[4].

In practice, a communication to the public will in most cases include some protected works. A live music concert which is so communicated, will, for example, include (at least) the copyright in the musical compositions which are performed, and (where broadcast) the copyright in the broadcast itself (ie the programme carrying signal). Inevitably, there will also be a number of other rights to consider, such as the copyright in any artistic works used in set design, and any performers' property or non-property rights arising in respect of performances rendered by the musicians.

Although internet-based transmissions to the public are not, on the whole, 'broadcasts', some such transmissions are included within the definition of a 'broadcast' set out in the CDPA, including the simultaneous transmission of live events[5]. It follows that if acquiring rights to transmit a live event on an internet streaming service, it is necessary to ensure that wide rights to 'communicate to the public' are obtained.

1   See **paragraph 1.02**.
2   See **Chapter 11**.
3   See **paragraph 11.02**.
4   See **paragraphs 11.19** ff.
5   See **paragraph 6.08**.

Broadcasts, public performance and communication to the public

24.16 A public performance of a broadcast may be effected by the operation of receiving equipment (eg a television screen or other monitor), but the person who sends the transmission is not responsible for such a public performance, and nor is a performer whose performance may appear in the transmission[1].

Although it is a restricted act to play or show a broadcast in public, there is an exception where the audience have not paid for admission[2].

So, for example, showing a broadcast on a television screen in the bar of a hotel to which the public have not paid for admission does not infringe the copyright in the broadcast, although a licence would be required in respect of any films, musical compositions and sound recordings (except sound recordings owned by the broadcaster) included in the broadcast[3]. It seems that the exception will apply even if such a performance takes place, for example, in the bar of a theatre to which the public must pay for admission, since in that case the public have not paid specifically for the privilege and ability to watch the screen. The liability is triggered if the payment in question is made for the right to watch the performance on the screen. In such a case the copyright in the broadcast (and its contents) will be infringed unless the performance is properly authorised. The infringement is caused by the venue in question, which is then liable to be sued not only by the broadcaster, but also by the owners of the copyright in all the works included in the broadcast[4].

It is worth noting that this exception to copyright infringement only applies to broadcasts and not to any other communication to the public. So, for example, the proprietors of a bar which is open to members of the public who have not paid for admission will infringe copyright if they publicly show an 'on demand' transmission (such as a VOD film) in their bar without an appropriate licence to do so.

The provision of television screens and connected entertainment in hotel rooms amounts to communication to the public of the broadcasts and other content in question, even though a hotel room is a private place in a personal sense, because the public in general are admitted to hotel rooms on payment, and the rooms are successively filled with guests. Without the necessary licences the hotel owner will be infringing copyright in any films shown, the music within those films, and the rights in the broadcasts themselves. This use would constitute a communication to the public even if only one guest might view a given piece of content, since the simple act of making available content, regardless of whether it is actually accessed, is a communication to the public[5].

1 CDPA s 19(4); see **paragraph 6.07**.
2 See **paragraph 8.35**.
3 See **paragraphs 23.10 and 24.12**.
4 See **paragraph 6.07**.
5 See **paragraph 6.08**.

Broadcasts

Satellite broadcasts in the EEA

24.17 The provisions of the CDPA regarding the protection of satellite broadcasts referred to above[1] should be mirrored in the legislation of all EEA Member States, since the 'country of origin' principle was introduced by the Satellite and Cable Directive[2]. The significance of the principle is that an owner or licensee of the rights in a copyright work in one Member State can license the broadcast by satellite of the work from that state to a footprint covering the whole of the EEA. The DTH reception in countries where there are other copyright owners or licensees of the work does not infringe the rights of such owners and licensees[3].

This position is to be contrasted with the position in relation to cable retransmissions of these broadcasts[4].

1   See **paragraph 24.11**.
2   See **paragraph 13.02**.
3   Subject to the exception referred to at **paragraph 24.20** for co-production agreements.
4   Which are considered further at **paragraph 24.18**.

Cable retransmissions of local/national wireless broadcasts

24.18   Until recently a wireless broadcast from the UK (but not from elsewhere in the EEA) could, under certain circumstances, be received and immediately retransmitted by cable without infringing copyright in the broadcast, or works included within the broadcast[1].

The position changed with the repeal of s 73 of the CDPA. The repeal raises some practical issues, including how to deal with underlying rights in cable retransmissions. The UK government has expressed the view that that issue is best left to negotiations between the various stakeholders. It is noted, however, that the stakeholders involved have very different views on this issue.

1   CDPA s 73 (repealed by the Digital Economy Act 2017 s 34).

Cable retransmissions of broadcasts from other EEA states – the 'cable retransmission right'

24.19   Inclusion of a wireless broadcast in another communication to the public (eg a cable retransmission) will infringe the copyright in the broadcast[1]. However, the CDPA, as amended by the 1996 Regulations, contains special provisions in relation to the cable retransmission of broadcasts originating from elsewhere in the EEA, which impact upon the rights of copyright owners.

The CDPA recognises the right of the owner of any literary, dramatic, musical or artistic work, film or sound recording, to grant or refuse authorisation for cable retransmission of a wireless broadcast from another EEA Member State in which the work is included[2]. This right is known, in the CDPA, as 'the cable retransmission right'[3]. However, each such owner (other than the maker of the broadcast) is required to exercise his rights against the cable operator only through a licensing body[4].

If the copyright owner has not transferred management of his cable retransmission right to a licensing body, the licensing body which manages rights of the same category (eg AGICOA for film producers, PRS for musical compositions, Phonographic Performance Limited (PPL) for sound recordings) will be deemed to be mandated to manage his rights[5]. A number of other bodies have established collection services for members, including ALCS (writers) and ComPact (producers)[6]. The copyright owner will be deemed to have the same rights and obligations resulting from any relevant agreement between the cable operator and the licensing body as do copyright owners who have transferred management of their cable retransmission rights to that licensing body[7]. The copyright owner must exercise his rights against the licensing body within three years of the date of the cable retransmission[8].

An important exception to the principle of collective licensing is made in the case of rights exercisable by the maker of the initial broadcast, whether in relation to the broadcast itself, or any works included within the broadcast[9].

So, if a UK cable operator wishes to retransmit a Dutch satellite television broadcast which includes a film, only (a) the Dutch broadcaster (in respect of cable retransmission rights he controls), or (b) AGICOA or a similar body, could claim for breach of copyright in the cable retransmission right and remuneration from the UK cable operator even though the film owner is not a member of AGICOA. The film producer will be able to claim its share of AGICOA revenues attributable to the retransmission of the broadcast of the film under normal AGICOA rules, within three years of the date of the cable retransmission as if it had been a member of AGICOA at that date.

Again, these provisions of the CDPA implement the Satellite and Cable Directive and as such should be largely mirrored throughout the EEA.

1   See **paragraph 6.08**.
2   CDPA s 144A(1).
3   CDPA s 144A.
4   CDPA s 144A(2).
5   CDPA s 144A(3).
6   See **paragraph 12.01** and **Appendix 1** for contact details.
7   CDPA s 144A(4).
8   CDPA s 144A(5).
9   CDPA s 144A(6).

Satellite broadcasting of films and international co-productions

24.20   International co-production agreements for films normally provide that the respective production companies retain copyright ownership of the film in their own countries. The effect of the provisions described in **paragraph 24.12** is to cut across such arrangements (since one producer can license the broadcast by satellite of the film for reception in homes across Europe including the country of the co-producer, thus damaging the value of the film rights in that country). The 1996 Regulations sought to alleviate the problem this created for film producers by providing that, where a co-production agreement has been concluded before 1 January 1995 between two or more co-producers of a film, one of whom is a national of an EEA state, and the provisions of the agreement grant to the parties exclusive rights to exploit all communication to the public of the film in separate geographical areas, the person to whom the exclusive exploitation rights in relation to the UK have been granted may not make any satellite broadcast of the work from the UK without the consent of the other party to the agreement 'whose language-related exploitation rights would be adversely affected by that broadcast' if the agreement does not 'expressly or by implication address satellite broadcasting from the UK'[1].

So, if a co-production agreement came into existence before 1 January 1995 between a UK film production company and a French film production company for the co-production of a film under which each party retained the right to communicate the film to the public in its own territory, neither producer could exercise the satellite broadcasting rights in the film from its own territory by way of a DTH broadcast intended to be received by the public in the other producer's country without the other's consent. In practice, in circumstances where this provision may apply, it would be prudent for the person acquiring satellite broadcasting rights to procure the agreement of all co-producers to the broadcasting agreement in addition to the usual warranties and indemnities.

1   1996 Regulations, reg 29.

Encrypted transmissions

24.21 Some satellite television transmissions are encrypted and are intended for reception by cable television systems, hotels and designated SMATV systems only. Accordingly, decoders are not made available to the public. The reception of a broadcast includes reception of a broadcast relayed by means of a telecommunications system[1]. Since a cable television system is a telecommunications system, such transmissions are 'capable of being lawfully received by members of the public'. However, they do not come within the definition of 'broadcast' because the decoders for those transmissions are not made available to the public and, accordingly, the transmissions do not qualify for copyright protection as broadcasts. Nevertheless, the CDPA does protect such transmissions from fraudulent reception[2].

1   CDPA s 6(5).
2   See **paragraph 24.23**.

Satellite broadcasting and cable agreements

24.22   There are potentially at least five types of agreement which a channel provider usually enters into in relation to a satellite or a cable transmission which have copyright implications:

• *An agreement for the provision of services on a transponder, space segment capacity or a transponder lease*: the transponder lease may be made with a packaged transmission services provider such as Arqiva, Globecast or BT, or one of the other licensed UK uplink station operators, or directly with the satellite operator such as EUTELSAT or Société Européenne des Satellites (the owners of ASTRA). In the context of digital satellite transmissions, digital compression allows the transmission of several channels of television programming via each single transponder. The transmissions to the satellite must be from a single uplink station of all the channels intended for one transponder. However, the signals to the uplink station can be provided by different programme providers. Thus, the owner or lessee of a whole transponder may enter into sub-leases with other channel providers to take their digital transmissions to uplink to the satellite. Where these transmissions are pay television services, it is necessary to also secure subscription management systems and for a common encryption system to be used. So, the programme provider which is not itself a transponder lessee, may enter into a single agreement to cover uplink transponder services and the provision of a subscriber management system.

  Although the transponder lease provides services to the lessee which are basically passive (in that the role of the transponder is to receive and retransmit the channel provider's signal from the uplink station), it is customary for the satellite owner and operator to impose certain conditions on the channel provider relating to the content of its programmes, for example, to ensure that the programming complies with the provisions of the appropriate regulator, does not infringe copyright and is otherwise lawful. Indeed, the satellite operator may reserve the right to 'turn off' the transponder if the channel provider is in breach of these conditions.

  The CDPA provides that the person making the broadcast is 'the person transmitting the programme, if he has responsibility to any extent for its contents, and to any person providing the programme etc'[1]. Whether or not the satellite operator is 'broadcasting' the channel provider's signal within the meaning of the CDPA depends on whether monitoring the programme and taking the right to close down transmissions for reasons relating to its content constitutes 'responsibility to any extent for its contents'. If so, the satellite operator will be one of the broadcasters and is liable to be sued by the copyright owners of the material in the signal who have not licensed use of their material in the broadcast by the programme provider.

Accordingly, the channel provider should be prepared to indemnify the uplink station operators and satellite operators against any actions that may be taken against them as persons making the broadcast in the event of the broadcasts constituting a breach of a third party's copyright.

It is normal in transponder leases for the lessor to be granted the right to record the channel provider's signals for monitoring purposes as the recording, by whatever means, of copyright work infringes the restricted act of making copies[2]. The CDPA does provide that copyright is not infringed by the making of certain recordings for the purpose of monitoring and regulating UK television broadcasters[3], however, these provisions do not extend to monitoring by a multiplexer or a satellite owner and operator. It is unlikely that the channel provider will be able to obtain any relaxation of this requirement by the satellite operator and accordingly will need to ensure that programme acquisition agreements, and indeed agreements with any copyright holder providing the copyright material which is used in broadcasts, give permission for copying for monitoring purposes.

- *An agreement with the uplink station to transmit the service to the satellite*: uplink services are often combined into a single agreement with the provision of transponder capacity with a bundled transmission services provider. The agreement between the uplink station and the channel provider will only have copyright consequences if, like the satellite operator, the uplink station can be said to 'have responsibility to any extent' for the contents of the programme. If the uplink station agreement contains warranties as to the content of the programme by the channel provider and the uplink station reserves the right to monitor the signals and to cut off the transmission to the satellite in the event of a breach of the warranties then it may be difficult for the uplink station to argue that it has no responsibility for the programme contents. In these circumstances, like the satellite operator, the uplink station will expect indemnities from the channel provider against third party claims for breach of copyright contained in the programme signals.
- *Agreements with the suppliers of the programme material*: these so-called 'programme acquisition agreements' will include a number of restrictions on the use by the channel/content provider of the programmes. This is partly because the licensors may have limited rights in the copyright elements in the programme and partly because certain uses may trigger additional (or residual) union payments or other licence fees. If the agreement is for a satellite broadcast and the channel provider's signal is encrypted

and intended for reception in a limited part of the satellite footprint, the channel provider should be required (insofar as possible within the boundaries of competition law)[4] not to issue nor to permit the issue of decoders capable of decoding the signal outside the licence area. The channel provider will be well advised to seek the widest possible rights in this regard.

The contract should specifically permit copyright for technical monitoring purposes by uplink stations, satellite operators and cable stations.

Public performances before paying audiences will usually be forbidden, or subject to special terms.

• *Carriage agreements*: traditionally, a distribution platform (such as a cable operator, satellite distributor or IPTV operator), when entering into an agreement with a channel provider, will be required to agree not to cut the channel's programmes, nor to record them and transmit them at a different time, nor to add anything to the programmes.

A carriage agreement will also typically include the right for the platform to distribute programming on a VOD basis together with any other required ancillary rights. In turn, the platform operator will require the channel provider to warrant that it has obtained all the necessary licences from all the copyright owners of the material in the channel's programmes, and to indemnify the platform operator against any copyright infringement proceedings that may be brought against the platform operator, consequential upon his transmitting materials supplied to him by the channel provider. If shops, hotels and other places are subscribers to the distribution service, because of the likelihood of public performances taking place, the agreement should state that the programmes are licensed for such types of performances.

The platform operator must also enquire whether the channel provider has obtained blanket licences from the appropriate copyright collection societies which extend to the inclusion of the material in its programmes, failing which it will have to apply for such licences himself[5]. In practice it is common for the platform to impose the liability to obtain these licences (at least for linear distribution) on the channel provider.

Platform operators will (and should) require an exception from the restrictions upon the recording of any part of the programmes to permit them to record for monitoring, since they are obliged to keep copies of all their programming for monitoring purposes. This exception is not, strictly speaking, necessary as a matter of law because the keeping of copies for these purposes will not infringe copyright in any work[6].

The channel provider may also require that the channel is not discriminated against when compared to other channels on any EPG.

In the context of digital and interactive services, operators will need to reserve the right to enable subscribers to insert or overlay on the television screen (sometimes over the programme) the EPG, icons, text and other content identifying the channel and other interactive services. The channel provider will want to restrict the operator from overlaying these interactive elements itself (ie without the subscriber's prompt). The operator will need to re-size, re-position and frame content to the extent necessary to enable subscribers to access interactive content on the service.

As technology has developed in recent years, these agreements have evolved and become heavily negotiated and much more complex.

- *Finally, an agreement with the subscriber management system operator* is required. A detailed consideration of this agreement is beyond the scope of this *User's Guide* but this may often form part of a carriage agreement and be handled, at least in part, by the platform operator.

1   CDPA s 6(3)(a).
2   See **paragraph 6.04**.
3   See **paragraph 8.31**.
4   See **Chapter 13**.
5   See **Chapter 12**.
6   See **paragraph 8.32**.

Fraudulent reception of transmissions

24.23 The CDPA has long included provisions which make it a criminal offence to dishonestly receive broadcasts. These provisions were revised by the Conditional Access (Unauthorised Decoders) Regulations 2000, SI 2000/1175 ('2000 Regulations') (which implemented into UK law the provisions of the Conditional Access Directive[1]), and by the 2003 Regulations.

The intention of the Conditional Access Directive (and hence the 2000 Regulations) is to provide protection against illegal devices which are designed or adapted to give access to a 'protected service' without the authorisation of the service provider. Protected services are television broadcasting, radio broadcasting and 'information society services' offered to the public *within the EU*, which are provided against remuneration (such as the payment of subscriptions) and on the basis of 'conditional access'. Internet-based services which place conditions on access are included within this meaning.

The CDPA (as amended) provides for a combination of civil and criminal remedies in respect of the fraudulent reception of broadcasting[2].

To best comprehend the provisions, it is important to understand the terminology used. The CDPA contains the following definitions[3]:

- *apparatus* is widely defined (as previously) to include 'any device, component or electronic data (including software)';

- *conditional access technology* means 'any technical measure or arrangement whereby access to encrypted transmissions in an intelligible form is made conditional upon prior individual authorisation';
- *decoder* means 'any apparatus which is designed or adapted to enable (whether on its own or with any other apparatus) an encrypted transmission to be decoded';
- *transmission* means any programme included in a broadcasting service or an 'information society service which is provided from a place within the UK or any other Member State'[4];
- *unauthorised,* in relation to a decoder, means that the decoder is designed or adapted to enable an encrypted transmission, or any service of which it forms part, to be accessed in an intelligible form without payment of the fee (however imposed) which the person making the transmission, or on whose behalf it is made, charges for accessing the transmission or service (whether by the circumvention of any conditional access technology related to the transmission or service or by any other means).

1   Directive 98/84/EC of the European Parliament on the legal protection of services based on, or consisting of, conditional access.
2   CDPA ss 297–298. Supplementary provisions as to fraudulent reception are contained in CDPA s 299.
3   CDPA s 297A(4).
4   See **paragraph 24.02**.

Fraudulently receiving programmes

24.24 A person who dishonestly receives a programme in a broadcasting service provided from a place in the UK with the intention to avoid payment of any charge applicable to the reception of the programme commits an offence and is liable on summary conviction to a fine[1].

This offence was considered in the *Murphy v Media Protection Services Ltd* litigation[2], which involved a publican who had imported a Greek satellite decoder card to show Premier League football matches in her pub in Southsea, Hampshire. Ms Murphy had purchased the decoder card but was using it to contravene geographical limitations (decoder cards issued by the Greek television provider, NOVA, were authorised for use in the Greek territory only, BSkyB being the Premier League's exclusive licensee for the UK and Ireland) and to avoid paying a subscription to BSkyB.

In *Murphy*, the Administrative Court held, on appeal from the Portsmouth Crown Court and following a reference to the CJEU, that:

- Ms Murphy's viewing cards were not illicit devices within the meaning of Art 2E of the Conditional Access Directive (had they been such devices, they would have fallen within the scope of that Directive and different considerations would have come into play);

- by virtue of Art 56 of the Treaty on the Functioning of the European Union, which contains a prohibition on restrictions on the freedom to provide services within the EU, s 297(1) of the CDPA could not be applied to Ms Murphy's use of the cards in question;
- the territorial restrictions imposed on the use of Ms Murphy's NOVA viewing cards were unlawful under EU law;
- Ms Murphy had paid for her card, she had not avoided any charge applicable to its use and had not acted dishonestly;
- Ms Murphy's convictions should be quashed[3].

The court made clear in *Murphy* that the issues of EC law raised in that case do not affect prosecutions resulting from, by way of example, the dishonest use of decoder cards which are 'pirate' or counterfeit or which have been stolen[4].

1   CDPA s 297.
2   The appeal from the decision of the Portsmouth Crown Court resulted in four judgments of the Administrative Court and a reference to the CJEU. The Administrative Court judgment dated 21 December 2007 ([2007] EWHC 3091 (Admin)) considered the interpretation of CDPA s 297 from an English Law perspective.
3   [2012] EWHC 466 (Admin).
4   See [2008] EWHC 1666 (Admin) at paras 63–65.

Unauthorised decoders

24.25 A person commits a criminal offence if he:

'(a) makes, imports, distributes, sells or lets for hire or offers or exposes for sale or hire any unauthorised decoder;

(b) has in his possession for commercial purposes an unauthorised decoder;

(c) installs, maintains or replaces for commercial purposes any unauthorised decoder; or

(d) advertises any unauthorised decoder for sale or hire or otherwise promotes any unauthorised decoder by means of commercial communications[1].'

The provisions referred to at (b) to (d) cover activities prohibited by the Conditional Access Directive.

Any person who commits one of the above offences will be liable to either:

- (on summary conviction) imprisonment for a term not exceeding six months or a fine not exceeding the statutory maximum, or both; or
- (on indictment) imprisonment for a period of not more than ten years or an unlimited fine, or both[2].

The defendant will have a defence if he can show that he 'did not know, and had no reasonable grounds for knowing, that the decoder was an unauthorised decoder'[3].

The rights and remedies available to the providers of information society services and conditional access services were also altered by the 2000 Regulations[4].

Any person who:

- makes charges for the reception of programmes included in a broadcasting service provided from a place in the UK or other Member State;
- sends encrypted transmissions from the UK or any other Member State; or
- provides conditional access services from the UK or any other Member State,

will be entitled to the same remedies against the infringer as a copyright owner has with regard to a breach of copyright (including delivery up and seizure)[5].

It is noteworthy that copyright holders themselves are not provided with a right of action, although where the copyright holder directly provides the service (eg through a password restricted website providing access to his work) he is likely to be entitled to a remedy as an information service provider.

The infringer will not be liable for damages if it can be shown that at the time of the infringement he did not know, and had no reason to believe, that his acts infringed these rights[6].

1   CDPA s 297A(1).
2   CDPA s 297A(2).
3   CDPA s 297A(3).
4   CDPA s 298.
5   CDPA s 298(1), (2).
6   CDPA s 298(5).

Search warrants and forfeiture

24.26 The CDPA was also revised by the Copyright, etc and Trade marks (Offences and Enforcement) Act 2002 to include:

- a power to issue search warrants authorising the entry and search of premises, using reasonable force as is necessary[1]; and
- a right to require forfeiture of unauthorised decoders[2].

These rights and remedies are available against any person who commits one of the criminal offences described above.

1   CDPA s 297B.
2   CDPA s 297C (England, Wales and Northern Ireland) and s 297D (Scotland).

Broadcasting copyright works, communication to the public and fair dealing

Spoken words

24.27 Literary works include words 'written, spoken or sung'[1]. So, words spoken extempore (such as during an interview) will constitute a literary work at the time they are recorded, and the author of the literary work will be the speaker[2]. However, the CDPA contains an exception to copyright infringement, so that where a record of spoken words is made, in writing or otherwise, for the purpose of reporting current events or communicating to the public the whole or part of the work, the use of this recording (or copies of it) will not infringe the spoken 'literary work'[3] provided that a number of conditions are met[4].

We have considered the general exceptions to copyright infringement elsewhere in this *User's Guide*[5], but in essence, the reading or recitation in public by one person of a published literary or dramatic work, provided that it is only a reasonable extract from the work, will not infringe copyright, if it is accompanied by a sufficient acknowledgement[6]. Similarly, the making of a recording of such a public reading or recitation, or the inclusion of such a recording in a communication to the public will not infringe copyright in the literary or dramatic work, provided that the programme consists mainly of other material (ie public readings or recitations) the use of which is exempt from copyright infringement[7].

1   See **paragraph 2.02**.
2   See **paragraph 2.05**.
3   CDPA s 58(1).
4   See **paragraph 8.20**.
5   See **Chapter 11**.
6   CDPA s 59(1); see **paragraph 8.21**.
7   CDPA s 59(2); see **paragraph 8.21**.

Published editions in interactive services

24.28 Copyright subsists in the typographical arrangement of published editions of literary, dramatic or musical works[1]. The term of the copyright is 25 years from the end of the calendar year in which the edition was first published[2]. Inclusion in a communication to the public is not a restricted act in relation to this subject matter.

1   See **paragraph 2.11**.
2   See **paragraph 5.15**.

Computer programs

24.29 Service providers may provide interactive services which include games or e-commerce opportunities. A computer program is protected as a literary work[1]. It follows that including a computer program in a communication to the public will require an appropriate licence from the copyright owner of the computer program concerned[2]. Similarly, the right to use any software conveyed to subscribers should be limited by the terms of a licence to the minimum content necessary to receive and utilise the service.

1   See **paragraph 2.02**.
2   For a detailed consideration of computer software generally, see **Chapter 28**.

Musical compositions

24.30 Communication to the public is an act restricted by copyright in relation to both musical works and literary works such as song lyrics[1], and these rights are vested in PRS by virtually every UK composer[2].

In the context of the broadcasting industry, PRS, in turn, negotiates 'blanket' licence agreements with broadcasters and cable operators which grant the right to broadcast *all* PRS repertoire music as part of their radio or television services.

The form of these blanket agreements is different in each case, and if agreement cannot be reached as to licence terms, the matter may be referred by the actual or prospective licensee to the Copyright Tribunal, which has the power to determine what are the fair commercial and other terms of such licences[3]. Either party can appeal to the court on a point of law against a decision of the Tribunal.

PRS blanket licence agreements require licensees to keep detailed records of all music transmitted, so as to enable PRS to divide its revenue between its members by reference to the number of times that its members' compositions are performed. Consequently, when it makes or acquires programming, the broadcaster needs to ensure that detailed 'cue sheets' identifying the music included in the programme are created and delivered, so as to enable it to make appropriate returns to PRS.

The basis of the royalty under the PRS blanket broadcasting licence varies. Smaller broadcasters are licensed on a rate card basis, while larger broadcasters negotiate their licence terms individually. For the majority of television licences the royalty is a lump sum which is usually adjusted yearly. The exception to this is music channels which are charged on a percentage of revenue basis, subject to a lump sum minimum.

For commercial radio the PRS charge is based on a percentage of broadcasting revenue plus a lump sum annual royalty fee.

PRS fees are payable for the right to transmit the PRS members' compositions. The right to transmit sound recordings which embody those compositions is entirely separate and must be acquired separately from PPL.

The right to copy a musical composition by making recordings of it, as distinct from the right to publicly perform the composition or to include an existing recording in a broadcast, is also one of the restricted acts applicable to musical compositions. Most music publishing companies appoint MCPS[4] as their agent to administer the right to record their musical compositions. A radio or television station which needs to record music (eg to include in a programme it intends to transmit) must pay a fee to MCPS unless it is able to use the so-called 'ephemeral' right exception[5]. Television stations, BBC radio and most independent radio stations have blanket licence arrangements with MCPS which are bundled into their blanket PRS licences. Some independent radio stations rely on the ephemeral right, but on the whole, broadcasters are not prepared to rely on the exception because of the requirement to dispose of recordings within the requisite period.

The MCPS blanket licence does not apply to the recording of any complete dramatico-musical works, nor to excerpts from such works unless:

- the total duration is no longer than 20 minutes and does not involve a complete act;
- the use is not a 'potted version' of the complete work;
- the excerpt is not presented in a dramatic form.

Use of such works outside a blanket licence is usually licensed direct by the copyright owner or licensee of the work.

In each case, the broadcaster should ensure that his blanket licence will cover all his anticipated activities. To the extent that it does not cover such activities, further payments will be required to be made by the broadcaster. It is worth noting that until August 2017 no licence was required by a cable operator for the inclusion in its service of music in certain broadcasts which are intended for reception in the cable operator's area. This exception was repealed so that all transmissions by cable in any area now require a full set of licences, and certain internet retransmission service operators who claimed the exception also applied to their activities (on the grounds that cable included the internet) can no longer make that claim.

The producer of any television programme will also need to take a licence from the copyright owner of the right to synchronise, or copy, any musical compositions he wishes to use in the soundtrack of the programme. This right is considered in detail elsewhere is this *User's Guide*[6].

In the context of the internet, different licensing models apply for the use of musical compositions; these are considered in detail at **paragraph 20.07**.

1   See **paragraph 6.08**.
2   See **paragraph 20.07**.
3   See **Chapter 12**.
4   See **paragraph 20.08**.
5   See **paragraphs 8.31** and **24.14**.
6   See **paragraph 22.10**.

Sound recordings of musical compositions and music videos

24.31 As with musical compositions, the acts restricted by copyright in relation to sound recordings include communication to the public[1]. A licence is therefore required to permit a television or radio station to broadcast a sound recording, and the broadcast rights in the great majority, if not all, of the commercial sound recordings produced in the

UK are vested in PPL[2]. There are 'blanket' licensing arrangements in force between PPL and the broadcasting organisations, so that separate licences are not required in respect of each sound recording used.

To the extent that a broadcaster uses commercial sound recordings to accompany interactive service channels, a PPL licence will also be required to facilitate these uses[3].

Record companies produce videos principally (but not exclusively) for the purposes of exploitation on television. VPL issues licences for the dubbing and broadcast of such videos. Most of the terrestrial and satellite television stations have been issued with licences by VPL. Licences for music videos can also be obtained direct from the record companies concerned.

Issues concerning the dubbing of commercial sound recordings into television programmes, and concerning PPL and VPL generally, are considered in detail elsewhere in this *User's Guide*[4].

Different issues apply in the context of taking licences to include sound recordings in internet and mobile services; these are considered in detail in **paragraph 20.23**.

1   See **paragraph 6.08**.
2   See **paragraph 20.22**.
3   See **paragraph 20.22**, any PPL licence regarding interactive services will be subject to certain limitations in relation to the use of the sound recording of part of such service.
4   See **paragraphs 22.11, 20.22** and **20.23**.

Fair dealing

24.32 The restricted acts in relation to a broadcast, as with other categories of copyright work, include communication to the public[1]. So, it is a breach of copyright to include in a communication to the public any part of another broadcast, or other categories of copyright work, which have copyright protection in the UK, without the owner's consent.

An exception to this principle arises in respect of 'fair dealing'. In the context of making a communication to the public of a copyright work, 'fair dealing' for the purpose of criticism and review, and (except in the case of photographs) for reporting news events is permitted[2].

For these purposes, 'criticism' may extend to matters other than literary criticism, such as ideas contained in the work, or events surrounding it. In *Time Warner Entertainments Co Ltd v Channel 4 Television Corpn plc*[3], the inclusion of a film clip amounted to 'fair dealing' in the context of a programme that considered the merits of the decision to withhold a work from distribution in the UK. The question in each case will be whether the use is genuinely one of criticism or review[4].

In the context of news reporting, *BBC v BSB Ltd*[5] held that, in the circumstances, BSkyB's transmission of excerpts from BBC broadcasts of World Cup football matches, to which the BBC had the exclusive broadcasting rights in the UK, constituted fair dealing for the purpose of reporting current events. The excerpts varied in length from 14 to 37 seconds and were used in successive news bulletins over the period of 24 hours following the match in question. They were accompanied by a verbal report of the incidents and an acknowledgement of the source of the film. Scott J accepted that for the purposes of the CDPA, fair dealing is largely 'a matter of impression'.

This case led to the adoption of a non-legally binding code of 'off air' news access between the main broadcasters in the UK which, has subsequently been reviewed[6].

1 See **paragraph 6.08**.
2 See **paragraph 8.04**.
3 [1994] EMLR 1, CA.
4 See **paragraph 8.04**.
5 [1992] Ch 141.
6 Fair dealing is discussed in detail in **Chapter 8**.

Digital products – infringements

24.33 Digital products may consist of protectable works. It follows that issues relating to the infringement of copyright works, moral rights and performers' rights should be considered when assessing whether a digital work infringes third party rights. These issues are considered in detail elsewhere in this *User's Guide*[1].

1 See **Chapters 6, 7, 8, 10** and **15**.

Incidental inclusion

24.34 The incidental inclusion of copyright works in a broadcast will not infringe the copyright in such works. Nor is copyright infringed by the communication to the public of anything (eg a television programme) whose making is not an infringement of copyright because of the 'incidental inclusion' exception. However, where musical works are included, the position is qualified, so that a musical work (and the recording of the work) will not be deemed to be 'incidentally included' if it is deliberately included[1].

1 See **paragraph 8.08**.

Digital content – linking and framing

Linking

24.35 Websites typically contain links to other sites, providing easy access to material made available online by third parties. The terms 'hyperlinking' or 'linking' cover activities including inline linking and deep-linking, as well as embedded linking and framing (which are dealt with separately below).

As noted at **paragraph 24.01**, authors of copyright protected works have the exclusive right to communicate their works to the public. In certain circumstances, the provision of a hyperlink to a copyright protected work may constitute an unauthorised 'communication to the public' and therefore an infringement of the copyright in that work. This is an area of law that has been the subject of a number of references to the CJEU.

The key CJEU cases on linking are *Svensson*[1] and *GS Media*[2]. However, before considering those cases it is useful to briefly reference earlier CJEU decisions which have considered the communication to the public right.

Those earlier cases establish that the concept of communication to the public includes two cumulative criteria: (a) an act of communication of a work; and (b) the communication of that work to a public. In order to determine whether there is a communication to the public within the meaning of the legislation it is necessary to consider a number of fact-sensitive criteria.

The concept of the 'public' refers to an indeterminate number of potential viewers and implies a fairly large number of people. To be categorised as a 'communication to the public', a protected work must be communicated using specific technical means different from those previously used or, failing that, to a 'new public', being a public which was not considered by the copyright owner when it authorised the initial communication to the public of the work.

In *TVCatchup*[3], the CJEU confirmed that any retransmission of a terrestrial television broadcast via the internet will constitute a communication to the public. It also confirmed that where the means of retransmission is different to the original communication, it is not necessary to show that the transmission is to a 'new' public.

In *Svensson,* the CJEU confirmed that where a work has been transmitted by the same technical means as the initial communication, the subsequent communication has to be to a 'new public' in order for the linking to constitute an infringing act.

Svensson concerned a website (Retriever) that provided services to subscribers about news items, or other matters of interest to them, by providing clickable links to those items. The authors of some of the articles in a Swedish newspaper which had been published in hard copy and online with the authors' consent, made complaint about the fact that the Retriever website was making available/communicating their articles to the public by providing clickable links to the online newspaper. It was therefore a case where the works had been transmitted by the same technical means as the initial communication.

On the facts of *Svensson* there was no 'new public' since the works in question were already freely accessible to all internet users without restrictions in the form of a paywall or similar. The court concluded that the provision on a website of hyperlinks to works freely available on another website does not constitute an infringement of the communication to the public right.

The principles established in *Svensson* in respect of linking were subsequently clarified in *GS Media* and restricted to circumstances where the copyright content is already freely available with the consent of the copyright owner.

GS Media concerned the provision of links to photographs that had been leaked and placed on a file storage service without the authorisation of the copyright owner. The CJEU held that where a user 'knew or ought to have known' that providing the link would enable access to unauthorised content, the provision of the link will constitute a communication to the public. In circumstances where the link is provided for profit, such knowledge is presumed. It is also clear that if the link allows users to circumvent access restrictions (eg a paywall), the provision of the link will constitute a communication to the public.

Linking to copyright content may attract liability for other offences under UK law where, for instance, it can be established that the linker authorised[4] and/or acted jointly with others to provide access to an unauthorised copy of a work, or where the hyperlinks provided enable end users to make unauthorised copies of a copyright protected work.

Authorisation (and joint tortfeasorship) in the online context was considered in detail in *Newzbin*[5]. The defendant operated a website that provided facilities allowing users to search for and acquire unlawful copies of the claimants' films. The High Court held that in authorisation by supply cases, the following factors should be considered: (a) the nature of the relationship between the alleged authoriser and the primary infringer; (b) whether the equipment or other material supplied constitutes the means used to infringe; (c) whether it is inevitable it will be used to infringe; and (d) the degree of control which the supplier retains and whether he has taken any steps to prevent infringement. These factors may or may not be determinative depending upon all the other circumstances.

The principles established in *Newzbin* have since been applied in subsequent cases that have considered authorisation of user infringement by the operators of pirate websites[6].

1   *Svensson v Retriever Sverige AB (Case C-466/12).*
2   *GS Media v Sanoma (Case C-160/15).*
3   *ITV Broadcasting Ltd v TVCatchup Ltd (Case C-607/11).*
4   CDPA s 16(2). See also **paragraph 6.02**.
5   *Twentieth Century Fox Film Corp v Newzbin Ltd [2010] EWHC 608 (Ch).*
6   See **paragraphs 24.49** ff.

Framing

24.36 Another method of providing connections between sites is 'framing' or 'embedded linking'. A web page may be subdivided into different portions, enabling the user to, for example, view a second site through a 'window' in a portion of the web page. Framing is achieved through the creation of links on the linking site to the web page/website where the framed content originates. The 'framed' content, whilst appearing to the user to be made available by the linking site, will be hosted on and streamed from the website whose content is being framed.

The 'framing' of content enables the operator of the linking site to add its own material (often advertising) in the 'frame' around the window to the second site, and to cover up material featured on the second site.

Framed content was considered by the CJEU in *Bestwater*[1]. *Bestwater* confirms that the conclusions reached in *Svensson* (see **paragraph 24.35**) are not altered where the content is framed/embedded:

> 'The mere fact that a protected work, freely available on an internet site, is inserted into another internet site by means of a link using the "framing" technique, such as that used in the case in the main proceedings, cannot [be] classified as "communication to the public" within the meaning of Article 3(1) of [the 2001 Directive] since the work at issue is not transmitted to a new public or communicated [by] a specific technical method different from that of the original communication.'[2]

Framing provides enhanced possibilities for material to be juxtaposed in a way which confuses the user as to the origin of the material in question, or constitutes a derogatory treatment. Hence issues of passing off and moral rights infringement may also be relevant[3].

1   *BestWater International GmbH v Michael Mebes, Stefan Potsch (Case C-348/13).*
2   Order of the Court of 21 October 2014, ECLI:EU:C:2014:2315.
3   See **Chapter 10** for a detailed consideration of moral rights.

Digital rights management systems

24.37 The development of digital technologies has enabled rights holders to exert a greater level of control over the online distribution of their copyright protected works within the framework of secure digital rights management ('DRM'). The ability to exercise this level of control is seen by many as increasingly important as a greater proportion of the population has access to broadband networks and content can be copied and shared with ever greater ease and speed. However, DRM is not without its opponents and even some larger companies (including Apple Inc in respect of all music on its iTunes service) now make DRM-free content available. The acronym 'DRM' refers to the digital management of rights, and is not to be confused with the separate, but nevertheless key, process of managing digital rights.

DRM is all about achieving three principal objectives which help to ensure that consumption of content always occurs within a rights holder's permitted framework, and that the chances of piracy are significantly reduced:

(1) there is a need to *identify* content, ensuring that each and every piece of content is associated with a unique number or code. This is not a new concept and has been around in sectors such as publishing for some time, with the ISBN and DOI systems;

(2) there is a need to *describe* data. By attaching 'meta data' to digital content, it is possible for the rights holder to indicate information about that content such as the author or the date and place of publication. This is useful for consumers, but also facts such as copyright information are key data in association with *rules*, the final aspect of managing digital rights;

(3) it is necessary to attach *rules* to the accessing and exploitation of data. Rules about the flexibility of each piece of content need to be set by the rights owner. These can range from simple statements such as 'do not copy' to complex logic formulations involving content-expiry and re-distribution parameters. Many of the control mechanisms which detail the permitted activities mirror the scope of the intellectual property licence that has been granted to the user, however, the freedom of rights holders to encroach into the realms of activities permitted in respect of copyright-protected works under applicable UK and EU legislation is what some groups regard as inconsistent with fundamental copyright laws.

In practical terms, DRM may assist rights holders with any or all of the following:

- filtering/classification – distinguishing certain types of content from others;
- authentication – being confident that only authorised users can access the content;
- broadcast monitoring – by embedding codes in the works, monitoring the timing and frequency of their appearance in broadcast signals;
- forensic tracking – allowing the work to 'remember' where it has been accessed, or to report home with these details;
- copy prevention – resisting (or restricting) attempts to duplicate the work;
- e-commerce/linking – triggering transactions or suggesting other transactions upon access; and/or
- copyright communication – ensuring end-users are aware of the identity of the rights holder.

DRM in the technical sense is the term given to any method of 'wrapping' content in order to achieve one or more access-related objectives. It is used primarily to encrypt content in order to prevent unauthorised access (necessary where unauthorised re-distribution is likely). DRM can also be used to provide parties in the delivery chain with a guarantee of integrity and authority via the use of digital signatures and/or watermarking (although identifying marks such as watermarks can still be applied without correspondingly applying DRM encryption measures)[1]. In respect of the latter it might be useful to be able to prove, as is possible, the source of the content and to integrate a mechanism for tracking content which might be 'in the wild' and otherwise reproduceable.

Figure 1 is a diagrammatic representation of a potential DRM framework for mobile super-distribution.

In this system, the content (for example, video) starts its life on the content server (top left) operated either by the rights owner or its licensee. Consumers may download the content, which is encrypted and contained within a DRM wrapper, over the internet to their mobile handset. However, the content is unwatchable until activated by calling upon a third party DRM broker, acting under licence from the operator of the content server to issue the end user with a licence for the video file. The consumer acquires an individual licence (with whatever restrictions the content owner chooses) in return for payment. Rights holders can be comfortable with the consumers being able to forward the content to other handset users, as the content will remain in the DRM wrapper requiring the purchase of a separate licence for each consumer (the licence is invariably attached to the consumer's computer or the consumer himself, rather than each instance of the content).

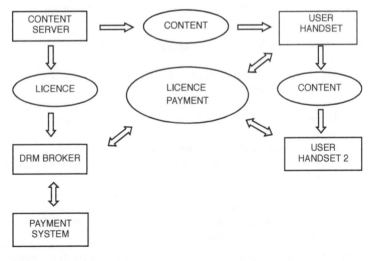

Figure 1

DRM systems are only useful where they are effective. If encryption technology is hacked, and either modified, to allow free access, or content meta data is changed, to change the scope of the 'rules', the system is rendered much less useful to rights holders. The 2001 Directive[2] and 2003 Regulations include various provisions to support the use by rights holders and the prevention of circumvention by third parties of DRM systems. The 2001 Directive also explicitly permits the use by rights holders of DRM systems (referred to as technological protection measures) within the context of the fair dealing exceptions (subject to certain conditions)[3].

Anti-circumvention legislation serves as a technical addition to the exclusive rights granted by traditional copyright law. Many have argued that these protections effectively grant a new exclusive right of 'access' for copyright owners, which moves well beyond traditional concepts of copyright protection[4]. This has also created public resistance to some protection measures. Those wishing to employ technical protection measures need to be aware of the law's provision of fair dealing and other access rights[5].

1 Apple Inc, as discussed above, does not use DRM technology on music distributed through its iTunes library but such content is still watermarked so that each purchaser can be identified.
2 Directive 2001/29/EC; see **paragraphs 24.38** ff.
3 See, for example, Recital 35, 2001 Directive relating to fair compensation for rights holders having to take account of any DRM measures used.
4 Lawrence Lessig is one well-known academic whose published works discuss such issues. See **paragraph 1.14**.
5 See **Chapter 8**.

Circumvention of protection measures

The 2001 Directive

24.38 Anti-circumvention provisions are laid out in the 2001 Directive, which deals with technological protection measures and implements the anti-circumvention legislation previously legislated for at an international level by the WIPO Copyright Treaty[1] and WIPO Performances and Phonograms Treaty[2]:

- *Article 6.1* of the 2001 Directive requires that Member States 'provide adequate legal protection against the circumvention of any effective technological measures, which the person concerned carries out in the knowledge, or with reasonable grounds to know, that he or she is pursuing that objective'.
- *Article 6.2* of the 2001 Directive requires Member States to:

'provide adequate legal protection against the manufacture, import, distribution, sale, rental, advertisement for sale or rental, or possession for commercial purposes of devices, products or components or the provision of services which:
(a) are promoted, advertised, or marketed for the purpose of circumvention of, or
(b) have only a limited commercially significant purpose or use other than to circumvent, or
(c) are primarily designed, produced, adapted or performed for the purpose of enabling or facilitating the circumvention of, any effective technological measures.'

- *Article 9* of the 2001 Directive emphasises that the provisions of the Directive are without prejudice to other legal provisions in this sphere. Thus, rights holders must continue to respect data protection law (for example, when tracking usage information by reference to individual identities) and the provisions of other relevant EU legislation such as the Conditional Access Directive[3], which prohibits the manufacture and distribution of pirate decoders.

- *Article 6(3)* of the 2001 Directive defines 'technological measures' as 'any technology, device or component that, in the normal course of its operation, is designed to prevent or restrict acts, in respect of works or other subject-matter, which are not authorised by the rightholder of any copyright or any right related to copyright ...'. In practice, examples of technical measures would include access control technologies, such as encryption systems employed by satellite TV broadcasters or scrambling, and copy control technologies, such as anti-copying systems included on DVDs and eBook readers.

  Technological measures are to be deemed 'effective' where the use of a protected work is controlled by the rights holders through application of an access control or protection process, such as encryption, scrambling or other transformation of the work which achieves the protection objective[4].

- *Recital 48* to the 2001 Directive states that: 'Such legal protection should respect proportionality and should not prohibit those devices or activities which have a commercially significant purpose or use other than to circumvent the technical protection.'

1   WIPO Copyright Treaty of December 20, 1996.
2   WIPO Performance and Phonograms Treaty of December 20, 1996.
3   Directive 98/84/EC
4   Article 6(3) of the 2001 Directive.

The CDPA and protection against circumvention

24.39 These requirements are implemented into the CDPA by the 2003 Regulations.

Section 296 provides for civil remedies in respect of the circumvention of technical devices applied to computer programs[1].

Sections 296ZA to 296ZF provide for remedies in relation to works other than computer programs, as follows:

- s 296ZA provides for civil remedies in respect of acts of circumvention of effective technological measures;
- s 296ZB provides for criminal offences in respect of devices and services designed to circumvent effective technological measures;
- s 296ZC contains provisions in relation to search warrants and forfeiture;
- s 296ZD provides for rights and civil remedies in respect of devices and services designed to circumvent effective technological methods;
- s 296ZE provides third parties with a remedy where effective technological measures prevent 'permitted acts'.
- s 296ZF contains interpretative provisions in respect of ss 296ZA to 296ZE.

The following paragraphs consider the UK provisions in further detail.

1   CDPA s 296 already provided protection against those manufacturing and dealing with devices designed to circumvent copyright-protection. The effect of the 2003 Regulations was to enhance this protection. As noted above, s 296 now relates only to computer programs.

Circumvention of technical devices applied to computer programs

24.40 Under the CDPA, as amended by the 2003 Regulations, copyright owners and exclusive licensees of copyright, owners and exclusive licensees of any intellectual property right in the technical device applied to the computer program, together with persons authorised to issue or communicate the computer program to the public, have rights analogous to those of copyright owners, in respect of an infringement of copyright[1], where:

'(a) a technical device has been applied to a computer program; and
 (b) a person (A) knowing or having reason to believe that it will be used to make infringing copies –
    (i) manufactures for sale or hire, imports, distributes, sells or lets for hire, offers or exposes for sale or hire, advertises for sale or hire or has in his possession for commercial purposes any means the sole intended purpose of which is to facilitate the unauthorised removal or circumvention of the technical device; or
    (ii) publishes information intended to enable or assist persons to remove or circumvent the technical device.'[2]

'Technical device' is defined as 'any device intended to prevent or restrict acts that are not authorised by the copyright owner of that computer program and are restricted by copyright'[3].

There are a number of cases in which the High Court of England and Wales has considered s 296 in the context of Sony Playstations. In one such case[4], the High Court considered whether chips, which by-passed the console's authorisation process of finding codes embedded into discs on which Sony's computer games were stored, had been specifically designed or adapted to circumvent the form of copy-protection employed. The chips also had legitimate uses. The court held that the chips were circumventing technological protection measures for the purposes of s 296, and that it did not matter that they had other uses which did not permit copyright infringement.

In a subsequent decision[5], the High Court considered whether a silicon chip had the 'sole intended purpose' of unauthorised circumvention of a technical device where, in addition to such unauthorised circumvention, the chip could also have a legitimate purpose (such as the making of a back-up copy under the exception at CDPA s 50A(1)[6]). The court held that nothing had been pleaded which would allow such a defence to come into play. The Sony Playstation games in issue were held on CDs and DVDs, which were robust and could not be wiped clean and, in the unlikely event that they were damaged or destroyed, Sony agreed to replace them. There was therefore no necessity to make back-up copies.

Two cases concerning a Nintendo games console further inform the application of s 296:

- In *Nintendo Company Ltd v Playables Ltd*[7], the High Court considered claims brought under both s 296 and s 296ZD of the CDPA. The court held that the boot-up software, the shared key encryption and scrambling technology installed into the console amounted to 'effective technological measures' for the purposes of s 296ZD; that although s 296 uses the expression 'technical device' instead of 'effective technological measures', it is clear that the definition is a wide one; it needs to be kept in mind that the focus of s 296 is on circumvention – the fact that a device may be used for a purpose which does not involve infringement of copyright does not mean that the sole intended purpose is not the unauthorised circumvention of a technical device; it is not necessary to show: (a) that the defendant knew any particular program was to be copied; or (b) that the means would only be used for making infringing copies.

  On the facts, the court held that it was clear both that the 'technical devices' had been applied to the copyright computer programs in the Nintendo DS and its game cards and that the relevant elements of the defendants' products had the sole intended purpose of circumventing those technical devices. The other requirements of the section were also made out.

- In *Nintendo Company Ltd v PC Box Srl*[8], the CJEU held that technological measures which were partly incorporated in the physical housing of the games and partly in the games consoles, fall within the meaning of 'effective technological measures' under Art 6(3) of the 2001 Directive if their objective is to prevent or limit acts adversely affecting the rights of the holder protected by them[9]. Given the wide definition of 'technical device' in s 296, there is reason to believe that the same approach is to be applied in respect of that provision[10].

1 CDPA s 296(2).
2 CDPA s 296(1).
3 CDPA s 296(6).
4 *Sony Computer Entertainment Inc v Owen [2002] ECDR 27.*
5 *Sony Computer Entertainment Inc v Ball [2005] FSR 9.*
6 See **paragraph 8.13**.
7 *Nintendo Company Ltd v Playables Ltd [2010] FSR 36.*
8 *Nintendo Company Ltd v PC Box Srl (Case C-355/12) [2014] ECDR 6.*
9 See ibid at paragraph 28.
10 See *Copinger & Skone James on Copyright* (17th edn) at para 15–13.

Circumvention of technical measures in relation to works other than computer programs (civil remedies)

24.41 In the context of copyright works other than computer programs, the CDPA, as amended by the 2003 Regulations, affords copyright owners and exclusive licensees of copyright, together with persons authorised to issue or communicate the same to the public[1], rights analogous to those of copyright owners in respect of an infringement of copyright, where effective technical measures have been applied to a copyright work and a person does anything which circumvents those measures, 'knowing, or with reasonable grounds for knowing, that he is pursuing that objective'[2].

Technological measures are defined as 'any technology, device or component which is designed, in the normal course of its operation, to protect a copyright work other than a computer program'[3].

In order to be protected under s 296ZA, a measure must be 'effective'. The CDPA states that a measure will be effective if it achieves the intended protection by either the copyright owner exercising control of the work through either: (a) an access control or protection process such as encryption, scrambling or other transformation of the work; or (b) a copy control mechanism[4].

The right does not apply to circumventions 'for the purposes of research into cryptology' unless the research, or information deriving from it, prejudicially affects the copyright owner[5].

Additional rights are afforded to the same categories of person where effective technological measures have been applied to a copyright work (other than a computer program) and where a person:

'manufactures, imports, distributes, sells or lets for hire, offers or exposes for sale or hire, advertises for sale or hire, or has in his possession for commercial purposes any device, product or component, or provides services which –

(i) are promoted, advertised or marketed for the purpose of the circumvention of, or
(ii) have only limited commercially significant purpose or use other than to circumvent, or
(iii) are primarily designed, produced, adapted or performed for the purpose of enabling or facilitating the circumvention of,

those measures'[6].

1   CDPA s 296ZA(3).
2   CDPA s 296ZA(1).
3   CDPA s 296ZF(1).
4   CDPA s 296ZF(2).
5   CDPA s 296ZA(2).
6   CDPA s 296ZD(1).

Criminal sanctions regarding devices and services designed to circumvent technical measures

24.42 Anyone who manufactures for sale or hire, imports (otherwise than for his private and domestic use), or (in the course of business) sells, lets for hire, offers, exposes or advertises for sale or hire, possesses or distributes 'any device, product or component which is primarily designed, produced or adapted for the purpose of enabling or facilitating the circumvention of effective technical measures' commits an offence[1]. The same offence is also committed if a person distributes any such device other than in the course of business 'to such an extent as to affect prejudicially the rights of the copyright owner'[2].

Similar offences are committed by a person who provides, promotes, advertises or markets a 'service the purpose of which is to enable or facilitate the circumvention of effective technical measures'[3]. The offence will arise if the activity takes place in the course of a business or otherwise where the activity is conducted to such an extent as to prejudicially affect the rights of the copyright owner[4]. An exception is made for activities undertaken for the purpose of national security or in the detection of a crime[5].

It is worth noting that it is only the activities in relation to devices and services which are designed to circumvent technological measures that potentially attract criminal liability. The act of circumvention in and of itself does not attract criminal liability.

A person accused of an offence under this part of the CDPA has a defence if he can establish that he did not know or did not have reasonable grounds for believing, that the relevant device, product, component or service enabled or facilitated the circumvention[6]. It follows that if a person wishes to rely on such a defence the burden will be on him to prove his lack of guilt.

The penalties for this form of activity are (on summary conviction) imprisonment for a term not exceeding three months and/or a fine not exceeding £5,000, and (on indictment) imprisonment for a term not exceeding two years and/or an unlimited fine[7].

Section 296ZC modifies the offences under s 297B (search warrants) and s 297C (forfeiture of unauthorised decoders) such that they also apply to the offences under s 297ZB.

1 CDPA s 296ZB(1).
2 Ibid.
3 CDPA s 296ZB(2).
4 Ibid.
5 CDPA s 296ZB(3).
6 CDPA s 296ZB(5).
7 CDPA s 296ZB(4).

Fair dealing and circumvention

24.43 Article 6.4 of the 2001 Directive provides a remedy to a party where technical protection measures have been applied by a rights holder to a copyright work (other than a computer program) with the effect of restricting that party's ability to exercise fair dealing or any other permitted act in respect of the work. The 2003 Regulations implemented that remedy into UK law by providing that, in such circumstances, a party prevented from exercising fair dealing can issue a notice of complaint to the Secretary of State[1], who in turn will investigate the matter, and depending on the investigation's outcome, can direct that a rights holder make access available to the party giving notice.

Notably, this remedy is not available in respect of works made available to the public on agreed contractual terms in such a way that members of the public may access them from a place and at a time individually chosen by them (ie where works are made available via an on demand service and such activity is regulated by contract)[2].

Failure to comply with any directions from the Secretary of State will amount to a breach of statutory duty by the rights holder.

1 CDPA s 296ZE(2).
2 CDPA s 296ZE(9).

Case law relevant to ss 296ZA to 296ZE

24.44 The decision in *Nintendo Co Ltd v PC Box Srl*[1] brings attention to a potential limitation on the scope of protection offered by Art 6 of the 2001 Directive (and hence CDPA ss 296ZA–296ZE). The CJEU held that the scope of protection is confined to technological protection measures that are put in place to prevent or eliminate acts where the third party would ordinarily require authorisation from the rights owner. A third party would therefore not be liable for circumventing technological protection measures where the act they are undertaking does not require authorisation, such as using a console to play a non-infringing game that is not owned or licensed by the console's rights owner. The CJEU stated that national courts should consider the proportionality of the measures taken by the rights owners to protect against unauthorised acts and 'may, in particular, examine how often those devices, products or components are in fact used in disregard of copyright and how often they are used for purposes which do not infringe copyright.'

1   *Nintendo Company Ltd v PC Box Srl (Case C-355/12).*

Rights management information

24.45 In addition, the 2001 Directive required additional protection to be made available to protect rights management information.

Article 7.1 of the 2001 Directive requires Member States to provide for adequate legal protection against any person knowingly performing without authority any of the following acts:

- the removal or alteration of any electronic rights management information; and
- the distribution, importation for distribution, broadcasting, communication or making available to the public of works or other subject matter from which electronic rights management information has been removed or altered without authority, if such person knows, or has reasonable grounds to know, that by so doing he is inducing, enabling, facilitating or concealing infringement of any copyright or any rights related to copyright.

For the purposes of the 2001 Directive, the expression 'rights management information' means any information provided by rights holders which identifies the work, the author or any other rights holder, or information about the terms and conditions of use of the work. Removal or amendment of this information may allow the work to be accessed or copied outside of the terms of any express or implied end user licence. In some cases, tampering with rights management information could amount to liability for circumvention of protection measures (see above).

These rights are incorporated into the CDPA by s 296ZG, which provides for civil remedies against a person carrying out such unauthorised acts.

Online piracy and enforcement

24.46 Forms of online piracy have diversified over time, both as a result of advancements in technology and due to the mutation of pirate business models in response to changing jurisprudence and amendments to the law.

Peer-to-peer (P2P)

24.47 Historically, P2P has been one of the most widely used means for the dissemination of infringing material online.

A P2P network is a grouping of computers in which any of the participating machines may act as clients (requesting data), servers (offering data) and/or 'servents' (both a client and a server). Once part of a P2P network, users are able to share both content and computer resources by virtue of direct connections between machines (without the use of central servers). The immediate advantage of P2P sharing is that content spreads much more quickly due to its availability from multiple sources.

Use of the P2P architecture to share digital music files was popularised by the Napster system. Napster Inc operated a centralised P2P system. As well as providing the P2P software, it operated a central index server, which responded to user requests for specific content by identifying all peers on the network with the correct content file. The central index server thus played a vital role in enabling users to locate, share and transfer digital content, albeit that no infringing content was ever stored on the server.

Although Napster Inc did not itself copy or distribute music files, a number of major record companies sued the company in the US for facilitating the direct infringement of their exclusive rights of distribution and reproduction by end users[1]. It was alleged that Napster was liable for contributory infringement (on the basis that, with knowledge of the infringing activity, it induced or materially contributed to the infringing conduct of its users and facilitated the identification and download of files). It was also alleged that Napster was vicariously liable for its 'users' infringements as it had the right and ability to supervise the infringing activity as well as a direct financial interest in prolonging them. In these respects, it was claimed that Napster had the ability to *control* the activity, by allowing or filtering out the music files, and also that Napster earned advertising revenue based upon the popularity of the service.

Napster relied on three major defences. First, it argued that its users were not infringing copyright (on the basis that filesharing between users fell within the 'fair use' defence contained in US common law and US statute[2]). Second, it argued that even if its users were infringing copyright, Napster could not be liable for contributory or vicarious infringement because not all of its subscribers were using the service for infringing purposes (the so-called 'Betamax defence')[3]. Third, it argued that, as an ISP, it had the benefit of 'safe harbour' provisions under the US Digital Millennium Copyright Act (DMCA), which grant certain immunities to ISPs.

The court found that Napster's vast number of subscribers were essentially receiving free music in circumstances where they would otherwise have had to pay for it and were therefore 'reaping economic advantage' from their use of Napster (which militated against a finding of 'fair use'); that '... any potential non-infringing use of the Napster service was minimal or was connected to the infringing activity'; and that Napster could and would have to control or supervise consumers' use of its service. The court also questioned whether Napster qualified as an ISP in any event.

An important distinction between the *Napster* case and that of *Sony Corporation and Universal Studios*[4] (and *Amstrad*[5]) was Napster's involvement in the ongoing operation of the centralised P2P network.

Following the Napster litigation other types of P2P network emerged using 'decentralised' architectures which removed the need for central servers. However, this move did not absolve P2P operators of liability in all cases. In *Grokster*[6] the US Supreme Court held that two P2P operators (Grokster and Streamcast) were liable for inducing infringement. Key to that decision were the findings that the operators were plainly aiming to satisfy a known source of demand for copyright infringement left by the demise of Napster; had failed to develop filtering tools or other mechanisms to diminish infringing activity; and made money by selling advertising space that was dependent on mass penetration. In a subsequent US case, Lime Group LLC was found to have encouraged infringement through its distribution of the LimeWire file-sharing program[7]. Determinative factors were LimeWire's awareness of substantial infringement by users; its efforts to attract infringing users and to enable and assist users to commit infringement; its dependence on infringing use for the success of its business; and its failure to mitigate infringing activities through existing technology.

1   *A&M Records Inc v Napster Inc, 114F: Supp 2d 896 (NC Cal 2000).*
2   'Fair use' is a general statutory exception to copyright infringement available in the US by which copyright is not infringed by copying for purposes such as (but not only) criticism, comment, reporting, scholarship and research. However, such copying must be within certain parameters in order to enjoy this exception to the general copyright rules. In determining this, the US court will look at: (a) the character and purpose of the copying – was it, eg for commercial, non-profit or educational purposes? (b) What is the nature of the work in question? (c) How much of the work was used; was it a substantial part of the work? and (d) What is the effect of the use on the potential market for the work? In addition, the US Audio Home Recording Act of 1992 contains a particular 'fair use' provision allowing music to be recorded for 'private' or 'non-commercial use'.
3   *Sony Corpn v Universal Studios Inc, 446 US 417 (1984).* The Supreme Court of the United States ruled that a producer who merely distributed a product that had substantial lawful use could not be held contributorily liable for infringements undertaken by third parties using the product. The decision is akin to that of the House of Lords in *CBS Songs v Amstrad Consumer Electronics plc [1988] 2 All ER 484* concerning twin deck tape recorders.
4   Ibid.

5   *CBS Songs v Amstrad Consumer Electronics plc [1988] 2 All ER 484.*
6   *Metro-Goldwyn-Mayer Studios Inc et al v Grokster Ltd et al 545 US 913 (2005).*
7   *Arista Records LLC v Lime Group LLC 715 F Supp 2d 481, 507 (SDNY 2010).*

BitTorrent

24.48 Following the *LimeWire* case (see **paragraph 24.47**), the BitTorrent P2P protocol emerged as a primary means for distributing unlicensed digital media files online. Key elements of the BitTorrent protocol are:

- torrent files, which provide the information necessary for users to download shared files using P2P software. Each torrent file relates to an associated content file. The torrent file does not contain the content itself;
- a 'tracker', which monitors computers that have all or some of the pieces that make up the content file and co-ordinates distribution of the content amongst peers;
- a torrent site, which publishes the information necessary to share the content file;
- BitTorrent client software, which is installed by the user, and retrieves and opens torrent files and uses the information in the torrent file to communicate with the tracker server and identifies all peers who are able to share the file.

Some BitTorrent systems bypass the need for a centralised tracker by enabling peers to find each other and share content in a decentralised way, such as through the use of magnet links.

The operation and use of BitTorrent sites that are focused on the distribution of unauthorised copyright content may give rise to several acts restricted by copyright. This has been considered by the High Court of England and Wales in a number of cases[1] in the context of site blocking applications. The court's findings in those cases were that:

- users who *upload* unauthorised copyright material infringe the communication to the public right within the CDPA s 20;
- users who *download* unauthorised copyright material infringe copyright by copying within the CDPA s 17;
- the website operators infringe copyright by communicating copyright works to the public[2]; by authorising the users' infringing acts of copying and communication to the public; and are jointly liable with such users.

The CJEU has subsequently ruled that the making available and management of a BitTorrent indexing website that enables users to locate copyright works via P2P file-sharing networks constitutes a communication to the public under Art 3(1) of the 2001 Directive[3].

1 *Dramatico Entertainment Ltd v British Sky Broadcasting [2012] EWHC 268 (Ch), [2012] 3 CMLR 14; EMI Records Ltd v British Sky Broadcasting Ltd [2013] EWHC 379 (Ch).*

2 The claimants in *Dramatico Entertainment Ltd v British Sky Broadcasting* did not allege communication to the public by the operators of The Pirate Bay as the CJEU reference in *Football Dataco Ltd v Sportradar GmbH (Case C-173/11)* was pending at the time that the application was made.

3 *Stichting Brein v Ziggo BV, XS4ALL Internet BV (Case C-610/15).* The case concerned The Pirate Bay BitTorrent indexing site.

The piracy landscape

24.49 The methods for distributing and accessing unauthorised digital media files online are by no means limited to P2P and BitTorrent technologies. This ever-evolving landscape includes (amongst other things):

- cyberlockers, which may be used to host infringing content;
- streaming sites, which collate and index links to content such as films, TV programmes and sports broadcasts;
- 'Popcorn Time' applications, which operate as BitTorrent clients to provide access to audio-visual content, and associated websites; and
- set-top boxes, media players, add-ons and mobile device apps, which enable access to infringing streams.

In *Stichting Brein v Jack Frederik Wullems*[1], the CJEU ruled that the sale of multi-media devices with 'add-ons' that contained links to websites streaming unauthorised film, TV and sporting content infringed copyright. The court held: (a) that the sale of such devices infringe the communication to the public right set out in Art 3 of the 2001 Directive; and (b) that copies made in the course of streaming content from such media players do not benefit from the exception for temporary copies set out in Art 5(1) of the same Directive.

1 Case C-527/15.

Direct action against infringers

24.50 In the UK (as elsewhere in the world) rights holders have taken legal actions against the operators of platforms that are engaged in large-scale copyright infringement. The *Newzbin* case[1] is of particular significance. The case was brought against the operator of the Newzbin site, a Usenet indexing website which searched for, indexed and categorised content posted to Usenet service providers, including film and television content.

The case demonstrated the court's willingness to apply copyright law to the online environment so as to give protection to content owners. It confirmed that the operators of websites that have: (a) a close connection with their users; (b) that focus on infringing content; (c) that can control what content their users can obtain; and (d) that can take active steps to prevent infringement, are likely to be regarded as infringers. The case also confirmed that liability for communication to the public may be established where the site does not actually transmit content but actively intervenes to make available protected content hosted elsewhere. As discussed in ealier sections of this *User's Guide*, this reasoning has been further developed by the CJEU jurisprudence.

The online environment presents enforcement challenges, however. Infringers can operate anonymously from anywhere in the world to reach a global audience. Identifying the underlying operator can in very many cases be difficult and bringing proceedings against the operators is not always effective. These difficulties were acknowledged by the High Court in *Cartier*[2]. Rights holders are therefore increasingly exploring other means of disrupting infringing operations.

1   *Twentieth Century Fox Film Corpn v Newzbin Ltd [2010] FSR 21.*
2   *Cartier International AG v British Sky Broadcasting Ltd [2014] EWHC 3354.*

Online intermediaries

24.51 EU law requires members states to provide intermediaries with certain immunities and obligations. The immunities are those set out in Arts 12–14 of the E-Commerce Directive[1], which provide a 'safe harbour' for an intermediary when it is providing certain technical services. The safe harbours are considered in the sections below.

These same provisions make clear that the safe harbours do not prevent a court from requiring the intermediary to terminate or prevent an infringement. It has been recognised that intermediaries are often best placed to bring an end to infringements of intellectual property rights. On this basis Member States are required to ensure that injunctive relief is available against intermediaries. This was first enacted in Art 8(3) of the 2001 Directive as regards copyright. When harmonising the relief available for IP infringements generally, the same right was made to cover other intellectual property rights by Art 11 of the Enforcement Directive[2].

1   Directive 2000/31/EC.
2   Directive 2004/48/EC.

Intermediary injunctions

24.52 Article 8(3) of the 2001 Directive provides that Member States must ensure that rights holders are in a position to apply for an injunction against intermediaries whose services are used by a third party to infringe copyright or a related right. The Recitals to the 2001 Directive recognise that: '[i]n the digital environment, in particular, the services of intermediaries may increasingly be used by third parties for infringing activities. In many cases such intermediaries are best placed to bring such infringing activities to an end'. The Recitals also state that the sanctions provided for 'should be effective, proportionate and dissuasive'[1].

Article 8(3) is transposed into UK law by s 97A of the CDPA[2], which states that: 'The High Court (in Scotland, the Court of Session) shall have power to grant an injunction against a service provider, where that service provider has actual knowledge of another person using their service to infringe copyright'.

A service provider is defined in reg 2 of the Electronic Commerce (EC Directive) Regulations 2002[3] as 'any person providing an information society service', which in turn is defined as 'any service normally provided for remuneration, at a distance, by means of electronic equipment for the processing (including digital compression) and storage of data, and at the individual request of a recipient of a service'.

There are four matters that need to be established for the court to have jurisdiction to grant an order under CDPA s 97A: (a) that the respondent is a service provider; (b) that users and/or the operators of the target website (or target server) infringe copyright; (c) that users and/or the operators of the target website (or target server) use the services of the respondent to do that; and (d) that the respondents have actual knowledge of this. Thereafter, the court is required to consider issues of proportionality and discretion.

These matters have been considered by the High Court in a line of cases beginning with *Newzbin2*[4]. *Newzbin2* concerned a successful blocking action brought by a number of film studios against British Telecommunications plc, the UK's largest internet service provider (ISP). BT was required to block access by its residential broadband subscribers to the Newzbin2 website (a successor website to the site that was considered in the *Newzbin* case). The result was later extended to other major UK ISPs by a series of further applications.

Orders to the like effect have since been made against all the major UK ISPs directed to various file-sharing and streaming websites[5]. The first 'live' blocking order was granted in 2017[6]. That order requires the defendant ISPs to block access to streaming servers which stream live Premier League matches to UK consumers during certain specified periods.

The threshold conditions and discretionary principles to be applied to website blocking applications were considered by the Court of Appeal in *Cartier*[7] in the parallel context of trade mark infringement. The Court of Appeal upheld orders granted pursuant to s 37(1) of the Senior Courts Act 1981 requiring the major UK ISPs to block subscriber access to a number of counterfeit-selling websites. The Court of Appeal accepted that the following discretionary principles must be considered: the relief must be: (a) necessary; (b) effective; (c) dissuasive; (d) not unnecessarily complicated or costly; (e) avoid barriers to legitimate trade; (f) be fair and equitable and strike a 'fair balance' between the applicable fundamental rights; and (g) be proportionate. A further appeal has been made in *Cartier* on the issue of costs, which is due to be heard by the UK Supreme Court in January 2018. Both the High Court and the majority of the Court of Appeal had held that the ISPs should bear the costs of implementing the blocking orders in *Cartier*, referencing (amongst other things) the CJEU decisions in *Scarlet*[8] and *UPC v Constantin*[9].

Site blocking orders have been granted against ISPs in a number of territories both within Europe and beyond. To date, the applications have tended to focus on ISPs. The position of search engines is considered below.

1 Recitals 58 and 59.
2 Inserted by the Copyright and Related Rights Regulations 2003, SI 2003/2498.
3 SI 2002/2013.
4 *Twentieth Century Fox Film Corpn v British Telecommunications plc [2011] RPC 28.*
5 See, for example, *Dramatico Entertainment Ltd v British Sky Broadcasting Ltd [2012] 3 CMLR 14*; *EMI Records Ltd v British Sky Broadcasting Ltd [2013] EWHC 379 (Ch)*; *Football Association Premier League Ltd v British Sky Broadcasting Ltd [2013] EWHC 2058 (Ch)*; *Paramount Home Entertainment International Ltd v British Sky Broadcasting Ltd [2013] EWHC 3479 (Ch).*
6 *Football Association Premier League Ltd v British Telecommunications plc [2017] EWHC 480 (Ch).*
7 *Cartier International AG v British Sky Broadcasting Ltd [2016] EWCA Civ 658.*
8 *Scarlet Extended SA Société Belge des Auteurs, Compositeurs et Editeurs Scrl (SABAM) (Case C-70/10).*
9 *UPC Telekabel Wien GmbH v Constantin Film Verleih GmbH (Case C-314/12).*

Search engines and metatags

SEARCH ENGINES

24.53 Search engines provide a key means by which users can discover, locate and navigate content that is available on the internet. Search engines operate by 'crawling' and indexing web pages and provide an interface enabling internet users to interrogate the search engine's index in order to find web pages and websites of interest. In response to a user search query, the search engine's algorithm processes the indexed information in order to return search results, including links to online locations, that are deemed most relevant to the search query entered.

There has been much debate over whether search engines should be responsible, or indeed liable, for content listed in their search results.

In certain circumstances, search engines will take voluntary action to remove (delist) material from their search results or otherwise demote content so that it is less visible to search engine users. For example, following the CJEU's ruling in *Google Spain*[1], European residents can invoke the so-called 'right to be forgotten' ie to request the removal of search results returned in response to queries that include their name if the results are inadequate, inaccurate, no longer relevant or excessive. The right to be forgotten is founded on data protection laws/misuse of personal information.

In the context of copyright, search engine operators will in certain cases remove links from their search results in response to the US DMCA (Digital Millennium Copyright Act) 1998 take down requests. The largest providers of search engine services in the UK have also signed up to a voluntary Code of Practice on Search and Copyright[2] under which they will demote sites demonstrated to meet certain stated criteria set out in the Code.

Outside the UK, search engine operators have been required by the courts to delist websites on the basis of intellectual property infringement. In *Allostreaming*[3], the Paris Regional Court ordered Google, Yahoo! and Bing to delist 16 pirate websites. The order was made on the basis of the French implementation of Art 8(3) of the 2001 Directive. In *Equustek*[4], the Supreme Court of Canada upheld an order requiring Google to delist certain search results on a worldwide basis. The delisting order stemmed from earlier proceedings brought against Canadian defendants to which Google was not a party.

1   *Google Spain SL and Google Inc v Agencia Española de Protección de Datos (AEPD) and Mario Costeja González (Case C-131/12).*
2   9 February 2017.
3   *Association des Producteurs de Cinema v Auchan Telecom SAS* (Paris Regional Court, 28 November 2013); upheld by the Paris Court of Appeal by judgment dated 15 March 2016. Google settled prior to the Paris Court of Appeal judgment.
4   *Google Inc v Equustek Solutions Inc*, 2017 SCC 34 (28 June 2017).

METATAGS
24.54 Metatags appear in the HTML code of websites and facilitate the searching of content by reference to key words included in the tag. Those key words may in themselves be protectable. Commonly, for example, they may include names or brands in which trading goodwill has been established or which are registered as trademarks. If so, the inclusion of such marks in a metatag may infringe such rights[1]. However, it is unlikely that words or phrases included in a metatag could amount to an actionable infringement of copyright[2].

1   See, for example, *Road Tech Computer Systems Ltd v Mandata (Management and Data Services) Ltd [2000] ETMR 970.*
2   See **paragraph 3.02**.

The 'safe harbour' defences

24.55 One of the central questions which has had to be addressed by legislators is the extent to which an online service provider should be liable for illegal or infringing material included within its service. In addressing this question, a distinction has been made between service providers who have knowledge of, and exercise control, over the content that they make available and those that may be acting as a passive recipient or communicator of information made available by others.

Articles 12–14 of the E-Commerce Directive provide for certain immunities from liability (or so-called 'safe harbour' defences). The 'safe harbours' operate to exclude service providers from liability for certain activities which arise out of their transmission and/or storage of information (including copyright works) in their electronic networks.

The rationale of these provisions was to protect service providers in respect of activities which are:

> 'limited to the technical process of operating and giving access to a communication network over which information made available by third parties is transmitted or temporarily stored, for the sole purpose of making the transmission more efficient; this activity is of a mere technical, automatic and passive nature, which implies that the information society service provider has neither knowledge of nor control over the information which is transmitted or stored.'[1]

One of the concerns that the E-Commerce Directive tried to allay was the apparent disparity between the laws of separate Member States in relation to the liability of service providers and how this could detract from the smooth functioning of the Internal Market. The E-Commerce Directive forms part of an EU legislative framework which also comprises the 2001 Directive and the Enforcement Directive (both of which are referred to elsewhere in this Chapter).

The 'safe harbour' defences apply to information society service providers[2] in respect of the following three forms of activities:

- acting as mere conduit (Art 12);
- caching (Art 13); and
- hosting (Art 14).

These same provisions make clear that the 'safe harbours' do not operate to prevent the grant of an injunction against an intermediary requiring it to terminate or prevent an infringement.

Articles 12–14 of the E-Commerce Directive are implemented by regs 17–19 of the Electronic Commerce (EC Directive) Regulations 2002. There is little difference between the wording of the respective provisions.

---

1   Recital 42, E-Commerce Directive. The CJEU has determined that Recital 42 also applies to 'hosting', notwithstanding that the language is more obviously directed to the 'mere conduit' and 'caching' defences (see Cases C-236/08 to C-238/08 *Google France and Google*).

2   An information service provider is defined in the E-Commerce Directive (by reference to Art 1(2) of Directive 98/34/EC (as amended by Directive 98/48/EC)) to mean 'any service normally provided for remuneration, at a distance, by electronic means and at the individual request of a recipient of a service'.

Acting as a mere conduit

24.56 The mere conduit defence is aimed at services which consist of 'transmission in a communication network' or the 'provision of access to a communication network'. When information is carried through a communication network, the provider of the service may not be liable for the information transmitted (on the basis that it is acting as a mere conduit) provided that it did not: (a) initiate the transmission; (b) select the receiver of the transmission; or (c) select or modify the information contained within the transmission[1].

The mere conduit defence only applies where the storage of any information transmitted is automatic, intermediate and/or transient in so far as this only takes place for the sole purpose of carrying out the transmission and the information transmitted is not stored for longer than is reasonably necessary for the transmission. This defence is most obviously intended to protect service providers offering internet access, such as broadband providers[2].

In a case concerning the posting of defamatory material on websites hosted by third parties, the English High Court appeared to accept that an internet service provider that provided only internet access to the individuals who had posted the material could benefit from the mere conduit defence. However, the court also accepted evidence that, where the service provider is providing a web-based e-mail service where messages are retained on the service provider's server until they are deleted by the recipient (and hence not stored only on an 'intermediate' or 'transient' basis, and are frequently stored for a period longer than is reasonably necessary for their transmission), the service provider is more likely to be regarded as 'hosting' the information and thus fall outside the mere conduit safe harbour[3].

In an Irish case[4] concerning injunctive relief sought against a commercial internet access provider (UPC Communications Ireland Limited) to address infringing P2P file sharing, the court was satisfied that UPC was a mere conduit. This was on the basis that UPC did not initiate any P2P transmission; the P2P swarms selected who was to receive the transmission; and, in the course of transmission, the information was not selected or modified. However, the court held that 'tacking on an advertisement to a transmission, or modifying it so that some of it is lost, as opposed to being transmitted slowly, would disable the mere conduit defence'[5].

In the *Newzbin2* case[6], it was accepted that, so far as was relevant to that case, BT acted as a 'mere conduit' within Art 12 of the E-Commerce Directive and reg 17 of the 2002 Regulations[7].

1   Article 12(1) of the Directive on Electronic Commerce (Directive 2000/31/EC), 'the 2000 Directive'.
2   The wording of the defence found in Art 12 is mirrored in reg 17 of the 2002 Regulations.

3   *Bunt v Tilley [2006] EWHC 407* (see, in particular, para 49).
4   *EMI Records (Ireland Ltd) v UPC Communications Ireland Ltd [2010] IEHC 377.*
5   Ibid, para 108.
6   *Twentieth Century Fox Film Corpn v BT Telecommunications plc [2011] EWHC 1981 (Ch).*
7   Ibid, para 99.

Caching

24.57 'Caching' is the process whereby service providers place information in temporary storage to improve the efficiency of the transmission of information. An example of caching is the technical process which enables internet providers to speed up the delivery of web pages to internet users by making a temporary copy of a web page that is requested by a user.

There are a number of conditions that need to be satisfied for the defence to apply. The service provider must:

*   not modify the information transmitted;
*   comply with conditions on access to information and any rules in relation to the updating of information (in accordance with those recognised and used in the industry);
*   not interfere with the lawful use of technology to obtain data on the use of the information;
*   expeditiously remove or disable access to the cached information on obtaining actual acknowledge of the fact that the information at the initial source of the transmission has been removed from the network, or access to it has been disabled, or that a court or administrative authority has ordered such removal or diasablement[1].

In *Bunt v Tilley*[2], it was conceded by BT that the caching defence was not be available to it where it hosted the Usenet newsgroups (message boards) on its servers; the newsgroup postings were stored for a period of time, usually amounting to a few weeks, to enable BT's users to access them; and where, although BT did not operate the newsgroups, it had the ability to remove postings from its newsgroup server[3].

In *Metropolitan International Schools Ltd v Designtechnica Corpn*[4] the English High Court considered that the automatic process by which Google displays 'snippets' of information about websites returned in its search results 'often involves a process of selection and "editing", albeit automatic, in order to provide a brief summary of the primary content on the relevant web page', which 'might be classified as "modification of the content"'[5].

In another case involving Google[6], this time concerning thumbnail images stored in a cache and automatically displayed in response to relevant search queries, the High Court held that the conversion of the original image into a thumbnail (requiring reduction of the image's size and definition) did not amount to modifying the information. The court held that: 'for an image to be modified the information and impression given to a viewer must be altered by, for example, the alteration of the image itself or the addition of something, including text, to it'[7].

1 Article 13(1) of the 2000 Directive. The wording of the defence is mirrored in reg 18 of the 2002 Regulations. In respect of actual knowledge, reg 22 of the 2002 Regulations states that when a court is considering whether a service provider has actual knowledge, it should take into account all matters which appear relevant in the circumstances and shall have regard (among other things) to whether the service provider received a notice; and whether the notice included the name and address of the sender of the notice, the details of the location of the information in question, and details of the unlawful nature of the activity or information in question.
2 *Bunt v Tilley [2006] EWHC 407*.
3 Ibid, para 68.
4 [2009] EMLR 27.
5 Ibid, para 92.
6 *Mosely v Google Inc [2015] EWHC 59 (QB)*.
7 Ibid, para 39.

Hosting

24.58 When a service provider stores information provided by a recipient of its service, it is 'hosting' this information. A good example is where a service provider hosts a website containing a message board that is used by subscribers to its services. In these circumstances, and where the recipient of the service is not acting under the authority or control of the service provider, the provider will not be liable for the information stored provided that:

- it does not have actual knowledge of illegal activity or information and, as regards claims for damages, it is not aware of facts or circumstances from which illegal activity or information is apparent; or
- upon obtaining such knowledge or awareness, it acts expeditiously to remove or disable access to the information[1].

The CJEU has given guidance on the application of the hosting defence:

- In *L'Oréal v eBay*[2], the CJEU confirmed that the defence is not available where the service provider, 'instead of confining itself to providing that service neutrally by a merely technical and automatic processing of the data provided by its customers, plays an active role of such a kind as to give it actual knowledge of, or control over, those data'[3]. The court went on to hold that where the service provider is aware of facts or circumstances on the basis of which a diligent economic operator should have identified the illegality in question and acted to remove or disable access to the relevant information, the hosting defence will be unavailable.

- In *Google France*[4], which concerned the Google Adwords service, the CJEU emphasised the importance of whether the party seeking to rely on the defence played an active role, ie a role which would give it knowledge or control over the data stored and thereby prevent it from playing a role which was merely technical, passive and automatic. Failure to remove or disable access to the data upon gaining knowledge of the infringement will preclude reliance on the defence, even where there was no active role.
- In a subsequent case, the CJEU held (unsurprisingly) that a newspaper which publishes its content online is not a mere 'host' of that content[5].

Equivalent provisions[6] are contained in the DMCA which introduced 'safe harbour' protection against copyright infringement for service providers who act as an unknowing conduit for infringing material, without controlling or supervising the material in question. The US legislation requires service providers to act expeditiously to remove offending material upon receipt of a notice in terms prescribed by the DMCA. An infringement notice forwarded to a US based service provider can be an effective method of ensuring that infringing material is removed from a website. However, that process will be onerous and impractical where a website is focused on infringement.

1   Article 14(1) of the 2000 Directive. The wording of the defence is mirrored in reg 19 of the 2002 Regulations.
2   *L'Oréal SA v eBay International AG (Case C-324/09)*.
3   Ibid, para 113.
4   *Google France and Google (Cases C-236/08 to C-238/08)*.
5   *Sotiris Papasavvas v O Fileleftheros Dimosia Etairia Ltd (Case C-291/13)*.
6   The US legislation is significantly different from its European/UK counterpart. The US provisions have been considered in, for example, *Viacom v YouTube*, *Disney v Hotfile* and *Columbia Pictures v Fung*.

Applicable law and jurisdiction

24.59 The internet is a worldwide medium. Mobile services, although addressable, permit subscribers to 'roam' into different jurisdictions. Where a service is capable of being received in a territory, it is possible for liability to arise in that corresponding jurisdiction.

Broadly, in the case of copyright infringement, the law applicable to determining whether an infringing act has taken place will be the law of the territory in which the act actually takes place.

Exactly which country has 'jurisdiction' over the matter (ie where a case can be tried) is an important issue when considering whether to bring an action against an infringer and if so where to bring it. The answer is not always obvious. There are particular problems in applying legislation conceived for print publishing to online exploitation of audio-visual works.

The basic rule of jurisdiction in the EU and most of the European Free Trade Area[1] countries is that a defendant should be sued in its country of domicile[2].

In England, the effective service of proceedings (ie the equivalent of what was known as a writ) on a person or legal entity is the basis of the court's jurisdiction in the matter. This means that only if the claim can be properly served on that person can the court accept jurisdiction. If the infringer is domiciled within England (including if it only has a subsidiary office in England), the claim can always be served on him. If the infringer is domiciled outside England, it may still be possible to serve the claim on him. There are two categories of such service: service without permission; and service with the permission of the court:

- *Service without permission:* in the courts of EU countries and the EFTA countries (apart from Liechtenstein), the Brussels Regulation[3] and the Lugano Convention[4] respectively (together, the 'Conventions') govern jurisdiction. For the purposes of this section, countries which are a signatory to one of the Conventions will be termed 'Convention countries'. If: (a) the Conventions apply to give the English court jurisdiction over a matter; (b) there are no existing proceedings relating to the same acts and between the same parties within any Convention country; and (c) the defendant is domiciled within a Convention country or party to an agreement conferring English court jurisdiction, then the claimant can serve proceedings in that matter without the court's permission[5].

  The basic rule under the Conventions is that the defendant should be sued in its country of domicile: that is, in the court nearest to where the defendant resides or does business or (if the defendant is a company) where it is incorporated[6]. (The nationality of the defendant is not relevant.)

  However, in cases of tort (which would include copyright infringement) the Conventions additionally confer jurisdiction on the courts of the Convention country where harmful events occurred or may occur. These may therefore be alternatives to suing the defendant where he is domiciled.

- *Service with permission:* if there are existing proceedings in a Convention country which relate to the same acts and are between the same parties, or if none of the defendants are domiciled within a Convention country, permission will be required before proceedings can be validly served. There are detailed grounds which govern when permission will be given. The grounds most relevant to copyright infringement (although others may be relevant on the facts of each case) are that:

  – an injunction is sought to restrain or compel acts within England;

- damage has been sustained within England; or
- damage has resulted from an act committed within England.

In the context of the internet, for example, if a party places infringing material on a server outside England, an English court may have jurisdiction in relation to that infringement. If, for example, the party is domiciled in England (including if it only has a subsidiary office in England) it can be sued there; and if the infringement causes harm in England, the claimant can bring proceedings there.

Internationally, there has been a movement away from the simple approach that because a service is capable of reception in jurisdiction B, that country may have jurisdiction to hear an action brought in connection with it, despite it being transmitted from jurisdiction A. Increasingly, courts have focused on factors such as which territory the service is targeted at and whether the site is marketed in the territory in question. The issue has been the subject of a significant amount of litigation, a detailed examination of which is beyond the scope of this edition of the *User's Guide*.

1   Iceland, Norway and Switzerland.
2   Broadly speaking, a person is domiciled in a place which is his ordinary or habitual residence. A company is domiciled in the country where it is incorporated.
3   Brussels Regulation (Regulation (EU) No 1215/2012) on Jurisdiction and the Recognition and Enforcement of Judgments in Civil and Commercial Matters (Recast).
4   Lugano Convention on Jurisdiction and the Enforcement of Judgments in Civil and Commercial Matters 2007.
5   Civil Procedure Rules r 6.33.
6   Brussels Regulation Art 2.

Practical protection measure: 'geoblocking' etc

24.60   In the case of internet exploitation it is very difficult to control who is accessing what content and where, and there is as yet no guaranteed way to avoid liability in a foreign jurisdiction. However, there are steps which may minimise risks for publishers of online content:

- *Subscription-based services*. It is possible to refuse subscriptions to persons outside the target area by barring certain postal addresses or countries of origin for credit cards. Unfortunately the fact that there are subscribers can also work against the publisher. For example, the judge in one Australian case[1] used the fact that the service provider was a subscription service to dispute Dow Jones' argument that it had no control over who read the features on its service.
- *User's IP address*. It is possible to bar access to certain users based on their location as determined by reference to the user's IP address. However, this mechanism can never be 100% successful as users can manipulate their address, for example by using proxy servers,

which makes a website think the internet address originates from a different country to than that from which it really originates.

1   *Dow Jones & Company, Inc v Gutnick M3/2002 (28 May 2002) (Australia).*

The EU Enforcement Directive

24.61 The objectives of the EU Enforcement Directive[1] are to harmonise national laws on the means of enforcing intellectual property rights and to establish a general framework for the exchange of information between the responsible national authorities. It is designed to ensure a level playing field for rights holders in the EU and to reinforce measures against offenders and thus act as a deterrent to those engaged in counterfeiting and piracy. Its scope is restricted to infringements 'for commercial purposes or which cause significant harm to rights holders'. The Directive is considered in detail elsewhere in this *User's Guide*[2].

1   Enforcement of Intellectual Property Rights Directive (2004/48/EC).
2   See **paragraph 7.24**.

Domain names – definition

24.62 Domain names are internet addresses that facilitate the identification and location of websites and computers on the internet. The domain name system converts readable domain names into internet protocol numbers, which are necessary for network equipment to communicate. The domain name is the key part of the system which provides a user with an address from which they can access a website. Inevitably, domain names have become valuable trading tools.

Ownership of a domain name is exclusive, leading to potential scarcity and, as a result, their potential increased value. There are, however, different domain name suffixes available on the internet. This means that for an individual or company with the same name there is opportunity for both to use an identical name but with different suffixes: eg '.com' or '.co.uk'. One useful role which domain name suffixes play is to indicate the location or geographical area where the domain name holder's business is registered or where they reside. For example, '.com. au' domains indicate that the business is registered in Australia. Such domain name suffixes as '.com.au' or '.co.uk' are known as country code top-level domains ('ccTLDs').

Top-level domains ('TLDs') can be sub-divided into ccTLDs and generic top-level domains ('gTLDs'), the latter being available universally on a global level with no (or very limited) restrictions.

The most recognised and commonly sought after TLDs are '.com' (which relates to corporate and commercial organisations), '.org' (relating to non-commercial organisations) and '.net' (these are available to internet service providers). Other TLDs include '.biz' and '.plc'. If any restrictions apply, they usually relate to purpose/specific use restrictions. For example, a non-profit-making organisation, such as a statutory body may be restricted from using the '.com' TLD.

In June 2011, ICANN[1] authorised the release of new generic top level domains as part of its New gTLD Program. In October 2013, the first New gTLDs were delegated and since then over 1,000 have been added on a rolling basis. Examples of New gTLDs include '.buy', '.live', 'taxi' and '.vet'.

1   See **paragraph 24.63**.

Domain names – registration

24.63 The Internet Corporation for Assigned Names and Numbers (ICANN) is the international non-profit corporation that oversees the assignment of both internet addresses and domain names. Registry operators are responsible for maintaining an authoritative master database of all domain names registered for each TLD. Registry operators may also fulfil the function of a registrar or may delegate that function to other entities. Domain name registrars are accredited by ICANN and certified by the registry operators to sell domains and process registrations.

Nominet UK Limited operates the official registry for '.uk' domains and administers registrations for, for example, '.uk', '.co.uk', 'org.uk' and '.me.uk' domains. VeriSign, Inc is the authoritative registry for all .com, .net, .name, .cc, .tv, .edu, .gov and .jobs domain names.

The domain name registration procedure is straightforward and conducted on a 'first come first served' basis. Applicants are able to register a domain name even though they may have no association with the registered name. Unsurprisingly, registration by people who have no connection with the name being registered has led to a number of disputes. Global brand owners view the availability of domain names which include their corporate name/brand as an essential part of their marketing and general brand strategies.

Registration rules for registering a ccTLD vary from country to country with some rules specifying that only businesses/individuals registered or residing in that particular territory can use them.

Information about who owns, and who is responsible for, a specific domain name is available through WHOIS services operated by registrars and registries. The purpose of WHOIS services is twofold: (a) to allow for the swift resolution of technical problems; and (b) to enable intellectual property rights to be enforced. However, it should be noted that it is possible for registrants (ie the person or entity who has registered a domain name) to hide certain information, such as their identity, by using a privacy agent. ICANN is in the process of implementing an accreditation programme for privacy and proxy service providers.

Registration lasts for ten years in total and within that period the registrar may offer initial and renewal registrations of one year. Most elements of registration (such as price, method of registration and renewal periods) differ from registrar to registrar.

Domain names – cyber squatting

24.64 Cyber squatting is the practice of registering internet domain names consisting of the names or marks of other businesses with the intention of selling the domain name on to that business.

Cyber squatters register domain names generally to disrupt the online capabilities of an organisation which has a legitimate interest in the registered domain name (mainly by directing web traffic to their domain/ website) and not to the 'legitimate' organisation's website, or by selling the domain name to such an organisation at an inflated price. This is often done with fraudulent intent.

High prices are named by the cyber squatters for domain names because of the value that organisations place on them. A domain name which reflects an organisation's business name or trade/service mark will greatly enhance the activities of an organisation that wants to offer online services, move into the e-business market, or promote its goods or services via the internet. The exponential rise of the internet as a key marketing and transactional channel offering global reach means that cyber squatters attempt to command high prices which greatly exceed their own costs in registering the domain name in the first place.

One of the first cases on this subject in the UK[1] concerned a defendant which had, without authorisation, registered domain names of numerous well-known enterprises, including Virgin, Sainsbury's, Marks and Spencer and Ladbrokes. The domain names were up for sale. The claimants sought an injunction to restrain passing off and trademark infringement. The court found that the main purpose of the defendant's registrations was systematically to prevent registration by the owners of the goodwill in the name and to extract money from the proper owner with the threat of either using the name or allowing someone else to do so. With regard to passing off, it was held that the proper owner was entitled to a final injunction to restrain such use, together with an order for the names to be assigned to the correct owners. In granting the injunction, the judge placed emphasis on the fact that the court was entitled to infer from the evidence that the registration itself (without any trading using the name) amounted to equipping the defendant with an 'instrument of fraud', because it inherently led to passing off.

However, the above decision does not create this presumption in all potential cases. In another case[2], the defendant was an internet consultant who registered the domain name 'fcuk.com.'. French Connection had registered the same initials as a trademark and used them in an advertising campaign, and applied for summary judgment for passing off. The application was refused because on the evidence the judge was not satisfied that there was no reasonable prospect of a defence to passing off (the defendant having claimed that the name was commonly used on the internet to denote pornography and that he had plans to use the name to attract traffic to his own site). The case illustrates that the courts will be reluctant to deal with 'cyber squatting' by way of summary judgment, except in flagrant cases.

A second case involving Marks and Spencer[3] was brought before the court along similar lines. An individual had pursued a consistent action of copying Marks and Spencer's website and reproducing it onto domain names he had registered with remarkably similar names to that of Marks and Spencer's official website. This understandably caused confusion amongst consumers using what they thought to be the official Marks and Spencer's site. The confusion extended to consumers using their credit cards on the sites, allowing their details to be used fraudulently.

The court found these websites to be in breach of Marks and Spencer's intellectual property rights and that the imitation of domain names could constitute both trademark and copyright infringement.

This case did, however, highlight that court orders which restrict the registration of a particular domain name may potentially be circumvented by cyber squatters registering similar, but equally misleading, domain names.

If the defendant can show some other legitimate purpose as to why he registered the domain name, then the domain name may not be an instrument of fraud. A defendant may thereby avoid liability in passing off even though the domain name is identical to a trade name of the claimant[4].

A domain name can still be an instrument of fraud, even if it is not inherently likely to lead to passing off because it is not so similar to the claimant's trademark, if the get-up of the website in total is adapted to be used for passing off and is intended to be so used[5].

There are other avenues for dealing with cyber squatting, aside from court proceedings. Complaints can be brought under the alternative dispute resolution procedures offered by, amongst others, Nominet UK, ICANN and WIPO[6].

---

1   *British Telecommunications plc, Virgin Enterprises Ltd, J Sainsbury plc, Marks and Spencer plc, Ladbroke plc v One in a Million Ltd [1999] 1 WLR 903, CA.*
2   *French Connection Ltd v Sutton [2000] ETMR 341.*
3   *Marks and Spencer plc v Craig Cottrell (unreported, 26 February 2001), High Court.*
4   *French Connection Ltd v Sutton [2000] ETMR 341.*
5   *EasyJet Airline Co Ltd v Tim Dainty t/a easyRealestate [2001] EBLR 104.*
6   See **paragraphs 24.65–24.67**.

Domain names – ICANN and dispute resolution procedures

ICANN

24.65 All ICANN-accredited registrars that are authorised to register names in the gTLDs subscribe to the Uniform Domain-Name Dispute-Resolution Policy ('UDRP'). The UDRP also applies to ccTLDs that have adopted the UDRP on a voluntary basis. The UDRP sets out procedures for the resolution of disputes between registrants and aggrieved third parties. Complaints made pursuant to the UDRP can be filed with one of a number of approved dispute resolution service providers. The procedure provides an alternative to bringing a claim in the courts.

The UDRP was adopted by ICANN in August 1999 and became fully operational in early 2000. In adopting this policy, the gTLD and ccTLD registrars incorporate the UDRP into their Registration Agreements thereby binding applicants to this means of dispute resolution.

The UDRP provides that a registrar will cancel or transfer a domain name registration if the domain name owner authorises them to do so, if the registrar receives a court order or binding arbitrator's decision or if the registrar receives a decision of an Administrative Panel requiring such action in any administrative proceeding.

Registrants who are bound by the UDRP are required to submit to mandatory administrative proceedings where a third party complainant files a complaint with the applicable administrative dispute resolution service provider asserting that:

- the registered domain name is identical or confusingly similar to a trademark or service mark in which the complainant has rights;
- the registered domain name holder has no legitimate rights or interests in that domain name; and
- the domain name was registered and is being used in bad faith[1].

An alternative process for resolving domain name disputes is the Uniform Rapid Suspension System ('URS'). The URS procedure was adopted by ICANN in 2013 and offers a cheaper and faster path to relief for rights holders. The complaint form is significantly shorter than the URDP complaint form, and a 500-word maximum explanatory statement is optional.

URS complaints may only be filed against domain names registered in a New gTLD. The URS is only available in 'clear cases of trade mark abuse' where there are no 'open questions of fact'. Unlike the UDRP, the URS does not allow for the transfer of the domain name to the complainant or cancellation by the registrar, only suspension. However, the URS does have an appeals process, which the UDRP does not offer.

The only organisation that conducts dispute resolution under the URS is the National Arbitration Forum ('NAF').

1   This is reproduced from the website https://www.icann.org/resources/pages/policy-2012-02-25-en, which offers a fuller explanation.

The World Intellectual Property Organisation (WIPO)

24.66 The WIPO service first began in December 1999. In administering its service, the WIPO Centre applies the UDRP.

A respondent to a complaint filed with WIPO has 20 days in which to respond. Once a defence is filed or the period for filing a defence expires, either one or three panellists (the 'Panel') are appointed by the WIPO Centre. The Panel then considers the facts of the case and arguments put forward by the respective parties, before delivering its decision. This decision is distributed to the parties, the relevant registrar, and ICANN.

If the Panel decides that a domain name should be cancelled or transferred then this must be carried out by the relevant registrar. However, as discussed above, such dispute resolution service is in addition to any court proceedings that can be commenced, and there is a 10-day period after the Panel's decision is delivered within which the losing party can commence court proceedings.

The service provided by the WIPO Centre is regarded as an effective and cost-efficient alternative to court proceedings. Complaints are usually concluded within two months, and there is a fixed fee for the dispute resolution service which can increase depending on the number of panellists involved and number of domain names being disputed.

WIPO is one of a number of organisations that conduct dispute resolution under the UDRP and ICANN. The other organisations include the NAF and the CPR Institute for Dispute Resolution ('CPR'), which are both based in the United States, and the Disputes.org/eResolution Consortium ('DeC') based in Canada.

The Nominet UK dispute resolution service

24.67 Nominet provides an alternative to commencing court proceedings involving disputed '.uk' domains if the complainant can show it has 'rights in respect of a name or mark which is identical or similar to the domain name' and that the registration or use of the domain name is an 'abusive registration'.

The Nominet resolution procedure differs from the UDRP, placing an emphasis on getting parties to resolve the dispute at the outset.

The first stage involves the complainant submitting a complaint to Nominet online, such complaint then being sent to the registrant of the domain name who has a set time to respond. If there is a response, the complainant has the opportunity to comment on it and then both parties may use Nominet's free mediation service to settle the dispute.

If this fails, stage two of the process may be undertaken. No fee is payable unless stage two is reached. At this stage (and following payment of the required fee), Nominet appoints an independent adjudicator (the 'Expert') who will decide whether action should be taken in relation to the domain name (ie whether it should be cancelled, suspended or transferred to the complainant). The Expert's decision is then communicated to both parties in writing.

Parties who have lost an Expert decision and want their case re-examined can make an appeal within ten working days of the decision being made. The appeal is heard by a panel of three Experts.

In addition to the remedies available using the Nominet service, the decision is also published on the Nominet website[1].

1   Further information is provided at https://www.nominet.uk/domains/resolving-uk-domain-disputes-and-complaints/.

Chapter 25

Artists, photographers, art galleries, art dealers and museums

Introduction

25.01 This chapter focuses on 'artistic works' and their exploitation. The phrase 'artistic work' has a technical meaning under the CDPA, and it is worth prefacing this chapter by saying that modern artists frequently use works in their art which do not fall within the technical definition of 'artistic work' (eg films, sound recordings, etc). Where it is the intention to use one of these other works, we recommend reference to the particular parts of this book dealing with issues arising in respect of those categories of work[1].

1   See in particular **Chapters 20** and **22**.

Definitions

25.02 Under the CDPA, the phrase 'artistic work' means:

'(a) a graphic work, photograph, sculpture or collage, irrespective of artistic quality,
(b) a work of architecture being a building or a model for a building, or
(c) a work of artistic craftsmanship.'[1]

In rare cases, an artistic work that is libellous, obscene, immoral or irreligious may be in copyright but may not be entitled to rely on copyright law for its protection[2].

1   CDPA s 4(1). See **paragraph 2.06** for a detailed discussion of this definition, and for the interpretation by the Supreme Court of the term 'sculpture' (*Lucasfilm Ltd v Ainsworth [2011] UKSC 39*).
2   See **paragraph 2.16**.

Ownership and infringement

25.03 It is important to distinguish between, on the one hand, the ownership of the object of art itself (eg the painting or sculpture), which is personal property, and on the other hand the ownership of the copyright in the 'artistic work' that the object of art embodies, which is intellectual property. Ownership of one does not entail ownership of the other[1].

Where a gallery or museum acquires a work of art, its ability to exploit its acquisition will depend upon whether (and, if so, to what extent) the copyright therein has been transferred or licensed to it. It is therefore vital for the gallery or museum to ensure that it properly acquires and catalogues the rights that it needs and that it carefully notes any such rights that are reserved to third parties.

In relation to infringement issues, in order to establish whether there has been a copyright infringement of an artistic work, it is necessary to establish that the latter falls within one of the categories of work in which copyright subsists[2], that the term of copyright is still ongoing[3], that a restricted act has been undertaken without the authorisation of the owner (ie a primary infringement has been committed)[4] and/or that an act which amounts to a 'secondary infringement' has been committed with 'guilty knowledge'[5], and that no exception or defence to copyright infringement is available to the defendant[6].

1   See **paragraph 9.01**.
2   See **paragraphs 2.01** ff.
3   See **Chapter 5**.
4   See **paragraphs 6.02–6.09**.
5   See **paragraphs 6.10–6.14**.
6   See **Chapter 8**.

Restricted acts – general

25.04 The acts restricted by the copyright in an artistic work (which, if committed without the consent of the copyright owner, will or may constitute primary infringement) are:

- *copying* the work, ie reproducing it in any material form[1];
- *issuing copies* of the work to the public[2];
- *renting or lending* the work to the public (other than a work of architecture in the form of a building or a model for a building, or a work of 'applied art')[3]; and
- *communicating the work to the public*[4] by electronic transmission.

It should be noted that exhibiting or selling an artistic work is not a restricted act, though it may constitute secondary infringement[5].

1   See **paragraph 6.04**.
2   See **paragraph 6.05**.
3   See **paragraph 6.06**.
4   See **paragraph 6.08**.
5   In connection with secondary infringement see *Nouveau Fabrics Ltd v Voyage Decoration Ltd [2004] EWHC 895*, which involved alleged copyright infringement of an artistic fabric.

Restricted acts – copying (two- and three-dimensional)

25.05 Copying an artistic work means reproducing it in any material form. This includes storing it in any medium by electronic means (eg in the memory of a computer[1]). The reproduction of an artistic work in any size, or the reproduction of a substantial part of an artistic work[2], may infringe copyright in the work, but there must be *actual* reproduction. The *re-use* of a copy of an artistic work made by someone else does not itself amount to reproduction, so re-use will not infringe copyright in the artistic work unless another restricted act (such as issuing to the public) is undertaken. So, it will not infringe copyright in an artistic work to make and sell a collage consisting of pictures of different artistic works cut out of magazines. However, if the collage-maker, for example, takes copies of his or her own work embodying the other artistic works, or issues those copies to the public[3], then he or she may be infringing copyright in the underlying artistic works which form part of the collage. A collage which utilises other copyright works may also result in an infringement of the moral rights of the earlier artist, if the use amounts to a derogatory treatment[4].

Reproducing a two-dimensional painting, drawing or engraving in three-dimensional form may infringe copyright in the two-dimensional original (eg toys; dolls; dresses; waxwork model tableaux; a tableau vivant of a painting). Similarly, making a two-dimensional graphic of a three-dimensional work of art such as a sculpture, a work of artistic craftsmanship or the model of a building, or the taking of photographs of such works, may infringe the copyright in them. There is an exception for such works when on permanent public display, and the exception applicable to buildings is expressed broadly, making infringement in this manner very unlikely[5].

1   See **paragraph 6.04**.
2   See **paragraph 7.06**.
3   See **paragraph 25.06**.
4   See **paragraphs 10.12** ff and **25.21**.
5   See **paragraph 8.24**.

Restricted acts – issuing copies to the public

25.06 Under the CDPA, *issuing copies* is deemed to include issuing the original[1]. However, once the artwork has first been issued to the public, the author's right may be deemed exhausted, and further sale of the work will not infringe the artist's copyright[2]. In a case before the Court of Justice of the European Union[3] which involved the copyright in posters that had been converted by the defendant into canvas transfers, it was held that the distribution right in that copyright had not been exhausted, as the object that incorporated the copyright work had, after initial marketing, been altered to such an extent that it amounted to a new reproduction of that work.

An art gallery may, for example, exhibit original photographs or engravings without infringing the copyright in those artistic works. However, if the gallery wished to reproduce copies of the works in, say, a catalogue which is issued to the public, this would infringe copyright in the artistic work unless appropriate authorisation is obtained, or unless the gallery can bring its use within the exemption from copyright infringement in relation to advertisements for the sale of artistic works[4]. A gallery may also wish to sell postcards or posters of the artistic work. Again, this may constitute an infringement both because it is a reproduction[5], and because it involves issuing copies to the public. Consequently any contract between a gallery and the artist should set out in detail the rights that the gallery wishes to exploit in the artist's work, and the means by which the artist will be remunerated for that exploitation. In the case of architecture, issuing copies means selling casts or models of the original – it does not include issuing photographs of the sculpture[6].

1   CDPA s 18(4).
2   See **paragraphs 6.05** and **13.04**.
3   *Art & Allposters International BV v Stichting Pictoright (Case C-419/13).*
4   See **paragraphs 8.25** and **25.09**.
5   See **paragraph 25.05**.
6   See **paragraph 6.05**.

Restricted acts – rental and lending of artistic works

25.07 The rental or lending of copies of artistic works to the public are acts restricted by the copyright in artistic works, subject to exceptions in the case of works of architecture and applied art[1]. Again, the making available of works for the purpose of exhibition in public does not constitute rental or lending[2], and the reference to the rental or lending of *copies* includes the rental or lending of the originals[3].

It should be noted that lending does not include making available artistic works between 'establishments which are accessible to the public'[4]. Therefore, galleries may lend artistic works to one another without the consent of the artist whether or not the purpose of the loan is public exhibition[5].

1   See **paragraph 6.06**.
2   CDPA s 18A(3)(b).
3   CDPA s 18A(6).
4   CDPA s 18A(4).
5   For the definitions of 'rental' and 'lending' and a discussion of this restricted act, see **paragraph 6.06**.

Restricted acts – communication to the public

25.08 Communicating an artistic work to the public by electronic transmission is an act restricted by copyright[1]. It includes the broadcasting of the work, and the making available to the public of the work in such a way that members of the public may access it from a place and at a time individually chosen by them.

1   CDPA s 20(1)(a); see **paragraph 6.08**.

Exceptions and defences to copyright infringement

25.09 Fair dealing with an artistic work for the purpose of private study will not infringe copyright[1]; nor, provided that (amongst other things) it is accompanied by a sufficient acknowledgment, will such fair dealing infringe copyright if it is in the form of quoting from the work, or for research for non-commercial purposes, or for the purpose of criticism or review, or (other than photographs) for the purpose of reporting current events, or for the purposes of caricature, parody or pastiche.

A number of specific exceptions also apply to artistic works. The most significant of these which affect art galleries appear in the CDPA at ss 62 (representation of certain works on public display) and 63 (advertisement of sale of artistic works)[2]:

- *Works on public display*[3]: in the case of buildings (including any part of a building, such as a room), and sculptures, models for buildings and works of artistic craftsmanship (ie not graphic works, photographs, sculptures or collages) which are 'permanently situated in a public place or in premises open to the public'[4], copyright is not infringed by:
    '(a)   making a graphic work representing it,
    (b)   making a photograph or film of it, or
    (c)   making a broadcast of a visual image of it'[5].
Issuing copies to the public, or communicating to the public anything made in accordance with s 62 is also permitted without infringing copyright[6].
- *Advertisement of sale of artistic work*[7]: it is not an infringement of copyright in an artistic work to copy it, or to issue copies to the public, for the purpose of advertising the sale of the work[8].

If a copy of a work permitted to be made pursuant to s 63 is subsequently 'dealt with' for another purpose (ie it is sold or let for hire, offered or exposed for sale or hire, or exhibited in public or distributed[9]), then that copy will be treated as an infringing copy with regard to that dealing and for all subsequent purposes. The provisions on secondary infringement of copyright will then apply[10]. Accordingly, whilst an art gallery may make copies of works for sale for the purpose of advertising them, it may not sell copies of the sales catalogue after the sale, without the permission of the copyright owners of the respective works reproduced in it.

1 See **paragraph 8.03**.
2 See **paragraphs 8.24** and **8.25**. Exceptions and defences to copyright infringement generally are considered in detail in **Chapter 8**.
3 CDPA s 62.
4 CDPA s 62(1).
5 CDPA s 62(2).
6 CDPA s 62(3).
7 CDPA s 63.
8 CDPA s 63(1).
9 CDPA s 63(2).
10 See **Chapter 6**.

Museums and galleries

25.10 Owners of museums, galleries and other premises who want to prevent visitors from reproducing photographs, paintings, drawings, engravings, sculptures, works of artistic craftsmanship or models of buildings that they are exhibiting seek to do so by making it a condition of entry to their premises that visitors may not take photographs, make drawings of them etc. This condition should be printed on admission tickets, and notices to the same effect should be prominently displayed, particularly near entrances. Although this will not give any copyright protection to the gallery owner or the artist, the condition will form part of the contract under which the visitor enters the premises. Breach of this contract may give the owners of the premises the right to sue for an injunction preventing reproduction of the photographs, drawings etc and also a right to damages. With the potential value to museums and art galleries of publication right[1], it is particularly important that they control photographers and the use of photographs of their exhibits.

The CDPA has been expanded[2] in order to extend to museums and galleries the rights of librarians and archivists to make copies of certain works for the purpose of preservation.

1 See **paragraph 25.23** and **Chapter 5**.
2 By the Copyright and Rights in Performances (Research, Education, Libraries and Archives) Regulations 2014, SI 2014/1372.

Incidental inclusion of artistic works in other copyright works

25.11 There will be no infringement of the copyright in an artistic work if it is included incidentally in a film, sound recording, broadcast or other artistic work or if the resulting work is issued, played, showed or communicated to the public[1].

So, paintings, drawings, and other artistic works can form part of the set of a film or televised drama without requiring any licence from the respective copyright owners, if the inclusion is incidental. Reproductions of the paintings of an artist in a television programme about that artist would probably not constitute incidental use.

1 See **paragraph 8.08**.

Artists' reserved right of reproduction

25.12 If an artist does not own the copyright in one of his or her works (because, for example, it has been assigned to a third party), he or she will nevertheless have a special statutory entitlement to continue to reproduce it in later works, provided that he or she does not repeat or imitate the main design of the earlier work[1].

1   CDPA s 64; see **paragraph 8.27**.

Duration of copyright

25.13 The term of copyright in artistic works is the life of the author plus 70 years from the end of the calendar year in which the author died. In the case of an artistic work of unknown authorship, copyright expires at the end of the period of 70 years from the end of the calendar year in which it was made; but if during that period the work is made available to the public, the copyright will instead expire at the end of the period of 70 years from the end of the calendar year in which it is so made available[1]. For these purposes the 'making available to the public' of an artistic work includes:

'(i)   exhibition in public,
(ii)   a film including the work being shown in public, or
(iii) communication to the public'[2].

But, in determining whether the work has been made available to the public, no account is to be taken of an unauthorised act.

Section 52 of the CDPA contained an exception that limited to 25 years the duration of copyright in artistic works that had been exploited with the copyright owner's consent by making, using an industrial process, articles that amount to copies of the work; but it was repealed in 2016[3].

1   Duration of copyright is considered in detail in **Chapter 5**.
2   CDPA s 12(5)(b).
3   Enterprise and Regulatory Reform Act 2013 s 74.

Ownership of copyright

25.14 Ownership of copyright generally, including artistic works, is considered in **Chapter 9**, but several points are particularly relevant to artistic works:

- *Commissioned work*: prior to the CDPA one of the exceptions to the general rule that the author is the first owner of a copyright was that copyright in commissioned photographs, portraits, engravings and sound recordings belonged to the commissioner, subject to any agreement to the contrary. Although the commissioner's copyright in photographs etc was removed by the CDPA, under the transitional provisions of the CDPA, copyright in photographs made after commencement (ie 1 August 1989) still belongs to the commissioner if the work is made in pursuance of a commission made before commencement of the Act.

- *Ownership of photographs*: prior to the CDPA, the owner of a photograph that had not been commissioned was the person who, at the time it was taken, was the owner of the material on which it was taken. The CDPA did not repeat this, and the position is now governed by the general rule that the author is the person who created the work. This will normally be the person who actually took the photograph. However, there may be circumstances where this is not the case. It might be the person who chose the camera angle, the type of film stock, the exposure or aperture setting, but did not actually press the button to activate the shutter. It follows that a photographer who wishes to ensure that he or she is the sole owner of the copyright in the resulting photograph would be well advised to ensure that the arrangements with those other people collaborating in the creation of the photograph confirm his or her ownership of the resulting copyright[1].

So, under the CDPA, the legal title to the copyright in, for example, wedding photographs which have been commissioned by the bride and groom will prima facie belong to the photographer as the author (or maker) of the photograph. However, the bride and groom still have some protection by virtue of the moral right of privacy[2].

For the purposes of determining the period of copyright attributable to a photograph taken before 1 August 1989, the author of the photograph is deemed to be the photographer, whether or not the taking of the photograph was commissioned.

1 See **Chapter 9**.
2 See **paragraph 10.24**.

Dealing with copyright in artistic works

25.15 Whenever the photograph or a work of art is commissioned, and it is intended that the person commissioning it should own the copyright in the work, as well as the object itself, it is essential that there be an assignment of copyright in writing signed by or on behalf of the owner. This does not have to be in any special form – a letter will suffice, providing that it is written in clear and unambiguous language[1].

The sale of a work of art does not automatically include the copyright in it[2]. Thus a gallery or dealer that acquires a work of art which is still in copyright does not necessarily acquire the right to reproduce it, or do any of the other restricted acts. To exercise such rights exclusively, there must be an assignment or exclusive licence of the copyright (or the relevant part of the copyright) in the work in writing, signed by or on behalf of the copyright owner. If a non-exclusive licence is required (eg to reproduce the work in a catalogue) it is still advisable to obtain a written licence, although an oral licence (which is capable of proof, and which is sufficient to amount to a contract) will be legally enforceable. A licence may also, depending on the circumstances, be implied by conduct[3]. If, for example, the copyright owner knows that a catalogue is being produced and allows the publisher to incur printing and distribution expenses before refusing a licence, it may be held that the former's failure to take action by warning the latter when it first knew of the gallery's intentions, constitutes an implied licence. Relying on an implied licence, however, is never recommended[4].

As we have noted, if the catalogue is purely for the purpose of advertising the sale of the artistic work, no licence will be required[5].

The rules regarding ownership of works produced in the course of employment apply to artistic works with no special exceptions[6].

In practice, galleries and museums have moved away from the practice of acquiring assignments of copyright. It is therefore crucial that they ensure that they are contractually entitled (by licences of copyright) to exercise those rights that they need.

1   Issues to be considered when dealing with an artistic work are considered in detail in **Chapter 9**.
2   See **paragraphs 9.01** and **25.03**.
3   Implied licences are considered at **paragraph 9.29**.
4   See **paragraph 9.29**.
5   See **paragraph 25.09**.
6   See **paragraphs 9.11** ff.

Collective licensing

25.16   If a museum or gallery wishes to sell postcards or other material reproducing paintings, drawings or reproductions of sculptures in its collection, it will need a licence not only from the owner of the copyright in the object concerned but also a licence or assignment of copyright from the person who produced the postcard or made the reproduction. The Design and Artists Copyright Society Ltd (DACS) has as members artists, designers and photographers and their estates, and collectively administers their respective copyrights. DACS has published scales of fees for reproduction of its members' works. It grants licences to the principal art publishers, broadcasters, poster printers and distributors and those who reproduce artistic works on merchandise (such as the Royal Academy of Arts) etc[1].

1   See **Appendix 1** for DACS' contact details.

International protection

25.17 As with the other copyright works, artistic works do not have to be registered in order to acquire copyright protection[1]. Strictly speaking, works of art need not carry the © symbol with the date of publication and the copyright owner's name in order to acquire protection under the Universal Copyright Convention. However, if there is any possibility of copies of a work of art being made available to the public in one of the few countries that are not parties to the Berne Convention, the requisite notice should, as a precaution, be affixed to the work, whatever its nature, to avoid the possibility that copyright protection may be lost in that country[2]. In every case the symbol should be affixed to reproductions of the work, if copies of the work are issued to the public. Accordingly, engravings, lithographs, sculptures and other works of art of which a number of copies are made for sale to the public should bear the © symbol etc. The safest course is to affix the © symbol etc to all works of art[3].

1   See **paragraph 9.20**.
2   See **paragraph 4.16**.
3   International protection for copyright works is considered in detail in **Chapter 4**.

Photographs

25.18 The following additional points regarding photographs and photographers should be noted:

• *Use of photographs*: unless a photograph has been commissioned for private and domestic purposes, and is therefore the subject of moral rights[1], there is nothing in UK intellectual property law to prevent a photographer taking and publishing a photograph of whomsoever he or she wishes, without making any payment to or obtaining any consent from the person(s) appearing in the photograph. But there may be problems under other areas of law such as data protection and breach of confidence, which fall outside the scope of this *User's Guide*.

• *Copies of other photographs*: even a snapshot is entitled to copyright protection[2]. However, if without consent a photograph consists entirely of another artistic work, such as a photograph of another photograph, it will infringe the copyright in the artistic work by reproducing it in a material form[3]. The second photograph will not be entitled to copyright protection, if it lacks the elements of originality and sufficient skill and labour that must be applied to it for it to acquire copyright protection[4]. To take a photograph of a scene identical to one depicted in a previous photograph is not as a general rule an infringement of copyright. But in the widely-reported case of *Temple Island v New English Teas*[5], which related to 'photographic works' (ie images manipulated by the author using photographic-imaging software, as distinct from 'mere photographs'), it was held that the claimant's artistic copyright in a photographic work depicting a red London bus crossing Westminster Bridge with a monochrome background had been reproduced by the defendants' image.

- *Positives and negatives*: the positive as well as the negative comes within the definition of a photograph in the CDPA, and positives made from the negative will constitute reproductions of the photograph for the purposes of the infringing act[6].

- *Video grab*: copying in relation to a film or broadcast includes making a photograph of the whole or any substantial part of *any image* forming part of the film or television broadcast[7]. However, an exception is made under the CDPA where the photograph is taken for private use from the television[8].

- *Correlation with dramatic works*: in a case relating to the infringement of copyright in photographs contained in a training manual[9], it was held that one photograph of a dramatic work in progress did not amount to a record of that work such as to create copyright in a dramatic work, and that a collection of such photographs could not record a sequence of techniques such as to give rise to copyright in the sequence as an overall dramatic work.

- A series of relatively recent cases have addressed the issue of the unlawful reproduction of photographs taken from websites[10].

- The Court of Justice of the European Union has held that the protection conferred on a portrait photograph by virtue of the Copyright Directive could not be inferior to the protection enjoyed by other works, including other photographic works[11].

1 See **paragraphs 10.24** ff.
2 See **paragraph 3.03**.
3 See **paragraph 6.04**.
4 See **paragraph 3.03**.
5 See *Temple Island Collections Ltd v New English Teas Ltd [2012] EWPCC 1*.
6 See **paragraph 3.06**.
7 See **paragraph 6.04**.
8 See **paragraph 6.04**.
9 *McCormack Training Ltd v Goldmark Training Services Ltd [2015] EWHC 41 (IPEC)*.
10 *Grisbrook v MGN Ltd [2010] EWCA Civ 1399; Hoffman v Drug Abuse Resistance Education (UK) Ltd [2012] EWPCC 2; Omnibill (Pty) Ltd v EGPSXXX Ltd (in liquidation) [2014] EWHC 3762; Absolute Lofts South West London Ltd v Artisan Home Improvements Ltd [2015] EWHC 2632 (IPEC)* and *[2015] EWHC 2608 (IPEC); Pez Hejduk v EnergieAgentur.NRW GmbH (Case C-441/13)*.
11 *Painer v Standard Verlags GmbH, Case C-145/10*.

Caricatures, parodies and pastiches

25.19 A work of art that satirizes or parodies another work in copyright may (subject to the statutory defence discussed below) infringe the copyright in the original work if it uses a substantial part of the original[1]. So, if a portrait were to be copied, and changed only by the addition of a moustache and spectacles, the copyright in the original portrait might be infringed.

The Copyright and Rights in Performances (Quotation and Parody) Regulations 2014[2] resulted in the addition of s 30A into the CDPA, providing that fair dealing with a work for the purposes of caricature, parody or pastiche will not infringe copyright in it.

1   See **paragraphs 7.05** and **7.06**.
2   SI 2014/2356.

Use in exhibitions of film, music and other works

25.20 The use of films, video, music and sound recordings in museums and galleries will require the licence of their respective copyright owners because their use of those works as part of an exhibition constitutes public performance[1].

1   Issues concerning public performance of copyright works are considered in detail at **Chapter 23**. See also **paragraph 6.07**.

Moral rights and artistic works

25.21 The following moral rights are applicable to artistic works generally[1]:

(a) the 'paternity right', or the right to be identified as author of the work[2];
(b) the 'integrity right', or the right to object to derogatory treatment of a work[3];
(c) the false attribution right[4]; and
(d) the right to privacy of certain photographs[5].

There are important exceptions to each of these rights and these are discussed in further detail in **Chapter 10**. Moral rights can be waived by the author in writing or otherwise[6]. It is also worth noting the following points:

- The paternity and integrity rights applicable to artistic works made before 1 August 1989 are limited, as to which see further **Chapter 10**.
- Of particular importance to those organising exhibitions of works of art are the provisions of the CDPA concerning the persons bound by the right of paternity[7]. The CDPA deals specifically with the way in which the right may be asserted in relation to the public exhibition of an artistic work[8]. In the case of an artistic work, the author's moral right of paternity is asserted when the author (or other first

owner of copyright in it) parts with possession of the original, or of a copy made by or under his or her control, on which the author is identified. The author may equally be identified, and therefore assert the right, by having his or her name on the frame, mount or other thing to which the artistic work is attached[9].

In addition, the paternity right may be asserted in a licence by which the author or other first owner of copyright authorises the making of copies of the work. To assert the right in relation to public exhibition of such copies, the licence must state that the author asserts his or her right to be identified in the event of the public exhibition of a copy made pursuant to the licence[10]. Anyone into whose hands comes the original or copy of an artistic work in respect of which the right to be identified has been made in relation to public exhibition of the work, is bound by the assertion[11]. This applies whether or not the identification on the work at the time the right was asserted is still visible. However, if the artist who is asserting his or her right to be identified has specified a pseudonym, initials or other particular form of identification, that form should be used.

The CDPA does not specify any particular way in which authors should be identified except to say that any reasonable form of identification may be used[12]. It is suggested that exhibition organisers should request the person providing an artistic work for exhibition to state in writing whether or not to his or her knowledge the right to be identified has been asserted and whether a particular form of identification has been specified by the artist. If it is desired for some reason to omit the identity of the artist, then a written waiver of the right should be obtained from the artist himself or herself – not the owner of the work – or, if he or she is dead, from the person to whom the right of identity has passed[13].

In *Tidy v Trustees of the Natural History Museum*[14], in considering whether the reduction in size of the claimant's cartoons by the Museum constituted a derogatory treatment, the court treated the question as being whether this was either a distortion or was otherwise prejudicial to the author's honour or reputation.

The moral right to privacy of photographs applies to the public exhibition of photographs[15]. Therefore, exhibition organisers should obtain a written statement from those providing photographs for exhibition to the effect that the photograph was not commissioned for private and domestic purposes. If, however, it *was* so commissioned, then consent for its exhibition must be obtained, not from the copyright owner (whose consent is not required in any event), but from the person who commissioned the taking of the photograph.

1 Moral rights are considered in detail in **Chapter 10.**
2 See **paragraphs 10.02–10.11.**
3 See **paragraphs 10.12–10.20**. For a rare example of the award of damages for the infringement of the integrity right in a photograph, see *Emma Delves-Broughton v House of Harlot Ltd [2012] EWPCC 29.*

4   See **paragraphs 10.21–10.23**.
5   See **paragraphs 10.24–10.26**. For an example of an unsuccessful infringement claim see *Trimingham v Associated Newspapers Ltd [2012] EWHC 1296*.
6   See **paragraph 10.29**.
7   See **paragraphs 10.02** ff.
8   CDPA s 78(3).
9   See **paragraph 10.08**.
10 See **paragraph 10.08**.
11 CDPA s 78(4).
12 CDPA s 77(8).
13 See **paragraph 10.29**.
14 (1997) 39 IPR 501.
15 See **paragraph 10.24**.

Artists' resale rights

25.22 On 13 October 2001 the Directive on Artists' Resale Rights[1] came into force. Its objective was to harmonise the market in modern and contemporary art by applying a resale right throughout the European Union ('the resale right'). On 14 February 2006 the Directive was transposed into UK law via the Artist's Resale Right Regulations 2006[2] (amended with effect from 1 January 2012 by the Artist's Resale Right (Amendment) Regulations 2011[3] following a period of various permitted derogations from the Directive). In the UK the resale right allows authors (who must be nationals of an EEA country or of a state whose legislation permits resale right protection for EEA authors and their respective successors) of original works of art (and, after their death, their respective successors) to receive, during the copyright period in the work, a royalty payment on a work of art each time it is resold by an art market professional such as an auctioneer, a gallery or any other art dealer.

Certain sales fall outside the resale right, such as a work being resold following it being bought directly from the artist less than three years before, and being sold for 10,000 euros or less. Sales between private individuals, and sales to public, non-profit making museums, do not trigger the payment of royalties.

The type of works covered by the resale right includes any copyright-protected work of graphic or plastic art such as pictures, collages, paintings, drawings, engravings, prints, lithographs, sculptures, tapestries, ceramics, glassware or photographs.

It is important to note that the resale right only applies when the sale price of a piece of art meets or exceeds the UK equivalent of 1,000 euros, and the royalty payment percentage is calculated on a sliding scale in a cumulative manner. The relevant collecting societies collect the royalty to then be distributed to the creators/authors/artists.

1   2001/84/EC.
2   SI 2006/346.
3   SI 2011/2873.

Publication right and museums and public galleries

25.23 The intellectual property right known as 'publication right', which was introduced into UK copyright law by the Copyright and Related Rights Regulations 1996 ('the 1996 Regulations'), is of particular importance to museums and public galleries[1].

Publication right applies to previously unpublished works whose copyright has expired. There is some ambiguity as to whether or not a work which has been exhibited in public is in fact unpublished, but on balance, such exhibition is likely to constitute publication when deciding whether or not the work is unpublished for the purposes of the 1996 Regulations.

Where a museum or art gallery publishes a work that has never been the subject of publication, it will be entitled to publication right in the work. Publication right gives the owner of an unpublished manuscript or other object embodying a work in which the copyright has expired the right to publish it for a period of 25 years from the end of the year in which the work is first published[2]. This is an exclusive right akin to copyright, and the same exceptions and rights apply to publication right as apply to copyright in an artistic work[3]. To qualify, it must be first published in the EEA and the publisher at the time of the publication must be a national of an EEA state[4].

It follows that museums should be extremely cautious before allowing publishers of art books to publish photographs of works in their collection, whether they be works of sculpture or works of artistic craftsmanship or graphic works, because by so doing they may lose the publication right therein which could otherwise be a useful source of revenue. If a museum decides to grant a publisher a right to publish the work, it should enter into a publishing agreement under which the museum is assigned publication right (or reserve it on the grounds that the museum is exercising publication right by arranging for the publisher to effect publication) and be paid appropriate royalties or other consideration.

Equally, when allowing photographers and publishers to take photographs of works in their collection, a museum or art gallery should ensure that copies of these photographs are deposited with it and that the rights of publication in such photographs should be clearly stated (by an agreement signed by the photographer or publisher) to be reserved by it.

1   See **paragraphs 5.13** ff.
2   See **paragraph 5.15**.
3   See **paragraph 5.13**.
4   See **paragraph 5.14**.

Chapter 26

Architects and architecture

Introduction

26.01 Works of architecture (ie buildings and models for buildings) are subject to a number of special provisions in the CDPA, which are considered in this chapter.

Definitions

26.02 The definition of 'artistic work' under the CDPA includes 'a work of architecture, being a building or a model for a building'[1], and a 'building' includes 'any fixed structure, and a part of a building or fixed structure'[2].

The plans, sketches, and drawings upon which works of architecture are based are also artistic works which have their own separate copyright[3], as do the notes prepared by the architect, which are protected as literary works[4].

Although there is no definition of 'fixed structure' in the CDPA, one decision which pre-dates the 1956 Copyright Act held that a garden, in that case a somewhat elaborately laid out garden, was a 'structure' and therefore a work of architecture[5].

The definitions of 'artistic work' and 'literary work' are so wide that they cover all the typical output of an architect's office: design sketches, blueprints, descriptive diagrams, working drawings, final drawings, artistic presentations, notes, both alphabetical and numerical, and reports.

1   CDPA s 4(1)(b).
2   CDPA s 4(2); see **paragraph 2.06**.
3   See **paragraphs 2.06** and **25.02**.
4   See **paragraph 2.02**.
5   *Meikle v Maufe [1941] 3 All ER 144.*

Restricted acts

26.03 The acts restricted by copyright applicable to works of architecture are the same as those applicable to any other artistic works[1], with certain special exceptions[2].

1   See **paragraph 6.02**.
2   See **paragraphs 26.11–26.14**.

Originality and artistic content

26.04 A work of architecture will not receive copyright protection unless it is original. However, the test for originality is not onerous. In essence, for these purposes 'originality' means 'originating from the owner'[1].

For architectural works, the inclusion of some distinctive design detail will certainly make the architect's task of proving infringement much easier. In *Stovin-Bradford v Volpoint Properties Ltd*[2], the courts were influenced by the fact that although many details of the architect's drawing were not reproduced in the constructed buildings, 'a distinctive diamond-shaped feature which gave a pleasing appearance to the whole' was reproduced.

Some distinctive design feature may also be important when it could otherwise be proved that the person sued was without any knowledge of the plaintiff's prior design, and that he produced identical solutions because of a similarity in circumstances. In the US case of *Muller v Triborough Bridge Authority*[3], for example, the US Supreme Court held that a copyright of the drawing showing a novel bridge approach designed to disentangle traffic congestion was not infringed by copying, because the system of relieving traffic congestion shown embodied an idea which could not be protected by copyright and was only the obvious solution to the problem.

1   See **paragraph 3.01**.
2   [1971] Ch 1007.
3   43 F Supp 288 (1942).

Duration of copyright

26.05 The protection of copyright in an artistic work extends for the lifetime of the author and a further period of 70 years from the end of the calendar year in which he died[1].

In the case of joint works, the 70 years begins to run from the end of the calendar year in which the last of the joint authors dies[2]. A joint work is one in which the work is produced by the collaboration of two or more authors in which the contribution of each author is not distinct from that of the other author or authors[3]. So, if a building is designed by two architects, but one is exclusively responsible only for the design of the doors and windows, so that it is possible to distinguish between the contributions of the two architects, the building will not be a joint work.

1   See **paragraph 5.02**.
2   See **paragraph 5.17**.
3   See **paragraph 9.08**.

Qualification

26.06 In order to qualify for copyright protection in the UK, the qualification requirements of the CDPA must be satisfied either as regards the author or the country in which the work was first published[1].

1   See **paragraphs 4.01** ff.

Publication in relation to artistic works, such as architecture

26.07 Under the CDPA, 'publication' essentially means the issue of copies to the public. However, in relation to works of architecture in the form of a building or an artistic work incorporated in a building, construction of the building is treated as equivalent to publication of the work[1].

The issue to the public of copies of a graphic work representing a building, or of photographs of a work of architecture in the form of a building, or a model for a building, a sculpture or a work of artistic craftsmanship, does not constitute publication for the purposes of the CDPA. Nor does the exhibition or issue to the public of copies of a film including the work, or the broadcasting of an artistic work. The inclusion of a model of a building in a public exhibition such as the Royal Academy Summer Exhibition, for example, would not amount to publication, nor would the inclusion of photographs of the model in a book[2].

1   See **paragraph 4.05**.
2   See **paragraph 4.06**.

Ownership of architectural works

26.08 Ownership of copyright in architectural works will usually first reside with the architect who actually drew the plan, drawing, sketch or diagram[1]. Property may be transferred in accordance with the principles referred to in **Chapter 9**.

However, it is possible for someone who did not actually put pen to paper to be a joint author of an architectural work. In *Cala Homes (South) Ltd v Alfred McAlpine Homes East Ltd*[2] an employee of Cala Homes supervised in detail the drawings for the designs and plans for houses which were actually undertaken by employees of a firm of technical draughtsmen. Notwithstanding he had not actually drawn anything, it was held he could be a joint author. This is, however, a factually unusual case[3].

1   Unless he is an employee; see **paragraph 26.09** and **Chapter 9**.
2   [1995] FSR 818.
3   See **paragraph 9.08** for a detailed analysis of this issue.

Employees and sub-contractors

26.09 As with any other artistic work, the copyright in architects' drawings, buildings or models produced by an employee in the course of his employment automatically vests in his employer, whether the latter is an architect in partnership, a limited company, or a public authority, in the absence of any agreement to the contrary[1].

Frequently, architects employ independent architects and artists to carry out parts of the drawing service as was the case in *Cala Homes*. Such persons are rarely employed under 'a contract of service' as distinct from 'a contract for services'. Employer architects should make it an express term of any sub-contractor's appointment that any copyright arising out of his work should vest in the employer.

Where a work is made by an officer or servant of the Crown in the course of his duties, the Crown will be the first owner of the copyright in the work[2].

1　See **paragraphs 9.11** ff.
2　See **paragraph 9.09**.

Ownership of drawings

26.10 Ownership of copyright in drawings should be distinguished from ownership of the actual material upon which they are drawn[1]. Although on payment of the architect's fees the client is likely to be entitled to physical possession of all the drawings prepared at his expense, in the absence of any agreement to the contrary, copyright remains with the architect, who also has a lien on (ie a right to withhold) the drawings until his fees are paid. If all copyright *is* assigned to the client, he may make such use of it as he wishes. Even if an architect does assign his copyright, he may reproduce in a subsequent work part of his own original design, provided that he does not repeat or imitate the main designs[2]. This provision enables an architect to repeat standard details which would otherwise pass to the client upon assignment of copyright.

1　See **paragraph 9.01**.
2　CDPA s 64; see **paragraph 8.26**.

Exceptions from infringement of architects' copyright: photographs and graphic works

26.11 Frequently, photographs of buildings designed by architects appear as part of advertisements by the contractors who constructed the buildings. As a matter of courtesy, the contractor usually makes some acknowledgement of the design, but he is not required to do so. Copyright in a work of architecture is not infringed by:

'(a)　making a graphic work representing it,
(b)　making a photograph or film of it, or
(c)　making a broadcast of a visual image of it'[1].

Copies of such graphic works, photographs and films can be issued to the public without infringing the copyright in the building as built.

It remains an infringement to copy the drawing or plan from which the building was constructed.

1   CDPA s 62(2); see **paragraph 8.24**.

Reconstruction

26.12 Copyright in a building, or any drawings or plans from which a building is constructed (with the authorisation of the owner) will not be infringed by anything done for the purpose of reconstructing the building[1].

1   CDPA s 65; see **paragraph 8.27**.

Fair dealing

26.13 A defence to an alleged infringement of copyright in an artistic work is 'fair dealing' for the purpose of criticism or review, provided that a sufficient acknowledgement is made to the earlier work[1] and provided that the work has been made available to the public[2]. As reproduction by photograph is the most likely method of illustrating a review and as a photograph of a building is specifically exempt from infringement[3], this defence of 'fair dealing' would appear to be needed only in the case of photographs or copies of *drawings* of buildings. A 'sufficient acknowledgement' is an acknowledgement identifying the building by its name and location, which also identifies the name of the architect who designed it. The name of the copyright owner need not be given if he has previously required that no acknowledgement of his name should be made. As certain self-appointed groups have now taken to awarding prizes for ugliness in design, some architects might find themselves in the unusual position of wishing to have no acknowledgement made of their connection with a design, although perhaps such publicity would hardly be 'fair dealing'.

Fair dealing with an artistic work for the purposes of research for a non-commercial purpose and private study is also a defence to an alleged copyright infringement provided that it is accompanied by a sufficient acknowledgment. However, there are limits on how, and how many, copies may be made[4].

1   See **paragraph 8.04**.
2   For further information on what constitutes making work available to the public see CDPA s 29(1A).
3   See **paragraph 26.11**.
4   See **paragraph 8.03**.

Special exceptions

26.14 Special exceptions are contained in the CDPA for copying for educational purposes and copying by libraries and archives and by public administration. These are considered in detail elsewhere in this *User's Guide*[1].

1   Generally, see **Chapters 8** and **18**.

Infringement

26.15 In brief, to prove infringement, a claimant must show:

- copyright subsists in his work;
- the copyright is vested in him;
- the alleged infringement is identical to his work in material particulars;
- the alleged infringement was copied from his work[1].

It is in the nature of architects' copyright that the alleged infringer must have had access directly or indirectly to the drawings. Infringement can therefore take a number of forms, considered in detail below.

1   Infringement of copyright is considered in detail in **Chapter 7**.

26.16 It is rare for drawings to be copied in every detail and copyright will be infringed in a drawing if a 'substantial part' is infringed[1]. This issue is considered elsewhere[2]. Substantial in this context refers to quality rather that to quantity. So, the reproduction of a distinctive diamond-shaped detail from a building design was enough to constitute infringement in the *Stovin-Bradford* case[3]. In *Signature Realty Ltd v Fortis Developments* the parties competed to purchase the same site. Prior to completion the claimant was granted planning consent based upon architectural drawings it had commissioned. The site was then purchased by the defendant who used the drawings obtained by the claimant. The claimant obtained an assignment of copyright from the architects and successfully sued for infringement[4].

1   CDPA s 16(3)(a).
2   See **paragraph 7.06**.
3   See **paragraph 26.04**.
4   [2016] EWHC 3583.

26.17 Reproduction of a drawing in the form of a building infringes the copyright in the drawing, even if no copy of the drawing itself is made by the infringer[1].

1   See **paragraph 6.03**.

26.18 How much of a work of architecture must be reproduced before there is an infringement? This is always a matter of degree and of examination of the facts in the particular case. It will be necessary to show that the subsequent building appears to substantially reproduce the earlier building[1]. The copyright in a building which is of an unusual design, and has considerable special detail, is more easily infringed than that of a very simple building using traditional forms and which is without much detail. The construction of a building with the same number of windows and doors and of approximately the same proportions in the case of, for example, a normal semi-detached house will not of itself constitute infringement. There must also be a causal connection – that is, the architect must have seen the original building, or a photograph or drawing of it[2].

Details of a building can also be infringed by reproduction. For example, a complex chimney arrangement, stair design or the like which is still in copyright may not be reproduced in a different building without a licence from the copyright owner (not necessarily the owner of the house). On the other hand, if the architect of a later chimney or staircase can show that he had drawn his inspiration from a common source, such as an even earlier building which is no longer in copyright, there will be no infringement.

1 See **paragraph 7.06**.
2 See **paragraph 3.05**.

26.19 Copyright in a work of architecture is not infringed by two-dimensional reproductions which are graphic works or photographs[1].

1 See **paragraphs 8.25**.

Licences: express licence

26.20 The Royal Institute of British Architects[1] publishes a Standard Form of Agreement for use in the appointment of an architect in connection with fully designed building projects[2]. The Conditions of Appointment which are appended to this Standard Form provide that: 'the Architect owns the copyright in the work produced by him'[3].

The standard form also provides that the architect asserts his right to be identified as the author of the artistic work/work of architecture which constitutes the architectural project[4].

In each case, the standard form agreement provides that the client shall have:

'a licence to copy and use and allow other consultants and contractors providing services to the architectural project to use and copy drawings, documents and bespoke software provided by the architect in performing the services ... but only for purposes related to the project on the site or part of the site to which the design relates'[5].

This licence is expressed to extend to the 'operation, maintenance, repair, reinstatement, alteration, extending, promotion, leasing and/or sale' of the project, but, unless a licence fee is agreed beforehand, the licence is not deemed to extend to use of the design for any extension built onto the architectural project, or to any other project[6].

The licence is also subject to a number of provisos. Most significantly, the architect is entitled to suspend the licence if the client is in default of paying fees[7].

RIBA also publishes amendments to the above terms for use in a 'design and build' situation, although these do not alter the copyright position as between client and architect referred to above.

Copyright may be expressly assigned to the client at some later stage, but it is usual to grant a licence authorising use of copyright subject to conditions rather than an outright assignment of all the architect's rights. An increasing number of public and commercial clients make it a condition of the architect's appointment that all copyright will vest in the client, but the architect should not consent to this without careful thought. It would seem reasonable that a client should not be prevented from extending a building and incorporating distinctive design features of the original building so that the two together should form one architectural unit.

So far as drawings are concerned, it must be remembered that drawings are the subject of copyright 'irrespective of artistic quality'[8] so that a prior express assignment of copyright to the client could theoretically grant him copyright in respect of even the most simple standard detail contained in the drawings.

1   RIBA, Tel: 020 7580 5533.
2   RIBA Standard Agreement 2010 (2012 Revision).
3   Conditions of engagement 6.1.
4   Conditions of engagement 6.1.
5   Conditions of engagement 6.2.
6   Conditions of engagement 6.2.
7   Conditions of engagement 6.2.3.
8   See **paragraph 2.06**.

Licences: implied licence

26.21 Courts will not imply a contractual term (including a licence) unless it is necessary to give efficacy to the intention of the parties[1]. Application of these rules of an architect's engagement suggests that an architect may impliedly be said to consent to the client making use of his drawings for the purpose for which they were intended (ie creating a building). If, therefore, the nature of the engagement is not a full RIBA service but, for example, obtaining outline planning permission and no more, the architect may be said to impliedly consent to the client making use of his copyright to apply for such permission. Again, if an architect is instructed to prepare drawings of a proposed alteration for submission to the client's landlord, the client may use the drawings to obtain a consent under the terms of his lease but not for any other purpose, and certainly not for the purpose of instructing a contractor to carry out the alteration work. Reliance on implied licences is never recommended.

1   See **paragraph 9.29**.

Alterations to architect's drawing and works of architecture

26.22 If a client alters an architect's plans or the completed building, the probability is that he will not therefore be in breach of the architect's copyright[1]. However, the client may not 'sell or hire' such buildings or plans as the unaltered work of the architect[2].

1   *Hunter v Fitzroy Robinson & Partners [1978] FSR 167.*
2   See **paragraph 26.25** below on moral rights.

Remedies for infringement: injunction

26.23 An injunction can be obtained to prevent the construction of a building that would infringe the copyright in another building, even if that building is part-built.

An injunction will not normally be granted if damages are an adequate relief. It is probable that a court would, in most cases, apply this rule in the case of an injunction to prevent the demolition of a building when the construction has substantially commenced. The decision of the court will depend upon all the facts and circumstances of the case[1].

1   See **paragraphs 7.12 ff.**

Remedies for infringement: damages

26.24 In *Potton Ltd v Yorkclose Ltd*[1] the defendants admitted that they had constructed 14 houses, in infringement of the claimant's copyright in a style of house named 'Grandsen'. The defendant's houses were substantial reproductions of the claimant's 'Grandsen' drawings and they had copied the drawings for obtaining outline planning permission and detailed planning permission. It was held that the claimants were entitled to the profits realised on the sale of the houses, apportioned to exclude profits attributable to:

- the purchase, landscaping and sale of the land on which the houses were built;
- any increase in value of the houses during the interval between the completion of the houses and their sale; and
- the advertising, marketing and selling of the houses.

In *Charles Church Developments plc v Cronin*[2] the defendants admitted that they had had a home built based on plans which were the copyright of the claimant. The distinction between this case and *Potton Ltd v Yorkclose Ltd* is that in the former case the houses were built for sale and had been sold, whereas in this case the house had not been sold and the claimants had obtained an injunction to prevent its sale. In the former case the claimants sued for an account of profits. In the latter case the claim was for compensatory damages for the loss caused by the infringement. The judge held that the measure of damages was a fair fee for a licence to use the drawings, based on what an architect would have charged for the preparation of drawings. The architect's fee should be calculated on the basis that the architect would have provided the whole of the basic services – in that case, 8.5% of the building costs.

The court may award additional damages as the justice of the case may require in cases of flagrant infringement, taking into account any benefit accruing to the defendant by reason of the infringement.

In the *Cala Homes* case[3], Mr Justice Laddie held that the breach of Cala's copyright had taken place flagrantly. He therefore held that it was an appropriate case for the court to exercise its discretion to award additional damages under the provisions of s 97(2) of the CDPA[4]. The damages would 'be designed to allow the court to register in terms of a financial penalty its disapproval of the behaviour of the infringer'.

In *Signature Realty v Fortis Developments*[5] a claim for additional damages under CDPA s 97(2) was rejected because there had been no flagrant use of the copyright. The defendant's benefit arose from the planning consent.

1   [1990] FSR 11.
2   [1990] FSR 1.
3   See **paragraphs 7.13** and **26.08**.
4   See **paragraph 7.13**.
5   [2016] EWHC 3583.

Moral rights

26.25 There are four basic categories of moral rights contained in the CDPA:

- the *right to be identified* as author;
- the right to object to *derogatory treatment* of work;
- *protection from false attribution* of work;
- the *right of privacy* of certain photographs and films[1].

The author of a work of architecture in the form of a building or a model for a building, has the right to be identified whenever copies of a graphic work representing it, or of a photograph of it, are issued to the public[2].

The author of a work of architecture in the form of a building also has the right to be identified on the building as constructed, or, where more than one building is constructed to the design, on the first to be constructed[3].

This right must be asserted by the author on any assignment of copyright in the work or by instrument in writing signed by the author. In the case of the public exhibition as an artistic work (for example, the inclusion of a model of a building in an exhibition), the right can be asserted by identifying the author on the original or copy of the work, or on a frame, mount or other thing to which the work is attached. If the author grants a licence to make copies of the work, then the right can be asserted for exhibitions by providing in the licence that the author must be identified on copies which are publicly exhibited[4].

There are certain exceptions to the right, of which the most important is that it does not apply to works originally vested in the author's employer[5].

The author of an artistic work has the right to object to his work being subjected to derogatory treatment[6].

In the case of a work of architecture in the form of a model of a building, the right is infringed by issuing copies of a graphic work representing it or of a photograph of a derogatory treatment of the work.

However, and most importantly, the right is not infringed in the case of a work of architecture in the form of a building. Nevertheless, if a building is the subject of a derogatory treatment, the architect is entitled to have his identification on the building as its architect removed[7].

In the case of works which vested originally in the author's employer, the right does not apply.

Similarly, in the case of an artistic work, a person has the right not to have its authorship falsely attributed to him. Thus, an architect can prevent a building which he has not designed being attributed to him as its architect[8].

1 Moral rights are considered in detail in **Chapter 10**.
2 CDPA s 77(4)(c).
3 CDPA s 77(5).
4 See **paragraph 10.08**.
5 See **paragraph 10.10**.
6 See **paragraph 10.15**.
7 See **paragraph 10.15**.
8 Moral rights are considered in detail in **Chapter 10**.

Chapter 27

Advertising agencies

Introduction

27.01 Advertising agencies are typically involved with almost every type of copyright, and reference should be made to the relevant chapters of this *User's Guide* in relation to different types of work, both online and offline[1]:

- *literary works*: advertising in newspapers and magazines[2];
- *dramatic works*: scripts of advertising films and television commercials[3];
- *musical works*: radio commercials and the soundtracks of television commercials[4];
- *artistic works*: posters, and magazine and press advertising[5];
- *sound recordings*: radio commercials[6];
- *films*: promotional films and television commercials[7];
- *published editions of works*: publicity publications which constitute editions of typographical arrangements[8].

There are, however, certain copyright issues which have a special bearing on the advertising industry, as discussed below.

1   See, generally, **Chapter 2**.
2   **Chapter 16**.
3   **Chapter 21**.
4   **Chapter 20**.
5   **Chapter 25**.
6   **Chapters 20** (Part II) and **23**.
7   **Chapter 22**.
8   **Chapter 15**.

Copyright in advertisements

27.02 The fact that work appears in an advertisement does not in principle detract from any right that it enjoys to protection under the

CDPA. For example, an advertising poster may well be entitled to qualify as an artistic work (as regards its artwork) and/or a literary work (as regards any text appearing on it)[1].

Whether an advertisement is entitled to copyright protection as a literary, artistic, musical or dramatic work will depend in each case on whether the skill and labour applied to its creation are sufficient to justify protection[2]. It is not the idea, but the resolution of the idea into material form, which is entitled to copyright[3]. For example, trade catalogues will in principle be entitled to copyright protection, provided that the criteria for protection are met. Although they are not 'literary' in the ordinary sense of that word, they will be treated as literary works in copyright law if they are in writing, and if original skill and labour have been expended upon their production. Their literary or artistic quality or merit is immaterial[4].

A distinction should be drawn between on the one hand those works which, like posters, are intended to be enjoyed as artistic works, and on the other hand those works which are intended to be applied to other articles, such as T-shirts, belt buckles, drinking glasses and the like. The law in such cases is complex, falling partly under copyright law and partly under design right.

1 See **paragraphs 2.02** and **2.06**.
2 See **Chapter 3**.
3 See **paragraphs 1.03** and **7.04**.
4 See **paragraph 2.02**.

Ownership

27.03 There are no special provisions in the CDPA regarding the ownership of copyright works produced for the purposes of advertising. It follows that the question of who owns advertising materials will be determined in accordance with the general principles outlined elsewhere in this *User's Guide*[1]. In brief, the copyright in an advertisement that consists of literary, artistic, dramatic or musical works will prima facie vest: (a) in its author; or (b) (if the author is employed, there is no agreement to the contrary and the work is made in the course of employment) in his or her employer[2]. Since alternative (b) in the foregoing sentence is unlikely to apply to the relationship between an advertising agency and its client, it follows that it will prima facie be the agency, and not the client, that owns the copyright in the advertisement, unless exceptional circumstances apply[3], for it is settled law that the mere fact that a contractor has been commissioned by a client to create a work is generally insufficient to entitle the client to the legal ownership of the copyright in the resulting work[4].

If an advertisement produced by an agency substantially copies material provided by the client, it will nevertheless qualify for copyright provided that it fulfils the requirements for protection[5]. Although the agency will (as against the client) own the copyright in the advertisement on the principles set out above, any use of the advertisement which amounts to a 'restricted act' may infringe the copyright in the client's material unless the use is authorised by the client[6].

1   See **Chapters 1** and **2**.
2   See **paragraphs 9.11** ff.
3   See further **paragraph 27.04**.
4   See **paragraph 9.12**.
5   See **Chapters 2** and **3**.
6   See **paragraphs 6.02** ff.

The client and copyright in advertising material

27.04 If a client changes its agency it is the custom of the industry for the agency to assign to its replacement the copyright in all the advertisements prepared by it for that client.

However, in the case of *Hutchison Personal Communications Ltd v Hook Advertising Ltd*[1] the agreement provided that Hook would:

> 'assign to you all and any copyright in all material produced or created for your advertising as is vested in us ... as and when requested in writing ...'

That case concerned the ownership of the material prepared by Hook for the 'pitch' for Hutchinson's work, and which was therefore prepared before the agreement was made.

Hook's material included a rabbit logo. It did not include material created before the advertising agent had been appointed. The logo, having been created before the date of the agreement, was not material caught by the clause even though it formed part of the advertisement. To catch the logo, Arden J said that the clause would have had to read:

> 'every copyright in all or any part of the material produced or created for your advertising'.

This case illustrates the importance of dealing explicitly with material created for the 'pitch' and with elements of the advertisement created for that client.

All employees of advertising agencies should be engaged under written contracts of service that vest in the agency the copyright in all material created by them in the course of their employment and, in addition, in all advertising material created by them at any time whilst they are employed by the agency, even if it is written outside working hours[2].

Similarly, when freelance artists, copywriters and other contributors are engaged by an advertising agency, they should also be required to sign agreements with the agency vesting the copyright in their contributions in the agency[3]. In addition, a waiver of all moral rights in their contributions should be obtained from such contributors[4].

A well-advised client should carefully consider the ownership position in relation to material created for it by an agency. In the event that the client wants to appoint a different agency to represent it at any time, it will need the ability to use material created by the first agent without restriction. This means taking either an assignment of copyright from the agent on the widest possible terms, or else an enforceable agreement to assign copyright at a later date on agreed terms, in the event that there is a 'parting of the ways'. A well-advised client will also seek contractual warranties and indemnities from its agency against the possibility that the agent has not obtained the copyright in any contributions made in the advertising copy by its staff or freelancers, and may require those agreements to be in approved form.

A very useful cautionary tale about the difficulties that clients may face is provided by the case of *Griggs v Evans*[5] in which the manufacturer of the famous 'Doctor Martens' boots commissioned an advertising agency to design its logo. It was only after lengthy litigation in the English High Court of Justice and in the Court of Appeal that the claimant secured an order that the copyright in the logo should be assigned back to it by the person to whom the agency's designer had transferred it. A more recent cautionary tale is provided by the INNOCENT smoothie case[6], in which High Court litigation was needed to obtain a court declaration that the client was the owner in equity of a logo designed by its agency. A different approach was adopted by the IP Enterprise Court in *Orvec International Ltd v Linfoots Ltd*[7], in which the court implied a term that photographs taken by the client's advertising agency should be the subject of a non-exclusive, and probably perpetual, licence therein. In this connection see further **paragraph 9.12**.

The Incorporated Society of British Advertisers[8], the Chartered Institute of Purchasing and Supply[9] and the Institute of Practitioners in Advertising[10] (of which the great majority of advertising agents are members) have issued suggested provisions for use in agency/client agreements.

1   [1996] FSR 549.
2   See **paragraph 9.12**.
3   See **paragraph 9.12**.
4   See **paragraph 10.29**.
5   *R Griggs Group Ltd v Evans [2005] EWCA (Civ) 11*.
6   *Fresh Trading Ltd v Deepend Fresh Recovery Ltd [2015] EWHC 52 (Ch)*.
7   [2014] EWHC 1970 (IPEC).
8   See www.isba.org.uk.
9   See www.cips.org.
10 See www.ipa.co.uk.

Unsolicited copyright material

27.05 Agencies are typically the recipients from time to time of proposed advertisements or ideas for advertisements from members of the public. There are dangers in using this material or even in allowing the agency's creative staff to see it. Employees of the agency may be working upon material very similar, if not identical, to that which has been submitted by a third party. In the event that the latter subsequently alleges an infringement of copyright, it could be difficult for the agency to prove that it had already begun to work on the idea before the material was received. And if the agency wants to use an idea submitted to it which is not entitled to copyright, it may still be in danger of being sued for breach of confidence by using the material.

It is therefore recommended that, to avoid such situations, a system is instituted whereby all incoming mail is sifted at an administrative (as distinct from creative) level, and that submissions from the public are automatically returned with a standard form letter explaining that the agency does not consider unsolicited ideas because it has its own creative staff.

Chapter 28

Software

Introduction

28.01 Programs 'instruct' a computer to undertake the tasks which are required of it – that is to say, the reception, storage, processing and retrieval of information.

Software is the expression used to include such programs and will include computer databases and files. 'Hardware' is a word coined by the computer industry to refer to items such as the chips and memory circuits used in the processors which store programs and information in the computer, and other similar storage devices, which, although part of the computer itself, have nevertheless been specially adopted for the particular program needs of that computer. This chapter deals with the protection available to computer programs, computer software generally and the information stored in computers.

Computer programs are generally excluded from patent protection under the laws of most European countries (including the UK).

In 1991, the EU adopted the Software Directive[1] on the legal protection of computer programs, which provided that Member States should legislate to protect computer programs as literary works, but not the ideas and principles which underlie them. The Software Directive was implemented into UK law by the Copyright (Computer Programs) Regulations 1992[2].

This Directive followed the Directive of 1986 on the legal protection of topographies of semi-conductor products which provided that Member States should legislate to protect the topographies of semi-conductor products. The UK implemented this latter Directive by according design right protection for semi-conductor products[3].

The manuals and papers relating to the programming and operation of computers will be protected as literary and artistic works[4]. No particular copyright problems arise in connection with these documents. The special problems are to be found in relation to the programs themselves and the information stored in computers.

Copyright provides no protection for bare concepts, or ideas[5]. Therefore, the concept of a particular algorithm, or an idea for a method of retrieving information will not be entitled to protection although the extent of this doctrine and its application raises difficult questions.

1 Council Directive 91/250/EEC of 14 May 1991 on the Legal Protection of Computer Programs.
2 SI 1992/3233.
3 See **paragraph 13.02**.
4 See **paragraphs 2.02** and **2.06**.
5 See **paragraph 7.04**.

Definitions

28.02 A *'literary work'* is defined by the CDPA as including a computer program, and preparatory design material for a computer program[1].

'Computer generated' means 'a work generated by computer in circumstances such that there is no human author of the work'[2].

'Adaptation' in relation to a computer program means an arrangement or altered version of the program or a translation of it[3].

'Translation', in relation to a computer program, includes a version of the program in which it is converted into or out of a computer language or code, or into a different language or code[4].

The definitions of *'artistic works'* and *'sound recordings'* are considered elsewhere in this *User's Guide*[5].

Expressions such as *'computer'*, *'program'*, *'system control'*, *'software'* and other examples of computer terminology have no definitions in the CDPA, and the courts will accept the computer industry usage as the source for definitions of such words. WIPO has prepared Model Provisions on the Protection of Computer Software which contain useful definitions of *'computer software'*, *'computer program'*, *'program description'* and *'supporting material'*. 'Preparatory Design Material' expressly included within the term 'computer program'[6].

1 CDPA s 3.
2 CDPA s 178.
3 See **paragraph 6.09**.
4 See **paragraph 6.09**.
5 See **paragraphs 2.06** and **2.07**.
6 Article 1(2) of the Directive; see *Nova Productions v Mazooma Games (2007) EWCH Civ 219*.

Types of work – literary and artistic works

28.03 Software, to the extent that it is recorded in writing or otherwise, will be protected as a 'literary work'[1]. For these purposes, 'writing or otherwise' has a very broad meaning, including any form quotation or code recorded in any medium[2].

Computer software, which is conveyed in the form of tapes or discs, even if it is never resolved into writing, will nevertheless qualify for copyright protection as a literary work. The CDPA provides that preparatory design materials for programs are also protected as literary works[3]. It is irrelevant if the program is in a higher or lower form language; or that there are no words, only numerals being used or that only a machine can understand it – it will, nevertheless, be a literary work.

The same principles apply to 'hardware', 'wired in' or 'firmware' programs, memory circuits (read-only memories, random access memories, bubble memories, etc), silicon chips, and to the information in the data bases of a computer, stored in the form of abstracts. If the program or data has been recorded, 'in writing or otherwise'[4], it will qualify as a literary work.

A computer print-out or manual will also be a 'literary work' or an 'artistic work' quite apart from the program itself and will therefore be entitled to copyright protection.

Protection under the Registered Designs Act 1949 or design right protection under the CDPA is not available to computer software although the topography of semi-conductor products is protected under the design right provisions of the CDPA.

1   See **paragraph 2.02**.
2   See **paragraph 2.05**.
3   CDPA s 3(1)(c), but note that this protection only applies when 'the nature of the preparatory work is such that a computer program can result from it at a later stage.'
4   CDPA s 3(2).

Copyright protection and originality

28.04 It is not necessary nor, indeed, possible to register a work in a copyright registry in the UK which has any standing under UK copyright law[1]. Nor is it necessary to publish a work for it to acquire copyright protection.

For a work to be entitled to copyright protection, it must be original. In short, its creation must originate from the author, and be the result of skill, labour or judgement[2].

If several companies work on the same problem at the same time, the one which arrives at the right algorithm first will be the owner of the copyright in that algorithm. Theoretically, other companies could arrive independently and spontaneously at the identical algorithm and also have copyright protection for their work, but this is unlikely[3]. Therefore, it is important to be able to prove the date upon which the algorithm – or any other element of the program – was first written. This can be done for example by depositing the material with a solicitor in a sealed package with a record of the date and time of receipt[4].

For software to be protected in the UK, it must satisfy several of the requirements of qualification set out in the CDPA[5]. What is protected is the form of expressions of the program itself. Other things that are conveyed by or described in the program such as 'ideas, procedures, methods of operation and mathematical concepts' are not protected[6]. The functionality is not protected.

The 'ideas' behind the software are also protected unless:

- they have no connection with the literary, dramatic, musical or artistic nature of the work; or
- they are not original or are so commonplace as not to perform a substantial part of the work, in other words the programming techniques are already well known and frequently used in software programming.

1   See **paragraph 9.20**.
2   See **paragraph 3.01**.
3   See **paragraph 3.05**.
4   See **paragraph 9.20**.
5   See **paragraphs 4.01** ff.
6   See *SAS Institute Inc v World Programming Ltd (2010) EWHC 1829.*

Ownership of copyright in computer programs

28.05 The only categories of copyright work within which computer programs may be protected are literary works and artistic works.

The basic rule is that the first owner of a literary or an artistic work is its author[1]. The CDPA also provides that the author of a work which is computer generated is taken to be the person by whom the arrangements necessary for creation of the work are undertaken[2]. An object code program is a computer-generated work, as will be a computer database (at least to the extent it is created by downloading from other databases).

Where a computer program is written by the programmer in the course of his employment under a contract of service, then the employer will be entitled to the copyright in the program, in the absence of any agreement to the contrary[3]. Where freelance programmers are used, copyright will vest in the freelancer. Accordingly, where appropriate, letters of engagement should specify that the copyright in material originated by freelancers will vest in and belong to the employer.

1   See **paragraph 9.02**.
2   CDPA s 9(3).
3   See **paragraph 9.11**.

Copyright in commissioned programs

28.06 It is usual for companies to employ computer bureaux or consultants to write program specifications and the programs for them.

In the absence of any contractual arrangements to the contrary, the copyright will remain in the bureau or consultant[1]. Therefore, customers should ensure that the terms of the contract with the consultant or bureau provide that the copyright in any programs specially written for them becomes their own or that they have, at the very least, a licence in the copyright in the program for the full period of copyright[2].

1   See paragraph 9.12.
2   See generally Chapter 9.

Ownership of computer output

28.07 Computer output is the result of the interaction between program and input. Behind this simple statement lie a number of complicated technical processes, which can involve up to three types of program:

- *source code*, written by the programmer;
- *a compiler, or interpreter*, which may have been written by the programmer but is quite often written by a different programmer;
- *object code,* which is the result of the translation of the source code by the compiler.

The hardware, which a program uses to produce output, will have its own copyright if it was originally recorded in a written form.

The output will, therefore, be the result of the interaction of programs and the data input by the user, each having its own copyright and usually with different owners.

Although the computer itself can be categorised as a tool (like a slide rule or paint brush), the program, as we have seen, is entitled to copyright protection. Dependent on the degree of skill and labour involved in the preparation of the data input, the output would seem to belong to the data provider.

In some cases (such as in the use of music writing software), it is relatively easy to see output as the work of the user (the computer and its software being a tool used to give effect to the creative act of the user). In other cases (such as in the use of programs which create music automatically) the user may have little or no input other than purely functional. In these circumstances the author will be the person by whom the arrangements necessary for creation of the work are undertaken[1].

1   See paragraph 28.05.

Duration of copyright

28.08 The period of copyright of a literary work and therefore of a computer program is the life of the author and 70 years thereafter. But in the case of computer-generated works, the copyright expires at the end of the period of 50 years from the end of the calendar year in which it was made[1].

1   CDPA s 12(3); see **paragraphs 5.01** and **5.04**.

Restricted acts applicable to computer software

28.09 Computer software is usually protected as a literary work[1]. The restricted acts applicable to a literary work are:

*   *copying* the work;
*   *issuing copies* of the work to the public;
*   *renting or lending* the work to the public;
*   *performing, showing or playing* the work in public;
*   *communicating* the work to the public;
*   *adapting* the work[2], or doing any of the above acts in relation to adapting the work.

1   As regards restricted acts generally, see **Chapter 6**.
2   See **paragraphs 6.02** ff.

Infringement by copying

28.10 Copying includes storing the work in any medium by electronic means[1]. It also includes making copies which are transient or are incidental to some other use of the work[2].

It follows that using computer software will involve copying in the sense of the CDPA, since running a computer program or loading a program into a computer memory both involve making copies (even though those copies may be transitory). As a basic principle, therefore, any use of software will need to be licensed[3].

In *IBCOS Computers Ltd v Barclays Mercantile Highland Finance Ltd*[4] a programmer who created programming for his employer later created similar programming (after leaving the company) in the same language. The court established that the new program contained elements copied from the old. Mr Justice Jacob rejected the defendant's claim that the similarities were a consequence of his use of well-established programming routines and holding that in circumstances where the facts suggest copying his style, arguments that the similarities arose from style should not be accepted when supported by independent evidence. Copying was found both within the individual programs concerned and in the overriding architecture of the software.

Particular problems arise in the case of computer software, where the 'look and feel' of a program may be duplicated even where the underlying program is based on an entirely different programming language. In the US, a number of cases have considered this problem but there is little English authority on the issue. Addressing the issue in *John Richardson Computers Ltd v Flanders*[5], however, Mr Justice Ferris considered the appropriate question to be whether the similarities between the two programs arose from the copying of a substantial part of the claimant's work. In answering this question Ferris J compared similarities between 'non-literal' aspects of the two programs, finding that copyright had been infringed. This decision has been subject to considerable criticism but remains good law.

The CJEU has held in *SAS Institute Inc v World Programming Ltd*[6] that copying of functionality by a lawful user of a copy of a program, without access to source code, will not infringe copyright in the program if the user complies with Art 5(3) of the Directive which provides an exception for a lawful user observing, studying or testing the functionality of the program to determine the underlying ideas and principles done while carrying out unauthorised acts.

At trial Mr Justice Arnold expressed the view that there was no infringement of copyright in a manual by reproducing compilations of formulae, keywords, default values, comments and optimisations from the SAS Manuals in the WPL Code[7].

1   CDPA s 17(2).
2   CDPA s 17(6); see **paragraph 6.02**.
3   However, see **paragraphs 28.15** ff in relation to permitted acts.
4   [1994] FSR 275.
5   [1993] FSR 497.
6   Case c-406/10 [2012] 3 CMLR 4.
7   [2013] EWHC 69.

'Substantial part'

28.11 For copyright to be infringed, it is necessary that a 'substantial part' of the work be copied[1].

If less than a 'substantial part' is used, there will be no infringement of copyright. Since a substantial part is not necessarily a reference to quantity but to quality, then if an essential part (even though a small part) of the program is copied this will constitute an infringement.

In one recent case, it was considered necessary when establishing whether a substantial part of a computer program had been copied to assess the skill and labour involved in the design and coding of the copied section against the skill and labour involved in the whole program[2].

1   See **paragraph 7.06**.
2   *Cantor Fitzgerald International v Tradition (UK) Ltd [2000] RPC 95.*

Issuing copies of software to the public

28.12 This restricted act is considered in detail elsewhere[1]. It is worth noting that the act is infringed by the importation into the UK or elsewhere in the EEA of copies of software which have been put on the market outside the EEA. In some parts of the world, computer software sells more cheaply than in the EEA, but this restricted act would be infringed by purchasing copies of programs put on the market in, say, the USA and reselling them in the UK without the authority of the copyright owner[2].

It is also worth noting that the CDPA contains a provision for the Secretary of State to grant licences where it seems the public interest requires it, based on the findings of any Competition Commission investigation.

1   See **paragraphs 6.04** and **14.04**.
2   See **paragraph 6.05**.

Rental and lending of computer software

28.13 The restricted act of rental and lending is considered in detail elsewhere[1]. Because it is so easy to copy computer software, copyright owners often refuse to permit their programs to be rented. However, there are a number of exceptions to the lending right[2].

Copyright in computer software is not infringed by the lending of copies of the work by an educational establishment or by a prescribed library or archive (other than a public library) which is not conducted for profit[3]. In order to try to limit the danger of copies being made unlawfully by persons borrowing computer software from educational establishments or prescribed libraries and archives, copyright owners should place on the software itself and on its packing notices to the effect that copyright will be infringed if any copy of the software is made. The notice can point out that use of the software by running it, loading it etc constitutes copying for copyright purposes. It would be wise to include these terms on a notice which is usually attached to software to the effect that when the shrink wrap is removed, the purchaser is deemed to have accepted the conditions of sale. This might deter libraries, archives and educational establishments from buying computer software for lending purposes, knowing that by so doing they will inevitably be in breach of the terms, because no use can be made of the software without infringing the restricted act of copying. If no such notice is placed on the software at the time of sale, it is more than probable that a court would hold that there is an implied licence to make copies for the purpose of using the software when it is sold to bodies which have the right to lend them under the provisions of the CDPA as amended by the Copyright and Related Rights Regulations 1996[4].

Shrink wrap notices can only be relied on by the copyright owner or licensee if the notice can be read on the outside of the packaging at the time of purchase[5].

1   See **paragraph 6.06**.
2   Generally, see **Chapter 8**.
3   As to what is meant by a prescribed library or archive, see **Chapter 18**.
4   SI 1996/2967; '1996 Regulations'.
5   See **paragraph 24.08**.

Infringement of software copyright by adaptation

28.14 In the case of computer programs, the CDPA provides that 'adaptations' means 'an arrangement or altered version of the program or a translation of it'.

By s 21(4) 'translation' in relation to a computer program includes 'a version of the program in which it is converted into or out of a computer language or code or into a different computer language or code'.

The reproduction of source code into object code effected by a compiler is a 'translation' for copyright purposes and will constitute an adaptation of a work[1]. The significance of this is to provide a copyright action to restrain unauthorised decompilation and compilation etc of programs, or 'reverse engineering', (ie the conversion of an object code into a source code enabling an examination of underlying programming techniques)[2].

1 See **paragraph 6.09** for a full analysis of the restricted act of adaptation.
2 Although note the fair dealing provisions at **paragraphs 28.15** ff.

Fair dealing with computer programs

28.15 Fair dealing is considered in more detail elsewhere[1]. However, in addition, the CDPA, in relation to computer programs, states that it is not fair dealing:

- to convert a computer program in a low-level language into a version expressed in a higher-level language; or
- incidentally in the course of so converting the program, to copy it[2]; or
- to observe, study or test the functioning of a computer program in order to determine the ideas and principles which underlie any element of the program (unless these acts are in accordance with s 50BA)[3].

1 See **Chapter 8.**
2 CDPA s 28(4).
3 CDPA s 28(4); see **paragraph 28.19** for the permitted acts defined in CDPA s 50BA.

Transfer of copies of works in electronic form

28.16 Purchasers of works in electronic form may copy, adapt or make copies of adaptations of them in connection with their use as if they had been purchased on terms which allow them to do such an act. The terms may be express or implied. The terms of purchase should expressly forbid such acts if the manufacturer does not want purchasers to copy or adapt such works[1].

1 See **paragraph 8.17.**

Back-up copies

28.17 It is not an infringement of copyright for a lawful user of a copy of a computer program to make any back-up copy which it is necessary for him to have for the purposes of his lawful use. A person is a lawful user of a computer program if he has a right to use the program. The right to use the program can be pursuant to a licence from the copyright holder or otherwise[1].

It is irrelevant whether or not there exists any term or condition in an agreement which purports to prohibit or restrict the act of making a back-up copy because such a prohibition would be void[2].

1   CDPA s 55A; see **paragraph 8.13**.
2   CDPA s 286A; see **paragraph 28.20**.

Decompilation

28.18 It is not an infringement of copyright for a lawful user of a copy of a computer program expressed in a low-level language:

- to convert it into a version expressed in a higher level language; or
- incidentally in the course of so converting the program to copy it (that is, to 'decompile' it) provided that the following conditions are met[1]:

  '(a) it is necessary to decompile the program to obtain the information necessary to create an independent program which can be operated with the program decompiled or with another program ("the permitted objective"); and

  (b) the information so obtained is not used for any purpose other than the permitted objective'[2].

These conditions are not met if the lawful user:

'(a) has readily available to him the information necessary to achieve the permitted objective;

(b) does not confine the decompiling to such acts as are necessary to achieve the permitted objective;

(c) supplies the information obtained by the decompiling to any person to whom it is not necessary to supply it in order to achieve the permitted objective; or

(d) uses the information to create a program which is substantially similar in its expression to the program decompiled or to do any act restricted by copyright'[3].

Again, any term or condition in an agreement which purports to prohibit the act which is permitted under s 50B will be void[4].

1   CDPA s 50B(1); see **paragraph 8.13**.
2   CDPA s 50B(2).
3   CDPA s 50B(3).
4   CDPA s 286A.

Observing, studying and testing computer programs

28.19 It is not an infringement of copyright for a lawful user of a copy of a computer program to observe, study or test the functioning of the program in order to determine the ideas and principles which underlie any element of the program if he does so while performing any of the acts of loading, displaying, running, transmitting or storing the program which he is entitled to do[1].

Where an act is permitted under CDPA s 50BA, it is irrelevant whether or not there exists any term or condition in an agreement which purports to prohibit or restrict such act[2].

1   CDPA s 50BA(1).
2   CDPA s 50BA(2).

Other acts permitted to lawful users of software programs

28.20 It is not an infringement of copyright for a lawful user of a copy of a computer program to copy or adapt it, provided that the copying or adapting:

'(a) is necessary for his lawful use; and
(b) is not prohibited under any term or condition of an agreement regulating the circumstances in which his use is lawful'[1].

Moreover, it is not an infringement of copyright to copy a computer program or adapt it for the purpose of correcting errors in it[2].

However, CDPA s 50C does not apply to any copying or adapting:

* permitted by making back-up copies[3];
* made in the process of decompilation[4]; or
* made in the process of observing, studying and testing computer programs[5].

Certain terms or conditions in agreements for the use of a computer program are deemed void by the CDPA, in particular, terms or conditions which seek to prohibit:

* the making of any back-up copy of the program which it is necessary to have for the purposes of the agreed use[6];
* the decompiling of the program when the conditions set out in s 50B(2) are met[7];
* the use of any device or means to observe, study or test the functioning of the program to understand the ideas and principles which underlie any element of the program[8].

1   CDPA s 50C(1).
2   CDPA s 50C(2).
3   CDPA s 50A.
4   CDPA s 50B.

5   CDPA s 50BA.
6   See **paragraph 28.17**.
7   See **paragraph 28.18**.
8   CDPA s 286A.

Moral rights not applicable

28.21 The rights to be identified as the author of a work and to object to the derogatory treatment of a work do not apply to computer programs[1].

1   See **paragraphs 10.10** and **10.18**.

'Seeded entries'

28.22 Obtaining proof of infringement of a program by deliberate copying can be very difficult in practice. One mechanism is to place 'deliberate mistakes' or bugs in programs so that if the program is copied, the deliberate mistake or bug will also appear, so providing evidence of copying[1].

1   See **paragraph 7.02** for a general consideration of this issue.

International protection

28.23 The copyright position of computer software and firmware outside the UK differs almost from country to country. The WIPO Geneva Copyright Treaty of December 1996 provided that:

> 'Computer programs are protected as literary works within the meaning of Article 2 of the Berne Convention. Such protection applies to computer programs, whatever may be the mode or form of their expression'[1].

Nevertheless, wherever international use is likely to be made of software, the owner of the copyright should seek to bolster his copyright protection with contractual protection. Contracts can go some way towards giving the same rights and remedies to a company supplying software and hardware as does copyright but only against the persons with whom such company enters into contractual relationships. Third parties making unauthorised use of the software are not affected by, and cannot be sued by, the owner of the copyright if the copyright law offers no protection in that particular country, irrespective of the copyright laws of the country in which the software originated.

In order to ensure maximum protection in countries not party to the Berne Convention, it is wise to affix the copyright symbol © plus the name of the copyright owner and the year of publication on all software[2].

The manufacturers of silicon chips usually put the copyright symbol etc on the actual chips themselves.

1   Article 4.
2   See generally **Chapter 4**.

Anti-spoiler devices

28.24 The computer industry (as well as the record and home video industries) uses devices which are designed to prevent the making of unauthorised copies of computer programs, sound recordings and films. These are known as forms of copy-protection, or spoilers. The CDPA contains provisions[1] intended to provide a cause of action to restrain the making, sale, importation or hiring of devices or means specifically designed or adapted to circumvent spoilers. Circumvention is dealt with in more detail elsewhere in this *User's Guide*[2].

1 CDPA s 286.
2 See **paragraphs 24.40** ff.

Part 3
Appendices

Appendix 1

Relevant organisations

[*All postal addresses are in the United Kingdom unless otherwise indicated.*]

AGICOA
1, rue Pestalozzi
CH-1202 Geneva
Switzerland
Tel: +41 22 544 83 00
Fax: +41 22 340 34 32
e-mail: info@agicoa.org
website: www.agicoa.org

Association of Professional Recording Services Ltd
PO Box 22
Totnes
TQ9 7YZ
Fax: 01803 868600
website: www2.aprs.co.uk

Authors Licensing and Collecting Society (ALCS)
1st Floor
Barnard's Inn
86 Fetter Lane
London
EC4A 1EN
Tel: 020 7264 5700
website: www.alcs.co.uk

British Academy of Composers and Songwriters (BASCA)
2 St Pancras Square
King's Cross
London N1C 4AG
Tel: 020 7636 2929
website: https://.basca.org.uk

British Actors Equity Association (known as Equity)
Guild House
Upper St Martins Lane
London WC2H 9EG
Tel: 020 7670 0200
Fax: 020 7379 7001
e-mail: info@equity.org.uk
website: www.equity.org.uk

British Copyright Council
2 Pancras Square
London N1C 4AG
Tel: 020 7582 4833
email: info@britishcopyright.org
website: www.britishcopyright.org

British Recorded Music Industry
Riverside Building
County Hall
Westminster Bridge Road
London SE1 7JA
Tel: 020 7803 1300
email: general@bpi.co.uk
website: www.bpi.co.uk

Compact Media Group Ltd
6–10 Whitfield Street
London
W1T 2RE
Tel: 020 7874 7480
Fax: 020 7383 7868
email: info@compact.media
website: http://compact.media

Copyright Licensing Agency Ltd
Barnard's Inn
86 Fetter Lane
London EC4A 1EN
Tel: 020 7400 3100
email: cla@cla.co.uk
website: www.cla.co.uk

DACS (Design & Artists Copyright Society)
33 Old Bethnal Green Road
London E2 6AA
Tel: 020 7336 8811
Fax: 020 7336 8822
website: www.dacs.org.uk

ERA (Educational Recording Agency)
1st Floor, Barnard's Inn
86 Fetter Lane
London EC4A 1EN
Tel: 020 7837 3222
Fax: 020 7837 3750
e-mail: era@era.org.uk
website: www.era.org.uk

Intellectual Property Office (IPO)
Concept House
Cardiff Road
Newport
South Wales
NP10 8QQ
Tel: 0300 300 2000
Fax: 01633 817777
email: feedback@ipo.gov.uk
website: www.ipo.gov.uk

Music Publishers' Association
2 Pancras Square
London N1C 4AG
Tel: 020 3741 3800
email: info@mpagroup.com
website: https://mpaonline.org.uk

Musicians' Union
60–62 Clapham Road
London SW9 0JJ
Tel: 020 7582 5566
email: info@theMU.org
website: www.musiciansunion.org.uk

NLA Media Access
Mount Pleasant House
Lonsdale Gardens
Tunbridge Wells TN1 1HJ
Tel: 01892 525 273
Fax: 01892 525 275
Email: copy@nla.co.uk

PPL (Phonographic Performance Ltd)
1 Upper James Street
London W1F 9DE
Tel: 020 7534 1000
email: info@ppluk.com
website: www.ppluk.com

PRS for Music
2 Pancras Square
London
N1C 4AG
Tel: 020 7580 5544
Fax: 020 3741 4455
website: https://www.prsformusic.com

Public Lending Right Office
The British Library
St Pancras
96 Euston Road
London
NW1 2DB
Tel: 01642 604699
email: plrcorporateservices@bl.uk
website: https://www.bl.uk/plr

Publishers' Association
50 Southwark Street
London SE1 1UN
Tel: 020 7378 0504
email: mail@publishers.org.uk
website: www.publishers.org.uk

Samuel French Ltd
24–32 Stephenson Way
London NW1 2HD
Tel: 020 7387 9373
website: www.samuelfrench.co.uk

Society of Authors
84 Drayton Gardens
London SW10 9SB
Tel: 020 7373 6642
website: www.societyofauthors.org

US Copyright Office
Library of Congress
Copyright Office
101 Independence Avenue SE
Washington
DC 20559-6000
USA
website: www.copyright.gov

Warner Chappell Production Music
Electric Lighting Station
46 Kensington Court
London W8 5DA
Tel: 020 7938 5550
email: london@warnerchappellpm.com

Writers' Guild of Great Britain
1st Floor, 134 Tooley Street,
London SE1 2TU
Tel: 020 7833 0777
e-mail: admin@writersguild.org.uk
website: www.writersguild.org.uk

Appendix 2

Table of Incidence of Copyright

I. Type of Work	Definition section	II. Term of copyright subject to reg 15(1) of the 1995 Regulations (see Chapter 5)	III. Restricted acts	IV. First owner (except Crown, Parliamentary and certain international organisation copyright)
1 Literary (Books, newspapers, magazines, catalogues, letters, tables or compilations (other than databases), computer programs, preparatory design material for computer programs, databases)	3(1)	Life of author plus 70 years Exceptions: (i) works of unknown authorship: 70 years from the end of calendar year in which made, or if during that period it is made available to the public, 70 years from the end of calendar year in which first made available to the public; (ii) computer generated works; 50 years from end of calendar year in which work was made; (iii) works of joint authorship: life of last author to die plus 70 years (s 12)	(a) Copying the work, ie reproducing the work in any material form (b) Issuing copies to the public (c) Renting or lending the work to the public (d) Performing, showing or playing the work in public (e) Communicating the work to the public (f) Making an adaptation (g) Doing, in relation to any adaptation, any of (a) to (f) (s 16)	(a) Author (ie the person who creates the work), or (b) If made in course of employment under a contract of service, employer will be first owner of all copyright (ss 9 and 11)

Appendix 2

I. Type of Work	Definition section	II. Term of copyright subject to reg 15(1) of the 1995 Regulations (see Chapter 5)	III. Restricted acts	IV. First owner (except Crown, Parliamentary and certain international organisation copyright)
Dramatic (Plays, operas, screen-plays, mimes, pantomimes, choreographic works, etc) Musical (Classical and popular songs, excluding words or action intended to be sung, spoken or performed with music. Does not include sound recordings of musical works) (s 3(1))	3(1)			
2 *Artistic works* (Graphic works, photography, sculpture, collages, architecture – buildings and models of buildings, works of artistic craftsmanship)	4	Life of author plus 70 years Works of unknown authorship, computer-generated works and works of joint authorship as 1 above (s 12)	(a) Copying the work, ie reproducing the work in any material form (b) Issuing copies to the public (c) Renting or lending copies of the work to the public other than: (i) a work of architecture in the form of a building of a model for a building, or (ii) a work of applied art (d) Communicating the work to the public	(a) Author, or (b) If made in course of employment under a contract of service, employer will be first owner of all copyright (ss 9 and 11)

I. Type of Work	Definition section	II. Term of copyright subject to reg 15(1) of the 1995 Regulations (see Chapter 5)	III. Restricted acts	IV. First owner (except Crown, Parliamentary and certain international organisation copyright)
3 Sound recordings (Recordings of sounds from which sounds may be reproduced, or a recording of a whole or part of a literary, dramatic or musical work from which sounds reproducing the work or part may be produced.	5A	(a) 50 years from the end of the year in which it was made, or (b) if released before end of that period, 50 years from end of calendar year in which released (s 13A)	(a) Copying the work ie reproducing the work in any material form (b) Issuing copies to the public (c) Renting or lending the work to the public (d) Playing or showing the work in public (e) Communicating the work to the public	The producer – the person by whom the arrangements necessary for the making of the sound recording are made (ss 9, 11(1) and 178)
4 Films (A recording on any medium from which a moving image may by any means be produced, and including the soundtrack)	5B	(a) 70 years from end of calendar year in which the death occurs of the last to die of: (i) the principal director; (ii) the author of the screenplay; (iii) the author of the dialogue; or (iv) the composer of music specially created for and used in the film (b) If the identity of (i) to (iv) is unknown, 70 years from end of calendar year in which the film was made, or if it is made available to the public during that period, then 70 years from the end of calendar year in which it is first so made available	(a) Copying the work, ie reproducing the work in any material form (b) Issuing copies to the public	(a) The producer (the person by whom the arrangements necessary for the making of the film are undertaken) and the principal director (ss 9, 11 and 178) (b) The employer if the film was made by the producer or principal director in the course of their employment (s 11(2))

Appendix 2

I. Type of Work	Definition section	II. Term of copyright subject to reg 15(1) of the 1995 Regulations (see Chapter 5)	III. Restricted acts	IV. First owner (except Crown, Parliamentary and certain international organisation copyright)
		(c) if there is no person falling within categories (i) to (iv), then 50 years from the end of the year in which the film was made (s 13B)	(c) Renting or lending the work to the public (d) Showing or playing the work in public (e) Communicating the work to the public	
5 Broadcasts ('An electronic transmission of visual images, sounds or other information...'. NB definition limited as set out in paragraph 2.09)	6	50 years from end of calendar year in which broadcast was made (s 14)	(a) Copying the work, ie reproducing the work in any material form (b) Issuing copies to the public (c) Playing or showing the work in public (d) Communicating the work to the public	The person making the broadcast, or in the case of a broadcast which relays another broadcast by reception and immediate retransmission, the person making that other broadcast (ss 9 and 11(1))
6 Published editions (In the context of copyright in the typographical arrangement of a published edition, means a published edition of the whole or any part of one or more literary, dramatic or musical works, except to the extent that it reproduces the typographical arrangement of a previous edition)	8	25 years from end of calendar year in which edition was first published (s 15)	(a) Copying the work, ie reproducing the work in any material form – means making a facsimile copy of the work (s 17(5)) (b) Issuing copies to the public	The publisher of the edition (ss 9 and 11)

Index

Index

Index

Index

Index

Index

Index

Index

Index

Index

Index

Index

Index

Index

Index